The IQ Controversy

The IQ Controversy,
the Media and Public Policy

Mark Snyderman
and
Stanley Rothman

Transaction Books
New Brunswick (USA) and Oxford (UK)

Library of Congress Catalog Number: 87-35403
ISBN: 0-88738-151-0
Printed in the United States of America

Library of Congress Cataloging in Publication Data

Snyderman, Mark.
    The controversy, the media, and public policy / Mark Snyderman
and Stanley Rothman.
        p.   cm.
    ISBN 0-88738-151-0
    1. Intelligence levels. 2. Intelligence levels in mass media.
3. Intelligence levels—Public opinion. 4. Intelligence levels-
-Government policy. I. Rothman, Stanley, 1927-   . II. Title.
III. Title: Intelligence quotient controversy, the media, and public
policy.
BF431.S615 1988
153.9′dc 19   87-35403

To my parents for all they have given.
—M.S.

To D.R.T. for helping me understand.
—S.R.

Contents

Preface   ix

Acknowledgments   xiii

1. Introduction: The IQ Controversy in Perspective   1

2. The Nature of Intelligence   43

3. The Heritability of IQ   79

4. Race and Class Differences in IQ   105

5. The Impact of Intelligence Testing   139

6. It's All There in Black and White:
   The Extent of News Media Coverage   175

7. No News Is Good News:
   The Nature of News Media Coverage   203

8. Conclusion: The New Sociology of Science   249

Appendices   261

Index   303

Preface

Very few questions have sparked more violent controversy in the past two decades than those relating to the nature of intelligence and intelligence testing.

In the 1950s it was widely agreed by both experts and the informed public that intelligence was something that could be measured by IQ tests, and that both the genetic endowment of the individual and his or her environment played a role in differences in measured intelligence.

During the 1960s and 1970s this view came under sharp attack. IQ tests were condemned as biased against both minorities and the poor. It was asserted that we do not know what intelligence is; that whatever it is, we do not know how to measure it, and that individual differences in intelligence, however measured, are primarily, if not entirely, a function of nurture rather than genetic endowment.

Today the critiques of IQ and intelligence testing have achieved the status of conventional wisdom among educated laymen. It is widely believed that newer scientific studies have discredited older views, which were based on bad, even dishonest, science, and that the great majority of scientists in the field of intelligence and intelligence studies support these studies. The new conventional wisdom has had important public policy consequences.

To determine the views of the relevant scientific community on these matters, we surveyed a broad sample of (primarily academic) experts in the field. We found that, whatever the conventional wisdom holds, most experts continue to believe that intelligence can be measured, and that genetic endowment plays an important role in individual differences in IQ. While experts believe that IQ tests are somewhat biased, they do not believe that the bias is serious enough to discredit such tests, and they believe that measured IQ is an important determinant of success in American society. Indeed, despite the discrediting of some of Cyril Burt's work on IQ heritability, the weight of evidence supporting such views, to judge from the scholarly literature, is probably greater today than it was in the 1950s.

In this book we are less interested in whether or not the experts are right than in exploring the reasons for the divergence of expert and public views and the influence of this divergence on public policy. The IQ controversy is examined in the context of our study of expert opinion. Expert opinion is then compared to news media reporting of such opinion, based on a detailed content analysis of coverage of the IQ controversy by the national media over a period of fifteen years.

We conclude that the public's view of the IQ controversy has been partly shaped by inaccurate media coverage, but that, more broadly, it has been shaped by changes in the nature of American liberalism and the key role of the civil rights issue in American life. The articulate public's perceptions of the opinions of experts in the field have been shaped far more by the general intellectual climate than by the actual views of the expert community.

This book consists of eight chapters. Chapter 1 discusses the history of the study of IQ and public controversy about it. Our survey of expert opinion is introduced in Chapter 2.

Chapters 2 to 5 summarize the controversy over the nature of intelligence, the question of heritability, group differences in IQ, and the use of intelligence tests. The scholarly and lay literature on these issues is reviewed and the views of our expert sample discussed. (A somewhat more technical, if briefer, discussion of the results of our survey can be found in Mark Snyderman and Stanley Rothman, "Survey of Expert Opinion on Intelligence and Aptitude Testing," *American Psychologist* 42, 2 (February 1987):137–144.)

Chapters 6 and 7 describe our analysis of news media coverage of the IQ issue.

Our findings are summarized in Chapter 8. In that chapter we also return to the central theme of the study, i.e., the social and political factors that influence the communication of information about controversial scientific issues to the public. We also draw some general conclusions about the changing role of science and scientists in decisions about public policy. We conclude that the growing influence of new strategic elites and the changing role of the mass media have had a profound effect on the communication of scientific information to the public.

The end of the book contains a series of appendices that generally contain more technical information about the expert survey and content analysis. Appendix A is a chronology of the development of notions of intelligence and intelligence testing and the controversy about these. Appendix E is of particular note because it contains the results of a survey of the attitudes of journalists and editors on the IQ question.

This book is one of a series of studies sponsored by the Center for the Study of Social and Political Change at Smith College. The studies focus on communication of scientific information about controversial issues to the public. Other areas that have been or are being studied include nuclear energy and environmental cancer. These studies, in turn, are part of a major exploration by the Center of the nature and direction of social and political change in the United States, directed by Stanley Rothman.

Our questionnaires, codebooks, and computer tapes have been deposited at the Roper Public Opinion Center at the University of Connecticut, as have the tapes and codebook of our content analysis.

Acknowledgements

The authors gratefully acknowledge the following scholars and publications for permission to use previously published material: Professor Thomas J. Bouchard, Jr. and *Science* for permission to use Figure 1 from T.J. Bouchard *et. al.* "Familia Studies of Intelligence: A Review", *Science* 212 (29 May, 1981), p.1056.

We thank James Davis, Sheldon White, and the pilot study respondents for their helpful comments during the development of the questionnaire, Kathleen McCartney and Douwe Yntema for their help with the statistical analyses, and Jacqueline Boudreau and Arianne Stubbs for their assistance in the preparation and mailing of the questionnaires and follow–ups. Alan McArdle played a key role in getting the data in final order and in developing the more complex statistical analyses.

Kudos to Ian Condry, Sally Connor, Michael Eastwood, Aimee Hamilton, Richard Malone, and Jane Weinzimmer for withstanding the ordeal of content analysis coding. Ole Holsti and Phil Stone lent their expertise to the development of the coding scheme. Patricia Davies helped the content analysis chapters along the path to readability. The entire project was aided by several conversations with Carol Weiss.

Special thanks to Richard Herrnstein for his invaluable comments on the questionnaire and the manuscript of the book, as well as for access to his voluminous files, and to Will Goldbeck, who deserves much of the credit for what's right with the content analysis, and none of the blame for what's wrong.

The following foundations provided financial support for our work: The Carthage Foundation, The Sarah Scaife Foundation, The Earhart Foundation, and The J. M. Foundation.

1

Introduction: The IQ Controversy in Perspective

The Challenge to Testing

In February 1969, the *Harvard Educational Review* (*HER*) published an article entitled "How Much Can We Boost IQ and Scholastic Achievement?" The author, University of California education professor Arthur Jensen, hypothesized that the apparent failure of large scale compensatory education programs intended to boost IQ and scholastic achievement could be traced to the largely heritable nature of intelligence. He also proposed that the average IQ difference between the black and white populations in the United States might be due in part to genetic factors.

Reaction to Jensen's article was swift and severe. The message scrawled on walls and placards and contained in handbills distributed by student protestors at Berkeley was that Jensen was a racist and a Nazi, and should be ousted from the university. Jensen's office was picketed, and his classes were regularly disrupted. Similar reaction met Jensen's attempts to give lectures at other campuses. For weeks, the student newspaper was filled with articles and letters concerning Jensen, most highly critical, many violently so. At one point, the activities of the Berkeley chapter of the Students for a Democratic Society (SDS) became so belligerent that the campus police thought it best to assign two plainclothes bodyguards to accompany Jensen around campus.[1]

At Harvard, letters to the *Crimson* also attacked Jensen, but many protests were directed at the *HER* for having published the article. Perhaps anticipating the inflammatory effect of Jensen's arguments, the *HER* had solicited, prior to the publication of Jensen's article, commentaries by seven expert critics. These were published in the following issue (Spring). But even the editors of the *HER* had not anticipated the full force of the reaction to Jensen, and they were unprepared to handle it. Deciding that the seven scholarly rebuttals published in the spring were insufficient, the editors included additional critiques in the Summer 1969 issue of the journal. Many of these, by their uncivil and arbitrary nature, were far below the standards of an academic journal. The editors released a statement claiming that they had never asked Jensen to deal with the racial issue in his article, an assertion Jensen was easily able to refute by producing a copy of *HER*'s original solicitation letter including an outline specifically mentioning racial differences in intelligence. When all else failed, the *HER* editors temporarily stopped selling copies of the issue containing Jensen's article, even refusing to sell reprints to Jensen himself.[2]

Reaction from Jensen's professional colleagues was, at best, mixed. Many decried the uncivil treatment being accorded Jensen, and publicly defended his right to express his views, while declaring their own disagreement with his conclusions. Others expressed their agreement with Jensen in personal letters and conversations, but were unwilling to do so publicly. The strongest and most prominent professional statements were decidedly anti–Jensen.[3] The Society for the Psychological Study of Social Issues (SPSSI), a division of the American Psychological Association (APA), released a five page statement to all the major news services outlining their disagreement with virtually all of the major points in Jensen's article.[4] A group called Psychologists for Social Action urged Jensen's expulsion from the APA. The 1969 convention of the American Anthropological Association (AAA) passed a resolution condemning Jensen's position on racial differences and encouraging members to fight racism through the use of "all available outlets in the national and local media."[5]

The uproar surrounding Jensen's thesis was not limited to college campuses. As the AAA had hoped, the national and local news media were quick to pick up on the story, emphasizing Jensen's conclusions about racial differences. The *HER* editors themselves played a crucial role in fostering press coverage, sending press releases and copies of the article and rebuttals to many newspapers and popular magazines. The media wasted no time in giving full coverage to Jensen. By June 1969, the *New York Times* already had devoted several articles to Jensen's arguments and the ensuing protests, and each of the three major newsweeklies had published at least one article on Jensen's theory that blacks are "Born Dumb."[6] Local newspapers throughout the country provided similar coverage. When the *New York Times Magazine* published a lengthy article entitled "jensenism, n. The Theory that IQ Is Determined Largely by the Genes" in August 1969, not only had a new word entered the media vocabulary, but the *Times Magazine* received more letters than it had for the publication of any article in its history, and more letters than the paper had received on any issue since the assassination of President Kennedy.[7] The *Times Magazine* published fifteen of the letters over a two–week period. Many of them not only attacked Jensen for his positions on the heritable nature of intelligence, and the possible genetic causes of race differences in IQ, but also criticized intelligence tests in general as biased and meaningless as measures of intelligence.

The Controversy and Its Effects

The content of the *Times Magazine* letters is an indication that the public controversy had become much larger than Jensen and his hypotheses. The past eighteen years has seen a steady stream of attacks on intelligence and aptitude tests, both from political organizations and from within the psychological and educational communities. It is frequently claimed that tests are culturally biased, invalid, irrelevant, stigmatizing, and restrictive of opportunities. Test makers have been accused of exerting unwarranted control over test takers' lives, and of engaging in secretive and unfair practices. Organizations like the National Education Association (NEA), the NAACP, and the Association of Black Psychologists (ABP) have called for a complete moratorium on standardized tests. Ralph Nader has been active in recent years in criticizing the Educational Testing Service (ETS), makers of the Scholastic Aptitude Test (SAT) and other admissions tests, for perpetuating class distinctions, and their own wealth, through biased and meaningless tests. Books with titles like *The Science and Politics of IQ*, *The Testing Trap*, *The Myth of Measurability*, and *The Mismeasure of Man* have added fuel to the fire by questioning the entire testing enterprise.[8] Nor has this criticism subsided. An October 1985 press conference announced the formation of "FairTest," an organization whose purpose it is to "examine the examiners." John Weiss, the executive director of Fair-Test explained that "[e]very year the educational and career opportunities—and self perceptions—of over 10 million Americans are forever altered by psychological exams. Most of these standardized multiple-choice tests are culturally biased and poorly designed."[9]

The result of much of this criticism has been substantial change in test use practices in the three major areas in which intelligence and aptitude tests have traditionally been used: elementary and secondary schools, employment, and admission to schools of higher education. As a matter of general practice in elementary and secondary schools, there is reason to believe that tests of intelligence and general aptitude are not as frequently given, or as often used, as they once were. In a 1964 nationwide survey conducted by the Akron, Ohio, Public Schools, 100% of large –city and –county test directors polled reported using group ability (intelligence and aptitude) tests in elementary school grades 4 through 6, and in junior high grades 7 through 9. A 1977 follow-up survey found that the frequency of test use had declined dramatically, to 23.4% in grades 4 to 6 and 35.1% in junior high school.[10]

Much of the change in group intelligence and aptitude test use is a result of a growing educational trend away from the separation of students into ability groups, known as tracking. Consequently, as even many of testing's strongest proponents have agreed, without the necessity of separating students by ability level much of the need for systematic intelligence and aptitude testing vanishes. After all, how useful is knowledge of a student's IQ to a teacher whose primary concern is that the student master the class material? There is, on the other hand, the danger that these numbers (IQ and aptitude test scores) can be misinterpreted and misused by those without the proper training. Some have expressed the fear that knowledge of intelligence test scores may actually be harmful to the student, creating unrealistic expectations of either too little or too great academic achievement.

The movement away from tracking, and from the use of intelligence and aptitude tests in making tracking decisions, was given a substantial boost by a 1967 federal court decision. *Hobson v. Hansen*[11] was the first in a series of court cases involving testing that have had a major impact on testing practices. In *Hobson*, the ability grouping system then in existence in the Washington, D.C., public schools was challenged as being racially discriminatory as defined in Title VI of the Civil Rights Act of 1964. The principal piece of evidence for racial discrimination was the disproportionate enrollment of black children in lower ability groups. Testing became an issue in the case because it was determined that scores on group–administered aptitude tests were an important element in the placement decision. On average, black students scored lower on these tests than did white students. Judge Skelly Wright was thus forced to examine the validity of these tests. Expert testimony from both sides of the case made it clear that the aptitude tests used were not, nor were they intended as, measures of innate ability, but were intended as tests of acquired skills that are influenced by a child's cultural and educational background. To Judge Wright, that black children scored lower on such tests was tantamount to racial bias, and he ruled in favor of the plaintiffs, striking down the D.C. tracking system, and placing a stigma on intelligence and aptitude tests.

The onus of the *Hobson* decision was felt clearly in *Larry P. v. Wilson Riles*,[12] the most important court case to date involving IQ tests. In November 1971, the parents of seven black children brought suit against the State of California in the United States District Court for the Northern District of California, claiming that their children had been incorrectly placed in classes for the educable mentally retarded (EMR) on the basis of culturally biased IQ tests. The plaintiffs, under the instigation and with the assistance of the Bay Area Association of Black Psychologists, the Urban League, and the NAACP Legal Defense Fund, among others, presented as evidence of racial discrimination the fact that black children were represented in EMR classes in San Francisco in numbers far in excess of their proportion in the school district as a whole, as well as the claim that the challenged intelligence tests were the primary determinant of EMR placement. An injunction was sought, calling for the elimination of all culturally biased tests, a reevaluation of all black EMR children, and the establishment of a quota so that black children would no longer be disproportionately assigned to EMR classes. The case was heard by Judge Robert Peckham.

There is an important distinction between the *Hobson* and *Larry P.* cases, other than that only the latter was a challenge to tests directly. *Hobson* involved large–scale administration of group intelligence and aptitude tests in an application of questionable value, ability grouping. In *Larry P.*, on the other hand, individually administered intelligence tests, universally recognized as more valid and reliable than group tests, were being attacked precisely where they had previously been thought to be most useful, for diagnosis of and educational planning for special needs students.

Judge Peckham accepted the data on disproportionate EMR enrollment as prima facie evidence of discrimination, thus shifting the burden of proof to the defendants to show a rational connection between the tests and their alleged use. As a result of the preliminary hearing, Judge Peckham concluded that the state had failed to meet this burden, and ruled that the school system had violated the students' rights to equal protection. He granted a preliminary injunction in 1972 enjoining any future placement of black children into EMR classes on the basis of intelligence tests. In 1974, that injunction was broadened to include the elimination of intelligence testing of all black children in California, and a year later the state board of education extended the moratorium to the use of intelligence tests for the placement of all students into EMR classes.

The full trial began in October 1977 and lasted over seven months. Twenty–six expert witnesses were called by both sides, in an attempt to establish the validity, or invalidity, of IQ tests for EMR placement. The court's decision, which did not come until 1979, was essentially the same as in the preliminary hearing. Judge Peckham found cultural bias in tests to be the most reasonable explanation for the disproportionate number of blacks in EMR classes, and concluded that the state had once again failed to establish the validity of intelligence tests for this purpose. The judge therefore ruled that the plaintiffs had met their burden of proving discrimination on the part of the state, and enjoined the state from using any IQ tests for the placement of black children into EMR classes without the prior approval of the court. In addition, the court's decision required that the status of all black children currently enrolled in EMR classes be immediately reevaluated, and that EMR enrollment be monitored so that the proportion of all minority children in California's EMR classes reflected their proportion in the school population. In 1984, Judge Peckham's decision was upheld by the United States Court of Appeals for the Ninth Circuit.[13]

Ironically, as Judge Peckham was reaching his decision, California was in the process of completely revising its system of special education in order to bring it in line with the federal Education for All Handicapped Children Act of 1975. This law calls for more individualized programs of instruction for handicapped children, as well as education in regular classrooms whenever possible. Under the Master Plan for Special Education, as it was then called, California no longer has anything resembling EMR classes or the EMR classification; labels are now applied to types of instruction, not to the students, and very few handicapped students are completely separated from their non–handicapped classmates. Moreover, the state keeps no records of the proportion of students of various racial and ethnic backgrounds enrolled in these programs. All of this means that until late 1986, intelligence tests continued to be used in California as one element of an extensive program of evaluation and special education curriculum planning for both black and white students, and the *Larry P.* ruling was virtually unenforceable.[14]

In December 1986, Judge Peckham issued a directive banning state administration of intelligence tests to all black children referred for special education. In May 1987, Mary Amaya received a letter from the public school in Rialto, California, asking her permission to test her son, Demond Crawford, for possible placement in special education classes. The letter contained a postscript explaining that because Demond is black, the school psychologist would be unable to give him an intelligence test. Ms. Amaya became angered that her child was being deprived of a complete analysis of his problems in school. Unconvinced by explanations of test bias from the NAACP and Larry P.'s attorney, Ms. Amaya took her case to the United States Civil Rights Commission, who in July 1987 began gathering facts about the case of Demond Crawford.[15] The outcome of this investigation and any legal action Ms. Amaya may pursue could have a profound effect on the use of intelligence tests in special education.

At present, it is difficult to gauge the overall impact of the *Larry P.* decision on the use of individually administered intelligence tests for special-needs students. Comprehensive data on such test practices are sorely lacking. We do know that these tests can no longer be used for the diagnosis of the special education needs of black children in the California public schools. Moreover, following the appellate court decision, a challenge to test use in federal district court in any state in the Ninth Circuit (Arizona, Idaho, Montana, Nevada, Oregon, and Washington) would probably lead to a similar ban in those jurisdictions. It is also likely that the fear of litigation has had a chilling effect on test administration in other school districts, particularly where black students are involved.

The legal procedure in test challenge cases, where adverse impact (generally interpreted as lower average scores by blacks or other minorities on tests used to make allocative decisions) is taken as prima facie evidence of discrimination, was established in a 1971 Supreme Court case involving employment testing, *Griggs v. Duke Power Co.*[16] In fact, charges of racial discrimination in employment practices through the use of biased aptitude tests have been the most common and most successful form of legal challenge to tests in recent years. The ease with which employment tests are struck down derives from the *Griggs* case, in which the court placed the burden of proof upon the employer in cases of adverse impact to show that the test in question is "a reasonable measure of job performance," and should be used despite inequalities in test score between groups. The court left unanswered the question of precisely what such a measure entails, but the Supreme Court and lower courts in subsequent cases have established the practice of showing "great deference" to the Equal Education Opportunity Commission (EEOC) *Guidelines on Employment Testing Procedures*. (The EEOC is charged with enforcing Title VII of the 1964 Civil Rights Act, dealing with unfair labor practices, and is the recipient of thousands of complaints of unfair test use each year.)

This custom has dealt a virtual death blow to the use of aptitude tests in employment (of seventy Title VII cases decided by federal courts between 1971 and 1976, 80 percent were won by the plaintiffs).[17] The EEOC *Guidelines* rely heavily on the APA *Standards for Educational and Psychological Tests*, which establishes validation criteria meant primarily for test developers with the resources to conduct large-scale validation studies involving hundreds of subjects. Individual employers, on the other hand, can rarely afford to conduct such studies, and so must rely on the validation supplied by the test maker, which generally demonstrate the tests' ability to predict performance on a wide variety of jobs of generic description. The courts have, in general, been unwilling to accept such validation in cases where there is adverse impact; employers have been required to show comprehensive validation data specific to the job or jobs in question.[18]

One result of this legal precedent, and the climate of fear produced by government advisories on test use,[19] may be the development of fairer and more valid employment tests. A more common reaction seems to be the elimination of employment testing by many firms (a 1976 survey of 200 companies found that 42% were using employment tests, compared to 90% doing so in a similar survey in 1963)[20] in favor of other selection procedures (interviews, biodata, etc.) that the courts are willing to accept. That these legally accepted criteria all predict job performance less well than aptitude tests led one testing expert to quip, "It's O.K. to be fairly stupid, but not O.K. to be unfairly stupid."[21]

Employment testing in the public sector, which is far more common than in private industry, has also suffered a decline as a result of litigation. A major setback to civil service testing came with the 1981 consent decree involving the federal government's Professional and Administrative Career Examination (PACE). A suit brought against the U.S. Civil Service Commission in 1972 alleged discrimination against black applicants through the use of the Federal Service Entrance Examination (FSEE), a test of verbal and quantitative reasoning used for employment in over 200 federal jobs.[22] While the case was on appeal in 1975, the Civil Service Commission replaced the FSEE with PACE, a carefully constructed and researched exam measuring five types of ability demonstrated to be important to performance in 118 jobs. The five subtests could be weighted differentially depending on the job in question. Despite its apparent well–documented validity, a 1979 Title VII challenge to PACE led to a 1981 consent decree that called for the elimination of the exam over three years. The federal government, like many other employers, finds itself moving toward separate, highly job–related exams for each job category.

In practice, just about the only employment tests that have been able to meet such challenges are those with high "face" validity, that is, actual work samples that look like the job being tested for. As a case in point, consider the New York City Police Department's sergeant's exam. In July 1981, an agreement was reached between the city, the federal government, and various minority groups within the police department in order to settle a series of civil rights suits charging that the sergeant's exam then in use discriminated against minority members. The settlement stipulated that a new test be developed, one specifically designed not to be discriminatory. The test was developed by a Florida firm chosen by the city with the approval of the other parties to the agreement. The new test, designed in consultation with experts from the city's police and personnel departments, cost $500,000 to develop and validate. The test was given to a group of over 11,000 police officers in July 1983. Slightly less than 11 percent of white officers passed the test, compared to only 1.6 percent of black and 4.4 percent of Hispanic candidates. Groups representing black and Hispanic officers charged that the test was racially biased and demanded that the results be thrown out. Mayor Koch expressed confidence that the test had been properly validated and was not biased, and announced that his administration would stand by the test results. The complainants filed related lawsuits claiming that the test was discriminatory and should be eliminated. In November 1985 the city announced that it would not use the results of the 1983 sergeant's exam, and instead would promote police officers on the basis of a quota system. This policy reversal followed a determination by city lawyers that they could not demonstrate to a court's satisfaction that the exam was sufficiently job related to warrant its use despite adverse impact. In particular, certain questions on the exam were deemed indefensible as job related because, for example, they required examinees to produce from memory information about the degree of seriousness of various crimes, data that sergeants could look up when actually on the job. The city subsequently began an investigation of how one–half million dollars could have been so misspent.

While thus far escaping direct legal challenge in court, aptitude test use in admissions to schools of higher education has been no less the subject of public criticism in recent years than has test use in elementary and secondary schools and in employment. In 1980, Columbia University student Allan Nairn and his associates, working under the auspices of Ralph Nader, published *The Reign of ETS*. In the book, criticisms traditionally reserved for standard intelligence tests are directed at tests used in admissions. Nairn et al. argue that tests like the SAT and the Law School Admissions Test (LSAT) are almost useless as predictors of performance in college or law school, are racially and socioeconomically biased, and are a fraud foisted on the public by the ETS in order to keep up profits and perpetuate their inordinate hold over test takers' lives.

The Reign of ETS, and a host of other books and articles, are part of the most recent trend in the IQ controversy: a move to lessen reliance on admissions tests. When a 1977 College Entrance Examination Board (CEEB) study panel suggested that the fifteen year decline in SAT scores among American high school students might be due in part to declining academic standards, the NEA, the country's largest teachers' organization, responded by naming the real culprit—the biased and invalid SAT.[23] In 1979, largely as a result of lobbying by the Nader organization, New York State passed a truth–in–testing law, requiring all admissions–test makers to release the contents and answers to their tests to the general public within a specified time after test administration. The law was passed over the objection of the testing industry, which argued that such a law would increase test costs and reduce test validity by preventing test makers from reusing questions of proven worth. (Whn the makers of the Medical College Admission Test [MCAT] threatened to remove their test from the state rather than attempt the nearly impossible task of constructing a completely new and equally valid exam on each administration, the legislators acquiesced by granting an exemption to the MCAT and certain other tests drawn from a limited corpus of knowledge.) Similar legislation was subsequently proposed in the U.S. Congress, forcing ETS to announce a policy of voluntary disclosure nationwide in order to undercut what they feared would be an even harsher law. (One of the goals of the new organization FairTest is to get such a national law passed.)

The effect of public debate on admissions test practices is difficult to gauge. In 1969, Bowdoin College in Brunswick, Maine, became the first major college in the U.S. to stop requiring students to submit SAT scores. While it hardly caused a tidal wave, Bowdoin has been joined by a handful of other colleges in recent years. Harvard College has considered a change in admissions policy whereby applicants would be able to submit achievement test scores in specified subjects in lieu of SAT scores. In 1985, the Harvard Business School announced that it would no longer require applicants to submit Graduate Management Admission Test (GMAT) scores, and Johns Hopkins Medical School adopted the same policy regarding MCATs. The moves by Harvard and Johns Hopkins may be prognostic, in light of these schools' traditional role as bellwethers in the educational community.

At present, however, it is not clear that the controversy has had much of an effect on admissions test use besides these isolated instances. For one thing, most colleges are not very selective. While virtually every four–year college in the United States requires applicants to submit either SAT or American College Testing (ACT) scores, the vast majority of college applicants are accepted by either their first– or second–choice schools.[24] Thus, it is only at a small number of the most selective colleges, and at graduate and professional schools, that admissions criteria are important at all. Of course, the most selective schools are also those attracting the most talented applicants. It therefore often becomes necessary for these schools to decide among a group of applicants, almost all of whom would probably succeed if admitted, on the basis of small differences in high school or college grades, test scores, or other factors. When talented students are denied admission to a prestigious university partially as a result of a small number of questions missed on a four–hour exam purported to measure "scholastic aptitude," complaints inevitably will be heard.

There is more to the controversy about admissions tests, however, than a handful of unsuccessful Ivy League applicants. The central issue in the public debate over intelligence and aptitude testing is that these tests, whether in the schools, on the job, or in admissions, are being used to allocate important resources and opportunities by ranking people according to "intelligence" or "aptitude" on the basis of a very small sample of behavior. Educational and occupational resources are limited, and decisions about their allocation must be made. Traditionally, Americans have attempted to make such decisions on the basis of merit, and tests have been seen as one objective criterion for doing so. Public controversy arises when the tests help produce allocative decisions that run counter to our ideals about fair and equitable treatment, namely, when there are significant group differences in the distribution of educational and employment opportunities. Hence, the outcry against Jensen, the *Larry P.* decision, and the current employment testing climate. The key to understanding the IQ controversy lies in the historical conflict between two strands in American thought, the desire for increasingly efficient and objective assessment, and the belief in human equipotentiality.

Early Developments

The publication of Charles Darwin's *On the Origin of Species* in 1859 was a seminal event in the development of intelligence and aptitude tests. Testing, of whatever form, has as its fundamental goal the measurement of individual differences. Tests of mental achievement, i.e., knowledge, had been used in the schools and in employment long before Darwin (the Chinese have had a system of civil service examinations for more than 3,000 years), but with the theory of evolution came an interest in differences in innate ability as well.

Darwin himself had little to say about psychological characteristics; he was more concerned with natural variation in physical structure and function. The application of Darwinian principles to the psychological realm therefore fell to Darwin's half–cousin, Francis Galton. A true Renaissance man, Galton made significant contributions in the fields of statistics, meteorology, geography, and criminology, among others. He is probably best known, however, as the founder of eugenics, the belief that humanity can be improved through selective breeding. Galton believed that important differences between people were largely the result of differences in inherited abilities. In support of his thesis, Galton published a genealogical study in 1869 entitled *Hereditary Genius*. Selecting a representative sample from various directories of famous men, Galton inquired into the status of their relatives. He found a much higher proportion of eminence within the families of his sample than would be expected by chance. Moreover, the closer the relative, the more likely that he or she was eminent, and the greater the similarity in the field in which eminence was achieved. While recognizing that the relatives of these high achievers most likely shared superior environments as well as superior genes, Galton was convinced that most of the differences in achievement between men were the result of differences in natural ability, primarily intelligence.

While biographical directories provided a useful indicator of natural ability, Galton needed a more direct measure. If eugenics was to become a practical reality, it was necessary to have a method for identifying those with natural talent at an early age. In attempting to develop such a measure, Galton began with the assumption, consistent with British empiricist tradition, that what we know is acquired through our senses. Differences in perceptual speed and acuity must therefore be crucial to differences in intellect. In 1884, initially as part of the International Health Exhibition in London, and later as part of the Science Museum in South Kensington, Galton set up an Anthropometric Laboratory. Visitors to the laboratory could, for a small fee, have various measurements taken and recorded. Besides gross physical measurements of height, weight, and so forth, the laboratory contained numerous measures of neurological and sensory functioning, such as simple reaction time, visual and auditory sensitivity, color perception, and steadiness of hand. Far from a carnival sideshow, Galton's laboratory was able to collect reliable data from over 9,000 individuals; this was the first attempt at the scientific measurement of individual differences in psychological characteristics. The work of summarizing these data by age, sex, etc., and of describing the interrelationships between the various measures and classifications, led to the development of important statistical techniques for measuring significance and correlation.

As Galton was making his reaction–time and sensory measurements at South Kensington, the first important work in experimental psychology was being conducted in the Leipzig laboratories of Wilhelm Wundt. Wundt used many of the same measurements as Galton, but to a different purpose. Wundt was interested, not in individual differences in mental functioning, but in the structure of the mind that was common to all individuals. One of his students, an American named James McKeen Cattell, was interested in studying individual differences in reaction time. While unable to interest Wundt in the idea, Cattell had heard of Galton's work in England and arranged to study with him. Following his tenure in England, Cattell returned to the University of Pennsylvania, where he became the world's first professor of psychology (psychology had previously been a subdiscipline of philosophy). At Penn, Cattell established the first university laboratory devoted to the psychological measurement of individual differences, work he continued at Columbia University. In 1890, Cattell coined the term "mental tests" to describe the series of strength, sensation, reaction–time, and memory tasks he and his students developed.[25] Cattell–type testing flourished during the next decade, which saw Cattell become the first chairman of the APA's Committee on Mental and Physical Tests.

The sensory and reaction–time approach to mental testing was hurt badly in 1901 by one of Cattell's own graduate students, Clark Wissler.[26] In the first correlational study of mental test results, Wissler obtained mental test scores and academic grades from over 300 Columbia and Barnard College students. He found virtually no correlation between mental test scores and academic grades. A professional controversy over the validity of the Wissler results and the Cattell tests ensued,[27] but quickly became moot as developments in France forever changed the face of mental testing.

In 1895 French psychologist Alfred Binet and his student Victor Henri published an article in Binet's newly founded journal, *L'Année Psychologique*, entitled "La Psychologie Individuelle." Binet and Henri outlined what they called an individual psychology. While general psychology was concerned with the general properties of "psychic processes," individual psychology had as its aim the study of how these processes differ from individual to individual, and between themselves within the same individual. To this end, the authors critically examined the then most popular method for studying individual psychic differences, the Cattell–type tests of simple sensory and memory processes. These tests were criticized as being too narrow in focus and too simple to produce meaningful individual differences. Binet and Henri proposed that the proper method for studying individual psychology required a wide variety of tests of different types in order to give a more complete profile of individual psychic functioning. Further, they argued that at least some of these tests must tap the higher mental functions, such as imagination and comprehension, for it is there that one finds most significant individual differences. Recognizing that the measurement of these higher functions would involve a certain loss of precision as compared to simple reaction time and memory tasks, the authors were nonetheless confident that the richness of the data would overcome any obstacles.

The Binet and Henri article drew the battle lines quite clearly between the Cattell and Binet schools of mental testing. As evidence accumulated, however, it became obvious where the future lay. Binet was able to draw support from work by Oehrn, Ebbinghaus, and others, showing that more complex memory tests were superior to simple tasks in discriminating the mental capabilities of students and mental patients. An 1899 article by Stella Sharp, a Cornell graduate student, directly compared Cattell–type to Binet–Henri–type tests in an experimental setting.[28] While skeptical about the overall value of individual psychology (Sharp was a student of E. B. Titchener, the leading American proponent of Wundt's school of general psychology), Sharp concluded that the Binet–Henri approach of using varied tests of higher mental functions was superior in the identification of individual differences.

Most of the data and methodology in favor of the Binet–Henri approach came from Binet himself. Throughout the 1890s Binet and his students developed tests of various higher mental functions such as verbal memory, suggestibility, and picture description, using French schoolchildren as subjects. In his writings, Binet suggested that when dealing with higher faculties such as imaginativeness, where there is no absolute scale of measurement, the only meaningful test measures are interindividual. In other words, test questions of this type must be scaled according to how examinees actually perform on the tasks. Another major advance in the development of the intelligence test came in a 1900 paper by Binet in which he developed a series of tests for "attention." He first asked a Paris schoolteacher for the five "most intelligent" and six "least intelligent" children in her class.[29] Binet began with a large series of tests, eliminating those that did not differentiate between the two groups of children. The practice of direct comparison to independent criteria was to become critical to later intelligence test development.

Binet's other major concern during this period was the unreliability of the methods then in use for the diagnosis and classification of those in hospitals for the mentally defective and for the identification of abnormal schoolchildren. These methods were anything but standardized, varying widely from examiner to examiner, and including such diverse measures as Binet- and Cattell–type mental tests, subjective impressions of cleanliness, and medical examinations. Little attempt had been made to regulate these practices or to determine if the tests being used were in fact related to intellectual functioning. Binet believed that he could apply his developing set of mental tests to these functions in a more systematic way.

His opportunity came in 1904, when the minister of public instruction set up a commission to study the educational problems of subnormal schoolchildren in Paris. In order for these children to receive the special education they needed, it was necessary to find an objective way of identifying those most in need of help. Binet and his student Theodore Simon were charged with developing such a test. The result of their efforts, the 1905 Binet–Simon scale, is generally considered the first usable intelligence test.[30]

The value of the Binet–Simon scale was derived from a series of features Binet had been working on during the previous decade:

- The test was, as Binet and Simon called it, a "Metrical Scale of Intelligence." The thirty test items were arranged in order of increasing difficulty, with difficulty levels established through standardization on both normal and subnormal children aged three to eleven in the Paris schools.

- The test items were age graded. It was reported, for example, that the average three–year–old made it through item 9, while five–year–olds correctly answered items through number 14 (standardization was only provided for odd–numbered years in the 1905 scale). Test scores were thus reported not in terms of an absolute level of intelligence, but by comparing a student's mental age (age–equivalent of highest question answered correctly) to his or her chronological age. Retardation or advancement was reported in years. (In order to eliminate nonlinearities in this method of reporting test scores—a five–year–old performing at the three–year–old level is actually more retarded than an eleven–year-old who tests as a nine–year–old—German psychologist William Stern, in 1911, proposed the use of the "mental quotient," in which a child's mental age is divided by his or her chronological age.[31] Today's intelligence quotient, or IQ, is derived from this measure, and is essentially the mental quotient multiplied by 100.) It was the genius of Binet to standardize mental age. Binet understood that intelligence, whatever it is, increases during childhood, and that it is more fruitful for a psychology of individual differences to concentrate on relative levels of intelligence than to try to measure such a nebulous concept in absolute terms.

- The scale items tested a wide variety of simple and higher mental functions in order to provide a more complete picture of the child's intellectual functioning. Thus, for example, item 1 measured simple visual coordination, in which the child had to move head and eyes in order to follow a lighted match passed before the eyes. In item 5, the child was required to remove a paper wrapper from a piece of chocolate. Item 11 asked children to repeat a series of three digits following oral presentation. Item 20 asked for the resemblance between groups of various named objects, such as a wild poppy and blood, or an ant, a fly, and a butterfly. Item 30, the most difficult in the scale, asked for the distinction between such abstract terms as "liking" and "respecting." The test thus provided a measure of general intellectual capacity, rather than of the more specific functions measured by earlier tests developed by Binet and others.

The most important feature of the Binet–Simon scale, of course, was that it worked. The 1905 scale, and even more so its 1908 revision, proved to be extremely useful for identifying the retarded. In addition, the Binet–Simon scale provided a general rank–ordering of normal and subnormal students that was consistent with other indicators of intelligence such as teacher and peer evaluations and ease of trainability, but did so in a more efficient and reliable manner than the other measures.

Typical of the reaction to the scales was that of H. H. Goddard, who in

1910 translated the 1908 scale into English for use in the United States. At first skeptical that one could measure global intelligence in the exact way Binet and Simon proposed, Goddard was amazed by the scale's accuracy when he began to use it at his Vineland, New Jersey school for feeble-minded children.

Another American psychologist particularly impressed by the Binet–Simon scales was Lewis Terman. As a graduate student at Clark University, Terman had been working on his own intelligence scale based on higher mental processes when the first Binet–Simon scale was published. In 1916, as a professor of psychology at Stanford University, Terman published the Stanford Revision of the Binet–Simon scale,[32] based partially on his own work and partially on the final 1911 revision (Binet died in that year) of the Binet–Simon. Terman's test, which in its subsequent revision has come to be known as the Stanford–Binet, became the standard by which all later intelligence tests have been judged.

The Army Tests and the First Controversy

The great need for reliable selection devices and the enthusiasm of the early American mental testers very quickly led to widespread intelligence test use in the United States in the years before World War I. The most common use was for the screening of children and the identification of the feeble-minded in public and private schools. Intelligence tests were also administered in other institutions, including hospitals, prisons and insane asylums. Many of these institutional applications were small-scale research projects, however. Large-scale intelligence and aptitude testing in the school and workplace was precluded by the expensive and time-consuming nature of individual test administration.

The status of mental testing changed dramatically with the first large-scale usage of group intelligence tests during World War I. The development of intelligence tests along the Binet–Simon model that could be administered to a large group simultaneously had been progressing slowly in the years preceding the war. As early as 1910, Binet and Simon had discussed the feasibility of group testing of army recruits.[33] The most notable progress was made by Arthur Otis, a student of Terman's at Stanford, who in 1917 developed an objectively scored paper-and-pencil test that Terman claimed produced scores almost identical to the individually-administered Stanford–Binet.[34] Otis' test served as an important model for the World War I Army exams. When the United States entered the war in 1917, Robert Yerkes of Harvard, then president of the APA, quickly mobilized psychologists to aid the war effort, and to promote the usefulness of their nascent enterprise. Among the committees formed was one chaired by Yerkes, on Methods of Psychological Examining of Recruits. Yerkes assembled in Vineland, New Jersey a group of America's leading mental testers, including Terman and Goddard, for the purpose of developing a group–administered test that would aid in placing recruits into appropriate jobs and could identify those incompetent to serve. The results of their efforts, as accepted for use by the army, were the Alpha and Beta exams. The Alpha contained questions in such areas as arithmetical reasoning, number series completion, and analogies—categories similar to those found in the Stanford–Binet and many present–day intelligence tests. The Beta, intended for use with illiterate recruits, contained similar questions, but in purely pictorial form.

Yerkes, and the Army Division of Psychology that he headed, supervised the administration of the Alpha and Beta to nearly 2 million Army recruits. The impact these test results had on the war effort is uncertain. While nearly 8,000 recruits were recommended for discharge as mentally incompetent, and thousands of others were assigned according to their test scores,[35] many Army officers were skeptical of the suddenly ubiquitous mental testers and their "scientific" instruments and refused to use the results. Nonetheless, that Yerkes and his group of testers were able to develop the tests and organize their administration to so many recruits under wartime conditions demonstrated the feasibility of large–scale group intelligence testing.

The success of the Army tests, at least from a logistical perspective, and the experience gained in developing these and more specific aptitude tests during the war, transformed psychology from an academic discipline into a profession. After the war, the new group–testing technology was applied on a regular basis in schools and industry. The rapidly expanding and changing American population and social structure of the first part of this century created a desperate need for efficient selection tools, and the mental testers were only too happy to help out. Mental testing, touted as the scientific solution to selection problems, fit nicely with popular Progressive ideas of reshaping society through the rational application of science. By 1921, 2 million American schoolchildren were being tested by one or another group intelligence test, mostly for placement in homogeneous classrooms (tracking).[36] Additionally, individually–administered tests continued to be widely used for the identification and placement of special–needs students.

The application of the new selection tools after World War I was particularly evident in employment, where the enthusiasm with which many employers accepted intelligence tests reflected a perception of the tests as major tools of efficiency. In the years immediately following the war, hundreds of companies began to use commercially available tests to make employment decisions, while only a handful of firms devoted the resources necessary to develop proper testing programs.[37] This state of affairs was partially the result of salesmanship by many of the mental testers, who were anxious to apply their new technology, even in cases where, as some of their colleagues warned, tests had not been sufficiently validated for the uses to which they were being put.

Besides putting psychology on the map, the Army tests had another consequence: they set off the first public controversy about intelligence testing. The Army data revealed that members of immigrant groups, on the average, scored lower than native–born Americans, and that immigrants from southern and eastern Europe (who were in general more recent arrivals) scored lower than those from northern and western Europe. Black recruits scored lowest of all. Moreover, based on the age–graded standards in use, the average mental age of all Army recruits was 13.

The immigrant data were seized upon by Carl Brigham, an assistant professor of psychology at Princeton, whose 1923 book *A Study of American Intelligence* is a racist treatise by any standard. Brigham argued that the Army data demonstrated the well–known inferiority of those of Mediterranean stock, as compared to the Nordic races of northern Europe. His conclusion was that the United States must restrict immigration from southern and eastern Europe in order to keep the American gene pool from deteriorating. While Brigham's book apparently had little influence in political circles, it is evidence that the same racism and xenophobia that produced the restrictionist Immigration Act of 1924 were amenable to the testing data. Similarly, popular eugenicist writers were quick to point to the average mental ability of Army recruits (despite the Army testers' own warnings that the numbers should not be interpreted too literally) as a warning that we must act quickly to improve our breeding stock. (The Army data fit nicely with the increasingly popular American eugenics movement; by the mid 1930s, 24 states had laws mandating sterilization for those with certain heritable defects, including feeble–mindedness.)[38] The reaction of many who found the conclusions being drawn from the Army results abhorrent was to attack not only the conclusions but the tests themselves.

Certain contemporary critics, most notably Stephen Jay Gould in *The Mismeasure of Man* and Leon Kamin in *The Science and Politics of IQ*, have sought to attack the testing edifice by exposing its racist foundations. They argue that the early mental testers propagated intelligence tests largely as a means of demonstrating the inherent superiority of middle– and upper–class whites, and that today's tests and those who support them represent the same agenda. A common tactic used by such writers is to describe in detail one extreme case, like Brigham, and then argue that it is typical of the mental–testing community as a whole. In fact, racism was probably less common among the early mental testers than among the rest of the population of the time. Once testing entered its period of most rapid and sophisticated development in the 1930s, there is no longer evidence of racist influence. The long history of attempts by mainstream psychometricians to develop culture–fair tests is one indication that tests have been more than tools for maintaining the status quo.

Frequently quoted in accounts of the inherent racism of testing is Kamin's description of H. H. Goddard's assessment of newly arriving immigrants at Ellis Island: "83% of the Jews, 80% of the Hungarians, 79% of the Italians, and 87% of the Russians were 'feebleminded.'"[39] Goddard does indeed report these numbers, but Kamin and those who cite him fail to tell their readers that Goddard did not believe the groups tested to be representative of immigrants from those countries, nor was he willing to attribute their feeble–mindedness to genetic causes.[40] It is also not the case that the Army testing data were in any way important to the passage of the Immigration Act of 1924, reports by Stephen Jay Gould and Leon Kamin notwithstanding. An examination of the relevant legislative history reveals that the Act would have been passed had the testing data never existed.[41] That the Gould/Kamin history is so uncritically reported in the news media and elsewhere is another example of the pervasiveness of anti-testing sentiment today.

The post–World War I mental–testing community, while obviously not willing to condemn testing as a whole, could be found on both sides of the debate over the Army data. Many psychologists and educators were critical of Brigham's book and of those who would draw strong conclusions from the obviously flawed Army tests.[42] It was pointed out, for example, that on six of the eight subtests of the Alpha the most common score was zero, an indication that the test was too difficult, and therefore meaningless as a measure of intelligence. Though intended as measures of native ability, it was clear that the tests were too dependent on specific cultural knowledge, a flaw particularly onerous to recent immigrants. Physical conditions varied across test administrations, often involving cramped quarters and inadequate lighting and acoustics. Mental age calculations were based on a supposed adult mental age of sixteen, even though few of the recruits had attended school past the age of fourteen. Many critics also pointed out that test scores of immigrant groups were higher the longer the groups had been in this country, indicating that much of the low scores of these groups could be attributed to an unfamiliarity with American culture. Brigham had taken these data to mean that recent immigrant groups were innately less intelligent than earlier ones.

In contrast to those both in and out of the psychological community who attacked the Army tests and their interpretations, Yerkes himself wrote the foreword to Brigham's book, noting that "[t]he author presents not theories or opinion but fact."[43] Moreover, many early psychologists were certainly amenable to the idea of innate differences in intelligence between racial and socio-economic groups. While not convinced by the Army data, Terman warned in 1922 that "No nation can afford to overlook the danger that the average quality of its germ plasm may gradually deteriorate as a result of unrestricted immigration."[44] He also argued, in discussing the results of the original standardization tests of the Stanford–Binet, "[t]hat the children of the superior social classes make a better showing in the tests is probably due, for the most part, to a superior original endowment."[45] Regarding racial differences, Terman hypothesized that when proper experiments on American Indian, Mexican, and Negro intelligence were conducted "there will be discovered enormously significant racial differences in general intelligence, differences which cannot be wiped out by any scheme of mental culture."[46]

The loudest popular voice raised against the mental testing movement was that of Walter Lippmann. In a series of articles in the *New Republic* in 1922 and 1923, Lippmann presented what the *New Republic* editors called an "analysis and estimate of intelligence tests."[47] Lippmann's primary target was the idea that intelligence tests were measures of innate mental ability, or of "intelligence" for that matter. He believed that this idea was being sold to the public by elitists (what he called the "New Snobbery") attempting to maintain the status quo (then, as now, test scores are higher in the upper classes), and by power–hungry psychologists who, with one examination, would be able to ascertain a child's immutable mental capacities. The *New Republic* published a reply to Lippmann by Terman, who, though surprisingly sarcastic in tone, was reasonable in substance. He explained that no psychologist believed the tests to be pure measures of mental ability (though to be sure genes were the most important factor), and that while certainly not perfect, intelligence tests were quite useful in doing the kinds of things one would expect an intelligence test to do. One doubts, however, that Terman's mean–spiritedness (in response to Lippmann's suggestion that environmental influences early in life might have a significant effect on intelligence, Terman proposed that Lippmann begin an investigation of the IQ effects of "different versions of Mother Goose")[48] did him much good in the public relations war.

The wave of public debate set off by the Army data ended by the mid 1920s, but the issues addressed—heredity vs. environment, the nature of intelligence, and the proper uses of testing—have remained important within professional circles, and, during the past twenty-five years, have again entered the public consciousness.

As public attacks on mental tests were subsiding, the testing movement was evolving from a largely experimental enterprise into a well–established professional endeavor. The 1920s and 30s saw a proliferation of intelligence and specific aptitude tests. Terman published his first revision of the Stanford–Binet, involving a standardization sample of over 3,000 adults and children, in 1937.[49] Two years later, David Wechsler published his first intelligence test, which was to become the Wechsler Adult Intelligence Scale, the most widely used individually–administered intelligence test for adults.[50] This period was also notable for the development of sophisticated statistical techniques for determining the reliability and validity of tests, the introduction of machine–scoring techniques, and the first large–scale adoption and twin studies for systematically investigating the relative roles of heredity and environment in intelligence. Additionally, several journals and professional organizations devoted to psychological measurement were founded, as were numerous test–publishing firms dedicated to the development and dissemination of psychological tests (by 1936 there were at least 96 different firms publishing tests).[51] As a result of this increasing professionalization, a general decline in Darwinian explanations of behavioral phenomena, and perhaps also because of their earlier experiences in the public domain, those who developed and studied intelligence tests became less bold in their proclamations about innate mental ability and the sources of group differences in IQ. Even Brigham admitted in 1930 that one can make no strong claims about group differences in intelligence.[52] The public seemed to pay little attention to any of these developments, except insofar as they found tests becoming an increasingly common part of their lives.

World War II and the Awakening of Public Consciousness

The potential demonstrated by the Army tests of World War I was realized during the Second World War, when the U.S. armed forces engaged in a massive testing program. More than 9 million recruits took the Army General Classification Test (AGCT), a test of general aptitude that, interestingly, the new breed of Army testers was very careful not to call an intelligence test. Unlike the Army Alpha and Beta, the AGCT clearly played an important role in selection and classification. Moreover, specific aptitude tests, like those given by the Air Force to screen potential pilots, proved to be tremendously useful in funneling those most qualified into expensive and time–consuming training programs.[53] As in World War I, the general perception, perhaps more accurate following the Second World War, was that the testing establishment had demonstrated that tests of mental ability were efficient decision–making tools.

After the war, the growth of testing continued at a rapid pace. In the schools, intelligence tests became a regular part of the curriculum, where they were used to segregate students by ability and for educational and career guidance. In a 1949 article in the *New York Times Magazine*, Benjamin Fine estimated that 20 million schoolchildren would be taking intelligence tests during the upcoming school year.[54] In college admissions, the SAT (introduced in 1926 and required by only a small fraction of colleges and universities before the war) was adopted, along with the ACT, by nearly every school in the nation. During the war years, the CEEB, sponsors of the SAT, dropped their earlier essay–type achievement test to concentrate on the multiple–choice SAT. The SAT was intended to be less dependent on any fixed curriculum than an achievement test, and thus more equitable.

Perhaps the largest effect of the wartime testing program was felt in employment. Surveys of American industry by Walter Dill Scott found that the percentage of companies using intelligence tests for hiring and promotion increased from 26 percent in 1940 to 63 percent in 1957.[55] The government helped, as the newly founded United States Employment Service made tests available at no cost to employers, and would even develop and standardize special tests in return for data supplied to the government.

The enlargement of intelligence and aptitude testing in employment after the war followed a decline in such testing during the 1920s and 1930s. Industrial leaders of the first part of the century had failed to heed the warnings of improper validation, and quickly found that their unvalidated tests weren't working. The Hawthorne Works project of the late 1920s, the first large–scale social–science study of industrial productivity, confirmed what employers were beginning to realize: that motivational and social factors are as important to certain kinds of productivity as is ability or external incentives. Military testing during the Second World War once again convinced employers of the usefulness of intelligence and aptitude tests. Ironically, there ensued another proliferation of commercially available employment tests, and overenthusiasm about test use on the part of both employers and test makers. As before, many in the testing field warned that employment tests were being overused.[56]

The original promise of intelligence tests was as a tool for increased efficiency in education and employment. In the postwar environment, tests held out a new hope: the means for achieving a more democratic society through the unbiased search for ability. Tests became a tool for achieving a social order based not on privilege or wealth, but on merit and ability.[57] During World War I, the validity of the tests was confirmed by the fact that officers, who were "obviously" more intelligent, outscored enlisted men on the Army tests. But the American mood had shifted by the end of World War II, and the emphasis on merit coexisted uneasily with a growing consensus among both the public and professionals that ability was equally distributed among all groups and social classes. It is not surprising, in the era of *Brown v. the Board of Education*, that a 1956 poll of American attitudes toward desegregation found that almost 80 percent of white Americans believed blacks to be their intellectual equals, compared to only half as many who believed the same thing in 1942.[58] The contradiction between the new view and the reality of group differences in test scores was resolved by the assumption that, as racial discrimination declined, minority groups would obtain scores on various measures of intelligence and achievement equal to those of other groups. Thus, intelligence tests were perceived as progressive instruments for helping the underprivileged to their rightful place.

The 1949 *New York Times Magazine* article by Fine is instructive as a barometer of the popular mood toward intelligence testing. Entitled "More and More, the IQ Idea Is Questioned," it is a rare (for the time) popular critique of testing, and an excellent example of the exception proving the rule. Fine was worried about overreliance on intelligence test scores at the expense of motivational variables in predicting student performance. He says of IQ tests, "Today . . . it is impossible to exaggerate their continued influence on American teaching methods."[59] After citing numerous instances of students outperforming their IQs, and exhorting educators not to put too much faith in imperfect instruments, Fine's damaging conclusion is: "In the classroom a pupil's capacity for learning, even if gauged only approximately, is one of the most important facts we can know about him and if IQ tests show a teacher what to expect in classroom performance then they have a definite validity. Only at all times we must remember that they cannot be relied upon exclusively."[60]

Accompanying the generally favorable attitudes toward intelligence testing of the postwar public was a lack of concern for the group difference issue, a subject that had been so important in earlier public debate about testing, and would be again. The only mention of group differences in intelligence in the Fine article is a discussion of attempts by University of Chicago sociologist Allison Davis to develop more culture–fair tests. Rather than attacking intelligence tests as biased, Fine mentions Davis' work merely as an indication that other factors besides native mental ability can affect a youngster's score. (In the professional community, Davis' work, like that of many others who attempted to develop culture–free or culture–fair tests, was generally seen as a noble but failed attempt—he was never able to develop a test that significantly reduced socioeconomic differences in test score but was still predictive of academic success.)

Further evidence that group differences in intelligence were not a significant public issue is the lack of public reaction to the article "Psychological

Tests–A Scientist's Report on Race Differences" in *U.S. News and World Report* in 1956.[61] Villanova psychology professor Frank McGurk argued that the significant black–white IQ difference apparent in the Army tests of World War I had not decreased at all during the following forty years, despite vast improvement in the social and economic conditions of black Americans. His conclusion was that the IQ difference could not be attributed to inferior black environment.

Unlike the public, the professional community was not willing to ignore such statements. A month after the McGurk piece, *U.S. News* ran a two–page statement signed by eighteen social scientists in which they denied that there was sufficient scientific evidence to justify the conclusion of significant genetic group differences in intelligence.[62] While there certainly was no shortage of scientific investigations of the group differences problem—Audrey Shuey's 1958 *The Testing of Negro Intelligence* reviewed over 200 such studies—public statements about genetic group differences were met with sharp critical reaction from the professional community. The atrocities committed in the name of the Nazi eugenic policies assured that any talk of genetic group differences was taboo. In addition to McGurk, Henry Garrett's description of the prevailing sentiment regarding group differences as "equalitarian dogma" was met with public censure by the SPSSI.[63] Audrey Shuey was unable to get a major scientific publishing firm to accept her book, which concluded that there was a significant genetic component to black–white IQ differences, and had to have it printed privately.[64] Similarly, when University of Chicago physiologist Dwight Ingle criticized fellow scientists for ignoring the possibility of genetic racial differences in intelligence in a 1964 *Science* magazine article, subsequent issues contained a host of hostile replies.[65] The acrimonious nature of professional debate on this topic went virtually unnoticed by a public generally pleased with current testing practices and outcomes.

Things began to change during the late 1950s and early 1960s, as three trends converged to alter perceptions about intelligence testing. The first was a shift in focus in the psychological community, particularly in developmental psychology. The increasingly popular work of Jean Piaget and his followers was placing the emphasis in the growth of cognitive structures on the child's interaction with his environment. More and more, psychologists came to understand that it was not a question of nature vs. nurture, but nature and nurture interacting. A child's intelligence, whatever its genetic component, could be significantly enriched or impoverished by the environment. The major treatise of this new philosophy was the 1961 book *Intelligence and Experience* by University of Illinois psychologist J. McV. Hunt. Hunt presented a great deal of evidence to support his position that intelligence was almost infinitely plastic. Hunt's book, and the ideas it represented, were enormously influential in both the scientific community and public policy circles, where, along with Benjamin Bloom's 1964 *Stability and Change in Human Characteristics*, it provided the scientific justification for the Head Start program.

The story of the beginnings of Head Start is an excellent example of how science may be usurped for political purposes. The original motivation for Head Start grew out of the increasing environmentalism in both the psychological community and political circles, and the consequent belief that poverty could be eliminated through education. The founders of the Head Start program saw it as a long–term social program aimed at many elements of the child's environment, including the family and community as much as the classroom. When the program was sold to the public and the policymakers, however, the politically more palatable quick fix was emphasized: two months in a special summer program would significantly raise the IQs of underprivileged children.[66]

The position that the environment can significantly affect intelligence, even where genetic factors are important, is one with which few social scientists would argue. But the new wave of the early 60s involved more than a mere emphasis on the environment. Somewhere along the way genetic factors were ignored. The long–standing psychological consensus that genes play a large role in within–group differences in intelligence had broken down. No one seemed to be denying outright that genes are important to intelligence, but there was almost a conspiracy of silence about the subject as psychologists and educators became the thankful recipients of millions of dollars of federal grant money aimed at raising the IQs of the underprivileged.

The second important trend of the era involved the public as much as the professionals. Perhaps inevitable in light of the tremendous enthusiasm with which America embraced testing after World War II, the 1960s saw a growing disenchantment with intelligence tests as tools for achieving a more democratic society. Popular books and articles began appearing in which tests were criticized as impure measures of intelligence, and the testing community was portrayed as an anti–democratic force with unjustified power over people's lives. Additionally, there were complaints of overreliance on and misinterpretation of test scores. Many parents and teachers, inadequately trained in psychometrics, succumbed to the magic of the IQ, and the belief that a single test score could tell them most of what they needed to know about a child's ability to succeed. In a way, the increasing complaints about testing were merely an extension of Benjamin Fine's earlier warnings, but now the public seemed more inclined to listen. In 1949, the tests represented the road to the good life; by the 1960s, it was clear that many people never got there.

Related to these developments, of course, was a growing public awareness of inequity in American society, and the will to do something about it. The civil rights movement awakened public consciousness to the deplorable social and economic circumstances of many minority groups, and equality became the watchword. Many of the inequities apparent in education and employment, like disproportionate black enrollment in EMR classes, involved resources and opportunities in which intelligence or aptitude testing played an allocative role. Persistent racial and socioeconomic IQ differences could only be interpreted as evidence of the cultural deprivation experienced by various minority groups and/or as the result of test bias.

There were, however, deeper issues involved. As Daniel Bell has argued in *The Cultural Contradictions of Capitalism*, liberal capitalist democracy in the United States had been built on notions of individualism, tempered by commitments to hard work and self–restraint derived from a Calvinist religious sensibility. Science and enlightenment had eroded the religious view, which defined work as a calling, and replaced it with the notion of work as something that would lead to ever greater individual material satisfaction. In contemporary America the latter notion had been replaced by the urge to achieve satisfaction through individual self–development and the consumption of meaningful experience.

The undermining of traditional bourgeois sensibilities, including commitments to self–restraint and appropriate patterns of authority, Bell argues, had been encouraged by intellectuals (broadly defined) in both Europe and America, and absorbed by the professional elites emerging in advanced capitalist societies. Bell stresses what he calls the "disjunction of realms." While the techno–economic realm calls for efficiency and meritocratic hierarchy, the cultural realm was now emphasizing the equality of all experience.[67]

To many of those on the Left, especially, IQ tests and even the notion of IQ came to be seen as the very epitome of a stratified, impersonal, bureaucratic, racist society. To attack them was also to mount a critique against that society in general.

Enter Jensen

A spark was applied to the tinder box created by these converging social trends by Arthur Jensen in early 1969. Perhaps torch is a better image, for Jensen did not merely speculate about taboo issues; "How Much Can We Boost IQ and Scholastic Achievement?" was directed at the heart of the current orthodoxy. The article begins "Compensatory education has been tried and it apparently has failed."[68] There follows a 123–page review of the scientific literature on the genetic and environmental determinants of intelligence. Among Jensen's conclusions: the failure of large-scale compensatory education programs to raise IQs significantly is best explained by the limitations placed on intellectual plasticity by an individual's genetic endowment. Based on the currently available evidence, Jensen placed the heritability of intelligence at about .80, meaning that 80 percent of the individual differences in IQ in the American population could be traced to genetic differences.

Though hardly belligerent in tone, Jensen was, by the nature of his statements, "girding himself for a holy war against 'environmentalists,'" as one commentator put it.[69] Coming as they did on the heels of the Westinghouse Learning Corporation report, which had concluded that the promised IQ gains from Head Start had not materialized,[70] Jensen's remarks were not likely to sit well with the psychological and educational establishment. Moreover, though he admitted that intelligence is not easily measured, Jensen argued for the validity and usefulness of intelligence tests, and was willing to accept the tests as measures of intelligence, a view counter to the growing disillusionment with testing among the articulate and informed public.

As much as these statements about IQ heritability and the validity of tests were likely to, and in fact did, incite critical reaction, nothing in Jensen's article was nearly as inflammatory as his speculations about the fifteen–point black–white IQ difference, a gap that has existed for as long as there have been useful measures of intelligence. Jensen found it "not an unreasonable hypothesis" that genetic factors are implicated in this difference. Admitting there was insufficient evidence to reach a strong conclusion, Jensen nevertheless felt that the existing evidence was more consistent with a hypothesis of genetic and environmental determination than with a strictly environmental explanation.

The virulent reaction to Jensen's article on college campuses and in the popular press marked the beginning of the modern IQ controversy. The furor over Jensen touched off a public debate over intelligence testing much larger than that created by the Army tests. The opposition to testing that had been prominent after World War I, and which had begun to surface again during the 1960s, came fully to the fore during the first half of the 70s. Besides the question of group differences in intelligence, the issues of test validity, the heritability of intelligence, and of course, cultural bias entered the popular literature. The 1970s saw a flood of popular books on testing, almost all of which were critical of Jensen and of intelligence tests in general. The news media helped to foster public debate by increasing their coverage of testing issues. During the first half of the last decade, nearly every general–interest magazine in the country had at least one article on the IQ controversy, concentrating primarily on the racial issue. The major newspapers, like the *New York Times* and the *Washington Post*, closely followed the exploits of the principals in this unfolding drama. And there was plenty to cover.

Among the more prominent players was Harvard psychology professor Richard Herrnstein. His entry into the debate is an example of how public controversies often feed upon themselves. Herrnstein, who is not a psychometrician, and who had never done any research on issues related to intelligence or testing, became interested in the topic through a chapter he had written for an introductory textbook, and through Jensen's article. He found particularly compelling Jensen's arguments about the substantial heritability of intelligence. Herrnstein began to read many of the original sources and became convinced that Jensen was correct. Herrnstein was also struck by the important role intelligence seemed to play in economic mobility in American society. In a 1971 *Atlantic* article entitled "I.Q.," Herrnstein argued that if intelligence is important in the race to get ahead, and if intelligence is largely heritable, then there will be genetic differences between members of different socioeconomic classes. He made no mention of the racial issue, per se, except to say that the most reasonable conclusion at present is that we don't know if genetic factors are implicated or not. Nonetheless, blacks are disproportionately represented in the lower classes, and it was easy to group Herrnstein with Jensen as yet another example of a long history of white elitists ready to use test scores and genetics as justification for an inequitable social structure.

As with Jensen, the reaction to Herrnstein was hostile. His classes were regularly disrupted, he was prevented from speaking at Harvard and at other campuses, even when he had come to speak about issues other than testing, and he was regularly called a racist. In the press and elsewhere, Herrnstein's name became linked with that of Jensen and Stanford physicist William Shockley. A 1971 American Anthropological Association resolution condemned "as dangerous and unscientific the racist, sexist or anti–working class theories of genetic inferiority propagated by R. Herrnstein, W. Shockley and A. Jensen."[71] The news media were fond of describing this unholy triumvirate as scientists holding controversial theories about the innate inferiority of blacks. In fact, Herrnstein had made no claims about the racial issue, and Jensen said nothing about inferiority, only lower intelligence.

Shockley was a different story. More blatantly political than Jensen or Herrnstein, Shockley, a Nobel Prize winner (as one of the inventors of the transistor), was probably more responsible than anyone for giving those on the pro–testing side a bad name. Even before the publication of Jensen's article, Shockley had been trying to get the National Academy of Sciences

(NAS) to sponsor research on group differences in intelligence. In tones smacking of earlier eugenicists, Shockley would speak of "dysgenic trends" in the American population, and at one point speculated publicly about paying people not to have children, the amount of payment to be determined by the individual's IQ; the lower the IQ, the larger the incentive not to breed. When, in 1980, millionaire inventor Robert Graham started his sperm bank for Nobel Prize winners, Shockley was one of the first to contribute and the only one to admit it publicly.

As Shockley toured the country propounding his views, the *New York Times* provided blow-by-blow coverage of the tumult. The NAS, which for years had refused to honor Shockley's call for research, surprisingly capitulated in 1971, but only in agreeing that racial differences should be studied. They declined to fund such research.

Testing Under Attack

While Jensen's *HER* article was the spark that touched off the IQ controversy, it would be a mistake to believe that there would have been no controversy without it. Criticism of testing was on the rise throughout the 60s; Jensen's article served to accelerate the pace and to focus attention on the racial issue. As early as 1968, however, the Association of Black Psychologists had called for a complete moratorium on standardized testing, charging that the tests were biased and were being used to stigmatize minority children. In 1972, the NEA passed a similar resolution. The controversy was, in fact, much broader than the theories of Herrnstein, Jensen, and Shockley.

Much of the growing disillusionment with testing was tied to another educational movement, towards mainstreaming. Mainstreaming refers to the teaching of handicapped children in the same classroom with their nonhandicapped peers, rather than in separate classes, and is mandated by Public Law 94-142, the Education for All Handicapped Children Act of 1975. In the years preceding the passage of 94-142, many educators had come increasingly to believe that teaching handicapped children (regardless of the type of handicap) in separate classes is stigmatizing and detrimental to the educational process. At the same time, as previously mentioned, there was a very strong trend away from tracking (ability grouping) among nonhandicapped children, the idea being that all children should, as much as possible, be given the same education. A large part of the problem with tracking and other forms of educational segregation is that students from certain racial and socioeconomic groups find themselves disproportionately in the excluded groups. As a primary tool by which tracking and placement decisions are made, intelligence and aptitude tests came under close scrutiny. The *Larry P.* decision is, of course, one example of where this examination led.

Among the numerous critiques of intelligence testing to appear during this period was a 1974 book, *The Science and Politics of IQ* by Princeton psychologist Leon Kamin. Like Herrnstein, Kamin had no experience with testing before the publication of Jensen's article. Ironically, Kamin became interested in the topic when, as chairman of the Princeton psychology department in 1972, he had to deal with the furor resulting from a scheduled talk by Herrnstein. When Kamin examined the intelligence literature for himself, he came to conclusions that were the opposite of Herrnstein's. Not only, Kamin decided, had the history of testing been one long attempt to keep minorities and the lower classes from usurping the privileges of those in power, but this politicization of science included the data on IQ heritability. Kamin claimed that there was no reasonable evidence for *any* heritable component to individual differences in IQ. This was a remarkable assertion in that it flew in the face of over fifty years of research that had almost unanimously concluded that IQ heritability was substantial. It has been noted that this consensus had been largely forgotten during the environmentalist dominated 60s, but it had never been directly disputed. In the acrimonious climate of the 70s, anything was possible.

As a result of his radical position, Kamin often found himself playing the part of the spokesman for the opposition in media accounts of the debate over IQ heritability. Although Kamin represented the most extreme possible position on the issue, the producers of *60 Minutes* and others were happy to set him up opposite Jensen or Herrnstein, giving the viewing and reading audience the impression that experts were, at best, undecided about the role of genes in intelligence.[72] That Jensen or Herrnstein were often chosen to represent the hereditarian position did not help matters, since they had already been associated with racism in earlier press reports.

The death blow for the hereditarian position, from the media perspective, came with the widely publicized scandal surrounding Sir Cyril Burt, the British psychologist who, late in life, apparently had faked data concerning the heritability of intelligence. Evidence of Burt's deceit began to surface in 1973 and 1974, but was not brought to the attention of the general public and the academic establishment as a whole until late 1976, when articles in the *Times* of London and *Science* magazine[73] (and subsequently the *New York Times* and the rest of the American print media) reviewed the evidence that Burt had invented data for twin studies of IQ heritability, and published, under the names of fictitious authors, papers supporting his own positions and attacking those of his critics. The immediate reaction from many of those most concerned about the IQ heritability issue was as irrational as it was predictable. Friends of Burt, and other believers in substantial IQ heritability, saw the attacks on Burt as another example of the smear tactics of left–wing environmentalists out to destroy the entire testing establishment. Environmentalists, on the other hand, accepted the evidence against Burt as proof that the hereditarian theory of intelligence was, from the beginning, a conspiracy against minorities and the poor.[74] That this mini–controversy ended with L. S. Hearnshaw's careful biography of Burt in 1979,[75] in which the author concludes that Burt most likely was guilty of intellectual fraud, did not help the protesting cause in the larger debate about IQ. The news media covered these events closely, emphasizing the damage caused to the hereditarian position by the loss of Burt's data. To be sure, the media were generally careful to point out that there were those who believed the loss of this data made little difference to the strength of the hereditarian claim, but the spokesmen for this position were usually Jensen or Herrnstein.

The Controversy as a Whole

At the heart of the IQ controversy is a clash between two sets of values central to American thought. The relative dominance of these values throughout the twentieth century has largely controlled the fate of intelligence testing in this country. As we have already pointed out this clash closely parallels what Daniel Bell has called the "disjunction of realms." This disjunction is reflected in the rational belief in intelligence and aptitude tests as efficient tools for the distribution of resources, coexisting with a cultural and political outcry against supposed individual and group differences in intelligence. The IQ controversy represents a clash of values, often within the same person, between a belief in a meritocratic hierarchy (efficiency) and the desire to see everyone succeed (equality).[76]

The desire for efficiency places the emphasis on differences between individuals, while equality concentrates on the similarities. Efficiency in a complex industrial society requires that resources and opportunities (education, employment, power) be allocated to those who will use them most productively, as defined by the production requirements (material, artistic, scientific, etc.) of the society. Among the skills most important to productivity in our society is intellectual aptitude of various sorts. In a capitalist system, value is placed on these skills through various rewards (money, prestige, etc.), which serve as incentives to assure that skills are propagated and resources properly allocated through competition. But the distribution of rewards through competition also carries with it the notion of dessert. Those who receive sought after rewards are, ideally, those who most deserve them, hence the notion of the meritocracy. But just as the aristocracy, originally meaning "rule by the best citizens," was corrupted into "rule by wealth and inheritance," so may "rule by the most deserving" (read "best citizens") contain the seeds of elitism and racism. Intelligence and aptitude tests may in fact be useful tools for the achievement of an efficient and productive society, but the system they help propagate carries with it the danger of an entrenched elite who can pervert these tools to maintain a notion of their own inherent superiority.

The egalitarian ideal is the antithesis of elitism and racism, and the subjugation of individuals and groups resulting therefrom. The democratic ideal that all men are created equal requires that under a capitalist system the competition be fair and that resources be allocated to those most deserving (to those who possess the necessary attributes and skills), irrespective of race, religion, ethnicity, wealth, and other factors thought to be irrelevant to optimum resource utilization. (Proponents of affirmative action and other quota systems argue that society will actually function more smoothly if some of these factors are taken explicitly into account in order to correct past inequities.) The danger inherent in egalitarianism is that a philosophy of human rights may be extrapolated into a theory of human nature. That individuals should be treated equally does not mean that all individuals are equal. Whether as a result of accidents of birth and environment, or through strength of will, people differ in abilities of all sorts, and it is possible that these abilities are not equally distributed among all possible subgroups of the population. Yet in a system where there is merit attached to certain attributes, regardless of their origin, inequity is easily perceived, even in situations where competition is fair and objective. When tests tell us that individuals and groups differ in average intellectual ability, there is a tendency to blame the messenger and cry "conspiracy," rather than accept what may be an unpleasant fact. The tendency toward apparently irrational response (if that is what much criticism of testing is) is heightened by the apparent racism and elitism (if that is what traditional pro–testing views are) of those who maintain that intelligence tests measure important attributes on which individuals, and possibly groups, differ genetically.

It might be argued that the dichotomy here outlined is undermined by the fact that the meritocracy is an egalitarian ideal, to be contrasted with the elitist aristocracy. This was true in the years following World War II, when tests were proclaimed as tools for achieving a meritocratic order based on fair competition between members of all groups. One of the products of the civil rights movement was a redefinition of fair competition. Fairness came to be defined in terms of outcomes (equal representation) rather than processes (equal opportunity). Not all of those who had supported the traditional meritocratic notions were willing to acquiesce in this change (particularly those who had benefited from the system), hence the conflict between meritocracy and egalitarianism. The terms are ours; no doubt testing's supporters would not consider themselves non-egalitarian, nor would its critics call themselves anti-meritocratic. The IQ controversy is not driven by the conflict between persons, however, but by the conflict between two essentially democratic ideals.

One can see, in the history of the IQ controversy previously outlined, the impetus of factors favoring the relative dominance of one or the other of these views. At the turn of the century, and through the First World War, the need to organize the chaos created by increasing industrialization, the growth of public education, and the rapid influx of myriad immigrant groups placed the emphasis squarely on efficiency, role specialization, and the identification of individual differences. The use and popularity of intelligence and aptitude tests increased rapidly, often more rapidly than the validity of the tests warranted. At the same time, the excesses of the meritocratic ethos, coupled with xenophobia toward immigrant groups and a long history of racism, led to the bastardization of the World War I Army testing results. The ensuing IQ controversy represents the first egalitarian backlash.

Between the wars, as eugenic and xenophobic attitudes waned, mental testers became more professional, the view of tests as tools of efficiency continued to hold the upper hand, and few complaints about testing were heard. The egalitarian ethic, on the rise after World War II, embraced the newly refurbished tests as means for a more equitable distribution of resources, and standardized testing enjoyed its greatest popularity. The love affair was short lived, however, as egalitarianism blossomed into the civil rights movement, and a heavily environmentalist view of human nature. Jensen, Herrnstein, and Shockley provided fodder for growing conspiratorial theories of the testing enterprise, and a new, more pervasive IQ controversy emerged. In recent years, the enemies of testing have gained important ground in this ongoing war.

It is the purpose of this book to examine more closely the important combatants and battlefields in the war over testing. Most of the fighting has taken place on two fronts: in the news media, and in public policy arenas. We have discussed how those opposed to testing appear to have made considerable gains in both domains. This may or may not be for the best. What is unfortunate about the public controversy over intelligence and aptitude testing is that it is so often uninformed. Much of the relevant discussion and decision making seems more influenced by political considerations than by the empirical literature on intelligence and testing. The recent history of this controversy is marked by the increasing subsumption of what is primarily a technical issue, the validity and usefulness of intelligence and aptitude tests, under political concerns.

Tests are an important public policy issue, as they continue to play a major allocative role in education and employment. Their politicization is therefore to some degree desirable; in a participatory democracy, citizens should have a say in how resources are distributed. Difficulties arise when this politicization so overwhelms the technical issues that it is forgotten that most members of society, including most of those charged with policy decisions, are ill equipped to deal with the technical questions involved. What has happened in the IQ controversy is that the expert voice has been misinterpreted and misrepresented, as science has been perverted for political ends. (The decision to use intelligence tests is a policy, and therefore political, decision, in which the technical question of test validity should play an important, but not necessarily decisive, part. The question of test validity, or test bias, on the other hand, is a purely technical one, and should not be influenced by political considerations.)

The news media have, of course, always appealed to experts in their coverage of controversies, but the tendency in the media is to paint everything in black and white, as if experts are equally split between two diametrically opposite positions. We have noted this tendency regarding the IQ heritability question. Furthermore, there is reason to believe that the media may have already decided what the experts think concerning IQ. When *Time* magazine tells us, as it did in 1977, that "the more tests that are devised, the more educators seem to doubt their validity,"[77] we are led to believe that those who publicly attack tests are echoing those most knowledgeable about them. Herrnstein has noted that every review of a book concerning intelligence testing in the *New York Times Book Review* between 1975 and 1981 is critical of testing, and that none of the reviewers is a trained psychometrician.[78]

In the legislatures and in the courts, expertise often takes a back seat to political considerations. The difficulties here are similar to those in the news media. As in the media, where controversy is presented as a clash between polar opposites, the adversary system, as practiced in legislative hearings and, to a greater extent, the courts, is not conducive to the acquisition of empirical knowledge. Rather than being presented with an objective assessment of the literature, legislators and judges hear the strongest possible case for what are often the most extreme arguments in a debate. Faced only with options at the extremes, decision makers must either adopt an extreme position or develop one of their own. Unfortunately, such decisions are often out of synch with the facts.

Consider, for example, the decisions reached by Judge Peckham in the *Larry P.* case, and by another federal district court judge, John Grady, in a highly similar case in 1980 (*PASE v. Hannon*).[79] As in *Larry P.*, Judge Grady was asked to enjoin the use of intelligence tests for the placement of black children into special education classes because these tests are racially biased. Remarkably, Judge Grady's decision was exactly the opposite of that reached by Judge Peckham. Grady concluded that these tests are not sufficiently biased to justify a discontinuation of their use. Examination of the transcripts of these cases reveals that each judge was presented with a great deal of technical information from experts testifying for both sides concerning the bias issue. Unable to reach a firm conclusion from this mountain of conflicting data, the judicial decisions reveal that the judges essentially ignored much of the expert testimony and reached their own conclusions about test bias based on two different criterion, both of which are equally wrong from a technical standpoint.

It is clear from Judge Peckham's decision and from his statements during the trial that he accepted as an incontrovertible fact that there is no difference in the "true" level of retardation between various racial and ethnic groups. Therefore, any test that purports to show such a difference must be biased. Such an argument is circular without other evidence for the assertion of equal levels of retardation, but it has the very useful property of ending discussion.

Having heard all the expert testimony about cultural bias in intelligence tests during the *PASE* case, Judge Grady decided that he couldn't decide. He therefore examined the tests in question on an item–by–item basis, and determined for himself how many items looked biased. Unlike Judge Peckham, who frequently cited expert testimony to back up his conclusions, Judge Grady was not convinced that the experts testifying at the trial were themselves being very objective. Unfortunately, Grady's method of measuring bias is useless without data on how test takers actually perform on each question. In the absence of what he felt to be reasonable expert testimony, and lacking expert knowledge himself, Judge Grady was forced into making a decision, on faulty grounds, that affected the lives of hundreds of schoolchildren.

The controversy surrounding intelligence and aptitude testing has important practical consequences, but the political nature of the controversy seems to have obscured that it is highly technical as well. When technical issues become important matters of public policy, whether in the courts, the legislatures, or the news media, the adversary nature of political debate will inevitably obscure an objective assessment of expert opinion. An accurate picture of expert opinion about intelligence and aptitude testing is therefore needed. Such a survey is not a means of settling the technical issues—scientific questions cannot be answered by consensus—but is an attempt to remain unbiased in the one element of an essentially political decision where objectivity is most important.

The next four chapters of this book will discuss the four major areas of contention in the IQ controversy: (1) the nature of intelligence, or, more accurately, what intelligence tests measure; (2) the heritability of IQ; (3) the nature of racial and class differences in intelligence test scores, including a discussion of the bias issue; and (4) the use and misuse of intelligence and aptitude tests. These chapters will include a summary of the positions held on each of the issues by the various constituents in the IQ debate. The discussion will focus, however, on the results of a large scale survey of expert opinion on controversial aspects of intelligence and aptitude testing. Many of the issues dealt with in the following chapters, and in the questionnaire, have not been the subject of much public discussion (i.e., news media coverage), but have been important elements in the longer and more comprehensive debate about testing in the scholarly literature. It is hoped that readers, particularly those charged with public policy decisions, will thereby gain a fuller understanding of the sources of contention in the IQ controversy and, most important, where the expert population stands on these issues. Chapters 4 and 5 also include an analysis of the relationship between the demographic and background characteristics of our expert sample, and their opinions about testing.

Chapters 6 and 7 describe the results of a content analysis of news media coverage of the modern IQ controversy. We have analyzed all coverage of testing–related issues appearing in ten major print and television news sources from the years 1969 (the year of Jensen's seminal article) to 1983, inclusive. The analysis concentrated on how the various controversial issues were presented and particularly, on how expert opinion about these issues was represented. Comparison between these results and those of the expert survey will provide a measure of news media accuracy on coverage of the IQ controversy. Additionally, Chapter 7 includes the results of a survey of journalist opinion about key testing issues, as well as ratings of news media coverage from our testing experts.

The concluding chapter presents a synthesis of the survey and content-analysis results and a more general discussion of the relationship between science and politics. We will also discuss the role of public opinion in the IQ controversy and the influence of the media, academia, and the general public on public policy.

It is important to note, before beginning a discussion of the important issues in the controversy, what this book is *not* about. We will not examine the controversy surrounding achievement tests—those tests intended to measure specific knowledge, rather than skills or abilities. There will, therefore, be no discussion of two recently disputed testing issues: minimum competency testing for students, and teacher competency testing. These tests are aimed at measuring the knowledge required for graduation and teaching, respectively, not aptitude or intelligence. There will, however, be considerable discussion of the much–debated aptitude–achievement distinction: What separates achievement from aptitude and intelligence tests, other than the test makers' intentions?

Additionally, we will not be concerned with newer and more radical conceptions of intelligence and testing such as Howard Gardner's "multiple intelligences," or Robert Sternberg's Triarchic Theory.[80] These recent developments are important contributions to the literature on intelligence that may very well lead to fundamental changes in the way we think about and measure intellectual skills, but they have very little to do with the issues of fundamental concern in the IQ controversy—the validity of tests, the heritability of IQ, the nature of group differences in test scores, test use and misuse—save the question of the nature of intelligence. Even here, these new approaches have yet to have much impact on the long–standing public discussion of what "intelligence" is. The same is true for most of modern cognitive science. Our primary concern is with the controversy over intelligence and aptitude testing, not with recent developments in the study of mental processes.

Notes

1. Arthur R. Jensen, *Genetics and Education* (New York: Harper & Row, 1972), p. 46.
2. Ibid., p. 24.
3. Although most of the more popular attacks on Jensen tended to be quite ad hominem, one of the few major exceptions has been Thomas Sowell, a conservative black economist. While Sowell has strongly criticized Jensen's conclusions, he has always treated him seriously and with civility. Thomas Sowell, *Race and Economics* (New York: David McKay, 1975).
4. SPSSI, "Statement on Current IQ Controversy: Heredity Versus Environment," *American Psychologist* 24 (1969):1039–1040.
5. Jensen, p. 39.
6. "Born Dumb?" *Newsweek* 31 March 1969, p. 84.
7. Jensen, p. 14; telephone interview with Lee Edson, author of "jensenism" article, 19 October 1985.
8. Leon J. Kamin, *The Science and Politics of IQ* (Potomac, MD: Lawrence Erlbaum, 1974); Andrew J. Strenio, *The Testing Trap* (New York: Rawson, Wade, 1981); Paul L. Houts, ed., *The Myth of Measurability* (New York: Hart Publishing, 1977); Stephen Jay Gould, *The Mismeasure of Man* (New York: Norton, 1981).
9. "New National Organization to Fight for Fair Standardized Tests," FairTest press release, 24 October 1985.
10. Carl Dimengo, "Basic Testing Programs Used in Major School Systems Throughout the United States in the School Year 1977–78," Akron Public Schools, March 1978.
11. *Hobson v. Hansen*, 269 F.Supp. 401 (D. D.C. 1967).
12. *Larry P. v. Riles*, 495 F.Supp. 926 (N.D. Cal. 1979).
13. *Larry P. v. Riles*, 793 F.2d 969 (9th Cir. 1984).

14. Telephone interview with Donna Bolen, Special–Education Consultant, California State Department of Education, 10 July 1984.
15. "IQ Tests Restricted by Race," *Washington Post*, 6 July 1987, p. A3; "Civil Rights Panel to Study California Ban on IQ Tests for Blacks," Associated Press, 13 July 1987.
16. *Griggs v. Duke Power Co.*, 401 U.S. 424 (1971).
17. Arthur R. Block and Michael A. Rebell, *Competence Assessment and the Courts: An Overview of the State of the Law* (ERIC ED 192 169), p. 16.
18. There may be some relief in sight for supporters of employment testing, as the EEOC, in response to increasing complaints about its unrealistic standards, announced in May 1985 that it is reviewing its *Guidelines* and may relax them. It would not pay to be optimistic, however, as the EEOC was close to relaxing it standards in 1976, only to be persuaded at the last minute by the NAACP to republish the original *Guidelines*. M. A. Pearn, *Employment Testing and the Goal of Equal Opportunity: The American Experience* (London: Runnymede Trust, July 1978), p. 28 (ERIC UD 019 829).
19. Mary L. Tenopyr, "The Realities of Employment Testing," *American Psychologist* 36 (1981):1121.
20. M. C. Miner and M. G. Miner, *Employee Selection Within the Law* (Washington, DC: The Bureau of National Affairs, 1978).
21. R. M. Guion, quoted in Pearn, p. 29.
22. *Douglas v. Hampton*, 338 F.Supp. 18 (D. D.C. 1972).
23. National Education Association, *Measurement and Testing: An NEA Perspective* (Washington, DC: Author, 1980).
24. R. T. Hartnett and R. A. Feldmesser, "College Admissions Testing and the Myth of Selectivity: An Unresolved Question and Needed Research," *AAHE Bulletin* 32 (1980):3–6.
25. J. McKeen Cattell, "Mental Tests and Measurement," *Mind* 15 (1890), p. 373 ff.
26. Clark Wissler, "The Correlation of Mental and Physical Tests," *Psychological Review, Monograph Supplement* 3 (1901).
27. Arthur R. Jensen, "Reaction Time and Psychometric g," in *A Model for Intelligence*, ed. Hans J. Eysenck (Berlin: Springer–Verlag, 1982), pp. 93–132; Langdon E. Longstreth, "Jensen's Reaction–Time Investigations of Intelligence: A Critique," *Intelligence* 8 (1984):139–160; Arthur R. Jensen and Philip A. Vernon, "Jensen's Reaction–Time Studies: A Reply to Longstreth," *Intelligence* 10 (1986):153–179; Langdon E. Longstreth, "The Real and the Unreal: A Reply to Jensen and Vernon," *Intelligence* 10 (1986):181–191; A. T. Welford, "Longstreth versus Jensen and Vernon on Reaction Time and IQ: an Outsider's View," *Intelligence* 10 (1986):193–195.
28. Stella E. Sharp, "Individual Psychology: A Study in Psychological Method," *American Journal of Psychology* 10 (1898–1899):329–391.
29. Alfred Binet, "Attention et Adaptation," *L'Année* Psychologique 6 (1900):248–404.
30. Alfred Binet and Theodore Simon, "Méthodes Nouvelles pour le Diagnostic du Niveau Intellectuel des Anormaux," *L'Année* Psychologique 11 (1905):191–244.
31. William Stern, *Die Differentielle Psychologie* (1911).
32. Lewis M. Terman, *The Measurement of Intelligence* (Boston: Houghton Mifflin, 1916).
33. Alfred Binet and Theodore Simon, "Sur la Nécessite d'une Méthode Applica-

ble au Diagnostic des Arriérées Militaires," *Annales Médico–Psychologiques,* (January/February 1910).

34. Daniel Resnick, "History of Educational Testing," in *Ability Testing: Uses, Consequences, and Controversies,* Part II, eds. Alexandra K. Wigdor and Wendell R. Garner (Washington, DC: National Academy Press, 1982), p. 182.

35. Matthew Hale, "History of Employment Testing," in *Ability Testing: Uses, Consequences, and Controversies,* Part II, eds. Alexandra K. Wigdor and Wendell R. Garner (Washington, DC: National Academy Press, 1982), p. 13.

36. Alexandra K. Wigdor and Wendell R. Garner, eds., *Ability Testing: Uses, Consequences, and Controversies,* Part I (Washington, DC: National Academy Press, 1982), p. 89.

37. Loren Baritz, *The Servants of Power* (Middletown, CT: Wesleyan University Press, 1960), p. 67.

38. Daniel J. Kevles, *In the Name of Eugenics: Genetics and the Uses of Human Heredity* (New York: Knopf, 1985).

39. Kamin, *Science and Politics of IQ.*

40. H. H. Goddard, "Mental Tests and the Immigrant," *The Journal of Delinquency* 2 (1917):243–277.

41. Mark Snyderman and R. J. Herrnstein, "Intelligence Tests and the Immigration Act of 1924," *American Psychologist* 38 (1983):986–995.

42. Edwin G. Boring, "Facts and Fancies of Immigration," *New Republic,* 25 April 1923, pp. 245–246; Percy E. Davidson, "The Social Significance of the Army Intelligence Findings," *Scientific Monthly* 16 (1923):184–193; M. B. Hexter and A. Myerson, "13.77 Versus 12.05: A Study in Probable Error," *Mental Hygiene* 8 (1924):69–82; Kimball Young, Review of *A Study of American Intelligence, Science* 57 (1923):666–670. See also Gould.

43. Robert Yerkes, Foreword to Carl C. Brigham, *A Study of American Intelligence* (Princeton, NJ: Princeton University Press, 1923).

44. Lewis M. Terman, "Were We Born That Way?" *World's Work* 44 (1922):655–660.

45. Terman, *Measurement of Intelligence,* p. 72.

46. Ibid., p. 92.

47. Lippmann–Terman debate reprinted in N. J. Block and Gerald Dworkin, eds., *The IQ Controversy* (New York: Pantheon Books, 1976), pp. 4–44.

48. Ibid., p. 37.

49. Lewis M. Terman and Maude A. Merrill, *Measuring Intelligence* (Boston: Houghton Mifflin, 1937).

50. David Wechsler, *The Measurement of Adult Intelligence* (Baltimore: Williams & Williams, 1939).

51. Philip H. Dubois, *A History of Psychological Testing* (Boston: Allyn and Bacon, 1970), pp. 112–120.

52. Carl C. Brigham, "Intelligence Tests of Immigrant Groups," *Psychological Review* 37 (1930):158–165.

53. Hale, pp. 23–24.

54. Benjamin Fine, "More and More, the IQ Idea Is Questioned," *New York Times Magazine,* 18 September 1949, pp. 7, 72–74.

55. Cited in Hale, p. 26.

56. Baritz, pp. 77–95, 139–166.

57. Theoretically, Americans had always believed that rewards should be distributed on the basis of effort and capacity, but the Protestant establishment

that controlled the major institutions of society had assumed that character and style were important in determining these essentials. In the aftermath of the war, this view changed rapidly, and tests of intelligence and aptitude were seen as mechanisms for insuring that the biases inherent in evaluating "character" no longer interfered with employment decisions or admission to prestigious colleges and universities. The change reflected a sharp decline in anti–Semitism, for, at that point, high achieving Jews had borne the brunt of such discrimination. Indeed, Jewish intellectuals and professionals were in the forefront of those pressing for decisions being made solely on the basis of objective measures of capacity and for the elimination of quota–like arrangements that had barred many of them from certain institutions of higher education. Indeed the shift to "objective" measures of aptitude was partly responsible for the rapidity with which Jews (and Japanese Americans) advanced in the post war period. Stanley Rothman and S. Robert Lichter, *Roots of Radicalism: Jews, Christians, and the New Left* (New York: Oxford University Press, 1982).

58. Herbert H. Hyman and Paul B. Sheatsley, "Attitudes toward Desegregation," *Scientific American* (December 1956):35–39.
59. Fine, p. 72.
60. Ibid., p. 74.
61. Frank C. J. McGurk,"'Psychological Tests–A Scientist's Report on Race Differences," *U.S. News and World Report* 21 September 1956:92–96.
62. Otto Klineberg et al., "18 Social Scientists Discuss: Does Race Really Make a Difference in Intelligence?" *U.S. News and World Report* 26 October 1956:74–76.
63. Henry E. Garrett, "The SPSSI and Racial Differences," *American Psychologist* 17 (1962):260–263.
64. R. Travis Osborne and Frank C. J. McGurk, *The Testing of Negro Intelligence*, Volume 2 (Athens, GA: The Foundation for Human Understanding, 1982), p. xiii.
65. Dwight J. Ingle, "Racial Differences and the Future," *Science* 146 (1964):375–379; comments in *Science* 146 (1964):1415–1418, 1526–1530, and *Science* 147 (1965):6–7.
66. Edward Zigler and Karen Anderson, "An Idea Whose Time Has Come: The Intellectual and Political Climate for Head Start," in Edward Zigler and Jeanette Valentine, eds., *Project Head Start* (New York: Free Press, 1979).
67. Daniel Bell, *The Cultural Contradictions of Capitalism* (New York: Basic Books, 1972); Lawrence M. Friedman, *Total Justice* (New York: Russell Sage Foundation, 1985).
68. Arthur R. Jensen, "How Much Can We Boost IQ and Scholastic Achievement?" *Harvard Educational Review* 39 (1969):2.
69. Lee J. Cronbach, "Heredity, Environment, and Educational Policy," *Harvard Educational Review* 39 (1969):90.
70. Westinghouse Learning Corp., *The Impact of Head Start: An Evaluation of the Effects of Head Start on Children's Cognitive and Affective Development. Executive Summary* (Washington, DC: Clearinghouse for Federal Scientific and Technical Information, June 1969) (ED 036 321).
71. American Anthropological Association, "Motions," *Newsletter* 13 (1972):12.
72. "The IQ Myth," *60 Minutes* segment, CBS, 26 June 1977.
73. Oliver Gillie, "Crucial Data Was Faked by Eminent Psychologist," *Sunday Times* (London), 24 October 1976; Nicholas Wade, "I.Q. and Heredity: Suspicion of Fraud Beclouds Classic Experiment," *Science* 194 (1976):916–919.

74. See, for example, "Correspondence" in the *Bulletin of the British Psychological Society* throughout 1977.
75. L. S. Hearnshaw, *Cyril Burt: Psychologist* (New York: Vintage Books, 1979).
76. This clash, at least as it affects opinion and policy toward testing, is not unique to capitalist society. The Chinese, who have used standardized tests in employment and education for over 3, 000 years, have twice during the past 40 years eliminated and then reinstated examinations for admission to schools of higher education. Each time the exams were eliminated as a result of complaints that certain economic and cultural groups were being disproportionately denied admission to these schools as a result of the tests, and each time the tests were reinstated in response to declining academic standards in the universities. The same pattern is to be found in the Soviet Union, and various Eastern European countries. After a period during which equal potentials were emphasized, scholars in these countries now maintain that differences in IQ are at least partly determined by the genes. Ana Teresa Gutierrez and Robert E. Klitgaard, *Higher Education and Admissions in the People's Republic of China* (Cambridge, MA: President and Fellows of Harvard College, 1982); H. J. Eysenck, "After Binet, Back to Galton," *Encounter*, (February 1983):74–79.
77. "Whatever Became of 'Geniuses'?" *Time* 19 (December 1977):89.
78. R. J. Herrnstein, "IQ Testing and the Media," *Atlantic Monthly*, (August 1982):68–74.
79. *PASE v. Hannon*, 506 F.Supp. 831 (N.D. Ill. 1980).
80. Howard Gardner, *Frames of Mind: The Theory of Multiple Intelligences* (New York: Basic Books, 1983); Robert J. Sternberg, *Beyond IQ: A Triarchic Theory of Human Intelligence* (New York: Cambridge University Press, 1985).

2

The Nature of Intelligence

I ain't no psychiatrist, I ain't no doctor with degrees,
but it don't take too much high IQ to see what you're
doin' to me.

—"Think" by Aretha Franklin and Ted White,
Fourteenth Hour Music, BMI, 1968

In March 1921, at a time when the practical application of mental testing was beginning a dramatic rise, and before the public controversy over the Army testing results had heated up, the *Journal of Educational Psychology* published a symposium on "Intelligence and Its Measurement," in which fourteen of the most important mental testers briefly expressed their views on the topic at hand.[1] A substantial majority of these experts appeared to be in agreement with what one tester called the "commonly accepted definition of intelligence" as mental adaptation to changing environmental stimuli (sometimes called the capacity to learn). Many also emphasized that intelligence is not a unitary trait, and that one must measure general intellectual capacity by sampling a wide variety of its interrelated subcomponents. The major source of disagreement between respondents concerned the breadth of adaptive experience to be considered "intelligent." For example, Lewis Terman felt that "[a]n individual is intelligent in proportion as he is able to carry on abstract thinking,"[2] and went so far as to castigate those whose "sense of psychological values" was so disturbed as to believe that "the individual who flounders in abstractions but is able to handle tools skillfully, or play a good game of baseball, is not to be considered necessarily *less* intelligent than the individual who can solve mathematical equations, acquire a huge vocabulary, or write poetry." At the other extreme, Brown University psychologist S. S. Colvin asserted that "intelligence tests should explore as many aspects of human ability as possible."[3] Most respondents agreed with Terman to the extent that they included some form of higher mental function, like abstract reasoning, problem solving, or decision making, in their definition of intelligence.

Besides the nature of intelligence, two further topics were frequently discussed by symposium participants. Regarding the ability of intelligence tests to measure intelligence, those experts holding broader definitions were naturally inclined to believe that tests were somewhat limited in content. Thus, for example, Terman's suggestions for improving tests primarily involved refinements of existing models, while Colvin asserted that true practicality would require tests of much broader scope. On the heritability issue, among those expressing an opinion, there was unanimous agreement that tests measured differences in both innate capacity and acquired knowledge, and that intelligence tests became better measures of capacity as individual differences in the opportunity to acquire knowledge were equalized.

Identical opinions on the heredity–environment issue were expressed by twelve mental testers polled by Frank Freeman in 1923.[4] This survey, published in the *Century Magazine,* covered a wider range of topics than the 1921 symposium. In addition to a statement about innate capacity and acquired knowledge, Freeman was able to get unanimous or near unanimous agreement to statements indicating the usefulness of intelligence tests, their validity as measures of general mental ability, and that group differences in intelligence are the result of differences in both environment and inheritance. Like the 1921 symposium, the consensus broke down when Freeman assessed agreement with the statement that general mental ability "represents ease of learning in the intellectual field." Experts could not agree as to what "the intellectual field" comprised. Some balked at the suggestion of even attempting to develop a precise definition of intelligence, claiming either that there were insufficient data or that the question was inconsequential compared to the issues of what the tests were measuring, and the possible uses to which they could be put.

The *Century Magazine* poll was published coincident with the first IQ controversy. The results of the poll were in striking contrast to the views expressed by the popular critics of the day, who claimed that intelligence tests had little to do with intelligence, and that differences in test scores were mostly the result of differences in training. Critics also portrayed mental testers, incorrectly according to the *Century* poll, as believing themselves to be in possession of pure measures of innate ability (see the discussion of Walter Lippmann's comments in Chapter 1). One area where the critics seemed to be right about the testers was their inability to agree on a definition of intelligence, at least in its particulars.

The disagreement among testing experts about a definition of intelligence apparent in the 1921 and 1923 polls may very well be an accurate representation of expert opinion at the time. It might also reflect the lack of any attempt to consolidate responses and look for underlying unity. Ironically, the technique best suited to discover such hidden structure, factor analysis, was developed as a result of the mental testing movement. Yet, it was sixty years before anyone attempted to apply factor analysis to opinions about the nature of intelligence. In 1981, Robert Sternberg and his colleagues published the results of a survey in which a group of laypersons and a group of psychologists conducting research on intelligence were asked how characteristic each of 250 behaviors is of an ideally intelligent person.[5] The ratings of the two groups were remarkably similar. More impressive, the ratings within each group could be largely explained by three underlying factors (components of intelligence). Among laypersons these factors were labeled "practical problem–solving ability," "verbal ability," and "social competence." Among experts they were "verbal intelligence," "problem–solving ability," and "practical intelligence." (Sternberg drew much of the impetus for his own Triarchic Theory, in which practical intelligence plays a prominent role, from the results of this survey.) The latter result lends credence to the contention of the APA ad hoc Committee on Educational Uses of Tests with Disadvantaged Students, in response to critics of testing, that "there is a consensus among psychologists as to the kinds of behaviors that are labeled intellectual."[6]

In 1986, Sternberg and Douglas Detterman published a book entitled *What Is Intelligence?*, an update of the 1921 *Journal of Educational Psychology* symposium, in which twenty–five contemporary experts on intelligence respond to the title question.[7] The results of the two symposia contain some striking similarities. In each case, there is a consensus of opinion about the nature of intelligence, in that the most frequently mentioned elements of intelligence are higher–level cognitive functions, such as abstract reasoning and problem solving. These attributes are mentioned by at least half the contributors in each symposium. Also prominent in both symposia, however, is disagreement over the breadth of the definition of intelligence, as is debate over whether intelligence is a general ability or a concatenation of many separate abilities.[8]

Unfortunately, there is little else we can say about consensus, or any other level of agreement or disagreement among experts on issues related to intelligence and aptitude testing. We have, at present, no concise description of the nature and variety of expert opinion on such issues as the origin and stability of intelligence, test use and misuse, bias in testing, and racial and economic group differences in IQ. The next four chapters of this book will describe the results of such a survey. We wish to emphasize again that this survey is not meant to settle the IQ controversy, but is merely an attempt to allow the expert voice to be heard in as objective a forum as possible.

Survey Methodology

The purpose of this research was to survey expert opinion about the IQ controversy. Because the controversy is a broad one, the population that constitutes "experts" is not immediately apparent. It was therefore necessary to define the population through the various considerations that guided sample selection. There were three primary considerations. First, the population was to be neither so broad that it contained a large proportion of individuals with little or no experience with intelligence or testing, nor so narrow as to include only those who might be considered to have a vested interest in testing. An example of the former would be all psychologists and educators, while the latter population might consist only of members of the National Council on Measurement in Education (NCME). NCME members undoubtedly are experts on testing, but there are many social scientists and educators who can reasonably be assumed to have knowledge of the academic literature on at least some aspects of the IQ controversy, but who do not deal with tests as an essential part of their work. We wished to include these individuals as well.

The second consideration in defining a population of experts was to include individuals with a wide variety of perspectives on the problem, even those who might have expertise on only a small part of the controversy. For this purpose, the population was divided into primary and secondary groups. Primary groups were those professional organizations whose members might be expected to be knowledgeable on several IQ–related topics. Secondary groups were organizations whose members were likely to know testing from only a narrow perspective. Primary groups included the American Educational Research Association (AERA), NCME, and the Developmental Psychology, Educational Psychology, Evaluation and Measurement, and School Psychology divisions of the American Psychological Association (APA). Secondary groups consisted of members of the American Sociological Association (ASA) identified as sociologists of education (included for expertise in the role of testing in society), the Behavior Genetics Association (for expertise in heritability), the Cognitive Science Society (for expertise on the nature of intelligence and cognitive abilities), and two other divisions of the APA, Counseling Psychology (for expertise in the use of tests in counseling), and Industrial and Organizational Psychology (for expertise in employment testing).

The final criterion was that the sample be weighted in favor of those with the most expertise, as indicated by research and publications on issues related to intelligence and testing. Therefore, only scholarly organizations were sampled. The sample was also weighted toward those organizations, and members of the organizations, thought to have the most expertise. Because members of primary groups were believed to have more overall expertise than members of secondary groups, twice as many members were selected from each primary group as from each secondary group. For those organizations where it was possible to separate Ph. D. from non–Ph. D. members, only members with doctorates were sampled. Within each division of the APA there are two classes of Ph. D. members, Members and Fellows. Members need only have a psychology Ph. D. Fellows must first have been Members, must have at least five years of experience in psychology beyond the Ph. D. , and must be nominated and elected by other APA members based on "evidence of unusual and outstanding contribution or performance in the field of psychology." Despite the fact that there are far fewer Fellows than Members within each division, half of the sample from each division was drawn from the Fellows and half from the Members.

The sample was drawn randomly, in the numbers indicated in Table 2.1, from the most recent available membership directory of each of the organizations. The final sample consisted of 1,020 social scientists and educators.

The questionnaire itself was divided into six sections. Four of these

TABLE 2.1
Composition of Survey Sample

Primary Groups	N
American Educational Research Association	120
National Council on Measurement in Education	120
American Psychological Association:	
Developmental Psychology	60 Fellows
	60 Members
Educational Psychology	60 Fellows
	60 Members
Evaluation and Measurement	60 Fellows
	60 Members
School Psychology	60 Fellows
	60 Members
Secondary Groups	
American Sociological Association: Education	60
Behavior Genetics Association	60
Cognitive Science Society	60
American Psychological Association: Counseling Psychology	30 Fellows
	30 Members
Industrial and Organizational Psychology	30 Fellows
	30 Members
Total	1,020

contained substantive questions about intelligence and testing, and two asked about various demographic and background characteristics of the respondents. The scope of the substantive questions was intended to include most areas of contention within the relevant academic literature, with an emphasis on areas of particular concern in the public debate.

The first substantive section, labeled "The Nature of Intelligence," will be the focus of discussion in this chapter. The remaining three substantive sections dealt with "The Heritability of IQ," "Race, Class, and Cultural Differences in IQ," and "The Use of Intelligence Testing," and will be considered in the following chapters.

The first of the two demographic sections of the questionnaire, "Professional Activities and Involvement with Intelligence Testing," was concerned primarily with measuring expertise and public exposure. This section also contained two multi-part questions of a more substantive nature. The first asked respondents to rate each of ten different news sources for accuracy in reporting issues related to intelligence and testing. The second asked for ratings of fourteen different authors as to the quality of their work on intelligence and testing.

The final section of the questionnaire, "Personal and Social Background," asked about the respondent's sex, age, marital status, ethnic and religious background, and childhood family income. Agreement or disagreement with a series of political statements, and a global political measure (liberal-conservative) were used to assess respondents' political perspectives.

Following pre-testing with various groups of testing experts, 1,020 questionnaires were mailed in September of 1984. A cover letter explained the purpose of the questionnaire (to help clarify confusion over testing), its importance in light of the widespread use and controversy over tests, and promised complete confidentiality (the questionnaire itself contained an ID number for the purpose of follow-up mailings). Because many respondents were not expected to have expertise in all areas of testing, the cover letter asked subjects to check the NQ (Not Qualified) response for any question they did not feel qualified to answer. This category also served for No Response/Don't Know.

Approximately two weeks after the initial mailing, postcard reminders were sent to all subjects who had not yet responded. About four weeks later, a second set of questionnaires was sent out to the remaining nonrespondents. The final response tally contained 661 completed questionnaires (65 percent). There was little variation in response rate between the various primary and secondary groups within the sample. Forty-nine subjects returned their questionnaires indicating they were not qualified to answer any of the substantive questions. Seventeen subjects were deceased or otherwise incapacitated, and twenty–seven subjects simply returned their questionnaires unanswered with no explanation.

Two hundred sixty–six, or 26 percent of the questionnaires were not returned at all. Phone calls were made to forty (15 percent) of these nonrespondents in order to determine if they differed in any important way from respondents and to ascertain their reasons for nonresponse. These subjects were asked some of the more important substantive and demographic questions, with mixed success; these were individuals who had already not responded to three mailings. Their responses to questions for which there were a sufficient number of answers for meaningful comparison were not significantly different from those of respondents to the mailed questionnaire. More informative perhaps were the reasons these subjects gave for not responding. All forty subjects answered this question. Twenty–three said that they were too busy to respond, and twelve did not feel qualified. Only six expressed any aversion to the questionnaire itself (respondents could give more than one reason). In all, given the nature of responses received from the phone sample, and their reasons for not responding to the mailed questionnaire, there seems little reason to believe that the results would look significantly different had the entire sample of 1,020 participated.

Professional Activities and Involvement with Intelligence Testing

The professional background characteristics of survey respondents are summarized in Table 2.2. The degree of expertise about intelligence and testing varies widely among respondents, but, on the whole, the sample is adequately characterized as expert. Approximately half of all respondents are faculty members at a college or university, and the bulk of the remainder classify themselves as psychologists or educational specialists

TABLE 2.2
Expertise of Sample

Characteristic	% of Respondents
College or university faculty	53.3
Other psychologist or educational specialist	36.1
Current research on intelligence or testing	55
Articles or chapters on intelligence or testing[a]	67
Speeches or lectures on intelligence or testing[a]	57
Served as news media source on intelligence or testing[a]	33
Administered individual intelligence test[a]	38.5
Administered group intelligence test[a]	29.3

[a]Within the previous two years.

working in some other capacity (e.g., in elementary and secondary education, for government, for the testing industry). Fifty–five percent are planning or carrying out research in some area related to intelligence or intelligence testing. The most common areas of research are the nature of intelligence, test development and validation, and testing in elementary and secondary schools.

Sixty–seven percent of respondents have written at least one article or chapter related to intelligence or testing, and 57 percent had given at least one such speech or lecture to other than a classroom audience during the previous two years. The mean number of articles written is eleven (median number of articles among all respondents is three), with articles written for an academic/professional audience about five times more common than those written for a general audience. The most common article topics parallel those for areas of research.

The central purpose of our research and this book is to test certain propositions about the changing patterns of communication of scientific controversy to an increasingly educated public. We hypothesized that in a number of areas, of which intelligence and aptitude testing is one, such communication is distorted, i.e., that the views of the relevant expert community are reported inaccurately to the attentive public by the elite media.

The distortion occurs because of the changing values and perceptions of the intellectual community, and the key role of an elite media that shares such values. This distortion is not a function of conscious bias, but rather of underlying assumptions that define the nature of reality to journalists and intellectuals alike.

In some areas, such as testing, we believe that the expert community has more or less accepted such distortions as inevitable. Since their scientific findings run counter to a conventional wisdom whose supporters are quite passionate, they have accepted a tradeoff that permits them to publish their findings in professional journals, but not for popular consumption. Under such circumstances they can continue their scientific work without the fear of being pilloried by the larger community and of being deprived of grants for research by government agencies and private foundations. So fully have many experts accepted this arrangement that they are angered by colleagues with whom they agree but who popularize their views and thus threaten their scientific work.

Thus, we maintain, a society that prides itself on its openness to scientific findings (which were once ignored or censored only by conservatives) now indulges in its own forms of subtle censorship by removing the discussion of some scientific issues from rational public discourse.[9]

To test these hypotheses our first task has been to summarize the views of the expert community as accurately as possible. The discussion that follows in this and the next three chapters, while including the results of our survey of expert opinion, will necessarily be broader in scope than the questionnaire itself. The questionnaire was concerned with only those topics where there is contention within the scholarly literature, or where there is significant public debate. A full understanding of these topics, however, requires a discussion of basic testing issues, including those for which there is a clear consensus among those who study tests.

Unfortunately, there are virtually no issues concerning testing on which *everyone* agrees. To take seriously all arguments about testing would put us in a position in which neither we nor our readers would any longer be able to distinguish the forest from the trees. While we are not in a position to judge the truth of expert statements in every area, our reading of the psychometric literature indicates that there are certain positions for which the empirical verification is so strong, and the scholarly consensus so overwhelming (e.g., that IQ is a significant predictor of academic success), that we feel justified in stating them as facts. The explicit sacrifice has been to trade off complete coverage of the most radical positions, both in and out of the expert community, for clarity of exposition. Our fundamental premise has been to take seriously as a scientific enterprise attempts to understand and measure intellectual functioning. Despite our attempts to remain objective, we realize that there are those to whom this entire project is worthless, or worse, because it legitimates what they see as an exercise in political oppression.

The Definition of Intelligence

According to Cyril Burt, the word "intelligence," originally from the Latin, was revived by Herbert Spencer and Francis Galton in the mid nineteenth century as a scientific term meaning "innate, general cognitive capacity": innate, meaning inherited, and not acquired through experience; general, as in ability applicable to a wide variety of circumstances; and cognitive, as opposed to motivational or emotional.[10] It was this definition Binet and Simon had in mind, Burt argues, when they developed the 1905 scale. Only later in the century did the term enter everyday language, becoming imbued with a proliferation of meaning.

An examination of the writings of Binet and Simon reveals that, like most test developers who have followed them, they were more concerned with measurement than definition. Though sometimes speaking of judgment as the basic factor in intelligence, Binet and Simon believed that sampling from a wide variety of mental processes would enable them to develop a complete picture of intellectual functioning, without having to worry about what intelligence really was. Many of the mental testers surveyed in 1921 and 1923 echoed these sentiments: theoretical questions about the nature of intelligence are neither as assessable, nor as important as inquiry into what it is that intelligence tests measure.

Sixty years of subsequent research on mental abilities has made it clear that "[i]ntelligence . . . is easier to measure than to define."[11] There exists today an extremely broad spectrum of theories and definitions of intelligence, ranging from purely biological descriptions based on speed of neural transmission to overarching theories like that of Howard Gardner, in which there is not one, but seven different intelligences encompassing virtually the entire realm of human abilities.[12] To many, this state of affairs undermines the entire testing enterprise. Walter Lippmann's 1923 assertion that "[w]e cannot measure intelligence when we have never defined it"[13] has been echoed by scores of critics in the intervening years.

The response of many who develop and validate intelligence tests has been to show great deference to the operational definition that intelligence is whatever intelligence tests measure.[14] This is not to say that modern psychometricians have blindly accepted so naive a doctrine. There is great concern among those who study intelligence tests about the relationship of test results to various lay and technical definitions of intelligence, as well as with the development of new theory and methodology in intelligence testing.[15] And there is certainly no shortage of definitions of intelligence offered by modern theoreticians, as the Sternberg and Detterman symposium demonstrates. Taking operationalism seriously merely shifts the focus away from the relationship between intelligence tests and "intelligence" broadly defined. Instead, a definition of intelligence is derived from the various methods by which tests are validated, in particular the relationship test results bear to some specifically defined criteria. The operationalist response was stated explicitly by T. Anne Cleary and her colleagues on the APA ad hoc committee when they claimed that "there is a consensus among psychologists as to the kinds of behaviors that are labeled intellectual," and that this consensus is both exemplified and defined by the great similarity of content of modern intelligence tests.[16]

An important distinction must be made at this point. Traditionally, there has been a split within psychology between those interested primarily in the nature of intelligence and cognitive abilities (cognitive scientists) and those whose interest in intelligence is closely tied to the ability to measure it (psychometricians). This split is apparent in a comparison of the 1921 and 1986 symposia on the definition of intelligence. The fundamental difference between the two symposia is in the greater elaboration of definition in 1986. In general, the later definitions are more detailed and highly structured, drawing on data and theory from a variety of disciplines, including developmental psychology, neurobiology, the study of mental retardation, and artificial intelligence. This elaboration derives from fundamental changes in the way intelligence is studied. In 1921, intelligence was the province of the mental testers, and symposium participants were principally concerned with the construct as it related to measurement and prediction. In 1986, many of those who study intelligence, and who contributed to the symposium, are not psychometricians, and it is common for these scientists to be more concerned with theory than with measurement.

This book is concerned with the controversy over intelligence and aptitude testing; it is not intended as a survey of cognitive science, or of theory on intelligence divorced from testing issues. Our discussion of the nature of intelligence is, therefore, more closely tied to the relation between the concept and its measurement (i.e., traditional psychometric concerns, exemplified by the 1921 symposium participants) than to the more broadly defined conceptions of cognitive theorists (like many of those in the 1986 symposium). As noted at the end of chapter 1, these newer conceptions, which may radically change both the theory *and* measurement of intelligence, have, as yet, had little impact on the IQ controversy.

In any case, the definitions provided by the 1921 and 1986 participants are not radically different. Higher–level processes, like abstract reasoning and problem solving, figure prominently in both sets of definitions (several 1986 definitions include executive processes, a computer–age term referring to higher–level control functions). Robert Sternberg and Cynthia Berg have tallied the various attributes of intelligence mentioned by contributors to the two symposia, and find that these two sets of frequencies correlate 0.50.[17] The important distinction, for our purposes, is that the conceptions of intelligence most relevant to the IQ controversy are those, from whatever era, that are fundamentally concerned with measurement.

N. J. Block and Gerald Dworkin in their edited book *The IQ Controversy* present an essay of their own entitled "IQ, Heritability, and Inequality" that is perhaps the best available statement of the major arguments against intelligence tests in the areas of the nature of intelligence and IQ heritability.[18] In the first part of their essay, the authors attack the operationalist doctrine, primarily for its atheoretical nature. They argue that the development of meaningful tests of intelligence cannot proceed independently of a theory of intelligence. One must have at least some idea of what intelligence is in order to create an intelligence test. Without a theory, Block and Dworkin claim, psychometricians have had to rely heavily on intuitive notions of intelligence in the initial construction of tests. Subsequent validation has primarily consisted of correlation with previously accepted tests. (This may account for Cleary et al.'s "consensus.") Thus, the historical development of intelligence testing has been a "*technological*, not a scientific process."[19] The intuitive notions on which this technological process is based might bear little resemblance to what intelligence really is (if there were a unified theory). In a true scientific process, measurement and theory must progress together. (Terman made essentially the same point in 1916.)[20] In the absence of theory, technological progress produces better and better ways to measure quantities whose relationship to "intelligence" is unknown.

Operationalists may offer some defense by pointing out that it is not the relationship between test scores and "intelligence" that is important. That relationship is defined by the principal tenet of operationalism. What is important is how test scores relate to certain other criteria like success in school and in the job market. As Terman warned in 1921, "the validity of a new test should not be judged entirely by its correlation with existing tests, however good these may be. There must be continued search for useful outside criteria."[21] But one must still have some independent notion of intelligence by which to decide the usefulness of an external criterion. Terman continues, "On the other hand, in our anxiety to escape the evils of a closed system we must guard against indiscriminate and ill–considered use of outside criteria. To condemn an intelligence test because it yields low correlations with success as a mill hand or streetcar motorman is an example of this error."[22] Obviously, being a good motorman requires little of what Terman considers intelligence. The point is, *some* independent notion of intelligence is necessary in order to decide whether a test that predicts success as a mill hand or streetcar motorman should be considered a good test of intelligence. That such a test might correlate poorly with other intelligence tests is inadequate grounds for rejection unless there are independent reasons for believing the other tests are better measures of intelligence.

In the end, the real conflict between those who criticize the atheoretical nature of intelligence testing and testing's supporters comes down to how much fuzziness in the definition of intelligence is to be tolerated. Critics point to the lack of a unified theory or universally agreed upon definition of intelligence. Defenders seem content with the high correlation between scores on disparate tests, as well as the strong relationship between test results and almost any common sense criterion of intelligence.

Unfortunately, many strong believers in the validity of intelligence tests use the word "intelligence" rather more freely than they should. Authors will often discuss both the technical and intuitive definitions of intelligence in the same document, and the reference of any particular appearance of the word is often ambiguous. The impression given by such writings is misleading: that one's intuitive idea of intelligence, and the results of intelligence tests, are synonymous.

Intelligence is a fuzzy concept that requires a fuzzy definition. As Douglas Detterman put it in comparing the 1986 symposium results to those from 1921:

> Though the definitions provided by this symposium may be more refined, substantial disagreement on a single definition still abounds. It is probably foolish to expect this symposium, or even one held 65 years from now, to come to a unanimous conclusion. A concept as complex as intelligence probably cannot be captured by a single definition without gross oversimplification.[23]

1. It has been argued that there is a consensus among psychologists and educators as to the kinds of behaviors that are labeled "intelligent." Do you agree or disagree that there is such a consensus?

Respondents are inclined to agree that there is a consensus. Fifty–three percent either somewhat or strongly agree, compared to 39.5 percent who disagree in some manner. The remaining 7.5 percent did not respond to the question. These results do not demonstrate, of course, that a consensus actually exists (question 3 is directed at that issue), but it is the case that most of the experts in our sample have the perception that they are working within a commonly accepted framework.

2. Do you believe that, on the whole, the development of intelligence tests has proceeded in the context of an adequate theory of intelligence?

Our expert sample is predominantly in agreement with this fundamental critique. Fifty–four percent of those surveyed answer "No" to this question, compared to 34 percent who answer "Yes." The remaining 12 percent do not respond. The obvious follow–up question, which, unfortunately, we did not ask, is "Does this make any difference to the validity of the tests?" To Block and Dworkin, the lack of a unified theory of intelligence severely reduces the validity and usefulness of intelligence tests. Most experts in our sample agree with the premise of this argument. Results from the remainder of the questionnaire, however, demonstrate that these experts do not share Block and Dworkin's pessimistic conclusion about tests.

3. Important elements of intelligence.

Respondents were asked to check all behavioral descriptors listed (there were thirteen, and space for writing in others) that they believe to be an important element of intelligence. This question attempts to assess directly the nature of consensus about the definition of intelligence.

Results are shown in Table 2.3. Response rate was 93 percent. Descrip-

TABLE 2.3
Important Elements of Intelligence

Descriptor	% of Respondents Checking as Important
Abstract thinking or reasoning	99.3
Problem solving ability	97.7
Capacity to acquire knowledge	96
Memory	80.5
Adaptation to one's environment	77.2
Mental speed	71.7
Linguistic competence	71
Mathematical competence	67.9
General knowledge	62.4
Creativity	59.6
Sensory acuity	24.4
Goal-directedness	24
Achievement motivation	18.9

tors fall into one of three well–defined categories: those for which there is near unanimity (greater than 96 percent agreement among those who answered the question)—"abstract thinking or reasoning," "the capacity to acquire knowledge," and "problem solving ability"; those checked by a majority of respondents (60–80 percent)—"adaptation to one's environment," "creativity," "general knowledge," "linguistic competence," "mathematical competence," "memory," and "mental speed"; and those rarely checked (less than 25 percent)—"achievement motivation," "goal–directedness," and "sensory acuity." The most commonly added behavioral descriptors are "social or interpersonal competence," "spatial ability," and "integrative capacity," though none of these is added by more than 2 percent of respondents.

These results should not be taken as providing a definition of intelligence. A list of traits is not a rigorous scientific definition, and it certainly isn't a unified theory. Nonetheless, two important points can be made. First, as in previous surveys already cited, there is considerable disagreement about the breadth of the definition, such that, for example, a substantial minority of respondents disagree that mathematical competence and creativity should be included. It is these sorts of disagreements that fuel debate about the nature of cognitive abilities.

Accompanying the disagreement about the scope of the definition of intelligence is very strong agreement at its core. It can reasonably be concluded that when different psychologists and educators use the term "intelligence" they are *basically* referring to the same concept, having to do with the capacity to learn and with more complex cognitive tasks like abstract reasoning and problem solving, and that they would generally exclude purely motivational and sensory abilities from this definition. These same threads run through both the 1921 and 1986 symposia. In many ways, Terman's 1921 definition of intelligence as abstract thinking remains at the heart of current thought about intelligence.

Apropos of our earlier discussion of the distinction between cognitive scientists and psychometricians, the survey sample was chosen to reflect expertise about a broad range of testing issues, and therefore includes a large proportion of psychometricians. There are, however, many other disciplines represented, including, for example, developmental psychologists and cognitive scientists (members of the Cognitive Science Society), who might be expected to bring very different perspectives to the question of the nature of intelligence. It is testimony to the generality of the results in Table 2.3 that comparison of responses between the various primary and secondary groups in the sample does not reveal a greater number of statistically significant differences on any of the elements of intelligence than would be expected by chance.

The results of the first three questions on the nature of intelligence present a mixed picture of the current psychological consensus. There appears to be basic agreement about the most important elements of intelligence, but considerable dissension about the details. These data support the majority opinion that intelligence tests have not been the products of unified and comprehensive theorizing.

It is not true, however, that the development of intelligence tests has proceeded in the absence of *any* theory. Besides the implicit theory that must accompany all test development, explicit theories of intelligence, both old and new, abound, and there are many tests that have been developed in connection to particular theories.[24] Critics like Block and Dworkin argue that the piecemeal approach is not sufficient, and that for psychometrics to become a true science tests must develop hand–in–hand with a unified theory. In response, many proponents of testing point to the substantial degree of intercorrelation between performance on all tests of mental ability, regardless of their theoretical origins. The argument is made that, with or without a proper theory, all of these tests seem to be measuring the same basic abilities, loosely defined as "intelligence."

What Intelligence Tests Measure

4. Important elements of intelligence not measured.

As a direct assessment of the ability of intelligence tests to measure "intelligence," we asked experts about the fit between the tests and their own definition of intelligence. Respondents were asked to check each of the behavioral descriptors that they believe to be an important element of intelligence (from the preceding question), but that they do not feel is adequately measured by the most commonly used intelligence tests.

The results of this question are given in Table 2.4. (Note that the percentages given in this table are drawn only from those who had previously checked the descriptor as an important element of intelligence, and not from the entire sample.) Response rate was 87 percent. On the whole, respondents seem to believe that intelligence tests are doing a good job measuring intelligence, as they would define it. Of the ten behavioral descriptors checked as important elements by more than 60 percent of respondents, only two, "adaptation to one's environment" and "creativity," are checked by a majority as not adequately measured, and only one other, "capacity to acquire knowledge," is checked by more than 20 percent.

The "adaptation to environment" result reflects the common criticism that tests are much better at measuring traits important to success in school than general life skills. It is also consistent with results from earlier surveys of expert opinion in which there was a consensus about intelligence as an adaptive skill, but disagreement about the variety of life circumstances under which adaptation should be called intelligent. Similarly, the "creativity" finding is not surprising in light of the poor correlation between tests of intelligence and tests of creativity. That tests of creativity are themselves poorly intercorrelated is evidence that behavioral scientists are unsure of what creativity consists, or where it fits in the constellation of cognitive abilities.[25]

More troublesome for supporters of testing is that 42 percent of those who believe "capacity to acquire knowledge" is an important element of intelligence, which includes virtually all respondents, do not believe it is adequately measured by intelligence tests. As with the previous question, the results of question 4 are more meaningfully interpreted at a very general level—that experts believe intelligence tests, while far from perfect, are for the most part measuring what they should be measuring—than at the level of specific behavioral terms, where ambiguities abound.

Some distinctions in terminology are warranted at this point. We will use the terms "IQ test," "intelligence test," and "test of general mental ability" interchangeably. As noted, IQ, which stands for intelligence quotient, was first defined by the German psychologist Stern as the ratio of mental age (tested age on an age–graded intelligence test) to chronological age. In order to eliminate nonlinearities resulting from changes in chronological age (a six–year–old whose mental age is retarded two years will have a much lower IQ than a twelve–year–old with the same degree of retardation), IQ is now defined as having a mean of 100 in each age group, and a standard deviation of either 15 or 16 (depending on the test). Thus,

TABLE 2.4
Important Elements of Intelligence Not Adequately Measured by Intelligence Tests

Descriptor	% of Respondents[a] Checking as Not Adequately Measured
Abstract thinking or reasoning	19.9
Problem solving ability	27.3
Capacity to acquire knowledge	42.2
Memory	12.7
Adaptation to one's environment	75.3
Mental speed	12.8
Linguistic competence	14
Mathematical competence	12.1
General knowledge	10.7
Creativity	88.3
Sensory acuity	57.7
Goal-directedness	64.1
Achievement motivation	71.7

[a]Respondents include only those who had previously indicated that descriptor was an important element of intelligence.

an eight–year–old whose score is one standard deviation above the eight-year-old mean on the Stanford–Binet test has an IQ of 116. This method of calculating IQ necessitates proper standardization for the population being tested.

Intelligence tests may be distinguished from aptitude tests. One tradition, which we will not honor, is to call all group tests of general ability aptitude tests, reserving the terms intelligence and IQ test for individually administered examinations. The more critical distinction is that aptitude tests are usually fairly homogeneous surveys of specific abilities, such as mathematical or musical skill. Intelligence tests, on the other hand, measure a wider variety of skills necessary for academic success. Intelligence tests may, either through design or subsequent factor analysis, yield, in addition to a measure of general intelligence, subscores corresponding to more specific abilities like verbal comprehension and numerical reasoning. Such tests are quite similar to multiple aptitude batteries, which consist of a broad range of specific aptitude tests. In the discussion that follows, intelligence tests are treated as tests of general cognitive aptitude. Additionally, we will use "IQ" as a shorthand for scores on all intelligence and general aptitude tests.

A great deal of confusion has been generated in the popular literature concerning the difference between intelligence or aptitude tests and tests of scholastic achievement. Much of this confusion may be warranted by the fact that scores on intelligence and achievement tests are highly correlated. Nonetheless, a distinction may be made, at least at the level of intentions.

Achievement tests are intended to ascertain the degree to which an individual has mastered a certain body of knowledge. Such tests are generally evaluated for content validity (the degree to which the questions actually contact the body of knowledge in question—see below). Intelligence and aptitude tests are designed to measure the extent of certain abilities or skills possessed by the respondent that are predictive of success in future endeavors, most notably academics. In addition, intelligence tests usually measure a much broader range of behaviors than achievement tests, and require knowledge learned in the more distant past.[26]

At one level, *all* cognitive tests are tests of achievement. A newborn infant can no more solve a block design problem on an intelligence test than it can name the state capitals on a geography achievement test. The necessary skills in both cases must be learned. The important distinction is between those skills and abilities thought to be acquired over a lifetime, and to be applicable to a wide variety of cognitive tasks, and specific bodies of knowledge generally acquired in a classroom setting. It may be pointed out, however, that this distinction often does not hold in practice, as, for example, in the ubiquitous vocabulary questions on intelligence tests. Test makers may respond: How better to test an ability like verbal comprehension than to ask vocabulary questions? The assumption is that all test takers will have had sufficient exposure to the relevant environmental stimuli for differences in acquired vocabulary to accurately reflect differences in verbal comprehension. Nonexposure is thought to introduce error distributed randomly across respondents. If these assumptions are incorrect, the test will be biased (see below).

In fact, aptitude and achievement tests often look very similar. The greater the environmental experience test takers are assumed to share, the more aptitude tests will look like achievement tests. The most notable example of this phenomenon, and one that has caused a great deal of controversy in recent years, is the Scholastic Aptitude Test (SAT). Despite the test's title, the Educational Testing Service (ETS) has become quite wary of calling the SAT a test of academic aptitude, stressing instead "developed abilities." This has put the ETS in the strange position of simultaneously arguing that its test measures developed abilities, but that coaching programs aimed at raising SAT scores don't work.[27] (See Chapter 5 for more on the debate over SAT coaching.) The SAT does consist largely of questions tapping specific knowledge about vocabulary, algebra, and geometry. Nonetheless, to the extent that test takers have been exposed to similar high school curricula, the SAT will work like an IQ or aptitude test in the population being tested. No doubt this correlation would break down if the test population consisted of many test takers who had not completed two years of high school.

Anne Anastasi has described a "Continuum of Experiential Specificity" among ability tests. On the highly specific end of the continuum are course–oriented achievement tests tied to particular academic instruction. On the highly general end are so–called "culture–fair" tests (see Chapter 4) such as the Ravens Progressive Matrices, consisting of abstract series–completion problems involving little or no language or other culturally–specific knowledge. Verbal–type intelligence and aptitude tests fall in the middle of this continuum.[28]

Robert Gordon has noted that much of the high correlation between aptitude or intelligence and achievement tests can be accounted for by the fact that most test takers have had equivalent exposure to relevant stimuli:

> When all individuals have had more or less equal exposure to school instruction, even a highly specific achievement test can function approximately as an aptitude or intelligence test in measuring individual differences ... The greater sensitivity of properly constructed achievement tests than of IQ tests to instruction is seldom demonstrated by giving them, along with intelligence tests, to individuals half of whom have had no instructions at all in the subject at hand. This would be wasteful and expensive, but it would break down the correlation between the two type of tests.[29]

Another reason intelligence and achievement tests correlate so well is that intelligence tests are designed that way. Intelligence tests are validated to a large degree by their ability to predict academic success. Such success includes grades, teacher evaluations, and scores on achievement tests. The logic behind this strategy is that one should require a test designed to measure certain abilities necessary for scholastic achievement to predict scores on scholastic achievement tests. Difficulties arise, according to certain critics, when the high correlation between intelligence and achievement tests is used to argue that intelligence tests measure important skills.[30] These arguments hold little weight, they claim, because the tests were designed to produce such correlations.

Such criticisms are not what drives the aptitude–achievement debate, however. At the heart of this controversy is the perception that an intelligence or aptitude test score is a relatively permanent feature of the individual. The desire to blur the aptitude–achievement distinction by claiming that intelligence and aptitude tests measure nothing but "acquired knowledge" is an attempt to reduce the potential stigmatizing effects of the IQ and to emphasize the plasticity of intelligence. (These claims are also frequently made in the context of a cultural bias argument: since intelligence tests are primarily measures of environment–specific knowledge, test takers with more exposure to the white middle–class environment for which the tests are weighted are at an unfair advantage.) It is an outgrowth of the environmentalism of the 1960s and 70s. As an attempt to alleviate stigmatization and grief, this redefinition is commendable, but at the scientific level it is based on a false distinction. The acquired, and therefore malleable, knowledge it is claimed intelligence and aptitude tests are actually measuring is contrasted with the innate, and therefore fixed, skills and abilities intelligence and aptitude tests are supposed to be measuring. In fact, as will be made clear in the next chapter, all skills, abilities, and knowledge are dependent on both genes and environment, and all are modifiable through environmental change. That the environmental change necessary to raise IQ significantly is much greater than that needed to raise one's score on a French language achievement test is an important distinction, and cannot be glossed over by arguing that all tests measure acquired knowledge.

5. Compared to success on achievement tests, does success on intelligence tests among American test takers generally depend less, more, or about the same amount on acquired knowledge?

This question is deliberately ambiguous, and was included because arguments about testing are commonly phrased this way in the popular press. One can maintain that "acquired knowledge" is anything not directly coded into the genes, in which case all behavioral indices measure it to the same degree. The popular conception seems to be, however, that "acquired knowledge" refers not to acquired skills and abilities, but to specific pieces of information, and is to be contrasted with "innate abilities"; the notion that genes and environment are both necessary to the development of all aspects of behavior seems to have been lost in public discussion.

By whatever definition they may be using, experts tend to disagree that intelligence and achievement tests are alike in their dependency on acquired knowledge. Fifty–nine percent believe that intelligence tests depend somewhat or much less on acquired knowledge, 25 percent say it is about the same, and 7 percent say acquired knowledge is more important to intelligence tests than to achievement tests. Eight percent did not answer the question. Because of the ambiguity, these results are only meaningful as a response to similarly worded, and equally confusing, arguments.

In the design and evaluation of intelligence tests there are two issues of primary importance; reliability and validity. Reliability refers to the consistency of test scores when an individual is given the same or similar items under similar test conditions. It is generally measured in one of three ways: by administering the same test on two different occasions (test–retest, also known as stability), by administering two forms of the same test on either the same or different occasions (alternative form), or by comparing scores on different items within the same administration of a test (split–half, or internal consistency). (Conceptually, reliability and stability are distinct, stability referring to the consistency of test scores over time. Stability coefficients are often calculated after the unreliability of the test—even identical tests given to the same person at a single test administration will not produce identical scores—has been corrected for. In practice, tests with high reliability also tend to be highly stable.)[31] The most common numerical estimate of reliability is the reliability coefficient, the correlation coefficient between the test scores being compared. For individually-administered intelligence tests, reliability coefficients rarely are below 0.80.[32]

The importance of reliability in the evaluation of intelligence tests is obvious. Regardless of what the test is measuring, one would have little confidence in a scale whose estimates varied widely under highly similar testing circumstances. Such variation is usually attributed to measurement error, and one of the goals in the development of any scaling instrument is to produce as error–free measurement as possible.

Interpreting intraindividual variations in test scores as measurement error assumes that whatever is being measured is itself quite stable. This assumption is probably correct for the circumstances under which most reliability (or stability) coefficients are calculated, that is, within the same, or two closely spaced, test sessions. When the same individual is tested over longer periods of time, test scores are not always very stable. Some of this instability is a function of measurement error, but genetic and environmental factors producing real changes in intelligence are also believed to be at work. IQ scores are norm referenced; IQ is computed by comparing an individual's score to those of others in the same age group. Changes in IQ with age therefore reflect changes in an individual's ranking; that absolute level of intelligence increases with age has already been controlled for.

Prior to age three, scores on tests of mental development are quite unstable and are usually rather poor predictors of adult IQ.[33] At four or five, scores begin to become more consistent and are found to correlate between 0.50 and 0.70 with adult IQ.[34] The highest levels of stability are obtained after age eight, when correlations between repeated intelligence tests given over quite large time intervals, corrected for unreliability, are between 0.90 and 1.0.[35] Jensen compares these changing patterns of correlations to those associated with changes in height, body weight, and physical strength, and concludes, "although the IQ is certainly not 'constant,' it seems safe to say that under normal environmental conditions it is at least as stable as developmental characteristics of a strictly physical nature."[36]

6. How stable is the attribute(s) being measured by intelligence tests, compared to a purely physical characteristic such as height, when each is expressed relative to the population mean?

Intelligence, as measured by intelligence tests, is viewed as less stable than height. Seventy-seven percent of experts surveyed say intelligence is somewhat or much less stable, 11 percent say it is equally stable, and only 2 percent indicate it is somewhat or much more stable. Ten percent did not respond.

There is an interpretational problem with this question, as many respondents indicated that they were not sure at what age to make the comparison. The phrase "relative to the population mean" was intended to refer to the same-age population mean, as is standard practice in the scoring of intelligence tests, and thus the question refers to the entire life span. It is clear, however, that many respondents were not answering the question we were asking.

Of greater relevance to the question of what intelligence tests measure is the issue of validity. Anne Anastasi, in her standard text *Psychological Testing*, identifies three basic forms of validity: content, criterion, and construct. "Content validation involves essentially the systematic examination of the test content to determine whether it covers a representative sample of the behavior domain to be measured."[37] This form of validity is of greater relevance to tests of scholastic achievement and specific aptitudes than to general intelligence tests. When one wishes to measure mathematical achievement, for example, the relevant behaviors (body of knowledge) are clearly defined, and the test may be evaluated against those behaviors. Intelligent behavior is not so easily defined (as we have seen), and tests of intelligence must be compared either to some external criteria thought to be related to intelligence, or to some theoretical construct.

"Criterion-related validation procedures indicate the effectiveness of a test in predicting an individual's behavior in specified situations."[38] Criterion validity represents an important, and for those who discount existing theories of intelligence, the only, method of evaluating tests of general intelligence. As noted, IQ is quite predictive of success in school, having an average validity coefficient (correlation coefficient corrected for unreliability) of between 0.50 and 0.60 with later measures of academic success like grades and achievement test scores.[39] The value of this coefficient decreases at higher levels of schooling, so that IQ is a much better predictor of success in high school, for example, than in college or graduate school.[40] Much of this decrease in correlation may be the result of range restriction effects; the range of IQs among those still in school decreases with years of schooling, thus reducing correlation coefficients. IQ correlates about 0.60 with highest grade of school completed.[41]

Christopher Jencks and his colleagues have reviewed evidence linking IQ to occupational status, as measured by the educational requirements and salary levels of various occupations, among white nonfarm American males. The correlation between adolescent IQ and adult occupational status is quite high, averaging between 0.50 and 0.60.[42] It has been argued, however, that IQ has its effects on occupational status indirectly, via educational attainment;[43] that is, those with higher IQs get better jobs primarily because these jobs require applicants to have completed more years of schooling. In contrast, most of the correlation between IQ and income, which is slightly greater than 0.30, is independent of the effects of amount of schooling completed.[44] Finally, a recent review of predictive validity of various measures of job performance by John and Ronda Hunter reports that the correlation between tests of general cognitive ability and job competence varies with job requirements, but is in all cases substantial (greater than 0.30). The mean predictive validity (correlation between test scores and job competence) across all job categories studied is between 0.50 and 0.60, with validity being slightly higher for ease of job training than for job proficiency as measured by supervisors' ratings.[45]

In line with our earlier discussion, we may say that intelligence, as measured by intelligence tests, consists of some set of skills that are very important for success in school and moderately important for success in the job market. This assumes, of course, that intelligence tests are measuring skills, and not merely class or racial variables, i.e., that the tests are not biased.

The substantial correlations between childhood IQ and eventual occupational status and income might lead one to conclude that whatever intelligence tests are measuring, it is important for success in our society. Correlation is not necessarily causation, however, and the social mobility hypothesis (the idea that success is largely determined by one's abilities, including intelligence as measured by IQ tests) has been challenged on the ground that the correlation between IQ and various measures of success is spurious.

Those who disagree with the social mobility hypothesis generally concede that intelligence tests are good predictors of success in school. They argue that this indicates only that these tests measure a very narrow conception of intelligence, substantially related to the sorts of verbal skills valuable in school. In the real world, it is said, the importance of these skills is dwarfed by such attributes as persistence, and the ability to get along with other people. This argument has often been made in response to Herrnstein's conclusion that SES is partly heritable. The social mobility hypothesis forms an essential part of Herrnstein's syllogism (see Chapter 4).

Christopher Jencks has also argued that in addition to intermediary effects of educational attainment on the IQ–occupational status correlation, much of this correlation can be explained by the effects of parents' socioeconomic status (SES). Children's IQs correlate about 0.30 with parents' SES, as measured by a number of variables, including quality of home environment, income, and occupational status.[46] The correlation between fathers' and sons' occupational status is between 0.40 and 0.50.[47] It is thus possible that much of the correlation between IQ and eventual occupational status and income is merely a byproduct of inherited wealth. (We will return in Chapter 4 to the question of why those with higher SES have higher IQs.) In fact, Jencks et al. in their analysis of the determinants of success in America reveal that the variation (standard deviation) in occupational status among men with identical test scores is about 88 percent of the variation among all men. "This suggests that the United States cannot be considered a 'meritocracy,' at least if 'merit' is measured by general cognitive skills."[48] Jencks also cites data indicating that the intergenerational transmission of SES is little affected by IQ.[49]

Such evidence notwithstanding, the correlation between SES and IQ might involve causal effects running in both directions. Just as the quality of environment provided by parental SES will influence IQ, so might one's intelligence (as measured by the tests) determine one's own SES; social mobility may be in part a function of intelligence. Evidence for this supposition can be found in the fact that the correlation between adolescent IQ and later income increases with age. Moreover, Jerome Waller, in a 1971 study of 131 fathers and 170 of their sons, found a correlation of about 0.29 between father–son IQ differences and father–son SES differences; sons with higher IQs than their fathers were more likely to have higher SES, while sons with lower IQs generally moved down the socioeconomic ladder.[50]

7. In your opinion, to what degree is the average American's socio-economic status (SES) determined by his or her IQ?

The majority of respondents support the idea that the United States is somewhat of an intellectual meritocracy. Sixty percent feel that IQ is an important, but not the most important, determinant of SES. Twenty–one percent believe IQ plays only a small role in determining SES, and 3 percent feel it is not at all important. Only 2 percent rate IQ as the most important determinant of SES. There were 14 percent nonrespondents.

"The construct validity of a test is the extent to which the test may be said to measure a theoretical construct or trait."[51] Block and Dworkin's criticism of operationalism in intelligence testing is based on this concept. Without an idea of what intelligence is, there is no way of knowing if an intelligence test is what it claims to be. There are, of course, many theories of intelligence, and tests have been designed with the constructs of these theories in mind, but there still is no generally accepted theoretical account of intelligence.

Our earlier question about important elements of intelligence not adequately measured by intelligence tests is in fact a crude measure of opinion about construct validity; we attempted to assess the degree to which experts believe these tests measure certain theoretical constructs, such as "the capacity to acquire knowledge." A more common source of construct validation for intelligence tests is correlation with existing tests; if scores on two tests are highly correlated, then the tests are assumed to be measuring the same constructs. The success of this strategy is limited by the construct validity of existing tests. Unfortunately, many of these tests have not themselves been subject to construct validation. For example, the Stanford revisions of the Binet–Simon scales have been among the most widely used of such standards. The Binet–Simon test may have had some construct validity, as Terman and others noted in explaining its success, but these were post–hoc analyses. The test was adopted because of its criterion validity. Correlation with existing tests is done as a form of construct validation; if scores on two tests are highly correlated, then the tests are assumed to be measuring the same constructs. The success of this strategy is limited by the construct validity of existing tests.

Much construct validation of intelligence tests, and, in fact, much intelligence theory, comes from another source, statistical analyses of test scores. The interpretation of these analyses has been one of the most hotly debated topics in the intelligence literature. At the center of this debate are arguments over the existence and status of a general mental ability. Psychometricians disagree about the extent to which scores on intelligence and general aptitude tests reflect primarily a single aptitude, or a larger number of independent cognitive abilities.

Those who argue for the existence of a general mental ability rely heavily on the fact that virtually all tests of intelligence and mental aptitude are positively correlated.[52] This phenomenon was first noted in 1904, the year before the publication of the Binet–Simon scale, by English psychologist Charles Spearman.[53] Spearman, a disciple of Galton's, had been using the newly invented correlational techniques to investigate the relationship between various measures of intelligence: teacher and peer ratings, school grades, and sensory and memory test scores. Unlike Clark Wissler, Spearman was impressed by the substantial intercorrelation between the various measures (Spearman noted that Wissler's correlations were too low because he had failed to correct for the unreliability of his measures), and particularly by the very high positive correlations between grades of preparatory school students in each of six subjects, ranging from English and mathematics to music. Students who did well in one subject were likely to do well in all of them. Spearman hypothesized that this pattern could be explained by a single underlying factor, which he called general intelligence, or g.

With the advent of the first workable intelligence tests, Spearman was provided with an even greater data base, and his work on the structure of intelligence continued apace. In order to more precisely define the manner in which a pattern of correlations between tests reflected common underlying entities like g, Spearman invented a technique known as factor analysis, which has become the primary tool of construct validation in psychometrics. Factor analysis is a method by which the set of correlations between a large number of entities (in this case scores on different tests or subtests) may be redescribed in terms of a smaller number of factors. The analysis produces a set of factor "loadings" for each entity that reflect the degree to which the entity in question measures each factor. Thus, for example, a set of correlations between twenty aptitude tests may be described by four underlying factors. Each test measures the four factors to varying degrees, as indicated by their factor loadings.

Spearman found, as he had predicted, that most correlations between test scores he analyzed could be described in terms of one underlying factor on which all of the tests had fairly high loadings, i.e. g. Tests that had a large number of high correlations with other tests were said to be more "g–loaded" than those with a preponderance of lower correlations. From the results of many such factor analyses Spearman developed his two–factor theory of intelligence.[54] Any given cognitive activity (or performance on any test of mental ability) could be accounted for by g, the general intelligence factor common to all such activities (or tests), and by a special (or group) factor, s, reflecting abilities unique to that activity (or test).

Spearman's theory was adopted by many of the early mental testers as an explanation of their test results; as a measure of g, intelligence test scores took on even greater significance. Once tests were firmly established, the statistical analysis of intelligence tests scores became one of the primary means by which theories of intelligence were developed and validated.

Three important points about factor analysis should be noted. First, factor analysis is a purely statistical technique that does nothing more than redescribe a set of correlations. Factors are descriptive categories, or, at best, hypothetical constructs, and should not be thought of as actual underlying entities. Second, factor analysis produces a set of factors that redescribe the data—it does not interpret these factors. Interpretation is left to those who examine the results of the analysis, and is usually accomplished by noting the similarities between those entities that load highly on a given factor. Finally, there are an infinite number of factor analytic solutions for any set of correlations (which is not to say that these solutions are not unique to the set of correlations being analyzed). The solution arrived at depends on the value of certain parameters specified by the analyst, who has certain goals in mind. Spearman performed his analyses so that each test would have the highest possible loading on one factor. It should be understood, however, that Spearman's analyses would not have produced the results they did if the original set of correlations had not allowed it. If few of the tests correlated positively, or if there were many negative correlations, the analyses would not have been able to produce one factor on which most tests loaded highly.

Nevertheless, the preceding caveats make it clear that one may arrive at a large and varied number of reasonable solutions and interpretations from the same set of test score correlations. Factor–analysis theorists tend to fall in one of two camps: those who hypothesize a primary general intelligence factor and subsidiary factors of special abilities, and those who see intelligence as composed entirely of separate faculties.

L. L. Thurstone was the first to point out that the same set of test scores could be factor analyzed to produce, instead of one general factor, a small number of factors. Thurstone called these factors primary mental abilities, each of which has about equal factor loadings across all tests. He also noted that the interpretation given to g depends largely on the particular tests whose scores are factor analyzed. In 1935, Thurstone published *The Vectors of Mind*, in which he hypothesized that intelligence might consist of a relatively small number of independent faculties corresponding to different cognitive domains, each of which contributes to a greater or lesser degree to intellectual functioning in any particular situation. Based on his own research and test development, Thurstone was able to identify eight primary mental abilities: verbal ability, inductive or general reasoning, numerical ability, rote memory, perceptual speed, word fluency, spatial ability, and deductive reasoning. All but the last of these have been frequently corroborated by the work of other multi–factor theorists.[55] It is interesting that, despite his belief that intelligence should not be described in terms of a general factor, Thurstone later observed that his small number of primary factors were themselves intercorrelated, leading him to postulate a "second–order g."[56]

Perhaps the most extreme form of the multi–factor view is represented by the structure–of–intellect model of J. P. Guilford.[57] Guilford has postulated some 120 intellectual factors based on a theoretical scheme in which an intellectual activity may be described in terms of one of five types of mental operation, four types of content, and six types of product. The model does not deal with any general abilities. Guilford and his associates have developed tests that attempt to identify the factors hypothesized by the model. After twenty years of research and test development, ninety-eight factors had been identified.[58] That most of these factors are correlated has been a major criticism of Guilford's anti-g position.[59] Nonetheless, Guilford's work is a good example of how intelligence theory and measurement may progress together.

General intelligence theorists do not disregard the idea of separate mental abilities, but argue that tests of these abilities are so highly correlated that there must be some more general factor influencing performance on all of them. Hierarchical organization is common to many theories postulating a general intelligence factor.[60] Philip Vernon, for example, places g at the top of the hierarchy. The "major group factors," verbal–educational and spatial–mechanical, constitute the second echelon. Under these are certain "minor group factors," and finally specific factors unique to each test. The more any given test taps into abilities in the upper levels of the hierarchy, the more scores from the test will correlate with those from other intelligence and aptitude tests. John Carroll has noted that, because of the somewhat arbitrary nature of factor–analytic solutions, the models of Vernon and Thurstone are interconvertible.[61]

Another popular analytic solution is Raymond Cattell's distinction between fluid and crystallized general intelligence.[62] Fluid g involves nonverbal, culture–free skills thought to be greatly dependent on physiological structures. Crystallized g refers to acquired skills and knowledge that depend on educational and cultural factors, and on fluid intelligence. Fluid intelligence increases until adolescence, after which it declines, as physiological structures deteriorate. Crystallized intelligence increases throughout life until severe deterioration of physiological structures (fluid intelligence) late in life causes acquired knowledge to decrease as well. IQ tests like the Stanford–Binet and the Wechsler tests measure both fluid and crystallized intelligence. Achievement tests are better measures of crystallized than fluid intelligence, while Cattell has developed nonverbal tests that are almost entirely measures of fluid intelligence.

If we are to believe general intelligence theorists, g is the most important aspect of intelligence. But what is g? As a matter of fact, g is a label given to part of the output of a statistical analysis describing a high degree of intercorrelation between tests of mental ability. Anything else that may be said about g is an interpretation based on an examination of those tests that load highly on the "general intelligence" factor. We may *hypothesize* that tests that load highly on g are measuring some underlying general ability, but we only *know* that such tests correlate highly with many other tests.

Jensen has looked closely at those tests that load highly on g. These include tests of verbal similarities and differences, verbal analogies, series completion, figure analogies, and arithmetic reasoning. Tests that load poorly on g include speed of simple addition, rote memory tasks, and simple reaction time. Jensen reaches two conclusions from his examination: first, "g is not related to the specific contents of items or to their surface characteristics."[63] In other words, whatever is causing tests to correlate highly is a *general* characteristic. Second, "g seems to be involved in items that require mental manipulation of images, symbols, words, numbers, or concepts. Tests that merely call for recall or reproduction of previous learning or highly practiced skills are poor measures of g."[64] In addition, Jensen notes that the higher a test loads on g, the better it correlates with subjective impressions of intelligence. For these reasons, Jensen and others have hypothesized that tests of mental ability that correlate well with many other tests do so because they require a great deal of general intellectual ability.

Multi–factor theorists argue that the correlation between tests of different aptitudes is the result of an independent, but coexistent, set of abilities. They point out that it is possible to construct tests that measure these specific abilities, and that the correlation between these tests is far from perfect. The existence of idiot savants (mental retardates possessing extraordinary abilities in one specific area), and, more generally, the unique profile of intellectual abilities displayed by all persons, argue for the existence of independent attributes.[65]

8. Is intelligence, as measured by intelligence tests, better described in terms of a primary general intelligence factor and subsidiary group of special ability factors, or entirely in terms of separate faculties?

Despite the "arbitrariness" of factor analytic solutions, most respondents hold definite opinions on how to most meaningfully to describe intelligence test results. Fifty–eight percent favor some form of a general intelligence solution, while 13 percent feel separate faculties are a superior description. Only 16 percent think the data are sufficiently ambiguous as not to favor either solution. Nonresponse rate was 13 percent.

Opinions about g tell us what most experts believe about the structure of intelligence, at least as measured by intelligence tests. There is also a more practical consequence. The revised edition of the Wechsler Intelligence Scale for Children (WISC–R) and the Stanford–Binet are the two most widely used individually–administered intelligence tests. Their most important use is in education planning for special–needs students. Because these tests yield separate subscores for such skills as verbal and arithmetic reasoning, trained test administrators can diagnose specific deficits and help plan appropriate remediation programs. These tests also yield an omnibus IQ. That the subscales of these tests are substantially intercorrelated and that the tests are highly g–loaded means, at least for believers in g, that the single-score IQ is also a highly meaningful measure, as are global scores on other general aptitude batteries.

Issues of the structure of intelligence aside, examination of modern intelligence tests indicates that these tests are measuring some set of intellectual skills. The WISC-R, for example, is extremely reliable, has good concurrent and predictive validity, loads highly on g, and has been well standardized for American children.[66] The WISC-R consists of the following subtests: general information, word similarities, arithmetic, vocabulary, problem comprehension, digit span, picture completion, block design, object assembly, coding, and mazes. It would be difficult to argue that WISC-R scores do *not* reflect intellectual abilities.

Two further questions about intelligence tests seem relevant. First, to what extent do these tests measure other than intellectual factors? Second, what important factors are not measured by intelligence tests? In a sense, these questions are just another way of asking how intelligence test scores are related to "intelligence," but in a form that may be more answerable.

Tests that measure to any significant extent nonintellectual factors associated with SES, class, or culture are biased. The nature and extent of bias in intelligence tests will be discussed in Chapter 4. For now we may ask whether intelligence tests measure any personality, motivational, or emotional factors not generally thought to be part of intelligence. The answer depends, of course, on one's definition of intelligence, but few would argue that intelligence tests should be measuring such things as willingness to comply with instructions or emotional lability (though these attributes might be quite predictive of academic success). That intelligence tests are influenced by such factors is generally agreed upon by those who study testing.[67] The degree of this influence is uncertain. The evidence is quite clear, however, that the personal characteristics of the examiner, the rapport established between the examiner and the subject, the subject's physical and emotional state, and test anxiety can all influence intelligence test scores. For this reason, psychometric texts and test manuals contain numerous warnings and suggestions for creating as "objective" a testing environment as possible, and for taking extra-intellectual factors into account when interpreting test results. (It also explains why those who administer intelligence and aptitude tests, particularly to individuals, must be well trained.) While it may be impossible to determine the precise influence of these factors in any given case, those who fail to heed the warnings will certainly obtain less comprehensible, and less accurate, test scores.

Block and Dworkin argue that intelligence tests also measure such personality and motivational factors as persistence and attentiveness. These traits are presumably little influenced by an examiner's attempts to make the testing situation more amenable to meaningful measurement. The importance of persistence and attentiveness violates the notion of "intelligence" testing, according to Block and Dworkin, because such traits are clearly nonintellectual. But these authors also indicate that David Wechsler, developer of the WISC and WAIS, believed that attributes like persistence and attentiveness are part of general intelligence, defining intelligence as adaptive behavior. Thus we return to the problem encountered in the 1921 and 1986 symposia of how broadly such adaptive behavior is to be defined.

9. The importance of personal characteristics to intelligence test performance.

Respondents were asked to rate each of six personal characteristics for their importance to performance on intelligence tests. These characteristics are achievement motivation, anxiety, attentiveness, emotional lability, persistence, and physical health. Ratings were made on a 4–point scale, where 1 was "Of little importance," 2 was "Somewhat important," 3 was "Moderately important," and 4 was "Very important."

The results of question 8 are shown in Table 2.5. All characteristics are seen as at least somewhat important to test performance, though only attentiveness is more than moderately important. Nonetheless, expert respondents believe that intelligence test scores can be substantially affected by traits traditionally considered nonintellectual. The case is most clearly

TABLE 2.5
Importance of Personal Characteristics to Intelligence Test Performance

Characteristic	Mean Importance Rating[a]
Achievement motivation	2.87
	(.964)[b]
Anxiety	2.68
	(.901)
Attentivenesss	3.39
	(.744)
Emotional lability	2.52
	(.938)
Persistence	2.96
	(.872)
Physical health	2.34
	(.892)

[a]1 = "Of little importance," 2 = "Somewhat important," 3 = "Moderately important," and 4 = "Very important." b. Numbers in parentheses are standard deviations.

made for achievement motivation. While only 19 percent of respondents believe achievement motivation is an important element of intelligence (Table 2.3), this trait receives a mean rating of 2.87 on the 4–point scale of importance to test performance.

"A psychological test is essentially an objective and standardized measure of a sample of behavior."[68] An intelligence test is a measure of a sample of intelligent behavior. The representativeness of that sample is the province of test validation, with all its attendant ambiguities. In this society, intelligence tests sample behavior that is predictive of (and presumably important to) success in our school systems and in the job market. Other skills and attributes, which may be equally important to success, are little measured. (See Jencks et al. 's 1972 book *Inequality* for an excellent discussion of the importance of noncognitive traits to success.) Their exclusion may be due to the failure of testmakers to produce an adequate sample, but more likely is a reflection of the limits of even so nebulous a concept as intelligence. Sociability, physical attractiveness, artistic talent, motor coordination, creativity, and the need for power undoubtedly all contribute to one's success in Western society, yet none of these attributes are measured by intelligence tests to any significant degree. Nor would many people argue that they should be. Other abilities, like complex problem solving and mathematical reasoning, are not sampled by many intelligence tests, yet are generally thought to be part of intelligent behavior. The restrictions placed on the behaviors sampled by intelligence tests represent a balance between efficiency, greater predictive validity, and the limitations of even the most broadly defined notion of intelligence.

Summary

In general, expert opinion on the nature of intelligence runs contrary to the most common criticisms of testing. Most experts believe that psychologists and educators are in general agreement about the definition of intelligence. This agreement is demonstrated empirically for the basic elements of abstract reasoning, problem–solving ability, and the capacity to acquire knowledge. Considerable disagreement still remains about the variety of behaviors to include in a definition of intelligence. This discord about the precise structure of intelligence is reflected in the majority opinion that the development of intelligence tests has not been guided by a unified theory of intelligence, though it is unclear how a lack of theory relates to the validity of the tests. Respondents also feel that intelligence tests are doing an adequate job of measuring the important elements of intelligence, but that certain nonintellectual personal characteristics can have a significant effect on intelligence test performance. Experts disagree that intelligence tests are nothing but measures of acquired knowledge, but do indicate that whatever the tests are measuring it is not as stable as a purely physical characteristic such as height. Whatever intelligence tests are measuring, the majority of experts believe it is an important determinant of success in American society. Finally, experts believe intelligence, as measured by tests, to be best described in terms of general intelligence and subsidiary factors.

In response to the general question of the nature of intelligence, most psychometricians maintain some form of operationalism, being more concerned with validating tests than with theorizing about cognitive abilities. Cognitive scientists, on the other hand, rarely are concerned with "intelligence" and even more rarely attempt to quantify individual differences in cognitive abilities for use as decision–making tools. This traditional rift between measurement and theory accounts for much of the ambiguity concerning definitions of intelligence. But there is more to the public debate over the nature of intelligence than the particular cognitive traits to be included in some definition, or how these traits are related. Burt's definition of intelligence as "*innate* general cognitive capacity" emphasizes the heritable nature of intelligence and the belief that intelligence is a largely fixed characteristic of the individual. Critics fear that it is as measures of fixed capacity that intelligence and aptitude tests are intended and interpreted. That a two–hour paper–and–pencil exam purports to tell us something about our *inherent* worth is onerous to most of us. The status of intelligence as an innate characteristic is the subject of the next chapter.

Notes

1. E. L. Thorndike et al., "Intelligence and Its Measurement: A Symposium," *Journal of Educational Psychology* 12 (1921):124–147, 195–216, 271–275.
2. Ibid., p. 128.
3. Ibid., p. 137.
4. Frank N. Freeman, "A Referendum of Psychologists: A Survey of Opinion on the Mental Tests," *Century Magazine* 107 (1923):237–245.
5. Robert L. Sternberg et al, "People's Conceptions of Intelligence," *Journal of Personality and Social Psychology* 41 (1981):37–55.
6. T. Anne Cleary et al, "Educational Uses of Tests with Disadvantaged Students," *American Psychologist* 30 (1975):19.
7. Robert J. Sternberg and Douglas K. Detterman, eds., *What Is Intelligence?* (Norwood, NJ: Ablex, 1986).
8. Robert J. Sternberg and Cynthia A. Berg, "Quantitative Integration: A Comparison of the 1921 and 1986 Symposia," in *What Is Intelligence?* eds. Robert J. Sternberg and Douglas K. Detterman (Norwood, NJ: Ablex, 1986), pp. 157–158.
9. Other areas that have been or are being studied include nuclear energy, environmental cancer, and gender differences. For discussions of the historical the-

oretical issues as well as some of the case studies, see chs. ; S. Robert Lichter, Stanley Rothman and Linda Lichter *The Media Elite* (Washington, D.C.: Adler and Adler, 1986); Stanley Rothman, S. Robert Lichter, and Linda Lichter, *Elites in Conflict: Social Change in America*; Stanley Rothman and S. Robert Lichter, "Elites in Conflict: Nuclear Energy, Ideology, and the perception of Risk," *Journal of Contemporary Studies* 8,3 (Summer/Fall, *Transaction/Society* 23,3 (March/April, 1986), pp. 5–8.

10. Cyril Burt, "Mental Capacity and Its Critics," *Bulletin of the British Psychological Society* 21 (1968):11–18.

11. Arthur R. Jensen, "How Much Can We Boost IQ and Scholastic Achievement?" *Harvard Educational Review* 39 (1969):5.

12. Hans J. Eysenck, ed., *A Model for Intelligence* (New York: Springer-Verlag, 1982); Howard Gardner, *Frames of Mind: The Theory of Multiple Intelligences* (New York: Basic Books, 1983).

13. N. J. Block and Gerald Dworkin, eds., *The IQ Controversy* (New York: Pantheon Books, 1976), p. 28.

14. Edwin G. Boring, "Intelligence as the Tests Test It," *New Republic* 35 (1923):35–37.

15. cf. Eysenck; Robert L. Sternberg, ed., *Recent Advances in Research on Intelligence* (Hillsdale, NJ: Lawrence Erlbaum, 1982).

16. Cleary et al., p. 19.

17. Robert J. Sternberg and Cynthia A. Berg, "Quantitative Integration: A Comparison of the 1921 and 1986 Symposia," in *What Is Intelligence?* eds. Robert J. Sternberg and Douglas K. Detterman (Norwood, NJ: Ablex, 1986), p. 157.

18. N. J. Block and Gerald Dworkin, "IQ, Heritability and Inequality," in *The IQ Controversy* eds. N. J. Block and Gerald Dworkin (New York: Pantheon Books, 1976), pp. 410–540.

19. Block and Dworkin, p. 423.

20. Lewis M. Terman, *The Measurement of Intelligence* (Boston: Houghton Mifflin, 1916).

21. Thorndike et al., p. 131.

22. Ibid.

23. Douglas K. Detterman, "Quantitative Integration: The Last Word?" in *What Is Intelligence?* eds. Robert J. Sternberg and Douglas K. Detterman (Norwood, NJ: Ablex, 1986), p. 164.

24. For example, Raymond B. Cattell, "A Culture-Free Intelligence Test, Part I," *Journal of Educational Psychology* 31 (1940):161–179; Raymond B. Cattell, "Theory of Fluid and Crystalized Intelligence: A Critical Experiment," *Journal of Educational Psychology* 54 (1963):1–22; J. P. Guilford and R. Hoepfner, *The Analysis of Intelligence* (New York: McGraw-Hill, 1971).

25. Jerome M. Sattler, *Assessment of Children's Intelligence and Special Abilities,* 2nd ed. (Boston: Allyn and Bacon, 1982), p. 440.

26. Cleary et al., p. 21; Robert A. Gordon, "Labelling Theory, Mental Retardation, and Public Policy: *Larry P.* and Other Developments Since 1974," in *The Labeling of Deviance: Evaluating a Perspective,* 2nd ed., ed. Walter R. Gove (Beverly Hills, CA: Sage Publications, 1980), pp. 190–191.

27. David Owen, *None of the Above: Behind the Myth of Scholastic Aptitude* (Boston: Houghton Mifflin, 1985).

28. Anne Anastasi, *Psychological Testing,* 5th ed. (New York: Collier Macmillan, 1982), p. 395.

29. Gordon, p. 190.
30. Block and Dworkin, p. 445.
31. Arthur R. Jensen, *Bias in Mental Testing* (New York: Free Press, 1980), pp. 261–262.
32. Ibid., p. 270.
33. Sattler, p. 57.
34. Jensen, "How Much," p. 18; Sattler, p. 58.
35. Benjamin S. Bloom, *Stability and Change in Human Characteristics* (New York: Wiley, 1964), p. 61.
36. Jensen, "How Much," p. 19.
37. Anastasi, p. 131.
38. Ibid., p. 137.
39. Jensen, *Bias,* pp. 317–319.
40. Ibid., p. 319.
41. Christopher Jencks et al., *Inequality* (New York: Basic Books, 1972), p. 144.
42. Ibid., p. 185; Jensen, *Bias,* p. 341.
43. Otis Dudley Duncan, "Ability and Achievement," *Eugenics Quarterly* 15 (1968):1–11.
44. Christopher Jencks et al., *Who Gets Ahead?* (New York: Basic Books, 1979), p. 121.
45. John E. Hunter and Ronda F. Hunter, "Validity and Utility of Alternative Predictors of Job Performance," *Psychological Bulletin* 96 (1984):72–98.
46. John C. Loehlin, Gardner Lindzey, and J. N. Spuhler, *Race Differences in Intelligence* (San Francisco: W.H. Freeman, 1975), p. 169.
47. Jencks et al., *Inequality,* p. 179.
48. Jencks et al., *Who Gets Ahead,* p. 115.
49. Samuel Bowles and Herbert Gintis, "IQ in the U.S. Class Structure," *Social Policy* (1973):65–96; Samuel Bowles and Valerie Nelson, "The 'Inheritance' of IQ and the Intergenerational Reproduction of Economic Inequality," *Review of Economics and Statistics* 56 (1974):39–51.
50. Jerome H. Waller, "Achievement and Social Mobility: Relationships Among IQ Score, Education, and Occupation in Two Generations," *Social Biology* 18 (1971):252–259.
51. Anastasi, p. 144.
52. Jensen, *Bias,* pp. 314–315.
53. Charles Spearman, "'General Intelligence' Objectively Determined and Measured," *American Journal of Psychology* 15 (1904):201–292.
54. Charles Spearman, *The Abilities of Man* (New York: Macmillan, 1927).
55. Anastasi, pp. 366–369.
56. L. L. Thurstone, *Multiple Factor Analysis* (Chicago: University of Chicago Press, 1947).
57. J. P. Guilford, *The Nature of Human Intelligence* (New York: McGraw-Hill, 1967).
58. J. P. Guilford and R. Hoepfner, *The Analysis of Intelligence* (New York: McGraw-Hill, 1971).
59. Sattler, p. 39.
60. Cyril Burt, "The Structure of the Mind: A Review of the Results of Factor Analysis," *British Journal of Educational Psychology* 19 (1949):100–111, 176–199; A. R. Hakstian and R. B. Cattell, "Higher-Stratum Ability Structures on a Basis of Twenty Primary Abilities," *Journal of Educational Psychology* 70

(1978):657–669; Lloyd G. Humphries, "The Organization of Human Abilities," *American Psychologist* 17 (1962):475–483; Philip E. Vernon, *The Structure of Human Abilities,* 2nd ed. (London: Methuen, 1961).

61. John B. Carroll, "The Measurement of Intelligence," in Robert J. Sternberg, ed., *Handbook of Human Intelligence* (Cambridge, U.K.: Cambridge University Press, 1982), p. 73.
62. Raymond B. Cattell, "Theory of Fluid and Crystalized Intelligence: A Critical Experiment," *Journal of Educational Psychology* 54 (1963):1–22.
63. Arthur R. Jensen, *Straight Talk About Mental Tests* (New York: Free Press, 1981), p. 58.
64. Ibid., p. 59.
65. cf. Godfrey H. Thomson, *The Factorial Analysis of Human Ability,* 5th ed. (Boston: Houghton Mifflin, 1951); Gardner.
66. Sattler, pp. 146–150.
67. Anastasi, pp. 34–41; Sattler, pp. 329–333.
68. Anastasi, p. 22.

3

The Heritability of IQ

It is meaningless to ask how much of an individual's intelligence may be attributed to genetic factors and how much to environment. The development of intelligence, like any other aspect of a person's body and behavior (phenotype), is as completely dependent on genetic constitution (genotype) as on environment. Just as a fertilized ovum must develop into a trait-laden human being in the context of some environment, environmental stimuli cannot produce a set of traits without the proper genetic material. As Donald Hebb has put it, "To ask how much heredity contributes to intelligence is like asking how much the width of a field contributes to its area."[1] The inextricable nature of the gene–environment synthesis does not, of course, preclude the study of the mechanisms by which genes and environment interact; it simply eliminates the possibility of assigning any greater importance to one factor over the other. From this perspective, the nature/nurture "controversy" is no controversy at all. (A proper understanding of the role of genes and environment in the determination of phenotypic traits underscores the absurdity of statements, like that in the title of the *New York Times Magazine* "jensenism" article, that "intelligence is largely determined by the genes." Intelligence is determined *entirely* by both the genes and the environment.)

What is not possible to study within the individual is often measurable in the population; the importance of *differences* between persons in genes and environment to individual *differences* in any given trait is theoretically assessable. The chief measure of this relationship is heritability. Heritability is defined as the proportion of variation in a trait attributable to genetic variation, and varies between 0 and 1.0. When the heritability of a trait is 0, it means that all of the variation in the trait among members of the population under study is due to environmental variation. If, for example, the heritability of IQ was 0, it would mean that the difference in IQ between the genius and the retardate, or between any two people, was entirely the result of different environmental experiences. The heritability

79

of language spoken, or of religious preference, is probably very near 0. When the heritability of a trait is 1.0, the present range of environmental variation bears no relation to individual differences in the trait in the population under study. Eye color is an example of a trait whose heritability is very near 1.0. Virtually all human behavioral and physical characteristics for which appropriate studies have been done have heritabilities between these two extremes.

Several important points must be kept in mind when interpreting data on the heritability of IQ. First, heritability deals with *variation* in a trait, not with absolute level. It indicates the degree to which individual differences in some trait can be attributed to genetic or nongenetic differences. Thus, the average IQ of the population as a whole can significantly change as a result of some environmental or genetic changes without affecting the heritability of IQ. If everyone's IQ increased by 20 points, with no change in IQ *variation* (no change in anyone's IQ relative to that of others), heritability would remain the same.

In fact, James Flynn has presented evidence of massive gains in the average IQ of white Americans between 1932 and 1978.[2] (Because IQ is always standardized according to the population mean, the only way to calculate population changes across time is to look at those individuals who have taken at least two tests standardized at different times. Unfortunately, early standardization samples of the Stanford–Binet and Wechsler tests did not include blacks, and thus Flynn was able to compare only the scores of white test takers.) Yet IQ heritability estimates calculated during that time period did not change substantially, though estimates have been somewhat lower in recent years. One may hypothesize that as the general level of education has improved since 1932, so have the cognitive skills of the average American, without much affecting the distribution of intelligence.

The average level of intelligence in any population is obviously an important statistic, particularly in an increasingly technological society where the level of cognitive skills necessary to compete in the workplace continues to rise. While heritability analyses are independent of average level of IQ, they can tell us how easy or difficult it would be to make significant changes. By studying variation, we learn the relationship between individual differences in IQ and environmental differences between people, and thus have a better understanding of the amount of environmental change necessary to produce changes in IQ. Moreover, the study of variation in a trait like IQ may be of great consequence, irrespective of the population average. Intelligence and aptitude tests are used as decision–making tools in situations where educational and occupational resources are scarce; a competitive social structure is based on the differences among people in relevant abilities and attributes. Understanding the causes of these differences, and subsequently being able to do something about them, may thus have profound effects on the nature of competition and the distribution of resources and opportunities.

A second important point about heritability is that it is a population-specific statistic; it is unique to the particular population sampled. In a different population, or in the same population at a different time, a different heritability estimate for the same trait may be obtained as genetic and environmental variation change. The heritability of IQ is thus not fixed. As the variation in environmental experience relevant to performance on intelligence tests changes in any population, so will heritability. A very high heritability for IQ therefore does *not* mean that IQ cannot be substantially altered through environmental change. It means that under the present circumstances, a large environmental change (relative to present levels of environmental variation) is needed to produce substantial changes in IQ. It is completely possible that some new program of environmental manipulation could be introduced that would produce very large changes in IQ in certain segments of the population, thus significantly lowering heritability.

Third, heritable should not be confused with innate, or genetic. Consider the trait of number of limbs. Most of us have four, and we are inclined to say that this is a genetic trait, in that we inherit it from our parents. The heritability of number of limbs is, however, probably closer to 0 than it is to 1.0. This is because much more of the *variation* between people in number of limbs is the result of environmental variation (industrial accidents, surgical amputation, etc.) than it is due to genetic variation.

It is an error, of which mental testers historically have been guilty, to speak of a test as measuring innate intelligence. If the heritability of IQ was 1.0, one might be justified in claiming that *differences* in IQ reflect innate (i.e., genetic) *differences*, but it is not true that the *skills* measured by the test are "innate" any more than they are "environmental." The early mental testers did not make such careful distinctions in their descriptions of the tests. Binet himself believed that his scale measured a combination of "intelligence pure and simple" and environmentally determined achievements. Certain of the items in the scale, however, particularly those dealing with performance measures rather than verbal skills, he believed could "isolate from the scholastic effects the real native intelligence."[3]

Binet differed from many of his colleagues of the time who, while conceding that the new intelligence tests were not uncontaminated by environment, believed that intelligence itself was fixed and could not be significantly altered by environmental circumstances. Binet believed that intelligence, as measured by the tests, could be improved, and criticized the "brutal pessimism" of those who would forever consign the backward child to a subnormal life. In contrast, Goddard, Terman, and others who revised and enthusiastically administered the tests in various institutions in the United States believed themselves to be in possession of instruments that, while not perfect, provided a very good measure of innate intelligence. Lewis Terman's attitude was typical. Urging widespread intelligence testing in the schools, he argued in 1916 that such tests are "necessary to determine whether a given child is unsuccessful in school because of poor native ability, or because of poor instruction, lack of interest, or some other re-movable cause."[4]

Many critics of testing have pointed to statements of this sort as evidence that intelligence tests were, almost from the beginning, an attempt to main-tain a caste system based on supposed innate, and therefore permanent, differences in ability.[5] (Binet is usually excepted as an innocent whose good intentions were corrupted by others.) Whatever the intentions of the early mental testers, one would be hard pressed to argue that modern psycho-metricians hold such naive views of the role of genes in intelligence test performance. There is, however, widespread misunderstanding about this issue among the general public, which continues to view IQ tests as at-tempts to measure innate intelligence.

This misconception is largely responsible for the supposed stigmatizing effects of the IQ (see Chapter 5), as well as the propagation of other aspects of the controversy. One of the few topics on which expert witnesses on both sides of the *Larry P.* case were in agreement is that intelligence tests are *not* measures of innate ability; IQ is legitimately a function of an individual's environment. Judge Peckham ignored this evidence, arguing that since there is no difference in "true" (i.e., innate) levels of retardation between blacks and whites, tests reporting such a difference must be biased. To the judge, as to much of the general public, all environmental effects on test performance represent bias and are to be avoided.

As a final point about heritability analyses, it should be noted that the heritability of IQ is *completely independent* of what IQ means or what intelligence tests measure. The methods used to estimate the heritability of IQ are unrelated to the methods used to measure intelligence. Thus if one decided to measure intelligence via the length of the nose, one could obtain a heritability estimate for this intelligence measure. The validity of that estimate of the heritability of nose length (like the heritability of a score on a more standard intelligence test) is independent of whether nose length is an adequate measure of intelligence. Only if one were to claim to now have an estimate of the heritability of "intelligence" would the relation between nose length and intelligence be relevant. For this reason, this chapter is concerned with the heritability of IQ, and we will look at the quality of the evidence supporting this determination. The relationship of IQ to intelligence is the subject of Chapter 2.

Unfortunately, heritability is much easier to define than to measure. Heritability analyses are the province of the field of quantitative genetics. These analyses use as their data the correlations in the trait being measured, in this case IQ scores, between pairs of persons who differ in genetic and environmental relatedness. A common research design is to compare the correlations of monozygotic (MZ, or identical) twins, who have all of their genes in common, to those of dizygotic (DZ, or fraternal) twins who have approximately half of their genes in common. A higher correlation of IQ scores for MZ than for DZ twins is taken as strong evidence for a genetic source of variation. Karl Holzinger, in 1929, was one of the first to attempt a quantitative estimation of heritability for IQ based on twin data.[6] He suggested a model for heritability estimation based on the difference between the correlation of MZ twin IQs and the correlation of DZ twin IQs. Similar formulas have been proposed and applied to twin data more recently.[7] The difficulty with these analyses is that they make some rather simplistic assumptions about the sources of variation in IQ. In particular, they assume that the environments of MZ and DZ twins are equally similar, and that any difference between MZ and DZ correlations must be due to genetic factors. Greater similarity of MZ environments compared to DZ environments (parents, teachers, and peers may treat identical twins more similarly than they treat fraternal twins) is one of a number of possible sources of variation in IQ scores ignored by many heritability analyses. The enumeration and estimation of the precise sources of variation contributing to phenotypic variation (in this case variation in IQ across persons in a population) has been the principal stumbling block and major source of contention in the scholarly debate over the heritability of IQ.

Sources of Variation

An analysis–of–variance model, as the name implies, allows for a more careful examination of the sources of variation in a trait. Phenotypic variation may be partitioned as follows:[8]

$$P = G + E + f(G,E)$$

where P is phenotypic variation, G is genetic variation, E is environmental variation, and f(G,E) is some function of the joint effects of genotype and environment. Each of the elements on the right–hand side of the equaton is expressed as a proportion of 1.0. It may be seen that G is the same as heritability.

Genetic and environmental variation may be either within or between families. Siblings (other than identical twins) differ in both genes and environment. This is within–family variation. Total population variance consists of these differences and the differences between families. Heritability analyses reveal these sources of variation to differing degrees. For example, studies comparing MZ to DZ twins reflect primarily within–family variation. Adoption studies, in which children are moved from one family to another, reveal the differences between families.

Other genetic factors to be considered include assortative mating, dominance, and epistasis. Assortative mating refers to the fact that mating is generally not random with respect to genotype. To the extent that there is a positive correlation between the genotypes of those who mate, genetic variation will increase between families and decrease within families. Thus, if those with genes for higher IQ are mating primarily with each other, and those with genes for lower IQ are mating primarily with each other, the variation in genotypic IQ will increase across families in the population. (Note that "genes for higher IQ" and "genes for lower IQ" do not imply that there are specific IQ genes. If there is a substantial heritability for IQ, however, it means that genetic variation is associated with variation in IQ and, all other things being equal, certain genotypes will produce higher IQ phenotypes than others.) At the same time, children will look more like their parents. To understand this relationship, imagine the most extreme case of assortative mating, in which mates differed only in their sex–determining genes. Sons of such a pairing would be identical genetically to their father and daughters would be identical to their mother.

Dominance decreases the similarity between the phenotypes of parents and children. Genes come in pairs, and children inherit one of each pair from the father and one from the mother. If, for any given gene pair, a child inherits a dominant gene from one parent and a recessive gene from the other, only the dominant gene will be manifest in the child's phenotype, and the child will look less like the average of its parents. Phenotypic variation will increase within families and decrease between families. Dominance and assortative mating will therefore have opposite effects, and to some degree cancel each other out. This is fortunate, since very few analyses of IQ heritability take either factor explicitly into account.

Another factor serving to decrease parent–child similarity is epistasis, which is the result of the interaction of genes. The child inherits a unique combination of genes from its parents, and some of these may interact in ways not predictable from the simple additive combination of their separate effects. Epistasis refers to these nonadditive effects. Existing evidence indicates that epistasis is not an important factor in variation in IQ.[9]

Environmental variance consists of all between– and within–family differences in environment, including pre– and perinatal effects, and error variance (measurement error). In some models, environmental variance is defined as all variance not due to genetic factors, and thus includes f(G,E), the joint effects of genotype and environment. This makes no difference to heritability estimates as long as heritability is calculated by dividing purely genetic variance by total variance. The problem is that some models include these joint effects as part of genetic variance, thus inflating heritability estimates. There seems to be little agreement among those who conduct behavior genetics studies whether f(G,E) should be attributed to the genes or to the environment.

The joint effects of G and E can take two forms: covariance and interaction. Gene–environment covariance is represented by a correlation between genotype and environment. Three types of covariance have been identified,[10] passive, reactive, and active. Passive covariance occurs when parents who give their children genes for higher IQ, also give them more favorable environments. In reactive covariance, others, particularly teachers, may react to a child's abilities by providing more enriching environments for those with more talent. Finally, in active covariance, the child itself, as a result of genetic predisposition to higher IQ, may actively seek out more intellectually stimulating situations. Gene–environment correlation may also be negative, of course, as when teachers try to provide the most stimulating environments to those who seem to need them most.

Positive covariance will act to produce greater phenotypic variability than would be predictable from genetic and environmental variation alone. David Layzer has argued that covariation is always present to an unknown degree in human behavior–genetic studies, thus invalidating any attempts to separate genetic from environmental influences.[11] Nonetheless, many heritability analyses have attempted to estimate the extent of covariance. Robert Plomin and his colleagues have demonstrated that the problem is statistically soluble, but claim that the necessary data are at present lacking.[12] There is therefore a great deal of indeterminacy in covariance estimates, which can have a profound effect on heritability calculations. For example, Jencks et al., based on their analysis of sources of variation in behavior–genetic studies of IQ, calculated that gene–environment covariance accounts for 20 percent of total phenotypic variance, and derived a heritability estimate of 0.45.[13] Loehlin, Lindzey, and Spuhler suggesting alternative hypotheses of gene–environment relations in Jencks et al.'s data, produce an equally plausible covariance estimate of 15 percent, leading to a heritability calculation of about 0.60.[14] The situation is further complicated by studies that do not attempt to estimate covariance at all, leading to inflated estimates of G, E, or both.[15]

Related to covariance is gene–environment interaction, which refers to the differential effects of certain environments on certain genotypes. In other words, an interaction occurs when genotypes and environments are not additive in their effects. Thus, it may be that individuals with genes for lower IQ profit more from a certain environment than those with genes for higher IQ, or vice versa. Richard Lewontin points out that the presence of gene–environment interaction severely limits the usefulness of heritability analyses.[16] What is really desired, he argues, is the norm of reaction, which describes the phenotypic outcome of all possible gene–environment combinations. Since heritability analyses are based on only a small number of these combinations (those present in the population being studied), the results of any given analysis may only be generalized if each environment has the same effect on different genotypes—in other words, if gene–environment effects are additive. While there are few good tests of interaction effects, particularly in twin studies,[17] at least four reviews of the literature have been unable to find any evidence for significant gene–environment interactions in IQ.[18] To date, few heritability analyses of IQ have included a specific interaction term.

Philip Vernon has presented the following chart as a way of summarizing the several sources of variance contributing to phenotypic variation:[19]

G   between families
G   within families
AM   (assortative mating   G
between parents)
D   (dominance)

G–E   covariance (effects of
covariation between G and E)   f(G,E)
G–E   interaction

E   between families
E   within families   E
e   (error or unreliability variance)

The more accurately such factors as dominance, assortative mating, covariance, and interaction can be estimated, the more accurate will be subsequent measures of heritability. We have seen that early heritability analyses took none of these factors into account. Modern investigations have attempted to deal with these variables, some more completely than others.

The state of the behavior–genetic art is represented by biometrical analysis, which attempts to model the sources of variation among the numerous genetic and environmental relationships in any given behavior–genetic study.[20] Biometrical analysis is advantageous in that it allows for statistical tests of the extent to which each of the factors listed above is important to the analysis at hand. Indeterminacy persists, however, because sufficient data are not always available to conduct all the necessary tests, and because analysts may disagree about the way variance is partitioned in their original model. Jencks et al. were one of the first to apply a path analysis to behavior–genetic data in order to account for the relationship between the intelligence of parents and children. As mentioned, Loehlin and his colleagues were able to derive a very different heritability estimate from the same data by assuming that adoptive parents' intelligence affects the child's environment directly, rather than via the adoptive parents' genotype, as in Jencks et al.'s model. Such assumptions are largely arbitrary, and can produce quite varied results.[21]

The heritability analyses to be discussed vary in the degree to which they deal with different sources of bias, and in their underlying models. Moreover, the quality of behavior–genetic data has been limited by such factors as poor sampling procedures and the instability of test scores across age groups. It should not be surprising, therefore, that estimates of heritability also vary. The best one can hope for at this point is evidence for or against a significant genetic component of differences in test scores, and a range of heritability estimates.

The Data

Figure 3.1, taken from a 1981 review by Thomas Bouchard and Matthew McGue, summarizes the results of 111 behavior–genetic studies of measured intelligence, representing the vast majority of all such studies ever done.[22] Each point represents the correlation, from one study, between intelligence test scores of persons of the indicated genetic and environmental relatedness. The vertical bar through each distribution represents the median correlation from all studies of that type. Thus, for example, Bouchard and McGue present the results of 41 studies of the IQ correlation of DZ twins reared together (line 5 in the figure), representing 5,546 pairs of DZ twins. The median IQ correlation across these studies is 0.58.

A more meaningful statistic than the median is the weighted average, which takes into account differences in sample size between investigations, and is given in one of the columns on the right side of the figure. Correlation coefficients from studies involving larger numbers of subjects are given more weight in calculating the average correlation. For DZ twins reared apart, this average is 0.60.

The arrow under each distribution indicates the predicted correlation of a simple polygenic model, assuming that all phenotypic variation in IQ is due to additive genetic effects (no dominance or epistasis), with no assortative mating. IQ heritability under such a model is 1.0.

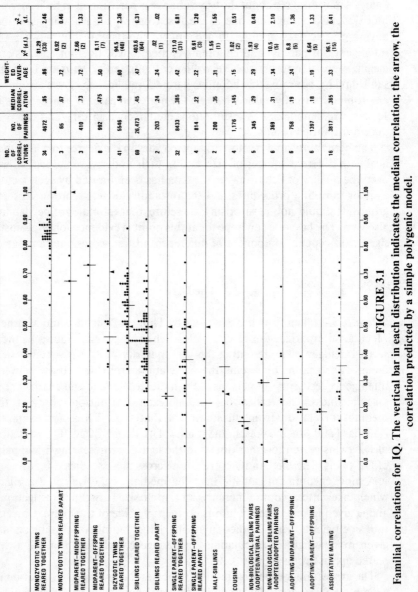

	NO. OF CORREL- ATIONS	NO. OF PAIRINGS	MEDIAN CORREL- ATION	WEIGHT- ED AVER- AGE	x^2 (d.f.)	$x^2 \div$ d.f.
MONOZYGOTIC TWINS REARED TOGETHER	34	4672	.85	.86	81.29 (33)	2.46
MONOZYGOTIC TWINS REARED APART	3	65	.67	.72	0.92 (2)	0.46
MIDPARENT–MIDOFFSPRING REARED TOGETHER	3	410	.73	.72	2.66 (2)	1.33
MIDPARENT–OFFSPRING REARED TOGETHER	8	992	.475	.50	8.11 (7)	1.16
DIZYGOTIC TWINS REARED TOGETHER	41	5546	.58	.60	94.5 (40)	2.36
SIBLINGS REARED TOGETHER	69	26,473	.45	.47	403.6 (64)	6.31
SIBLINGS REARED APART	2	203	.24	.24	.02 (1)	.02
SINGLE PARENT–OFFSPRING REARED TOGETHER	32	8433	.385	.42	211.0 (31)	6.81
SINGLE PARENT–OFFSPRING REARED APART	4	814	.22	.22	9.61 (3)	3.20
HALF-SIBLINGS	2	200	.35	.31	1.55 (1)	1.55
COUSINS	4	1,176	.145	.15	1.02 (2)	0.51
NON-BIOLOGICAL SIBLING PAIRS (ADOPTED/NATURAL PAIRINGS)	5	345	.29	.29	1.93 (4)	0.48
NON-BIOLOGICAL SIBLING PAIRS (ADOPTED/ADOPTED PAIRINGS)	6	369	.31	.34	10.5 (5)	2.10
ADOPTING MIDPARENT–OFFSPRING	6	758	.19	.24	6.8 (5)	1.36
ADOPTING PARENT–OFFSPRING	6	1397	.18	.19	6.64 (5)	1.33
ASSORTATIVE MATING	16	3817	.365	.33	96.1 (15)	6.41

FIGURE 3.1

Familial correlations for IQ. The vertical bar in each distribution indicates the median correlation; the arrow, the correlation predicted by a simple polygenic model.

Two facts should be noted about Figure 3.1 before the data are examined more carefully. First, there is a wide distribution of IQ correlations across studies examining similarly related individuals (i.e., the dots on each line are widely spread). Much of this variation may be attributed to differences in the populations being studied, but procedural differences, such as the type of intelligence test used, and the degree of environmental correlation between individuals being raised apart, undoubtedly contribute to the indeterminacy of the results. The variation among correlation coefficients should serve to reinforce the earlier caveat that precise heritability estimates are not possible.

The second important characteristic of the Figure 3.1 data is that they do not include the results of studies by Sir Cyril Burt. The story of Burt's apparent fraud is described briefly in Chapter 1. Remarkably, even if Burt did fake much of his data, he was careful to manufacture reasonable figures, as the inclusion of his results make little difference to the median values calculated across studies.[23]

Comparing the weighted average correlations to the simple polygenic predictions (the arrows), one finds some rather large quantitative discrepancies, but great similarity in qualitative trends. For example, average correlation decreases with degree of kinship (genetic relatedness) from MZ twins, to siblings reared together, to half–siblings, to cousins, to unrelated persons reared apart (not shown in Figure 3.1, but found to correlate very close to 0 in at least four investigations).[24] Precise quantitative agreement between the model and the data is not to be expected for a number of reasons, foremost of which is that the model assumes an IQ heritability of 1.0, and environmental variation is certainly important to differences in IQ. In addition, the correlation coefficients given are not corrected for unreliability of test scores (even two test scores from the same person will not correlate 1.0), and the simple model ignores factors such as dominance and assortative mating. The last row in Figure 3.1 indicates that the degree of assortative mating, at least at the phenotypic level, is substantial in the populations studied, as the IQ scores of mates have a weighted average correlation of 0.33.

While the qualitative agreement between genetic relatedness and IQ correlation in the kinship data described above is suggestive of a significant genetic contribution to variation in IQ, these data are at least consistent with a purely environmental hypothesis. As Kamin points out, the differences in genetic similarity between siblings and half–siblings, for example, may be confounded with differences in environmental similarity.[25] Siblings are probably *treated* more alike than are half–siblings, who are treated more similarly than cousins, and so on, and this may account for the differences in IQ correlations. The more informative comparisons to make are those in which genetic and environmental factors can be to some degree separated. Thus, it would be difficult for a strict environmentalist to explain why MZ twins reared apart should have more similar IQ scores than siblings reared together, or than unrelated persons reared together (adoptive pairings) for that matter.

In a sense, MZ twins reared apart (MZA) represent the ideal natural experiment in behavior genetics. These individuals have identical genes, and different environments, and therefore any difference in IQ must be due to environmental variation. The fact that there is so little difference (weighted average correlation, uncorrected for unreliability = 0.72) is taken as strong evidence for a significant genetic component to IQ. That MZ twins reared together show an even higher correlation (0.86) indicates that environmental variation is also important. But MZA studies are not without some rather serious flaws. For one thing, such individuals are rare: when Burt's data are excluded, the total number of MZA pairs ever studied is only 65 (though Bouchard is currently gathering data on another thirty-four pairs).[26] The primary criticism of MZA studies, however, has been that, though reared apart, the environments of the separated twins are often highly correlated.[27] For example, Kamin cites cases in which MZA twins were raised by relatives, lived in the same small town, and attended the same school. Also, adoption agencies often try to match parents to the characteristics of the child, and one would therefore expect MZ twins to end up in similar homes. Correlated environments are a problem for a genetic interpretation of MZA research because they might produce the high MZA IQ correlation in the absence of any genetic determination of variation. As Vernon notes, however, the correlated environment problem still can't explain, from an environmentalist standpoint, why MZA twins should show a higher IQ correlation than DZ twins reared together.[28] Surely even relatives living in the same town cannot supply environments as similar as one set of parents provide their own twin children.

Kamin has further attacked much of the MZA data, arguing that researchers did not take into account age effects on test scores, even though the twins tested varied widely in age.[29] Kamin performed a series of intricate age–corrections on these data, and claims to have eliminated most of the IQ correlation. Elsewhere in his book, similar statistical techniques are used to discredit other behavior–genetic studies purporting to show a significant genetic component to variation in IQ. Many authors find Kamin's analyses ad hoc and arbitrary,[30] though he is certainly not without his supporters.[31] It should be pointed out that Kamin is one of the few participants in the IQ debate who believes there is no reasonable evidence for *any* heritable component to IQ.

Another common technique used in estimating heritability involves the comparison of MZ and DZ twins, alluded to earlier. The greater similarity in IQ between MZ twins (average weighted correlation = 0.86), who share all their all genes, than between DZ twins (0.60), who share only half their genes, indicates genetic involvement in IQ variation. Critics have argued that much of the increased similarity of MZ twins is the result of MZ twins having more similar environments. Yet studies like that of Hugh Lytton in 1977, involving extensive observations and other measures of interactions between parents and their twin children, conclude that the greater environmental similarity of MZ over DZ twins is primarily a result, not a cause, of their behavioral similarity.[32]

Not shown in Figure 3.1 are data on the children of identical twins, who offer a unique opportunity for behavior geneticists because they are as similar genetically to the twin of their parent as they are to their parent, yet they presumably share little of their aunt or uncle's environment. Richard Rose and his associates have found that children's scores on the Wechsler Block Design test correlate almost as highly with scores of their co–twin aunt or uncle, as with those of their co–twin parent, while the correlation with the spouse of their co–twin aunt or uncle is zero.[33] These twin–family data, which also include correlations of test scores between cousins, who are as genetically related as half–siblings, yield heritability estimates in the range of 0.4 to 0.6.

In many ways the best source of behavior–genetic data comes from adoption studies, in which children are raised by parents to whom they are genetically unrelated. These investigations allow for numerous comparisons between parents and children relevant to the heritability issue. In addition, the many sources of data from individuals of known genetic and environmental relation are more amenable to accurate statistical estimation of sources of bias like dominance, covariance, and interaction.[34] While adoption research has not been as common historically as twin research, for example, recent years have seen the initiation of several large–scale adoption studies.[35]

The average weighted IQ correlation between an adopted child and its adopted parent, who supplies much of the child's environment and none of its genes, is 0.19. The IQ correlation between an adopted child and its natural parent, who supplies the child's genes and very little of its environment, is 0.22. The difference between these two numbers is not significant, and it suggests that differences in natural parents' genes contribute at least as much to variation in children's IQ as differences in environment supplied by adoptive parents. Consistent with the idea that both genes and environment are important is the fact that both the natural parent–adopted child and adoptive parent–adopted child correlations are less than the natural parent–natural child correlation (0.42).

Further evidence comes from a comparison between adopted children. Genetically unrelated children reared together have a weighted average IQ correlation of 0.34, consistent with a significant environmental component to IQ variation. On the other hand, full siblings, who share about half their genes, have an IQ correlation of 0.47 when reared together, and MZ twins, who share all their genes, have IQs that correlate 0.86. These comparisons strongly indicate that genetic variation is important as well.

As numerous as are the data sources from adoption studies, so are the potential problems. Some of the mostly commonly cited, and potentially serious, include: (1) the selective placement of children into homes similar to those in which they were born, leading to a correlation between natural and adoptive parental environments; (2) variation in the age of adopting—children in many studies are adopted quite late, meaning that they have had significant exposure to the natural parents' environment; (3) age and SES differences between natural and adoptive parents—adoptive parents are often significantly older and more prosperous than natural parents, which may produce systematic differences in upbringing (This is precisely the opposite of problem number 1. Ideally, natural and adoptive parental environments should be completely uncorrelated.); and (4) restriction of range of adoptive parents—particularly in older adoption studies, the adoptive parents tended to be mostly of above–average IQ and SES. This acts both to restrict environmental variation and thus produce higher heritability estimates, and to limit the generality of these estimates.[36]

While every adoption study suffers from one or more of these problems to some degree, the general quality of the research has been high enough, and the cumulative weight of the evidence so overwhelming, that virtually everyone who has studied these data agrees that they support the idea of a substantial genetic contribution to variation in IQ.[37] Needless to say, Kamin disagrees, and has engaged in published debate on the subject,[38] claiming that the problems listed above, and more, invalidate any evidence for heritability to be found in adoption studies.

9. Sources of heritability evidence.

Respondents were asked to check all sources of evidence from a list of five provided that they believed to be consistent with a significant non–zero heritability of IQ in the American white population. (Heritability estimates are population–specific, and most IQ heritability studies have involved only white subjects.) Sources of evidence were: kinship correlations, studies of monozygotic twins reared apart, monozygotic–dizygotic twin comparisons, twin–family studies, and adoption studies.

The results are reported in Table 3.1. Twenty–five percent of subjects did

TABLE 3.1
Sources of Non-Zero IQ Heritability Evidence

Source	% Indicating Reasonable Evidence
Kinship correlations-general comparisons between degree of genetic relatedness and IQ correlations	69.1
Studies of monozygotic twins reared apart	84.4
Studies comparing monozygotic twins to dizygotic twins	70.3
Twin-family studies comparing, for example, the children of monozygotic twins	55.3
Adoption studies	63.4

Note: 94% of respondents indicated at least one source as providing reasonable evidence of a significant non-zero heritability of IQ in the American white population.

not feel qualified to answer this question. Of those who did respond, 94 percent check at least one source of evidence, and each of the sources is checked by at least half the respondents. Support is greatest for studies of MZ twins reared apart (84.4 percent) and weakest for twin family studies (55.3 percent). The latter result is understandable, as twin family studies are a relatively recent development in the behavior genetics of IQ.[39] Taken together, these results are a strong indication that experts believe within-group differences in IQ to be at least partially inherited. They also demonstrate how far Kamin's position is from the psychological consensus.

Estimates of IQ Heritability

Despite the tremendous variation in the correlational data, and the numerous differences in models used, modern estimates of IQ heritability have fallen within a surprisingly narrow range, corresponding to a very substantial genetic component to differences in IQ. In his much–discussed *Harvard Educational Review* article, Jensen arrived at a heritability estimate of 0.80, as an average of estimates then in the literature. All of these estimates were based on non–biometrical analyses, however, meaning that they either ignored, or did not carefully account for dominance, assortative mating, covariance, and interaction. In a later publication, Jensen attempted to derive reasonable estimates for each of these factors from the published data (no interaction was assumed), and came up with a value of 0.65 for G, 0.28 for E, and 0.07 for covariance.[40] His covariance estimate is considerably lower than most other such calculations.

J. L. Jinks and D. W. Fulker performed a biometrical analysis of behavior–genetic data in 1970, in which they were able to test for the statistical significance of various biasing factors.[41] Their heritability estimate of about 0.72 is one of the highest in the modern literature. Two aspects of their analysis may account for this discrepancy. First, they used a more limited set of data than have Jensen and others, including only those studies for which statistical testing for covariance and interaction were possible. Second, Jinks and Fulker found no evidence for either significant interaction or covariance in any of the studies they analyzed. The latter finding is difficult to believe in light of both empirical research and common sense. Yet Jinks and L. J. Eaves, and Fulker and Hans Eysenck, using similar analyses, reached the same conclusion about larger data sets, estimating heritability at 0.68 and 0.69, respectively.[42]

The heritability estimate of Christopher Jencks and his collaborators has been perhaps the most widely discussed and reinterpreted of all analyses. Their results are G = 0.45, E = 0.35, and G-E covariance = 0.20. Subsequent reanalyses have produced higher estimates of G. Newton Morton performed a biometrical analysis on essentially the same set of data as Jencks et al., using a different model of (i.e., making different assumptions about) the way in which the genes and environments of parents, children, and siblings interact to influence IQ.[43] Morton's estimates are G = 0.67, E = 0.19, and G-E covariance = 0.14. As noted, Loehlin and his associates, by making only minor changes to the Jencks et al. model, derived estimates of G = 0.61, E = 0.24, and G-E covariance = 0.15. Neil Gourlay also provides a modified analysis of Jencks et al.'s data, in this case taking into account variation in genotype with age.[44] (It might seem counterintuitive that genes, which are fixed at birth, can vary with age. But genotype does vary with age, *in its effects on phenotype*, as genetic factors operate at different points in time throughout the development of the individual.) His estimates are similar to those of Loehlin et al.: G = 0.61, E = 0.21, and G-E covariance = 0.19. To the credit of Jencks and his coworkers, they recognized the arbitrary and indeterminant nature of much of behavior–genetic analysis, and reported their heritability estimate as ± 0.20.

The considerable agreement among many of these analyses, though impressive, should not lead one to give too much weight to precise heritability estimates. As discussed, variations in procedure between studies, including the tests given and the presence or absence of appropriate controls, and the indeterminacies of behavior–genetic analysis, make it much safer to argue that a considerable proportion of variation in IQ is due to differences in genes, than to claim that that proportion falls within any given range. As a case in point, most of the heritability analyses described above were based on data presented in a 1963 summary of behavior genetic studies of IQ by L. Erlenmeyer–Kimling and Lissy Jarvik (the forerunner of Bouchard and McGue's summary [Fig. 3.1]). Estimates of heritability derived from these data may be inflated because they included Burt's results, which, while generally similar to those of other investigations, are consistent with a slightly higher proportion of genetic variance.[45] Moreover, a review of the results of recent behavior–genetic studies, including particularly large-scale and statistically sophisticated adoption studies in Hawaii and Texas, indicates these data are consistent with IQ heritability estimates "closer to 0.50 than 0.70."[46]

10. Do you believe there is sufficient evidence to arrive at a reasonable estimate of the heritability of IQ in the American white population?

The vagaries of heritability estimation are reflected in that 50 percent of those who felt qualified to answer this question do not believe it is possible to arrive at a reasonable estimate. This response is, of course, very different from saying that the heritability of IQ is just as likely 0 as it is 0.50, as the results of question 9 indicate. Though many experts believe it is not possible to precisely specify IQ heritability, they are nearly unanimous in their belief that the heritability is substantially different from 0.

Among respondents to the questionnaire were thirty–four members of the Behavior Genetics Association, all of whom responded to question 10. This subgroup of experts is much more likely than the rest of the sample to believe that a reasonable estimation of IQ heritability is possible (76 percent "Yes" versus 48 percent "Yes" for non–BGA respondents, p < .001).

10a. White heritability estimate.

Only those respondents who felt there was sufficient evidence were asked to provide a heritability estimate.

The mean estimate for the 214 received is .596 (SD = .166), meaning that these experts believe that about 60 percent of the variation in IQ among the American white population is attributable to genetic variation.

11. Do you believe there is sufficient evidence to arrive at a reasonable estimate of the heritability of IQ in the American black population?

Given the dearth of appropriate studies, we expected the percentage of affirmative responses to be much lower here than on question 10. Indeed, only 26 percent of those who felt qualified to answer the question believe that a reasonable black IQ heritability estimate is possible.

11a. Black heritability estimate.

The mean heritability estimate for 101 received is .571 (SD = .178). A heritability of this magnitude means that approximately 57 percent of the variation in IQ *within* the American black population is the result of genetic variation. It says nothing about the possible causes of the average black–white difference in IQ. Within–population heritability bears little if any relation to the question of between–population differences. Misunderstanding of this distinction, which will be discussed more fully in the next chapter, has been the source of a large proportion of the highly emotional rhetoric that has characterized much of the IQ controversy, in which believers in a substantial within–group IQ heritability have been accused of assigning blacks to a permanent lower class.

The Meaning of Heritability Analyses

What is to be made of the apparent overwhelming consensus among experts that a substantial portion of existing variation in IQ is attributable to genetic variation? Of what value is such information? M. W. Feldman and Richard Lewontin argue that heritability analyses of phenotypic traits are of little use, since "no statistical methodology exists that will enable us to predict the range of phenotypic possibilities that are inherent in any genotype, nor can any technique of statistical estimation provide a convincing argument for a genetic mechanism more complicated than one or two Mendelian loci with low or constant permanence."[47] In other words, heritability estimates tell us only about the relation between variation in phenotype, genotype, and environment, and nothing about the particular phenotype to be expected from any given genotype–environment combination, particularly from environments outside the existing range of variation.

A description of the relations between phenotype and particular genotype–environment combinations, described earlier as the norm of reaction, can only be derived from an analysis of variation (heritability analysis) if additivity (noninteraction) holds between genotypes and environments.[48] This fact may be made clearer by looking at specific numbers. A heritability estimate for IQ of 0.60 means that, *on average* in the population under study, a 1–standard deviation (SD) change in IQ requires a 2 ½ SD change in IQ–relevant environment, but only a 1 ⅔ SD change in IQ–relevant genotype. The ability to predict from this information the effect of a 1–SD change in IQ–relevant environment on the IQ of any specific *individual* depends on the effects of environment being independent of genotypic level (no interaction). If there is gene–environment interaction, then prediction requires not only knowledge of the average relations, but specific information about the individual's genotype as well. Gene–environment interaction, Feldman and Lewontin argue, is a characteristic of the norm of reaction of most phenotypic traits. Analyses pur porting to show no interaction (see references above), they claim, are severely limited by the narrow range of environments studied. Thus, the only way to get an accurate picture of the functional relations between genotype and environment is through a mechanistic description of the processes underlying gene action, and not through a statistical analysis of population variation.

Sandra Scarr and Louise Carter–Saltzman answer Feldman and Lewontin's charges by pointing out that the latter authors ignore the important questions that heritability analyses *can* answer:

> Answers to questions about the current intellectual state of human populations, the distribution of intelligence, and the likely success of improving intellectual phenotypes through intervention with *known* environmental manipulations call for a statistical model of contemporary sources of variance in the population. Knowledge of evolutionary history, selection pressures, or enzyme activity at a few loci will not help. Nor will appealing to the unpredictable effects of yet–to–be–devised interventions help solve the problems of the here and now.[49] (emphasis in the original)

Feldman and Lewontin are correct, of course, in pointing out that heritability analyses tell us little, if anything, about untried environmental manipulations, nor do they allow much in the way of specific predictions. Scarr and Carter–Saltzman argue that it is nonetheless of value to have a better understanding of the general effects of manipulations within the existing range. This was precisely Jensen's intention when he attempted to answer the question "How much can we boost IQ and scholastic achievement?" Given the high degree of heritability of IQ (he estimated it at about 0.80), the answer was "not much, on average, within the existing range of environments." This, Jensen believed, could help explain the apparent failure of large–scale intervention programs like Head Start to boost IQ significantly.

Despite the Head Start results (the general pattern is an immediate ten– to twenty–point increase in IQ from the preschool projects, which does not last beyond the second or third grade, though long term gains in achievement are common),[50] others have reported dramatic IQ gains through environmental manipulation. The most widely cited studies in this area have been those by Harold Skeels and others at the Iowa Child Welfare Research Station beginning in the 1930s, and the Milwaukee Project of Richard Heber and his colleagues, conducted in the early 1970s.[51]

In 1945, and again in 1949, Marie Skodak and Skeels reported follow–up results of an adoption study in which children were adopted from low–IQ mothers and raised in high–quality environments, where their adolescent IQs were twenty to thirty points higher than their natural mothers'. This study, like others from the Iowa group, were criticized at the time by followers of Lewis Terman, who saw such results as antithetical to their own views of the largely genetic character of measured intelligence.[52] An article in the February 1940 *Psychological Bulletin* by Quinn McNemar of Stanford presents a critical examination of all the Iowa studies published to date.[53] In a style remarkably similar to that Kamin used thirty-four years later to debunk heritability research, McNemar launched an unrelenting attack on methodological and statistical flaws in the data purporting to show significant environmental influences on IQ. Much like Kamin, McNemar was eventually able to explain away all of the Iowa results. Unfortunately, this bit of scholarly legerdemain required not only extensive statistical reanalyses, but assumptions of the following sort: "Our guess is that the 'unknown' fathers of illegitimate children are apt to be intellectually superior to known fathers, the intellectual superiority being a factor in their remaining unknown."

Much of the naivete of McNemar and other critics in painting the debate in terms of "hereditarians" versus "environmentalists," and their unwillingness to accept evidence for *any* environmental influence, reflects an older view among mental testers of tests as measures of "innate" intelligence. A proper understanding of the role of genes and environment in the development of the phenotype was at that time just beginning to take hold in the psychological community, as the first behavior-genetic studies of IQ were being completed.

Had McNemar understood the true nature of heritability, he would not have been so alarmed by the Iowa data. As Jensen points out, the Skodak and Skeels data are consistent with a very high IQ heritability estimate.[54] Jensen notes that the proper comparison in this study is not between the child's IQ and the natural mother's IQ, but between the child's IQ and his expected IQ, had he been raised by his natural mother. Taking into account regression to the mean (children of parents with deviant IQs, whether high or low, will, on average, have IQs closer to the population mean), Jensen calculated the difference between actual and expected IQ to be about thirteen points. A gain of this magnitude is consistent with a heritability estimate as high as 0.80, given the not unreasonable assumption that the adoptive parents in the Iowa study provided an environment about two standard deviations better than the natural parents would have provided.

In an even more extreme case of environmental change, Skeels reports a twenty-five-year follow-up of a group of thirteen children adopted into normal homes from an extremely unstimulating orphanage. When adopted at age nineteen months, these children had an average IQ of 64, as did eleven other children who were left in the orphanage. Six years later, the adopted children had an average IQ of 96.[55] Consistent with this remarkable improvement, twenty–five years later the thirteen were found to be productive citizens with children of their own of average IQ. The eleven control subjects were either still institutionalized or were in very low–status jobs. As remarkable and heartening as these results are, even IQ improvement of this magnitude might be expected in a population with a high degree of heritability for IQ, given the extreme environmental deprivation suffered by the children in the orphanage.[56] Assuming that 40 percent of the variance in IQ is the result of environmental variation (heritability $= 0.60$), a two–standard deviation increase in IQ (32 points, as in the Skeels and Dye study) requires a 3.2–standard deviation improvement in environment.

One of the most frequently cited studies of the effects of environmental intervention on IQ is the Milwaukee Project. Beginning in the late 1960s, children at high risk for mental retardation (low parental IQ combined with a ghetto environment) were provided with intellectually enriched environments and proper nutrition and health care. The intervention began at three months of age and continued until the children entered grammar school. Richard Heber and his associates report that at age eight to nine, these children had an average IQ twenty–four points higher than that of a matched group of untreated controls. Though often cited as an example of the overwhelming importance of environment to variation in intelligence, an IQ differential of twenty–four points is probably not inconsistent with a large heritability, in light of the extensive nature of the intervention (children attended a training center seven hours a day, five days a week, for over five years, and the program also included education for the mothers), and the very poor environments experienced by control subjects.

Nonetheless, the Milwaukee Project results are among the most dramatic ever reported in an intervention study, and bear closer scrutiny. Philip Vernon has pointed out that the twenty–four–point IQ difference at age eight to nine was down from about thirty points at age six, and data from other intervention studies indicate that the two groups will score even more similarly later in life.[57] Moreover, the procedural details and complete results of the Milwaukee Project have never been reviewed in a professionally refereed journal. Yet these results continue to be widely cited, both in the popular press and in college textbooks. Robert and Barbara Sommer recently reported that nearly half of all abnormal and developmental psychology textbooks published since 1977 mention the Milwaukee study.[58] That the Milwaukee Project has not undergone professional review does not mean that its results are invalid, but the uncritical acceptance of this study is an indication that in the field of cognitive abilities, as in any other area of science, both professionals and nonprofessionals are more likely to accept results that are consistent with the way they feel the world *should* be.

(Richard Herrnstein has noted that in 1981 Richard Heber and an associate were convicted of numerous counts of diverting institutional funds,
and that they were sentenced to three years in prison.[59] The point of Herrnstein's revelation is not that the Milwaukee Project data are less valid
because Dr. Heber is a thief, but rather that Heber's conviction went unre-
ported by the same media sources that offered the Milwaukee Project data
as evidence for the overwhelming importance of environment over heredity in determining intelligence. It is unlikely that Arthur Jensen or Herrnstein himself would have been so kindly treated had they encountered
similar difficulties with the law.)

Difficulties with the Milwaukee Project notwithstanding, there is reason
to believe that environmental intervention can produce large IQ gains,
particularly in cases of severe deprivation. Jensen's statement about the
failure of compensatory education, in addition to being a largely rhetorical
device, was directed at large–scale intervention programs. In his 1969 article, Jensen reviews successful programs[60] that, like the Milwaukee Project,
involved intensive intervention (many hours each day over long periods,
and very low student–teacher ratios) and children whose normal environments put them at extreme risk of mental retardation.[61] Since the Jensen
article and the Milwaukee Project, there have been similar successes in
programs of this sort (though there still remains a question of how long
these children can maintain their IQ advantage over their nonprogram
counterparts without continued intervention).[62] Recent years have also
seen positive results in the teaching of thinking skills to both children and
adults, though global IQ is often not an outcome measure in such studies.[63]

The apparent substantial heritability of IQ is consistent with these successes, as it is with the failure of other programs in which the intervention
and/or deprivation was not so extreme. In addition to whatever heuristic
value heritability estmates may have in their own right, they also serve to
clarify the limits of our existing knowledge and the range of our present
possibilities. Meanwhile, the search continues for new and better ways to
improve intellectual skills. Because they do not deal with novel environmental manipulations, heritability analyses do not preclude the search for
new ways to improve intelligence. If anything, the knowledge that present
manipulations are not very effective encourages experimentation.

Notes

1. Donald O. Hebb, *A Textbook of Psychology* (Philadelphia: W. B. Saunders, 1958), p. 129.
2. James R. Flynn, "The Mean IQ of Americans: Massive Gains, 1932 to 1978," *Psychological Bulletin* 95 (1984):29–51.

3. Alfred Binet, quoted in Joseph Peterson, *Early Conceptions and Tests of Intelligence* (Yonkers–on–Hudson, NY: World Book, 1925), pp. 204 and 274.
4. Lewis M. Terman, *The Measurement of Intelligence* (Boston: Houghton Mifflin, 1916), p. 5.
5. Stephen Jay Gould, *The Mismeasure of Man* (New York: Norton, 1981); Leon J. Kamin, *The Science and Politics of IQ* (New York: Wiley, 1974); Clarence J. Karier, "Testing for Order and Control in the Corporate Liberal State," in *The IQ Controversy*, ed. N. J. Block and Gerald Dworkin (New York: Pantheon, 1976), pp. 339–373.
6. Karl J. Holzinger, "The Relative Effect of Nature and Nurture Influences on Twin Differences," *Journal of Educational Psychology* 20 (1929):245–248.
7. R. C. Nichols, "The Inheritance of General and Specific Ability," *National Merit Scholarship Research Reports* 1 (1965); Stephen G. Vandenberg, "What Do We Know Today About the Inheritance of Intelligence and How Do We Know It?" in *Intelligence: Genetic and Environmental Influences*, ed. R. Cancro (New York: Grune and Stratton, 1971), pp. 182–218.
8. J. L. Jinks and D. W. Fulker, "Comparison of the Biometrical Genetical, MAVA, and Classical Approaches to the Analysis of Human Behavior," *Psychological Bulletin* 73 (1970):312; Philip E. Vernon, *Intelligence: Heredity and Environment* (San Francisco: W. H. Freeman, 1979), p. 184.
9. Vernon, p. 183.
10. Robert Plomin, J. C. DeFries, and John C. Loehlin, "Genotype—Environment Interaction and Correlation in the Analysis of Human Behavior," *Psychological Bulletin* 84 (1977):309–322.
11. David Layzer, "Heritability Analyses of IQ Scores: Science or Numerology?" *Science* 183 (1974):1259–1266.
12. Plomin et al, pp. 317–320.
13. Christopher Jencks et al., *Inequality* (New York: Basic Books, 1972), pp. 266–319.
14. John C. Loehlin, Gardner Lindzey, and J. N. Spuhler, *Race Differences in Intelligence* (San Francisco: W. H. Freeman, 1975), pp. 300–302.
15. Plomin et al., p. 321.
16. Richard C. Lewontin, "The Analysis of Variance and the Analysis of Causes," *American Journal of Human Genetics* 26 (1974):400–411.
17. Plomin et al., p. 315; Sandra Scarr and Louise Carter– Saltzman, "Genetics and Intelligence," in *Handbook of Human Intelligence*, ed. Robert J. Sternberg (Cambridge, U.K.: Cambridge University Press, 1982), p. 820.
18. L. Erlenmeyer-Kimling, "Gene-Environment Interactions and the Variability of Behavior," in *Genetics, Environment and Behavior*, ed. L. Ehrman, G. S. Omenn, and E. Caspari (New York: Academic Press, 1972); Arthur R. Jensen, "IQs of Identical Twins Reared Apart," *Behavior Genetics* 1 (1970):133–148; Jinks and Fulker, p. 342; Plomin et al., pp. 314–317.
19. Vernon, p. 185.
20. L. J. Eaves, "Testing Models for Variation in Intelligence," *Heredity* 34 (1975):132–136; Jinks and Fulker.
21. Arthur S. Goldberger, "Pitfalls in the Resolution of IQ Inheritance," in *Genetic Epidemiology*, ed. N. E. Morton and C. S. Chung (New York: Academic Press, 1978).
22. Thomas J. Bouchard Jr. and Matthew McGue, "Familial Studies of Intelligence: A Review," *Science* 212 (1981):1056.

23. B. Rimland and H. Munsinger, "Burt's IQ Data," *Science* 195 (1977):248.
24. L. Erlenmeyer–Kimling and Lissy F. Jarvik, "Genetics and Intelligence: A Review," *Science* 142 (1963):1477.
25. Kamin, pp. 73–95.
26. Matt McGue et al., "Information Processing Abilities in Twins Reared Apart," *Intelligence* 8 (1984):239–258.
27. Kamin, pp. 33–56; M. Schwartz and J. Schwartz, "Evidence Against a Genetical Component to Performance on IQ Tests," *Nature* 248 (1974):84–85.
28. Vernon, p. 175.
29. Kamin, pp. 56–65.
30. D. W. Fulker, "Review of 'The Science and Politics of IQ' by L. J. Kamin," *American Journal of Psychology* 88 (1975):505–519; Sandra Scarr–Salaptek, "Review of Kamin's 'The Science and Politics of IQ,'" *Contemporary Psychology* 21 (1976):98–99; Peter Urbach, "Progress and Degeneration in the IQ Debate," *British Journal of the Philosophy of Science* 25 (1974):99–135, 235–259.
31. Jerry Hirsch, "To Unfrock the Charlatans," *Sage Race Relations Abstracts* 6 (1981):24–28; James M. Lawler, *IQ, Heritability and Racism* (New York: International Publishers, 1978), pp.165–172; R. C. Lewontin, Stephen Rose, *Not in Our Genes* (New York: Pantheon, 1984), pp. 83–129; Susan Orbach, Joe Schwartz, and Mike Schwartz, "The Case for Zero Heritability," *Science for the People* 6 (1974):23–25; Howard F. Taylor, *The IQ Game* (London: Harvester, 1980); Adam Vetta, "Concepts and Issues in the IQ Debate," *Bulletin of the British Psychological Society* 33 (1980):241–243.
32. Hugh Lytton, "Do Parents Create, or Respond, to Differences in Twins?" *Developmental Psychology* 13 (1977):456–459; Robert Plomin, Lee Willerman, and John C. Loehlin, "Resemblance in Appearance and the Equal Environments Assumption in Twin Studies of Personality," *Behavior Genetics* 6 (1976):43–52; Sandra Scarr and Louise Carter–Saltzman, "Twin Method: Defense of a Critical Assumption," *Behavior Genetics* 9 (1979):527–542.
33. Richard J. Rose et al., "Genetic Variance in Nonverbal Intelligence: Data from Kinships of Identical Twins," *Science* 205 (1979):1153–1155.
34. Jinks and Fulker; Plomin et al., "Genotype–Environment," p. 314.
35. Scarr and Carter–Saltzman, "Genetics and Intelligence," pp. 833–863.
36. H. Munsinger, "The Adopted Child's IQ: A Critical Review," *Psychological Bulletin* 82 (1975):623–659.
37. H. Munsinger; Scarr and Carter–Saltzman, "Genetics and Intelligence," pp. 833–863; Vernon, pp. 215–230.
38. Kamin; Munsinger; Leon J. Kamin, "Comment on Munsinger's Review of Adoption Studies," *Psychological Bulletin* 85 (1978):194–201; H. Munsinger, "Reply to Kamin," *Psychological Bulletin* 85 (1978):202–206.
39. Scarr and Carter–Saltzman, "Genetics and Intelligence," p. 831.
40. Arthur R. Jensen, "The Problem of Genotype–Environment Correlation in the Estimation of Heritability from Monozygotic and Dizygotic Twins," *Acta Geneticae, Medicae et Gemellologiae*, 1977.
41. Jinks and Fulker, p. 346.
42. J. L. Jinks and L. J. Eaves, "IQ and Inequality," *Nature* 248 (1974):287–289; D. W. Fuller and Hans J. Eysenck, "Nature and Nurture: Heredity" in Hans J. Eysenck, *The Structure and Measurement of Intelligence* (New York: Springer-Verlag, 1979).

43. Newton E. Morton, "Human Behavioral Genetics," in *Genetics, Environment, and Behavior*, ed. L. Ehrman, G. S. Omenn, and E. Caspari (New York: Academic Press, 1972).
44. Neil Gourlay, "Heredity Versus Environment: An Integrative Analysis," *Psychological Bulletin* 80 (1979):596–615.
45. D. C. Rowe and R. Plomin, "The Burt Controversy: A Comparison of Burt's Data on IQ with Data from Other Sources," *Behavior Genetics* 8 (1978):81–84.
46. Robert Plomin and J. C. DeFries, "Genetics and Intelligence: Recent Data," *Intelligence* 4 (1980):21.
47. M. W. Feldman and R. Lewontin, "The Heritability 'Hang–Up'," *Science* 190 (1975):1168.
48. Lewontin, pp. 409–411.
49. Scarr and Carter–Saltzman, "Genetics and Intelligence," p. 797.
50. A. Harrell, *The Effects of the Head Start Program on Children's Cognitive Development* (Washington, DC: U.S. Department of Health and Human Services, 1983); Westinghouse Learning Corporation, *The Impact of Head Start: An Evaluation of the Effects of Head Start on Children's Cognitive and Affective Development* (Athens, Ohio: Ohio University, 1969); S. H. White et al., *Federal Programs for Young Children: Review and Recommendations* (Washington, DC: U.S. Department of Health, Education, and Welfare, 1973).
51. Harold M. Skeels and H. B. Dye, "A Study of the Effects of Differential Stimulation on Mentally Retarded Children," *Proceedings of the American Association for Mental Deficiency* 44 (1939)pp. 114–136; Marie Skodak and Harold M. Skeels, "A Follow–Up Study of Children in Adoptive Homes," *Journal of Genetic Psychology* 66 (1945):21–58; Marie Skodak and Harold M. Skeels, "A Final Follow–Up Study of One Hundred Adopted Children," *Journal of Genetic Psychology* 75 (1949):85–125; Harold M. Skeels, "Adult Status of Children with Contrasting Early Life Experiences: A Follow–Up Study," *Monographs of the Society for Research in Child Development* 31 (1966); R. Heber et al., *Rehabilitation of Families at Risk for Mental Retardation* (Progress Rep.) (Washington, DC: U.S. Department of Health, Education, and Welfare, 1972); H. Garber and R. Heber, "The Milwaukee Project," in *Research to Practice in Mental Retardation*, ed. P. Mittler (Baltimore: University Park Press, 1977), pp. 119–127.
52. Vernon, p. 9.
53. Quinn McNemar, "A Critical Examination of the University of Iowa Studies of Environmental Influences Upon the IQ," *Psychological Bulletin* 37 (1940):63–92.
54. Arthur R. Jensen, "Let's Understand Skodak and Skeels, Finally," *Educational Psychologist* 10 (1973):30–35.
55. Skeels; Skeels and Dye.
56. Vernon, p. 208.
57. Ibid., p. 135.
58. Robert Sommer and Barbara A. Sommer, "Mystery in Milwaukee: Early Intervention, IQ and Psychology Textbooks," *American Psychologist* 38 (1983):982–985.
59. R. J. Herrnstein, "IQ Testing and the Media," *Atlantic Monthly*, (August 1982):70.
60. R. M. Darlington et al., "Preschool Programs and Later School Competence of Children from Low–Income Families," *Science* 208 (1980):202–204; John R.

Berrueta–Clement et al., *Changed Lives: The Effects of the Perry Preschool Program on Youths Through Age 19* (Ypsilanti, MI: High/Scope Press, 1984).

61. Arthur R. Jensen, "How Much Can We Boost IQ and Scholastic Achievement?" *Harvard Educational Review* 39 (1969):96–101.

62. M. B. Karnes, "Evaluation and Implication of Research with Young Handicapped and Low–Income Children," in *Contemporary Education for Children, Ages 2 to 8*, ed. J. C. Stanley (Baltimore: Johns Hopkins University Press, 1973); C. T. Ramey, D. MacPhee, and K. O. Yeates, "Preventing Developmental Retardation: A General Systems Model," in *How and How Much Can Intelligence Be Increased?* ed. D. K. Detterman and R. J. Sternberg (Norwood, NJ: Ablex, 1982).

63. Raymond S. Nickerson, David N. Perkins, and Edward E. Smith, *The Teaching of Thinking Skills* (Hillsdale, NJ: Lawrence Erlbaum, 1985); Arthur Whimbey, *Intelligence Can Be Taught* (New York: E. P. Dutton, 1975).

4

Race and Class Differences in IQ

No area of testing has been the subject of as much public concern, and outrage, as the issue of race and class differences in intelligence and aptitude test scores. That such differences exist is a matter of fact; disagreement occurs over how they are to be interpreted. The most common explanation, and the most common criticism leveled against tests, is that they are culturally biased. As the argument goes, average test score differences between racial and socioeconomic groups do not reflect real differences in intellectual ability, but rather that tests of mental ability are in large part measures of certain cultural variables. These variables have nothing to do with intelligence, it is said, but differ between racial and economic groups. Those who defend tests, on the other hand, argue that whatever bias there is is small, and that group score differentials primarily represent real differences in intellectual ability. In this view, claims of test bias constitute a case of blaming the messenger. The debate over cultural bias in testing has been heated and, in recent years, has frequently ended in court, where those claiming discrimination have found a sympathetic ear.

Among those who do not believe that bias can completely account for group differences in test scores, other explanations are proposed. Virtually everyone agrees that environmental factors are important. There are significant differences, on average, between various groups within our society in such important areas as child–rearing practices, nutrition, and quality of education. It would be foolish to think that these have no effect on intellectual skills. But the possibility has also been raised that genetic differences may play a causal role in group differences in test score.

The issue of genetic determinants, particularly regarding the black–white IQ difference, is at the heart of the modern IQ controversy; all other concerns about testing have taken on new significance following the furor over Jensen's postulation. To claim, in a political climate stressing the fundamental similarity of all groups, that blacks and whites differ genetically in any trait other than skin color is the most invidious of allegations.

Proposals by Jensen, Herrnstein and others that genes play a role in group differences in test scores have not only brought opprobrium upon these authors, but have spawned repeated and detailed allegations that the entire testing enterprise is an exercise in oppression. In a nation sensitized by the civil rights movement and the plight of minorities, the subject of genetic differences between groups has resisted rational public discussion.

The literature on group differences in IQ is almost exclusively concerned with the black–white difference and, to a lesser extent, the relationship between socioeconomic status (SES) and intelligence. While evidence exists for other racial and ethnic group differences in test scores (e.g., Asian Americans and Jews tend to have higher IQs than other Americans, while Puerto Ricans and Mexican Americans score lower on average),[1] they have attracted relatively little attention. The same is true of gender differences. There is no significant difference in mean IQ between men and women, but the standard deviation of IQ is about one point larger in men. Men also show a small but significant advantage on tests of spatial–visual ability and quantitative reasoning, while women, past the age of ten or eleven, tend to do better on tests of verbal ability.[2] There is also evidence that the black–white IQ differential is greater among men than among women.[3]

At this point, the data on the black–white differential in IQ are very clear. Results accumulated over many years, on many different types of intelligence and aptitude tests, indicate that American blacks average about one standard deviation (fifteen points on the WISC–R) lower in IQ than American whites.[4] These differences are usually not manifest until about age three or four (at the time that scores on intelligence tests begin to correlate substantially with adult IQ), and remain fairly constant throughout the school years.[5] There is some interaction with specific abilities, such that the differential is greater for performance than verbal tests, and is probably greater for more highly g–loaded tests.[6]

Children's IQs correlate about 0.30 with parents' SES, as measured by a number of variables, including quality of home environment, income, and occupational status.[7] The correlation of an individual's adolescent IQ with his own later occupational status is about 0.50, while correlation with income tends to increase throughout life, peaking between 0.30 and 0.40 around age forty.[8] The correlation between SES and IQ is slightly smaller among blacks than among whites; there is a race–by–SES interaction in IQ, such that the racial difference is less among lower socioeconomic groups.[9] The average IQ difference between blacks and whites of the same SES (i.e., the black–white IQ difference controlling for SES) is about 12 points.[10]

It is important to understand the relationship between race and class differences in IQ and IQ differences between individuals within the same racial and SES groups. Intelligence and aptitude tests are rather poor discriminators of race and social class. Race and class differences represent only a small fraction of the total variance in IQ (they have been estimated to account for only 22 percent of total WISC–R variance);[11] the overwhelming majority of variance comes from individual differences within racial and SES groups. In other words, if all Americans were of the same race and SES, we would still see almost 80 percent of the variance in IQ that we now see. This fact by itself is strong evidence that intelligence tests are primarily measures of something other than culture.

Group differences in test score are, of course, irrelevant at the individual level, where tests are used. Each racial, ethnic, and socioeconomic group contains within it individuals with the full range of test scores; knowing an individual's group affiliations provides little information about intelligence, aptitude, or whatever it is these tests are measuring. A 100 IQ for a black test taker means the same thing, on an unbiased test, as a 100 IQ for a white test taker; we need not be concerned with race in using these test scores. Nonetheless, as individual decisions accumulate, the average score differences between groups have a profound effect on the representation of these groups in certain key positions. Because scores on most intelligence and aptitude tests are approximately normally distributed, a one–standard deviation score differential, like that between blacks and whites, becomes particularly obvious at the tails of the distribution, where most selection decisions are made. For example, the percentage of blacks with IQs between 50 and 70 (a common criterion for EMR placement) is more than six times greater than the percentage of whites, while whites are over ten times more likely to have IQs above 130 or to score 650 or better (on a scale of 800) on the verbal portion of the Scholastic Aptitude Test. Group differences in test score are of concern not only because people do not like to be called stupid; these differentials have important effects on educational and occupational opportunities.

Bias in Intelligence and Aptitude Testing

The operationalist dictum that intelligence is whatever intelligence tests measure notwithstanding, group differences in intelligence test *scores* are not necessarily the same as differences in intelligence. There are several ways in which a test may be biased against a certain racial or socioeconomic group, and thus produce differences in test scores independent of any differences in the ability the test is attempting to measure. We shall examine the more important of these. First, however, it is crucial to understand what cultural bias is *not* and to distinguish between cultural disadvantage, culture specificity, and cultural bias.

Human beings possess a multitude of aptitudes and abilities. The importance placed on these skills will vary across contexts, as will the labels with which they are described. The graffiti seen as the malicious destruction of public property on the New York City subways may be viewed as art in the galleries of SoHo. So it is, in some sense, with intelligence. Those behaviors that are labeled "intelligent" or "intellectual" will vary across cultures, and across situations within a culture. The intelligence that standard intelligence tests measure consists primarily of those skills necessary to success in school in an industrialized society: linguistic, logical–mathematical, and spatial abilities. This definition of intelligence is to a large degree culturally relative. Most of us live in a culture in which great importance is placed on the development of linguistic, logical–mathematical, and spatial skills, one in which these skills form the core of our common–sense notion of intelligence.

To say that intelligence is a culturally relative concept is not to say that it is culture bound, or that these skills are only of importance in a very limited context. On the contrary, it is hard to imagine any definition of intelligence that did not include at least some proficiency in communication and logical thought, regardless of the culture providing the definition. Similarly, the possession of these "intellectual" skills confers a distinct advantage in contexts other than schools, most notably, on the job. Nonetheless, there are numerous other attributes, such as creativity, musical aptitude, and interpersonal sensitivity that are of great importance in our culture, and may be of even greater importance in others, that are not measured to any significant degree by intelligence tests. Intelligence is thus a concept that contains certain universally recognized attributes, and many that are relative to the culture in which intelligence is defined.

With this definition in hand, we can understand the distinction between cultural disadvantage and cultural bias. If an individual is raised in a subculture in which emphasis is placed on the development of skills and abilities other than those stressed by the dominant culture of the society, that individual may be at a disadvantage relative to members of the dominant culture on a test of those skills and abilities for which he was not adequately prepared. In other words, he may actually possess less of those skills and abilities by virtue of the subculture in which he was raised. If the test in question is accurately measuring the relevant skills and abilities it purports to measure, no matter how culturally determined those abilities might be, then our hypothetical individual is at a *cultural disadvantage* when it comes to performance on the test. One may argue about the fairness of a situation in which an individual is required to demonstrate skills for which he was inadequately prepared, but the fact remains that the individual in this example actually possesses less of those skills and abilities the test is measuring. A test may only be considered *culturally biased* if it does not accurately measure what it attempts to measure, such that members of certain cultures score differently than members of other cultures, *despite the fact that members of these cultures possess the relevant skills and abilities to the same extent.*

As an example, let us consider the yardstick as a measure of height. It is well known that the consumption of certain nutrients during childhood can have a profound influence on physical stature. Imagine two cultures that differ in the degree to which these nutrients form a part of their regular diet, such that culture A suffers a severe shortage relative to culture B. All other things being equal, members of culture A will, on the average, be shorter than members of culture B. Assuming we have a yardstick that is an accurate measure of height, members of culture A will be at a cultural disadvantage relative to members of culture B when it comes to "performance" on the yardstick. The yardstick is not, however, culturally biased, as it accurately measures height in both groups. If, on the other hand, we had a yardstick that systematically expanded or contracted depending on the cultural membership of the person being measured, we would say that the yardstick was culturally biased. Such a conclusion presupposes, of course, that we have other independent criteria by which to measure height.

Applying our example to intelligence and aptitude tests, members of certain groups may perform poorly on these tests because their cultural backgrounds have prevented them from adequately developing those skills and abilities that the tests are accurately measuring. (Whether certain racial, ethnic, and class groups actually represent separate cultures or subcultures is irrelevant, as long as these groups differ experientially, on average, in important ways.) These individuals are culturally disadvantaged. It is also possible that these individuals are performing poorly, despite the fact that they possess an abundance of the appropriate skills, because the test score is influenced by cultural factors other than those relevant to intelligence. Such a test is culturally biased. One way to distinguish between these possibilities, and determine that cultural differences in test score reflect bias, is to compare performance on the test to some other criteria of intelligence. If the groups in question do not differ to the same degree on these external criteria as they do on the test, there is reason to believe the test is biased. Such external validation is critically important, for it may be argued that the concept of intelligence being measured by intelligence tests is so culturally determined as to bear little or no relation to any meaningful notion of intelligence. If one were to construct a test of "intelligence" that consisted of nothing but questions about polo and yachting, certain members of the upper classes undoubtedly would test as most intelligent. But such a test would be a culturally biased measure of intelligence because performance on the test would correlate poorly with other indicators of intellectual ability, such as school performance and peer intelligence ratings. The test would not, however, be a biased measure of polo and yachting knowledge; members of lower socioeconomic classes would merely be at a cultural disadvantage. The point of this discussion is that cultural influences on test performance are inevitable, and do not necessarily represent test bias.

Apropos of cultural influence is the question of cultural specificity (or cultural loading) of intelligence and aptitude tests. Tests vary in the degree to which performance requires culture–specific knowledge. Jensen gives the example of a test of mental ability with questions drawn from a particular family's private experiences that might be highly valid in distinguishing the intelligence of siblings in the family but would yield random scores for all others taking the test. At the other extreme, Jensen proposes a test of mechanical problem solving that might be able to rank–order some important aspects of mental ability in all primates.[12] Thus, one may speak of a Continuum of Cultural Specificity among tests, analogous to Anastasi's Continuum of Experiential Specificity.

Examining tests actually in use, at the culture–specific end are those like the Peabody Picture Vocabulary Test (PPVT), which consists of a series of pictures representing various nouns, gerunds, and modifiers. Test takers are to answer yes or no as to whether a word presented corresponds to a given picture or series of pictures. The test has a high degree of validity within the United States, but because item difficulty is determined by the rarity of words in American English the test is of little use outside the United States.[13] At the culture–nonspecific or culture–fair end of the continuum are nonlanguage tests like the Ravens Progressive Matrices, consisting of abstract series–completion problems, which has been validated in dozens of cultures around the world.[14]

Even less culture specific, but more controversial, than the Ravens are tests of choice reaction time, in which the test taker has only to remove her finger from a button when one of a series of lights is illuminated. The speed with which the finger is removed from the button, reaction time, has been found to correlate significantly with scores on traditional intelligence tests and to display significant racial differences.[15] It should be noted that work on sophisticated reaction time measures of intelligence is in its earliest stages, and is not without its critics.[16]

Tests at both ends of the continuum, and at every point in between, show significant race and class differences in test score.[17] There have been, over the years, numerous attempts to develop culture–fair tests that do not produce group differences. Thus far, no test that shows equivalent scores across racial and socioeconomic groups has been demonstrated to be a valid measure of intelligence.[18] These tests do not correlate sufficiently with other criteria of intellectual ability to be of any practical use.

Cultural loading is not the same as cultural bias. A test is culturally biased only when the culture–specific knowledge it tests is not equally available to all test takers *and* that knowledge is not relevant to the performance criteria (e.g., success in school) against which the test is validated. In the United States, the PPVT has been validated for both black and white test takers. (Nonetheless, many of testing's strongest supporters, like Jensen, have called for the discontinuation of the PPVT and other vocabulary tests that rely on the rarity of items presented to distinguish between test takers, precisely because of the extreme cultural specificity of these tests.) This indicates that blacks and whites tend to have equivalent prior exposure to the items tested. Thus, a test can be highly culture specific and still be valid in the culture in which it was developed (like Jensen's within-family test).[19] The PPVT is not valid in most other cultures, however, and is therefore a biased measure of ability in those societies. The Ravens is valid in most cultures around the world, and predicts success in schools and on the job just as well for black as for white Americans, and for members of all social classes. The argument is made that tests like the Ravens are biased, despite their nonlanguage content, because black children, as a result of inferior schooling and different cultural practices, have less exposure to the kinds of abstract problem–solving tasks that these tests require. There is a good chance that the claim about schooling and culture is true. Even so, it is not an indication that the tests are biased, but rather that blacks are at a cultural disadvantage. In this culture abstract problem solving is a relevant dimension of intelligence, and those who experience inferior education will actually display fewer of these abilities.

With these caveats in mind, we now turn to some of the more common definitions of test bias.[20]

Bias as mean differences. This is really an improper definition, since by taking the existence of group differences as prima facie evidence of bias one begs the question. Such a definition assumes that intellectual ability is equally distributed among all races and classes, but this is precisely what intelligence tests given to different groups are trying to measure. As noted, no test that shows equal average scores for different SES or racial–ethnic groups has been shown to have any useful predictive validity. Given the large environmental differences between racial and economic groups in this country, it would be surprising if there *were not* mean differences in IQ between groups.

Bias as improper standardization. Another frequently mentioned, but equally inadequate concept of bias is improper test standardization. It is often claimed that tests that show a black–white difference were standardized only on a white population and are therefore biased against blacks. Tests like the WISC–R and Stanford–Binet are scaled so that the average score in the population will be 100, with a standard deviation of 15 (WISC–R) or 16 (S–B). Scaling is accomplished by giving the test to a large sample chosen to be representative of the population as a whole. It is true that early standardization samples of the Stanford–Binet did not include blacks and other minorities (it is not true of more recent standardization samples, nor of any other modern intelligence or aptitude test). That blacks and other minority groups were not included in these samples evinces an insensitivity on the part of early test developers, if not outright racism. But it has nothing to do with the question of whether the tests are biased. As a case in point, early intelligence tests were not properly standardized for Asian Americans, yet members of this group have generally scored higher than white Americans. Using a standardization criteria for bias, one would have to argue that intelligence tests are biased in favor of Asian Americans, and therefore against white Americans, for whom the test presumably was developed.

The fact is that standardization and restandardization, by themselves, have no influence on group differences in test score or their causes. If blacks, or any other group, score on the average x points lower (or higher) than whites, whether because the test is biased, or for more legitimate reasons, on a test standardized on an all–white population, they will still score x points lower (or higher) on a test standardized on a more representative population. Merely restandardizing a test, without actually changing any questions, will lead to a change in absolute, but not relative scores between groups, and will provide no new information as to the reason for group differences in average score.

12. In your opinion, is the fact that an intelligence test has not been properly standardized for a certain group, by itself, sufficient evidence that the test is biased against that group?

This question, like number 5, was included not so much for its heuristic value, but as a direct response to popular criticism. Probably more than any other question in the survey, the answer here is a matter of fact rather than opinion. It is difficult to imagine what test bias could mean if it is indicated simply because a certain group was not included in proper proportion in the standardization sample, since standardization itself has no effect on the content of the test. Nonetheless, one often reads that intelligence tests like the Stanford–Binet are biased against blacks because blacks were not properly represented in the standardization sample. Needless to say, experts disagreed. Seventy–one percent indicate that improper standardization is not sufficient evidence of test bias, while 12 percent do not respond to the question. What is very surprising is that the remaining 17 percent feel that improper standardization is sufficient evidence of test bias. It is possible that these respondents interpret "improper standardization" to mean something more radical than underrepresentation in the standardization sample, though it is unclear what this might be.

Bias as content. Tests are often thought to be culturally biased because many of the questions presuppose or test knowledge that is more common to certain cultural groups, particularly middle- and upper-class whites. Examples are given of particular test items involving objects and concepts supposedly more common among the middle and upper classes, like pottery and pacifism, or that ask for aesthetic judgments based on an Anglo-Saxon conception of beauty. Thus what is being tested, it is claimed, is not intelligence but cultural familiarity.

Intuition applied to specific test items, while appealing as a rhetorical device, does not constitute a legitimate criterion for test bias. One of the most frequently cited of the supposedly biased questions, taken from the WISC, is one in which children are asked what they would do if struck by a smaller child of the same sex. Striking the child back is considered an incorrect answer. On its face, the question seems highly culture loaded and culture biased. Black children miss this question far more often than do white children, and it is argued that retaliation may be an adaptive and therefore "intelligent" response for a ghetto child. Rather than being sufficient evidence of racial bias in the test, however, poorer black performance on this question is to be expected, given the lower overall average score of black children, regardless of whether the difference is a result of bias. The appropriate criterion for racial–content bias involves a comparison of item difficulty across *all* items between black and white children. Given that black children score lower overall, the important question becomes, is the *relative* difficulty of items significantly different for black and white children. In other words, is the rank–ordering of item difficulty among black children different from the rank–ordering among white children, indicating that certain items are particularly easier or more difficult for members of a given race. Culturally biased items should be more difficult than other items for members of groups outside the tested culture. In analysis of variance terms, there should be a significant race–by–item interaction on test scores. (Such an interaction is a necessary, but not sufficient, criterion for content bias, as there may be other reasons that black test takers do relatively worse on some items.)

At present, there is little or no evidence of such interaction in studies of the most commonly used intelligence and aptitude tests.[21] Item difficulty levels correlate between 0.95 and 0.98 between black and white test takers on these tests, indicating nearly identical relative difficulty.

In order to argue, in the face of such evidence, that significant racial content bias exists, one must maintain that virtually every item on a test like the WISC-R or Stanford-Binet is equally biased. This position was taken by two witnesses for the plaintiffs in the *Larry P.* case, Dr. Asa Hilliard, one of the psychologists who retested the plaintiff children, and Dr. Jane Mercer, a professor of sociology at the University of California at Riverside. Their arguments center around the existence of nonstandard English in the black culture and that black children are equally displaced from all aspects of white culture. We leave it to the reader to decide whether it is reasonable to believe that every item of a test including sections on vocabulary, general comprehension, block design, and picture completion is equally biased against American blacks.

Moreover, between-group comparisons of specific items independently judged to be most culturally loaded show that black subjects do no worse on these questions, compared to middle-class whites, than on any others.[22] (Ironically, the "fight" question cited above is one on which the black-white performance difference is smallest.[23] Removing this question from the test would actually penalize black test takers.) Overall, blacks seem to do somewhat worse compared to whites on nonverbal (those requiring only the manipulation of nonlinguistic symbols and objects) than on verbal intelligence tests.[24] If cultural bias is to creep into a test, it presumably has a better opportunity to do so through language than through abstract symbols, yet blacks do better on language tests.

Another measure of content bias involves factor analysis of various intelligence and aptitude tests. If factor-analytic solutions differ between black and white test takers, it may be supposed that these tests are measuring different entities in the two groups (see Chapter 2 for a discussion of factor analysis), and therefore are not equally valid measures of intelligence for blacks and whites. Once again, the empirical literature reveals no such differences in factor-analytic solutions.[25]

Despite the evidence, and the existence of numerous explanations of the impropriety of the item-by-item method of judging content bias, the piecemeal approach has been given the force of law. In 1976, the Golden Rule Insurance Company of Lawrenceville, Illinois, supported by the NAACP and Ralph Nader, brought suit against the Educational Testing Service (ETS) and the State of Illinois, charging that the Illinois Insurance Agent Licensing Test unfairly discriminated against blacks because the failure rate for blacks was higher than for whites. After eight years, in November 1984, the defendants agreed to end the suit by adopting what has come to be called the "Golden Rule" procedure in order to make the test fairer. This procedure requires that the ETS replace all test items on which black and white test takers differ in percentage correct by items measuring the same content, but on which blacks and whites differ least in performance. We have explained why such a procedure is not a proper measure of content bias. Consider, therefore, the very real possibility that a test subjected to the Golden Rule procedure is in fact not content biased. This implies that all valid test questions show approximately the same black–white differential, and that black test takers do possess, on average, less of the skills or knowledge measured by the test. The inevitable result of replacing questions from such a test with those that show a smaller differential is to make the test less valid as a predictor of job performance.

13. Racial content bias may be defined as either race by item interaction in test scores, or different factor analytic solutions between black and white test takers. According to either definition, how much racial content bias do you believe there is in the most commonly used intelligence and aptitude tests?

Ratings were made on a 4–point scale, where 1 was described as "An insignificant amount of content bias," 2 was "Some content bias," 3 was "A moderate amount of content bias," and 4 was "A large amount of content bias." The mean rating received from expert respondents is 2.13 (s.d. = .802, r.r. = 79%). This result indicates that, on average, experts believe there is a significant amount of racial content bias in intelligence tests, though less than what would be considered a moderate amount.

It is surprising, in light of our review of the empirical literature, that most experts think racial content bias is significant. We were similarly surprised by the results of the other bias questions. The end of this chapter and of the next contains a discussion of the relationship of demographic and background variables to substantive question responding. As the most politically sensitive questions in the survey, those dealing with race and class differences in IQ are also those most related to factors other than respondents' expertise, in particular, belief in equality of outcome in the economic realm.

Bias as differential validity/prediction. A test shows differential validity if scores for members of one group predict performance on some criterion, for example school grades, less well than do scores for members of another group. If IQ is found to correlate more poorly with school grades for blacks than for whites, the fifteen point (on the Wechsler tests) black–white IQ differential would not necessarily mean the same thing, in terms of test takers' abilities to succeed in school, as an equivalent IQ difference within the white population. IQ tests in this case are biased against blacks, in the sense that black IQs are less meaningful than white IQs. Such bias may be checked by comparing validity coefficients (correlation coefficient between test scores and criterion performance) between groups.

Technically, a discrepancy in validity coefficients is all that is meant by differential validity. However, the validity coefficient only measures the strength of the relationship between test score and criterion performance. A test that exhibits differential validity may still be useful, even for a group whose scores are less predictive, if validity coefficients remain high compared to other predictive measures. For example, if an aptitude test is found to correlate 0.50 with job performance for white applicants, but only 0.40 for black applicants, an employer might still want to use the test for all job applicants if including test scores along with other criteria provides better prediction of job performance, even for black applicants, than does the use of the other criteria alone.

A complete test of bias must look for equality of prediction, not just validity. In fact, a test may exhibit no differential validity, but evidence differential prediction, and therefore be biased. An IQ test that has the same validity coefficient for school grades for both blacks and whites predicts grades equally as accurately for each group. If, however, an equivalent score on this test predicts a higher grade point average (GPA) for black test takers than for whites, the test underpredicts black performance relative to that of whites. The test is biased against blacks because blacks with lower scores are likely to achieve GPAs equivalent to those of whites with higher scores. It is said that lower scores by blacks and Hispanics on many job tests reflect bias in the tests (differential prediction), because blacks and Hispanics will perform just as well on the job as whites with higher average scores.

The relationship between test scores and some criterion of performance may be represented by a separate regression equation for each group (racial, ethnic, class, etc.) taking the test. Differential validity concerns only differences in the correlation coefficient between groups. Differential prediction involves all three elements of the equation relating criterion performance to test score for each group: slope, intercept, and standard error of estimate. When a single regression equation is used (e.g., a single cutoff score is used for all applicants for some job or school) in a case where regression equations differ between groups, the test (or, more correctly, its use in this case) will be biased either in favor of one group (if the equation used is that for the group whose scores predict higher performance), against the other (if the other regression equation is used), or both (if, as is most likely, an average equation for all test takers is used).

There have been, in the last twenty years, scores of studies examining differential validity and differential prediction in a variety of intelligence and aptitude tests primarily dealing with the black–white difference, but involving SES and several other group comparisons as well. These data have been extensively reviewed by Arthur Jensen in his book *Bias in Mental Testing* by Robert Linn, as part of a National Academy of Sciences study of ability testing, and by John Hunter and his colleagues (black–white differences in employment testing only). These authors reach virtually identical conclusions. The results of differential validity studies vary across tests and criteria, but in most cases show no evidence of bias. IQ tests have comparable validity for black and white test takers in the prediction of elementary school grades. The correlation between SAT scores and freshman grades in college is slightly higher for whites than for blacks or Hispanics, but there is no disparity between groups differing only in SES. Scores on the Armed Services Vocational Aptitude Battery correlate more highly with final grades in Air Force technical training school for whites than for blacks. In contrast, there is little indication of differential validity in studies of performance in graduate and professional schools and in employment testing.

The results of studies of differential prediction are more consistent; the vast majority reveal no significant differences between blacks and whites in any of the most widely used intelligence and aptitude tests from elementary school through the workplace. When a difference is found, it is almost always in the intercept of the regression line, with the black intercept below the white. Such a difference implies that the use of the white or total group regression equation on the black population will result in *over*prediction of black performance. In other words, these tests are biased in favor of blacks. Similarly, the few studies that show differential prediction across SES reveal that tests overpredict the performance of low–SES test takers.[26]

14. On the whole, to what extent do you believe the most commonly used intelligence tests are biased against American blacks? In other words, to what extent does an average black American's test score underrepresent his or her actual level of those abilities the test purports to measure, relative to the average ability level of members of other racial or ethnic groups?

The question is directed at the rather technical concept of bias as differential prediction, but is worded in as straightforward a manner as possible. Ratings of bias for this question, as for the next, were made on a 4–point scale, where 1 was described as "Not at all or insignificantly biased," 2 was "Somewhat biased," 3 was "Moderately biased," and 4 was "Extremely biased." The mean bias rating for this question is 2.12 (s.d. = .787, r.r. = 84.1%), indicating that experts believe there is a small but significant amount of racial bias (differential prediction) in intelligence tests.

15. On the whole, to what extent do you believe the most commonly used intelligence tests are biased against members of lower socioeconomic groups? In other words, to what extent does the test score of an average lower socioeconomic group member underrepresent his or her actual level of those abilities the test purports to measure, relative to the average ability level of members of other socioeconomic groups?

The mean rating received for socioeconomic bias is slightly higher than for racial bias, at 2.24 (s.d. = .813, r.r. = 84.7%).

Bias as selection model. Selection model bias refers, not to bias in the test itself, but in how the test is used in some selection procedure. Whereas the criteria for bias in tests are generally well defined and agreed upon, bias or fairness in selection procedures remains a highly subjective matter. The perceived fairness of any given selection model is independent, however, of whether the test on which selection is based is itself biased. The many selection models proposed may be classified into three broad categories:[27] unqualified individualism, qualified individualism, and quotas. Models of unqualified individualism maintain that a selection strategy should pick from the pool of applicants those with the highest predicted performance, using whatever combination of variables yields the most valid prediction, even if one of these variables is racial or socioeconomic group membership. Tests with unequal but known regression equations for different groups (biased tests) may thus be used under unqualified individualism as long as the appropriate regression equation is used for members of each group. (Note that the use of separate regression equations for blacks and whites in tests that currently overpredict black performance will work to the detriment of black applicants compared to the use of a single, average equation.) Qualified individualism is identical to unqualified individualism with the one constraint that group membership should not enter into the selection procedure. With an unbiased test, qualified and unqualified individualism represent the same position, but with a biased test, the qualified individualist must either not use the test or sacrifice predictive validity for one or more groups. Quotas make this sacrifice explicit by trading off a certain amount of predictive validity in order to achieve other socially important goals, particularly more proportional representation of minority groups in schools and occupations. Other things being equal, the higher the predictive validity of the test, the greater the proportion of individuals from the lower scoring group who will fail once selected under a quota system in which the test score cutoff is lower for the lower scoring group.

Bias as the wrong criterion. Even though a test has equal predictive validity for different groups, bias in the use of the test may still exist if the criterion being predicted is biased. While such bias is technically not in the test, the test may be considered biased if it derives its meaning from such criteria. For example, a test of mechanical aptitude may be validated through correlation with supervisors' ratings in some mechanical training course. If the supervisors base their ratings to a large degree on the trainee's race or ethnic group, then the test may be considered a biased measure of mechanical ability, unless other unbiased validation criteria exist. A similar claim may be made against intelligence tests, which appear to have equal predictive validity for school performance among blacks and whites. If success in schools depends primarily on assimilation to white culture rather than intelligence, then IQ tests may be biased indicators of what they purport to measure. That most intelligence tests are validated against a large number of predictive and construct criteria makes this possibility unlikely, but one must still be wary of particularly culture–loaded validity criteria.

Bias in the validity criterion may also work to make an unbiased test appear biased. A test that is an equally valid measure of some ability in two groups will have differential predictive validity if the validity criterion is biased against one of the groups. A finding of differential predictive validity therefore does not automatically mean the test is biased, just as equivalent prediction or validity doesn't mean that it is not.

Bias as atmosphere. Atmosphere refers to a wide variety of external sources of bias, including coaching and practice effects, language or attitude of the examiner, and instructions or scoring. All of these elements may have an influence on test score, but they only represent bias if they differentially affect certain groups. Perhaps the most widely hypothesized of these biasing variables is race of the examiner. Jensen's review of thirty studies directed at this question found overwhelmingly nonsignificant results of race of examiner on black and white children.[28] Other variables, like coaching effects and examiner's attitude, have been shown to have small but significant effects on test scores, but no apparent differential effect across cultural groups. Some of these variables will be discussed further in the next chapter.

Bias as motivation. As noted in Chapter 2, N. J. Block and Gerald Dworkin have argued that intelligence tests are, to a significant degree, a measure of certain personality and motivational characteristics. Our expert sample agrees (question 8). Block and Dworkin further maintain that because these characteristics are nonintellectual, their influence on intelligence test scores seriously dilutes the IQ as a measure of "intelligence." In addition, because it is reasonable to expect that individuals from different cultural backgrounds will vary on average in the degree to which they display these personality and motivational traits, intelligence tests can be said to be biased against test takers from cultures that do not stress the tested traits.[29]

Jeff Howard and Ray Hammond, in a 1985 *New Republic* article, have made this argument explicit for black Americans.[30] Howard and Hammond distinguish between performance and ability, stressing that the black intellectual performance gap, as measured on the job, in school, and in test scores, does not reflect a deficit in intellectual ability. Rather, they claim, the performance gap is largely a behavioral problem caused by a tendency among members of the black community to avoid intellectual competition. This motivational/behavioral problem is, in turn, the result of a larger society that "projects an image of black intellectual inferiority" that is "internalized by black people." Moreover, "imputing intellectual inferiority to genetic causes, especially in the face of data confirming poorer performance, intensifies the fears and doubts that surround this issue."[31]

The bias–as–motivation problem requires for its solution a return to the question of the nature of intelligence. Howard and Hammond argue that performance on tests should be distinguished from intellectual ability, and that if motivational problems are solved, equivalent black and white intellectual ability will be demonstrated in test performance. They may be right, but, as they note, intelligence tests are behavioral measures of performance in the intellectual domain. The validity of these tests derives from their ability to predict performance in other intellectual domains. To the extent that the poorer black performance on tests is reflected in poorer black performance in school and on the job, the tests are not biased.

Block and Dworkin cite testing experts who claim that personality and motivational variables are a necessary part of intellectual performance, and the two authors thereby condemn tests as impure measures of "intelligence." Block and Dworkin refuse to accept the notion that intelligence is a behavioral (i.e., performance) concept, clinging instead to an idea of intelligence as pure, and therefore unmeasurable, intellectual ability. The "ability" intelligence and aptitude tests measure is not an abstract concept, but rather the ability to perform on certain intellectual tasks.

All of this is not to say that motivation cannot be a source of bias in intelligence tests. If blacks are, on average, less motivated to perform on intelligence and aptitude tests, and this motivational difference does not carry over to intellectual performance in other areas, then the tests may be considered biased indicators of black intellectual ability (as measured by performance). There are, at present, virtually no data relevant to this question.

16. Other biasing factors.

Surveyed experts were presented with a list of five factors that have been proposed at various times as differentially affecting the test scores of members of certain ethnic, racial, or economic groups. They were asked to rate the degree to which they believe each of the factors biases individually administered intelligence test scores. Ratings were made on a 4–point scale, where 1 was "Insignificant biasing effect," 2 was "Some biasing effect," 3 was "Moderate biasing effect," and 4 was "Large biasing effect." Mean bias ratings for the five factors are race of the examiner, 1.91 (s.d. = .758, r.r. = 85.9%); language and dialect of the examiner, 2.46 (s.d. = .865, r.r. = 86.2%); attitude of the examiner toward the group in question, 2.74 (s.d. = .932, r.r. = 85.6%); test taker anxiety, 2.63 (s.d. = .894, r.r. = 85.1%); and test taker motivation, 2.91 (s.d. = .925, r.r. = 85.6%).

It is interesting that two of the most commonly mentioned explanations for the black–white IQ difference, that black test takers perform more poorly with white examiners, and lack of motivation to perform well among black students, received the lowest and highest bias ratings, respectively. Perhaps the difference reflects the fact that a substantial body of empirical literature exists concerning the question of examiner race, while explanations in terms of test taker motivation remain largely hypothetical.

Overall, considering several definitions of test bias, expert respondents believe the most commonly used intelligence tests are somewhat biased against blacks and members of lower socioeconomic groups, with the highest bias ratings received for sources external to the test. Experts on bias, defined as those who were conducting research or had written at least one article or chapter on bias or group differences (N = 173), rated all of the sources of bias (questions 13–16) lower (less biasing effect) than did the rest of the sample, though the difference was significant (p < .01) only for test taker motivation (2.75 vs. 2.98, X^2 = 8.6, d.f. = 1, p < .004, 2–tailed).

Genetic Influences on Race and Class Differences in IQ

Given the large black–white and SES differences in IQ, anything short of a very large amount of bias will be insufficient to explain these differentials. The experts contend that there is some racial and economic bias in intelligence and aptitude tests. Even so, a substantial proportion, probably most, of the group differences in test score remains to be explained. It is a virtual certainty that environmental factors play a role; the difference in lifestyles between black and lower class children and middle–and upper–

class whites is too extreme not to have an effect on intellectual development. What is uncertain is whether these environmental differences are themselves a sufficient explanation of group differences in average test score. The alternative, that genetic factors also are important, remains the most contentious of all IQ–related issues.

Arthur Jensen hypothesized that genetic factors play a role in the black–white IQ differential. For this he was physically threatened, publicly censured, and called a racist by numerous parties. And he continues to be misrepresented to the present day. Anthropologist Melvin Konner, in his highly regarded book on biology and human behavior, *The Tangled Wing,* accuses Jensen of "[c]laiming to have shown that known race differences in intelligence were genetically based," when Jensen only hypothesized that genetic factors play a role.[32] ("Genetically based" sounds suspiciously like "genetic determination.") Konner then describes and criticizes a graph supposedly used by Jensen to argue for gene–environment interaction effects in the black–white IQ difference. But such a graph never appears in any of Jensen's writing; Konner has apparently set up a straw man in order to express his disagreement with Jensen's thesis. Numerous additional examples of such misrepresentation are available in Gould's *The Mismeasure of Man* and in several publications by the Cambridge, Massachusetts based organization Science for the People.[33]

In the news media and elsewhere, Jensen, and those who agreed with him, were accused of asserting the innate inferiority of blacks. This is a false but understandable accusation. It relates to two fundamental conceptions in American thought to which Jensen was perhaps insufficiently attendant. First, there is the general confusion, discussed in the last chapter, between genetic influence and innate, or "fixed," traits. The possibility of a genetic component to group difference in IQ in no way precludes a narrowing, or even elimination, of these differences; as long as the environment plays a role, anything is possible. This truth is generally ignored; talk of genetics runs counter to the belief in the essential equality of man.

Second, the question is one of *differences in IQ,* not inferiority. Individuals and groups differ in myriad physical and behavioral traits. To say that a particular person or group is inferior or superior is a moral judgment based on the value placed on these traits; objectively, people are only different. Arthur Jensen is a scientist who was discussing differences in a behavioral trait. (It would be fair to say that Jensen believes blacks, on average, to be *inferior in intelligence* but this belief is held by anyone who does not think cultural bias is a sufficient explanation of the black–white IQ differential, and it is not a statement about general worth.) The value placed on that trait is society's, not Jensen's. Somehow, intelligence, more than almost any other human attribute, is considered central to an individual's worth. If

Jensen had been discussing group differences in musical aptitude or ath-letic ability, his name would not be infamous. But to call someone tone deaf or clumsy has not nearly the impact of calling him stupid. Jensen has never maintained that blacks are any worse, or should be treated any differently as a group, because of their scores on intelligence tests; in fact, he has frequently asserted the opposite. Jensen may be accused of extreme callousness in baldly addressing so sensitive an issue; such an accusation has its merits. But to call Jensen, or anyone else who rationally discusses the empirical data on group differences in IQ a racist is grossly unfair.

Compounding the difficulties in maintaining rational discourse about group differences is the fact that genetic influences on race and class dif-ferences in IQ are extremely difficult to estimate. Within–group heritability, because it is tied to the particular environmental and genetic variation existing within the group, has little relevance to the causes of between–group variation. Jensen has argued that the high degree of heritability for IQ within the black and white populations makes it more *probable* that between–group differences have some significant heritable component as well.[34] Richard Lewontin and others disagree, citing exam-ples from genetic studies with other organisms demonstrating that high within–group heritability can be associated with almost any degree of ge-netic influence between groups.[35]

An example given by Lewontin is worth repeating here, as it helps clarify the important distinction between within–group heritability and between–group differences (a distinction more often blurred than understood in news media reports—See Chapter 7):

> We will take two handsful from a sack containing seed of an open–pollinated variety of corn. Such a variety has lots of genetic variation in it. Instead of using potting soil, however, we will grow the seed in vermiculite watered with a carefully made up nutrient, Knop's solution, used by plant physiologists for controlled growth experiments. One batch of seed will be grown on complete Knop's solution, but the other will have the concentration of nitrates cut in half. ... After several weeks we will measure the plants. Now we will find variation within seed lots which is entirely genetical since no environmental variation within seed lots was allowed. Thus heritability will be 1.0. However, there will be a radical difference between seed lots which is ascribable entirely to the difference in nutrient levels. Thus, we have a case where heritability within populations is complete, yet the difference between populations is entirely environmental![36]

Lewontin's point is that even if we know that the within–group heritability of IQ is substantial, this tells us nothing about the possibility of genetic between–group differences; they are independent questions. Jensen dem-onstrates, however, that high within–group heritability necessarily implies substantial between–group genetic influences, as long as the sources of environmental variation are the same between as within groups.[37] Large within–group heritability is only consistent with no genetic influence between groups if there is some source or sources of environmental variation that exists only between groups, like the variation in nutrients in Lewontin's example. But black and white Americans are two populations where such a source of environmental variation is very likely to exist: it falls under the general heading of "racial discrimination." Thus, if the environments of black and white Americans differ in ways that are not generally seen between families or individuals within the black and white communities, estimates of within–group heritability are of dubious relevance to the between–group question.

The major obstacle to the study of the causes of group differences is that it may be impossible to randomize or control the relevant environmental factors, and thus separate genetic from environmental sources of variation. How can one be sure, for example, that a black and a white child have been raised in similar environments, when genetically based racial differences remain obvious? Even black and white children raised in the same home may be treated very differently because of their skin color. Many experts in the study of genetics have argued that the nature of the situation makes it impossible to adequately assess the question of the genetic influence on group differences in psychological traits.[38]

This problem is obviously of more relevance to racial and ethnic group than to socioeconomic class differences. The evidence for a genetic component to differences in intelligence between classes is therefore less controversial. One can examine the effects of moving children of the same race from one social stratum to another without worrying about the children carrying with them physical markers of their biological parents' social class. E. M. Lawrence found a significant correlation between biological fathers' SES and the IQ of children raised in an orphanage, which was only slightly lower than the same correlation for children raised with their parents.[39] Similarly, Alice Leahy observed that the IQ of children adopted in infancy showed a much lower correlation with adopted parents' SES than is the case for children raised in their natural homes.[40] Thus it seems that at least part of the influence of a parent's SES on the child's IQ is independent of the environment the parent provides.

Further evidence for genetic IQ differences between classes is derived from the social mobility hypothesis, discussed in Chapter 2. The hypothesis is that one's intelligence, as measured by IQ tests, is an important determinant of one's eventual SES. We saw (question 6) that a majority of expert respondents are in agreement with this proposition. The apparent influence of IQ on SES, coupled with the substantial heritability of IQ in the general population, seems to imply that at least some of the IQ difference between classes is heritable. In an article in the *Atlantic* in 1971, Richard Herrnstein made the argument explicit, and slightly more general, in the following (abbreviated) syllogism: (Sociologist Bruce Eckland made essentially the same argument, also in 1971, in a strictly academic text, and thus received no notoriety.)[41]

1. If differences in mental abilities (as measured, for example, in intelligence tests) are to some extent inherited; and
2. if success in our society calls for those mental abilities;
3. then, success in our society reflects inherited differences between people to some extent.

Herrnstein is a firm believer in the social mobility hypothesis, arguing that our society is to a significant degree a meritocracy, in which ability is an important determinant of success. An important corollary to Herrnstein's syllogism is that as environmental factors relevant to the development of intelligence become more uniform (by being made as good as possible for everyone), the heritability of intelligence will increase, and the syllogism will hold with even greater force. Thus, Herrnstein concludes, the realization of egalitarian social and political goals will further stratify society into an increasingly hereditary meritocracy; as environments become more similar, differences in merit will depend more completely on differences in heredity. Assortative mating serves to accelerate this stratification.

Herrnstein's article, published only two years after Jensen's famous paper, touched off yet another storm of controversy and protest, much of it quite uncivil (See Chapter 1). A poster put out by the Committee Against Racism (CAR)[42] in Storrs, Connecticut, advertising a "National Conference on Racism and the University," shows a tree, whose roots are labeled "Racism, The Killer Weed." Hanging from the branches of the tree are the heads of six scientists: Herrnstein, Jensen, Shockley, Hans Eysenck (an English psychologist who has been a staunch supporter of Jensen), Daniel Patrick Moynihan, and Edward Banfield. Associated with each head is a balloon containing a quote from the scientist. Herrnstein's quote, from his *Atlantic* article, reads, "as technology advances, the tendency to be unemployed may run in the genes of a family about as certainly as bad teeth do now." The racism inherent in this statement is perhaps more apparent to the CAR than to those who have read Herrnstein's article.

17. Which of the following best characterizes your opinion of the heritability of socio–economic class differences in IQ?

Technically, this question is misworded, as one generally does not speak of the "heritability" of between–group differences, but rather the "source."

Nonetheless, the response options made it clear what we were asking. They were: "The difference is due entirely to environmental variation," "The difference is due entirely to genetic variation," "The difference is a product of both genetic and environmental variation," and "The data are insufficient to support any reasonable opinion." A majority of experts (55 percent) choose the genetic–environmental option, as opposed to 12 percent for strictly environmental. There were 15 percent no responses, and 18 percent do not feel there are sufficient data. Only one respondent attributes the difference entirely to genetics.

The study of genetic influences on racial differences in IQ is a more difficult problem than SES differences, in part because of difficulties in controlling relevant environments. But perhaps most of the problem arises because this area is so controversial and, it is believed, potentially dangerous that research "is subjected to the scrutiny of an electron microscope."[43] Traditional kinship studies, when they can be performed at all, are rather easily criticized as insufficiently controlled. The bulk of the evidence must therefore come from more indirect sources, a state of affairs that allows the data at present to support virtually any conclusion about the source of racial differences.

John C. Loehlin and his associates reviewed the relevant data in their myriad, and sometimes rather sketchy, forms in 1975.[44] Philip Vernon has updated this review, summarizing some thirty different types of evidence bearing on the source of racial differences in IQ.[45] The opinions reached in both reviews are essentially the same: the literature contains numerous poorly designed and executed studies. Nevertheless, black–white IQ differences probably reflect both environmental and genetic differences. All authors are careful to point out, however, that the data are not of sufficient quality or consistency to be considered conclusive. Jensen advocates essentially the same position, calling himself an agnostic for purposes of public policy, but maintaining a research hypothesis that both genetic and environmental factors are important.[46] Others (R. Darrell Bock and Elsie G. J. Moore, as well as Brian MacKenzie) have examined the relevant data and conclude that the most reasonable hypothesis is that racial differences in IQ are completely environmentally determined.[47] It may therefore be useful at this point to review some of the more important pieces of evidence pertaining to the genetic question.

As noted, within–group estimates of heritability are relevant to the between–group question only if all sources of environmental variation are the same within and between groups. Vernon has estimated that given a within–group heritability of 0.60 (heritability estimates are approximately the same within the black and white American populations), between–family environmental variance (actually, standard deviation) accounts for

6.3 IQ points (the remainder is within families, and is therefore not relevant to the black–white difference).[48] In order for the entire 15–point black–white difference to be accounted for by sources of environmental variation existing within groups, the average black environment would have to be 2.38 standard deviations worse (intellectually) than the average white environment. If such a large average disparity does not in fact exist, a completely environmental explanation for the black–white IQ difference must look to environmental (i.e., cultural) differences that do not exist within either population. Jensen has labeled these differences Factor X because, he says, they have not been clearly identified or agreed upon by those who argue that racial differences in IQ are entirely environmental.[49] Hypotheses about the effects of slavery and prejudice aside, Jensen sees such explanations, at present, as nothing more than ad hoc conjectures.[50] Others, most notably Sandra Scarr, disagree, citing evidence from systematic investigations of child–rearing practices that demonstrate real qualitative differences between black and white families.[51] These differences may also provide an environmental explanation for the lower IQs of black than white children whose parents have equivalent SES and IQ.

Less ambiguous, but still inconclusive, evidence for a genetic component to racial differences includes the following: (1) American Indians and Mexican Americans, despite equivalent or worse socioeconomic conditions than blacks, have higher average IQ scores; (2) Head Start programs, whose student population is almost entirely black, have failed to significantly raise IQs in the long run; and (3) improvements in black educational and environmental conditions over the past thirty years have produced no decrease in the IQ differential. Our earlier caveat about environmental manipulations applies to these last two points as well; that those manipulations that have been tried have not been successful does not imply that other environmental changes will meet with similar failure. These failures are consistent, however, with significant genetic influence on between–group IQ differences under the *existing* conditions of environmental variation. Moreover, the average IQ of both black and white Americans has improved over the past thirty years, but the black–white difference has not changed. Thus, while the education and environment of black Americans apparently have improved, so have that of whites, and the *differences* in black and white environment (at least as they relate to IQ) may be as great as ever.

Advocates of a completely environmental explanation of racial differences in intelligence may find support in the failure of studies that have attempted to link genetic markers of European or African ancestry to IQ to find any such relation. Similarly, there is little relation between IQ and lightness of skin color. (Studies linking IQ to degree of white ancestry have produced contradictory results.) Environmentalists might also point out that, in contradistinction to the failure of Head Start, more intense intervention programs with black children, like the Milwaukee Project, appear to have produced substantial IQ gains.

A study of racial differences in intelligence by Sandra Scarr and Richard Weinberg deserves special mention because it is one of the few such studies to utilize traditional behavior–genetic methodology.[52] One hundred thirty children from either black or interracial matings were adopted, most very early in life, into advantaged (mean annual income $16,000 in 1976, IQ 119) white homes in Minnesota. The adopted children, whose natural parents were educationally average, scored above the IQ average of the white population, but not as high as the adoptive parents' natural children. The authors found strong support for an environmental explanation in a comparison of the average adoptive child's IQ of 106 to the black population average (in the North Central United States) of 90. Black/interracial adoptees' IQs compare favorably to those of white adoptees in other adoption studies. Moreover, the earlier a child was adopted, the higher her eventual IQ.

The Scarr and Weinberg study has been criticized for a number of reasons, but primarily for poor sampling techniques, including recruitment of adoptive families on a voluntary basis and the possibility of selective placement by adoption agencies, so that a higher–than–90 IQ might have been expected from adoptees purely on genetic grounds.[53] The presence of both interracial and black adoptees poses particular problems for a strictly environmental interpretation, as the black partner of an interracial mating might be expected to have an IQ above the black population average (See the discussion of assortative mating in chapter 3). In fact, interracial adoptees had an average IQ of 109, compared to 97 for black adoptees. Scarr and Weinberg attribute this result to pre– and post–adoptive environmental differences rather than genetic factors, but if correct, these authors are merely indicting their own procedures.

18. Which of the following best characterizes your opinion of the heritability of the black–white difference in IQ?

The caveat about the wording of question 17 applies here as well. The response alternatives were also the same. In this case, a plurality of experts (45 percent), and a majority of respondents, believe the black–white IQ difference to be a product of both genetic and environmental variation, compared to only 15 percent who feel the difference is entirely due to environmental variation. Twenty–four percent of experts do not believe there are sufficient data to support any reasonable opinion, and 14 percent did not respond to the question. Eight of the experts (1 percent) indicate a belief in an entirely genetic determination. That a majority of experts who respond to this question believe genetic determinants to be important in the black–white IQ difference is remarkable in light of the overwhelmingly negative reaction from both the academic and public spheres that met Jensen's statement of the same hypothesis. Either expert opinion has changed dramatically since 1969, or the psychological and educational communities are not making their opinions known to the general public.

It is interesting to compare these results to those of a similar survey conducted by Robert Friedrichs in 1973.[54] Friedrichs polled 341 APA members as to their agreement or disagreement with the following quotation from Jensen: "[I]t is a not unreasonable hypothesis that genetic factors are strongly implicated in the average Negro–white intelligence difference. The preponderance of the evidence is, in my opinion, less consistent with a strictly environmental hypothesis than with a genetic hypothesis." Sixty percent of respondents either disagreed or tended to disagree, compared to only 28 percent who either agreed or tended to agree.

These results are deceiving for two reasons. First, the quotation presents to respondents what survey experts call a "double–barreled question." That is, there are two assertions contained in the quotation, and it is unclear to which subjects are responding. It is possible that someone might agree that genetic factors present "a not unreasonable hypothesis," but believe that the evidence still generally favors a strictly environmental explanation. This possibility is made more salient by the second and more damaging problem with the quotation: it is highly misleading. By taking the quotation out of context, the impression is given that by "genetic hypothesis" Jensen means a strictly genetic explanation, yet it is clear from the rest of his article that he is referring only to a hypothesis in which there is *some* genetic determination. Thus, respondents who believe that there is some genetic component to racial differences in IQ, but who misinterpret the quotation, will be inclined to disagree.

No doubt many readers are wondering at this point, "Why bother studying group differences in IQ? Our society must still treat each person as an individual with regard to educational and occupational opportunity, and group differences are irrelevant." It is true that we may never wish to make important decisions on the basis of group membership, but it is precisely because we are interested in individual liberties irrespective of race and class that we need to know why, for example, blacks are overrepresented in classes for the mentally retarded, or underrepresented in higher education or in certain professions. If these differences are in part genetic, or if they are the result of environmental factors outside the test, shouting "bias," and setting up a quota system whenever blacks do poorly on a test obscures a search for real solutions.

Many critics believe that the study of race and class differences in IQ is not necessarily irrelevant, but dangerous.[55] It is maintained that any practical consequences that may be the result of such research are far outweighed by the possible negative social effects. The existence of genetic differences in intelligence, or even their possibility, may be used to reinforce existing social inequities and to propagate additional racial and economic oppression. In fact, even a completely environmental explanation can lead one to trouble with these critics, as Scarr and Weinberg have been accused of "blaming the victim," by attributing the black IQ decrement to black culture.[56] Moreover, there is the Howard and Hammond argument that discussions of genetic differences profoundly affect black intellectual performance.

Scientists who discuss possible explanations of racial and class differences in IQ are accused of ignoring the moral issue of the social consequences of their work. Critics differ, however, in the degree to which they are willing to attribute racist sentiments to the investigators themselves. A common tactic, mentioned previously, is to argue for a historical continuum between earlier racist philosophies and modern investigations of individual and group differences—the politics of science.[57] At the very least, it is asserted, those who would not have their work used to support racist and elitist social policies must be extremely cautious in putting forth hypotheses about racial and class differences, lest there be misinterpretation.[58] In an ideal world, such conjecture and investigation would cease altogether.

Those in favor of investigating group differences reply that science and politics, while often interconnected, are not the same thing. Science is, and should be, concerned primarily with the discovery of facts. While many of these facts have social consequences, such consequences do not follow directly from the facts themselves, but depend critically on certain social values that are independent of scientific investigation.[59] The scientist should not, however, be unaware of the possible consequences of his work, and should exercise caution when putting forth politically dangerous hypotheses. Scientific knowledge, in and of itself, is a good thing, and this is particularly true when that knowledge concerns human behavior. In the long run, it is better to know all that we can about individual and group differences in socially relevant traits, and to base social policy on facts, than to rely on our often biased conjectures.

The Politics of Expert Opinion

Despite the desires of many to keep the scientific and political realms separate, scientists lead lives outside the laboratory and the library, and their opinions about scientific issues inevitably will be influenced by factors external to the data. It has been our hope that by surveying experts we will obtain an assessment of the "facts" about testing that is less tainted by extraneous motivations than has heretofore been the case. Our wishes notwithstanding, politics necessarily will color opinions about politically charged issues.

Nowhere is this clearer than when dealing with group differences in test score. To maintain that the black–white and SES IQ differentials are meaningful, even when the data appear to point that way, is to directly contradict the egalitarian ethic that all men are created equal and that the plight of minorities is entirely the fault of oppressors. Scientists who cross that line, either in arguing that tests are unbiased, or worse, in hypothesizing that genetic factors may be involved will meet with disapprobation from both the general public and from other scientists. Jensen and Herrnstein were widely castigated by the expert community, yet the majority of expert respondents agree with the Jensen and Herrnstein positions on genetics and group differences. When scientists enter the public realm, the response they receive from their fellows is as much influenced by the political as the empirical content of their statements.

In light of the way Jensen and others have been treated, we wondered how experts feel about their more controversial and higher profile colleagues. Respondents were presented with a list of fourteen social scientists, shown in Table 4.1, who have written about intelligence or intelligence testing, and asked to indicate their respect for the author's relevant work. Ratings were made on a 7–point scale, where 1 was "Very low regard" and 7 was "Very high regard."

Six of the listed scientists (Burt, Eysenck, Gould, Herrnstein, Jensen, and Kamin) have been prominent in the public controversy over testing, particularly group differences and the supposed racism inherent in the tests. The remainder are well–known psychometricians who have generally stayed clear of the fray. Response rates vary considerably across authors, but seem more a function of familiarity than of the author's position on any issue. The controversial authors, despite differing widely in their stances toward testing, are all rated lower (with greater variance) than those psychologists not prominently involved in the public debate. That Cyril Burt should be rated much lower than all of the other authors is understandable in light of the revelations about him after his death. Somewhat less understandable, considering responses to other questions in the survey, but consistent with the public record, the controversial authors who could be labeled pro–testing (Burt, Eysenck, Herrnstein, and Jensen) are all rated below the two anti–testing scientists (Gould and Kamin). (These differences are significant [$p < .01$, 2–tailed] for Burt, Eysenck, and Jensen; Herrnstein does not do significantly worse than Gould or Kamin.)

TABLE 4.1
Author Ratings

Author	Mean Respect Rating[a]	% Responding
Anne Anastasi	5.8 (1.1)[b]	78.2
Cyril Burt	2.43 (1.61)	72.3
Raymond Cattell	5.14 (1.33)	81.7
Lee Cronbach	5.89 (1.1)	82.6
Hans Eysenck	4.33 (1.56)	68.4
Stephen J. Gould	4.45 (1.73)	35.7
J. P. Guilford	5.55 (1.18)	82.6
Richard Herrnstein	4.14 (1.71)	44.6
Lloyd Humphreys	5.17 (1.29)	42.5
Arthur Jensen	3.68 (1.83)	87.1
Leon Kamin	4.36 (1.61)	39.6
Robert L. Thorndike	5.57 (1.21)	83.6
Philip Vernon	5.21 (1.18)	37.8
David Wechsler	5.72 (1.16)	86.7

[a]1 = "Very low regard," 7 = "Very high regard." [b]Numbers in parentheses are standard deviations.

The lower ratings for the public figures may be attributed to a general distaste for popularization and public controversy among the expert population. The difference between the pro- and anti-testing scientists is not so easily explained. For one thing, the more highly rated noncontroversial authors are all accurately characterized as pro-testing. Moreover, respondents tend to agree with Eysenck, Herrnstein, and Jensen on the group difference issues (belief in a genetic influence on both race and SES differences in IQ are significantly positively correlated with ratings for these authors). The abundance of very low ratings for those who publicly postulate genetic influences on group differences thus seems to reflect the views of both those who disagree with these positions and those who may agree but believe certain things are better left unsaid, at least publicly.

Both the mean and variance of ratings for controversial authors indicate that these ratings are related to factors other than the content of the authors' work. Our hypothesis is that expert opinions on all the questions concerning group differences are related to the political perspective of the respondents. The dilemma (disjunction of realms) between the data on group differences and political belief faced by a liberal psychologist must be greater than that faced by a conservative, who might be more inclined to value efficiency over equality of outcome.

Political perspective was assessed in two ways. First, respondents stated their agreement or disagreement with a series of six political statements. The statements dealing with U.S. economic exploitation, the fairness of the private enterprise system, affirmative action, the desirability of socialism, alienation caused by the structure of society, and the propriety of extramarital sexual relations. Responses to these statements were discovered, in a previous investigation incorporating many more such statements, to load highly on a factor representing overall political perspective.[60] Agreement was assessed on a 4– point scale, where 1 was "Strongly agree" and 4 was "Strongly disagree." For four of the six statements, the mean response is approximately at indifference. Respondents are somewhat more likely to disagree that "The United States would be better off if it moved toward socialism" and that "The structure of our society causes most people to feel alienated." The second measure of political perspective asked experts to indicate their global political perspective on a 7–point scale, where 1 was "Very liberal" and 7 was "Very conservative." Mean self–assessment on this scale is 3.19 (s.d. = 1.28, r.r. = 95.6%), putting this expert population slightly to the left of center.

Factor analysis of responses to the six statements and the global rating reveal that all questions, with the exception of the statement about extramarital affairs, load highly on a single factor (i.e., are highly correlated). The five statements and the global rating were therefore normalized and combined to form a political perspective supervariable. It is this variable that is used as a measure of overall political perspective. Note that the liberal position on the five included statements (e.g., belief in socialism, affirmative action, economic exploitation) can all be characterized as placing a higher value on equality of outcome than on economic efficiency.

The next chapter contains a detailed discussion of the relationship between political perspective and other demographic and background variables, and substantive question responding. It is worth noting here that political perspective is *not* significantly related to responses to most substantive questions. The exceptions include a handful of questions on the nature of intelligence and heritability, as well as several questions on test use and misuse (discussed in the next chapter), and *all* of the questions dealing with group differences discussed in this chapter. For every source of bias examined (questions 12–16), there is a significant positive correlation between liberalism and amount of bias attributed to tests, a result that makes the discrepancy between the bias ratings and our review of the empirical literature more understandable. Conservatives are significantly more likely than liberals to believe that genes play a causal role in race and class differences in IQ, and rate Burt, Eysenck, Herrnstein, and Jensen higher. Liberals, on the other hand, are more favorably disposed to Gould and Kamin than are conservatives.

Group differences in IQ are the driving force behind the IQ controversy and remain its most sensitive topic. Those who attack tests usually begin with this issue; those who defend them usually shy away from it. Experts surveyed indicate that there is some bias in intelligence and aptitude tests, but that it is insufficient to account for the totality of group differences in test score. Most respondents are of the opinion that genetic factors as well as environmental differences contribute to the black–white and SES differentials in IQ. These data are not, however, an accurate representation of the coldly rational scientific view. The United States has suffered through a long and ugly history of racism, and the past thirty years has seen the rise of a new egalitarian ethic. In its wake, there are certain topics that many scientists are unwilling to discuss publicly, and about which they cannot be totally objective.

Notes

1. Lee Willerman, *The Psychology of Individual and Group Differences* (San Francisco: W. H. Freeman, 1979), pp. 465–474.
2. Eleanor Emmons Maccoby and Carol Nagy Jacklin, *The Psychology of Sex Differences* (Stanford, CA: Stanford University Press), pp. 63–133; Arthur R. Jensen, *Bias in Mental Testing* (New York: Free Press, 1980), pp. 622–628.
3. Arthur R. Jensen, "The Race X Sex X Ability Interaction," in *Intelligence: Genetic and Environmental Influences*, ed. R. Cancro (New York: Grune and Stratton, 1971), p. 136.
4. Audrey M. Shuey, *The Testing of Negro Intelligence* 2nd ed. (New York: Social Science Press, 1966); R. Travis Osborne and Frank C. J. McGurk, *The Testing of Negro Intelligence, Vol. 2* (Athens, GA: The Foundation for Human Understanding, 1982).
5. John C. Loehlin, Gardner Lindzey, and J. N. Spuhler, *Race Differences in Intelligence* (San Francisco: W. H. Freeman, 1975), p. 235.
6. Ibid.; Arthur R. Jensen, "The Nature of the Black–White Difference on Various Psychometric Tests: Spearman's Hypothesis," *The Behavioral and Brain Sciences* 8 (June 1985):193–263.

7. Loehlin et al., p. 235.
8. Christopher Jencks et al., *Inequality* (New York: Basic Books, 1972), p. 144; Christopher Jencks et al., *Who Gets Ahead?* (New York: Basic Books, 1979), p. 121.
9. Jenson, *Bias*, p. 44.
10. Ibid.
11. Ibid., p. 43.
12. Ibid., p. 635.
13. Ibid., pp. 570–571; Anne Anastasi, *Psychological Testing*, 5th ed. (New York: Macmillan, 1982), pp. 284–285.
14. J. H. Court, *Researchers' Bibliography for Raven's Progressive Matrices and Mill Hill Vocabulary Scales*, 3d ed. (Adelaide, Australia: Flinders University, 1976).
15. Jensen, *Bias*, p. 704.
16. Langdon E. Longstreth, "Jensen's Reaction Time Investigations of Intelligence: A Critique," *Intelligence* 8 (April–June 1984): 139–160.
17. Jensen, *Bias*, pp. 635–714.
18. Philip Vernon, *Intelligence: Heredity and Environment* (San Francisco: W. H. Freeman, 1979), p. 310.
19. So too can a test be highly culture specific and invalid. Psychologist Robert Williams has developed a test he calls the BITCH (Black Intelligence Test of Cultural Homogeneity), designed to be a culture–specific test on which blacks outperform whites. See Robert L. Williams, *The BITCH Test* (St. Louis, MO: Black Studies Program, Washington University, 1972). Dr. Williams accomplished his objective; the test consists entirely of vocabulary questions concerning black slang. Unfortunately, performance on the test has not been demonstrated to correlate significantly with any other criterion of intelligence. See Jensen, *Bias*, pp. 679–681.
20. Adapted from Ronald L. Flaugher, "The Many Definitions of Test Bias," *American Psychologist* 33 (July 1978):671–679.
21. Jensen, *Bias*, pp. 552–580.
22. Vernon, p. 265; but see Jensen, *Bias*, pp. 530–533.
23. F. Miele, "Cultural Bias in the WISC," *Intelligence* 3 (1979):149–164.
24. Frank C. J. McGurk, "Race Differences—Twenty Years Later," *Homo* 26 (1975):219–239.
25. Jensen, *Bias*, pp. 533–552.
26. Ibid., pp. 465–516; Robert Linn, "Ability Testing: Individual Differences, Prediction and Differential Prediction," in *Ability Testing: Uses, Consequences, and Controversies*, part II, eds. Alexandra K. Wigdor and Wendell R. Garner (Washington, DC: National Academy Press, 1982), pp. 335–388; John E. Hunter, Frank L. Schmidt, and Ronda Hunter, "Differential Validity of Employment Tests by Race: A Comprehensive Review and Analysis," *Psychological Bulletin* 86 (1979):721–735.
27. John E. Hunter and Frank L. Schmidt, "A Critical Analysis of the Statistical and Ethical Implications of Five Definitions of Test Fairness," *Psychological Bulletin* 83 (1976):1053–1071.
28. Jensen, *Bias*, pp. 596–603.
29. N. J. Block and Gerald Dworkin, "IQ, Heritability, and Inequality," in *The IQ Controversy*, eds. N. J. Block and Gerald Dworkin (New York: Pantheon Books, 1976), p. 455.

30. Jeff Howard and Ray Hammond, "Rumors of Inferiority," *New Republic* 3686 (September 9, 1985):17–21.
31. Ibid., p. 19.
32. Melvin Konner, *The Tangled Wing* (New York: Harper Colophon, 1983), p. 400.
33. Stephen Jay Gould, *The Mismeasure of Man* (New York: W. W. Norton, 1981); Various, *Science for the People* 6 (March 1974); Various, *Biology as Destiny: Science Fact or Social Bias?* (Cambridge, MA: Science for the People, 1984).
34. Arthur R. Jensen, "How Much Can We Boost IQ and Scholastic Achievement?" *Harvard Educational Review* 39 (Winter 1969):80.
35. Richard Lewontin, "Race and Intelligence," *Bulletin of the Atomic Scientists* (March 1970):2–8.
36. Ibid., p. 7.
37. Arthur R. Jensen, *Educability and Group Differences* (New York: Harper & Row, 1973).
38. W. F. Bodmer and L. L. Cavalli-Sforza, "Intelligence and Race," *Scientific American* 223 (1970):19–29; Theodosius Dobzhansky, *Genetic Diversity and Human Equality* (New York: Basic Books, 1973); N. E. Morton, "Human Behavioral Genetics," in *Genetics, Environment, and Behavior*, eds. L. Ehrman, G. S. Omenn, and E. Caspari (New York: Academic Press, 1972).
39. E. M. Lawrence, "An Investigation Into the Relation Between Intelligence and Inheritance," *British Journal of Psychology, Monograph Supplements* 16 (1931).
40. Alice M. Leahy, "Nature–Nurture and Intelligence," *Genetic Psychology Monographs* 17 (1935):235–308.
41. Bruce C. Eckland, "Social Class Structure and the Genetic Basis of Intelligence," in *Intelligence: Genetic and Environmental Influences*, ed. R. Cancro (New York: Grune and Stratton, 1971), pp. 65–76.
42. The same organization placed a half-page ad in the October 18, 1973, *New York Times*, in which the "doctrine of racial supremacy" espoused by Jensen, Eysenck, Herrnstein, and Shockley is equated with that of the Nazis.
43. Sandra Scarr, *Race, Social Class, and Individual Differences in IQ* (Hillsdale, NJ: Lawrence Erlbaum, 1981).
44. Loehlin et al.
45. Vernon, pp. 242–332.
46. Arthur R. Jensen, "Obstacles, Problems, and Pitfalls in Differential Psychology," in *Race, Social Class, and Individual Differences in IQ*, ed. Sandra Scarr (Hillsdale, NJ: Lawrence Erlbaum, 1981).
47. R. Darrell Bock and Elsie G. J. Moore, *Profile of American Youth: Demographic Influences on ASVAB Test Performance* (Washington, DC: Government Printing Office, 1984), pp. 268–271; Brian Mackenzie, "Explaining Race Differences in IQ: The Logic, the Methodology, and the Evidence," 39 (November 1984):1214–1233.
48. Vernon, p. 267.
49. Jensen, *Educability*.
50. Jensen, "Obstacles."
51. Scarr; Willerman, pp. 462–465.
52. Sandra Scarr and Richard A. Weinberg, "IQ Test Performance of Black Children Adopted by White Families," *American Psychologist* 31 (1976):726–739.
53. Scarr.

54. Robert W. Friedrichs, "The Impact of Social Factors Upon Scientific Judgment: The 'Jensen Thesis' as Appraised by Members of the American Psychological Association," *Journal of Negro Education* 42 (1973):429–438.

55. e.g.,Block and Dworkin; Noam Chomsky, "Psychology and Ideology," *Cognition* 1 (1972):11–46; Jerry Hirsch, "Behavior–Genetic Analysis and Its Biosocial Consequences," *Seminars in Psychiatry* 2 (1970):89–105; Leon J. Kamin, *The Science and Politics of IQ* (Potomac, MD: Lawrence Erlbaum, 1974).

56. C. W. Oden Jr. and W. S. MacDonald, "The RIP in Social Scientific Reporting," *American Psychologist* 33 (1978):952–954.

57. e.g., Kamin; Clarence J. Karier, "Testing for Order and Control in the Corporate Liberal State," in *The IQ Controversy*, eds. N. J. Block and Gerald Dworkin (New York: Pantheon Books, 1976), pp. 339–373.

58. Block and Dworkin, p. 517.

59. Jensen, "Obstacles."

60. Stanley Rothman and S. Robert Lichter, "Personality, Ideology, and World View: A Comparison of Media and Business Elites," *British Journal of Political Science* 15 (1984):29–44.

5

The Impact of Intelligence Testing

Intelligence and aptitude tests measure samples of behavior, acquired under specific conditions in a relatively short period of time, that may be used to make predictions about behavior in a larger context. Test scores tell us how individuals differ from one another in the domain of intellectual functioning. They are often used as tools to aid decision making in such areas as curriculum placement, diagnosis for special education, educational and career counseling, college admissions, and the hiring and promotion of employees. In a society where there is competition for educational and occupational resources, the hope has been that tests can aid in the efficient distribution of these resources according to intellectual merit, rather than wealth or ancestry.

Concerns about what tests are measuring, about racial and class differences in test scores, and about how these scores are being used have led many to question the usefulness of intelligence tests as gatekeepers. The impact of tests on the education and occupations of Americans has come under increasing attack. Martin Holmen and Richard Docter identify what they call the "central criticism" of testing:

> At the heart of criticisms about tests and testing programs is one fact that is likely to help perpetuate at least some of the criticism: tests are often used as tools for the allocation of limited resources or opportunities. Put another way, educational and psychological tests are frequently designed to measure differences among individuals so that one person recieves a reward or privilege which another person is then denied.[1]

For many critics of testing, and other firm believers in a liberal democratic state, policies which allocate many of society's most precious resources, at least in part, according to one's answers on a brief multiple–choice exam are very disturbing. This is particularly true when these tests are seen as culturally biased and of limited applicability to real–world behavior. Tests only matter to the extent that they are used. Thus, perhaps the most important question we can ask about intelligence tests is "What good are they?" What effect do these tests have on those who are competing for limited resources, and on the rest of us who must live in the society thus created? This chapter will discuss, in the context of expert opinion, some of the uses and abuses of intelligence and aptitude tests, as well as the question of whether these tests offer any advantage over other gatekeeping methods. We will be concerned with the three primary uses for intelligence and aptitude testing: the individualization of education in elementary and secondary schools, admission to schools of higher education, and employment testing. Tests have proven useful in each of these contexts, but the potential for abuse is also great, as tests are used and interpreted inappropriately by those without an adequate understanding of their functions and limitations. The tradeoff between efficiency and the potential for abuse has been a central concern in litigation, legislation, and executive policy concerning intelligence and aptitude tests.

In addition to these issues, the last section of the chapter will discuss data on the demographic and background characteristics of the survey respondents as they relate to substantive question responding.

Intelligence and Aptitude Testing in Elementary and Secondary Schools

The past ten years have seen several attempts o measure the nature and extent of intelligence and aptitude test use in U.S. schools.[2] The results of these surveys are not always consistent, as there are significant differences in survey samples and the phrasing of questions. Nonetheless, it appears that between one–half and two–thirds of all public school districts administer group intelligence or aptitude tests to all students at least once during the period between kindergarten and twelfth grade. Two facts seem clear about these data. First, they represent a decline in test use over the previous ten or twenty years. In Chapter 1 we mentioned the results of two nationwide surveys, conducted by the Akron Public Schools, of large–city and –county test directors. The Akron surveys found that in certain grade levels, the use of group tests had declined from 100 percent in the 1964 survey to less than 40 percent in 1978.[3] (The percentages for 1978 test use in this survey represent test use during only three school years; other surveys that include all elementary and secondary grades generally indicate usage in excess of fifty percent.) Similarly, in a stratified random survey of over 5,000 American public high school students conducted in 1963 and 1964, Orville Brim and his associates found that 78 percent of students were confident they had taken at least one intelligence test during their lifetime.[4] None of the recent surveys of test use indicate percentages this high. The decrease in test use stems from a decline in tracking (ability grouping) in elementary and secondary schools coupled with an increasing perception that without a specific application like tracking information about the general level of intelligence or aptitude of most students is a relatively useless supplement to school grades and achievement test scores.

The second important fact about the use of group intelligence and aptitude tests to be gleaned from these surveys is that the level of actual test *usage* is far below the frequency of test administration. Beverly Anderson, in a survey of test use in fourteen western states published in 1982, estimates that about two–thirds of the school districts in these states administer group aptitude tests, but that about half of these do so as a result of public pressure or school board policy, and seldom or never use the results.[5] A 1979 Nationwide Teacher Opinion Poll conducted by the National Education Association (NEA) found that 64 percent of teachers had used group intelligence test score, and 59 percent had used group aptitude test scores, during the previous three years, but only 39 percent of each group had found these scores in any way helpful.[6] In the absence of specific applications, teachers and guidance counselors find aptitude and intelligence test scores of limited usefulness.

One application where intelligence tests continue to be useful is in diagnosis and special–education planning. This was, of course, the function of the original Binet–Simon scale. In cases where a student is having extreme difficulty in the classroom, it is common practice to use individually administered intelligence tests, in conjunction with a host of other tests and assessment devices, to diagnose the student's particular problems and to help tailor a curriculum to the student's needs. Thus, individually administered intelligence tests continue to be widely used in special education in elementary and secondary schools. Anderson found such usage to be common in all the western school districts surveyed,[7] though her survey was conducted before the 1984 appellate decision extending the *Larry P.* decision to seven western states.

Accompanying the use of intelligence and aptitude tests in schools is a lack of test sophistication by teachers. David Goslin's 1967 stratified random survey of approximately 1,500 elementary and secondary school teachers found that most had taken either no or only one graduate or undergraduate course related to psychological measurement, and that very few had ever attended a clinic or meeting in which they had been instructed in the use of, or theory behind, standardized tests.[8] A 1979 survey of American Federation of Teachers (AFT) members by James Ward found the situation little improved; one in five had no formal college training in testing and measurement, and only one in three received any further training while teaching.[9] Another recent survey of schoolteachers found that many did not know the meaning of percentiles in score reporting.[10] Most of Goslin's teachers admitted having little or no knowledge of what the following tests measure: WISC, Differential Aptitude Tests, California Test of Mental Maturity, and Lorge–Thorndike Intelligence Tests. This despite the fact that two–thirds of the high schools and a greater percentage of elementary schools surveyed reported giving group administered intelligence tests to at least some of their students. The bulk of teachers reported no experience with actual test administration, as this was generally handled by counselors and other administrators with more testing expertise.

That most elementary and secondary schools still administer intelligence and aptitude tests, coupled with an apparent lack of real understanding on the part of teachers of what intelligence tests are measuring, creates the potential for abuse of testing. Though such instances are difficult to document statistically, the following is a partial list of some of the abuses observed by those familiar with testing practices in schools:[11]

- Failure to give adequate instructions or to follow prescribed time limits in test administration.
- Administration under conditions of inadequate lighting and/or ventilation, or with other distractions to clear thinking and writing.
- Acceptance of test scores as absolute measures of aptitude or intelligence, without an understanding of the probabilistic and limited nature of legitimate predictions.
- Use of English–language test results for long–range predictions concerning students for whom English is a second language.
- Comparison of test scores between students while ignoring the limitations placed on such comparisons by the test's reliability and measurement error.
- Comparison of aptitude and achievement test scores as a measure of under– or overachievement, while ignoring test reliability and measurement error and differences in the domains of ability covered by each test. (Anderson and others have found such comparisons to be the most common use of group–administered aptitude test scores, besides tracking, in school districts where these scores are still taken seriously.)[12]
- Use of tests in making decisions for which they have limited or unknown validity.

19. Frequency of test misuse.

It is not uncommon for those who are otherwise supporters of standardized testing to complain about misuse and misinterpretation of test scores.[13] This question assesses expert opinion of the prevalence of errors

TABLE 5.1
Intelligence Test Misuse in Elementary and Secondary Schools

Source	Mean Prevalence Rating[a]	% Responding
Administration under improper conditions, such as failure to follow prescribed time limits, or in an environment with significant distractors	2.2 (.664)[b]	76.9
Use of English language test results for long-range predictions concerning students for whom English is a second language	2.41 (.74)	71.4
Comparison of test scores among students, while ignoring limitations set by test reliability and measurement error	2.8 (.76)	80.3
Comparison of intelligence and achievement test scores as a measure of under- or overachievement, while ignoring test reliability and measurement error, and differences in test domain	2.88 (.736)	79.3
Use of tests in making decisions for which they have limited or unknown validity	2.75 (.747)	80.8

[a]1 = "Rarely present," 2 = "Sometimes present," 3 = "Often present," and 4 = "Almost always present." [b]Numbers in parentheses are standard deviations.

in test use in elementary and secondary schools. Table 5.1 presents the mean prevalence ratings for each of five types of test misuse. Ratings were made on a 4–point scale, where 1 was "Rarely present," 2 was "Sometimes present," 3 was "Often present," and 4 was "Almost always present." Respondents believe all types of misuse to be at least sometimes present, with the highest ratings received for instances of overuse or overreliance on test scores that stem from ignoring test inaccuracies.

Those respondents who indicate that they work primarily in elementary or secondary education (N = 44) rate each form of test misuse as less prevalent than do the rest of the sample, but this difference is significant only for invalid decision making (2.43 vs. 2.78, p < .007).

All of the abuses listed above obviously are possible in other testing situations, but the consensus among those who have studied the problem seems to be that, with the exception of the use of invalid tests, abuses are most often found in schools, where test use is most frequent and test scores are available to many who don't fully understand them. The extent of the problem is impossible to estimate with any degree of accuracy, though experts believe such problems are at least sometimes present, but it is clear that some form of control is necessary to eliminate test misuse. Unfortunately, organizations like the American Psychological Association (APA) and American Educational Research Association (AERA), which have set up extensive guidelines for test preparation and use, are unable to enforce them in most elementary and secondary schools, where test users are not members of the relevant organizations. Nor can test publishers exercise much influence by refusing to sell their tests, as the FTC has ruled that test makers may not exchange information on known test abusers.[14] Recent court cases like *Larry P.* provide a costly and rather drastic measure of control through complete elimination of tests in certain applications, but even the courts offer limited regulation, as much test misuse does not violate any existing laws. In the end, the responsibility for proper testing falls with the school board and the community, who must ensure that those who use tests in decision making about students have an adequate understanding of their tools.

One of the great fears about test use, even among those who support testing, is that a child's knowledge of his intelligence test score, or the treatment he receives from others who know his score, may act to lower self–esteem and motivation, and, depending on how the scores are used, to stigmatize the child. The likelihood of such consequences is greatly increased when intelligence test scores are (incorrectly) interpreted by teachers and students as a measure of some immutable characteristic of the individual. Moreover, tracking in elementary and secondary schools, by which students are separated according to test score, may exacerbate the problem. Special–education classes for the mentally retarded represent an extreme form of placement through the use of tests. Evaluation, and subsequent effects on student self–concept, are a necessary part of any educational system, but intelligence and aptitude tests provide a particular danger because so much importance is placed on a single number.

While few would argue that intelligence and aptitude test scores do *not* affect self–esteem and motivation, the magnitude of this influence is difficult to measure. There have been many reports of significant positive correlations between test scores and self–concept, motivation, or expectancy, but causality remains ambiguous.[15] The evidence seems to indicate, however, that the influence of test scores on these affective variables is probably not large. (Causation in the opposite direction may not be very significant either, as the correlation may reflect the influence of a third variable, students' actual level of ability and success in school.) Brim and his associates found that high school students tended to greatly overestimate their own intelligence, as measured by test scores. This was particularly true of students with low scores. Fifty percent of students thought their scores were too low relative to their actual level of ability, while 45 percent thought their scores were accurate. Only 7 percent of the students reported lowering their self–estimates of intelligence as a result of their test scores, while 24 percent raised their estimates.[16]

Test scores are believed to influence student self–esteem and motivation via teachers' attitudes toward test results. A frequently mentioned example of test abuse involves teachers' interpreting test titles too literally. In particular, tests of aptitude or intelligence are said to be interpreted as measures of some fairly permanent aspect of the test taker. This fatalistic attitude is then conveyed to the low–scoring student. What evidence there is on this question is far from convincing. The majority of teachers in Goslin's survey indicated they believe scores on standardized intelligence tests are influenced at least as much by learned knowledge as by heredity. More than three–quarters of the teachers reported never having used intelligence test scores in any dealings with students, including the assigning of grades, advising on coursework, and reporting of scores to more than a few students.[17] (No doubt a more recent survey would find an even greater belief in environmentalism, and less reporting of test results to students.) Of course, teachers do not have to report test score results in order for those scores to influence the teacher's relationship with the student. It is interesting to note, however, that most teachers in the Goslin survey reported infrequent knowledge of student test scores. These data to some degree vitiate concerns over teachers' lack of test sophistication.

One study that continues to be widely cited as an example of the strong influence of nonintellectual factors on intelligence test scores is a 1968 experiment entitled *Pygmalion in the Classroom*.[18] At the beginning of the school year, elementary school teachers were given a list of several children who were predicted to show great gains in cognitive development, as indicated by a pretest. In fact, the names of the students were selected randomly from the students in the class. In an IQ test administered at the end of the school year, these children were found to have made significantly larger gains in IQ than their classmates. While the study was designed to show the effects of teacher expectancy on subsequent test score, it also demonstrates that a teacher's belief about a student's score may influence the student–teacher relationship. The experiment has come under attack for some rather severe methodological flaws,[19] and the IQ results have not been replicated, despite at least a dozen attempts to do so. A recent review of *Pygmalion* studies by S. W. Raudenbush reveals that the effects of teacher knowledge on student academic performance are well established, but that overall the effects of teacher knowledge on student IQ are of borderline significance, and that these effects are almost entirely restricted to situations where the teacher has had very little prior contact with the student, and only in the first and second grades.[20] What is unfortunate about *Pygmalion*, like Heber's Milwaukee Project, is that the IQ results continue to be reported so uncritically in academic texts and in more popular literature. That these results are consistent with an extreme environmentalist position regarding IQ ensures their continued popularity, despite their questionable empirical status.

20. On the average, how much effect do you believe a teacher's knowledge of a student's intelligence test score has on the student's academic performance?

Here we ask about the more general phenomenon of the *Pygmalion* effect on academic performance rather than the discredited IQ results. Answers were given on a 4–point scale, where 1 was "No significant effect," 2 was "Some effect," 3 was "A moderate effect," and 4 was "A large effect." The mean rating of 2.60 (s.d. = .85, r.r. = 87.7%) indicates that experts believe teachers' knowledge of test scores have, on average, a small to moderate effect on student academic performance. Such influence might be either positive or negative: low–scoring students might be harmed by teachers who spend more time with students who learn most easily, or they might benefit from teachers who concentrate their energies on students most in need of help.

21. On the average, how much of an effect do you believe a student's knowledge of his or her intelligence test score has on the student's academic performance?

This question represents one variant of the idea that students may be stigmatized by lower test scores. These scores may affect other aspects of student behavior as well. In the present case, the mean rating is 2.44 (s.d. = .788, r.r. = 84.9%) on the same scale used in the previous question. Once again, the effect of test scores on student behavior might be positive as well as negative.

As noted, most teachers report giving information about intelligence scores to only a few students. The majority of secondary–school teachers surveyed by Goslin in 1967 believed that specific information about intelligence test scores should only be reported to students in special cases. This secrecy may be due, in part, to a belief in the possible effects of test score on a student's self–esteem. Robert Ebel has identified three primary justifications for the long–standing tradition of secrecy in reporting test results.[21] First, complete information on the meaning of test results is too complex for those without the proper training. Second, those who don't understand the scores will misuse them. Third, it spares those who use the scores from having to explain and justify their decision making. In arguing for more openness in reporting test results, Ebel points out that decision–making processes should be accessible to those whom the decisions affect, and that much misuse can be avoided if the meaning of test results are explained carefully.

Certainly, there is great potential for abuse if IQ scores are reported to parents and students without a proper explanation of what the score represents. Many have suggested that such abuses can be minimized through the use of criterion–referenced rather than norm–referenced tests. Students are less likely to suffer a loss of self worth and parents are less likely to criticize tests (because they believe the tests are attempting to measure something about their child's innate worth) if scores are reported in terms of percentage of material mastered rather than by a comparison with other test takers. Unfortunately, criterion referencing is only applicable for achievement tests, not tests of aptitude or intelligence where there is no independent criterion to which performance can be compared. Since Binet, intelligence has been defined relative to the performance of others. Much misinterpretation of results may therefore be unavoidable unless those receiving the scores have a good understanding of the various concepts of reliability and validity as they relate to any particular intelligence test.

Test reporting practices have changed somewhat from the picture presented by the Brim et al. and Goslin studies due to the passage of the Educational Rights and Privacy Act of 1974. Also known as the Buckley Amendment, this law requires educational institutions receiving federal financial assistance to allow students or their parents access to the students' academic files, and also to ensure complete confidentiality. However, unless schools make a point of reporting intelligence test results along with a detailed explanation of their meaning, the law makes it more likely that parents and students will have access to IQ scores that they don't fully understand. For many nonprofessionals, the IQ continues to carry the aura of a linear scale of human worth. For this reason, and many of the others listed above, Jensen, one of testing's staunchest supporters, has joined critics in arguing against general IQ testing of all students as a regular part of the academic curriculum. He favors intelligence testing only for research and for diagnoses of mental retardation and other learning problems.[22] Recognizing that the identification of academic talent among the culturally and educationally disadvantaged is also a legitimate justification for intelligence testing, Jensen believes such testing should be carried out through group administration by an outside agency that only reports the scores of high–potential students.

There is a widespread belief that the potential stigmatizing effects of intelligence testing are greatest when tests are used for ability grouping, or tracking, in elementary and secondary schools. Creating homogeneous classrooms according to ability level has the intention of providing each student with a more individualized level of instruction. The primary reason for the great expansion in the use of IQ tests in schools following World War I was their use in the establishment of homogeneous classrooms.[23] Though there is still a strong belief among many educators that intelligence tests can be used to provide the appropriate education for each student's abilities, tracking per se is not as common as it was. Particularly at the elementary–school level, the evidence indicates that ability grouping has little effect on how much students learn. What positive effects there are generally occur with high–ability students; low–ability students actually seem to do worse when grouped only with students of similar aptitude.[24] These results, along with the perception that ability grouping is stigmatizing to those in lower ability groups, has led to a decline in the use of tracking in many schools.

In fact, the effects of tracking on student self–esteem and motivation are difficult to document. Being placed in the "dummies" class can't be good for either one's public or private image. (Euphemistic labels for ability groups like "bluebirds" and "cardinals" are unlikely to fool anyone.) The question is, however, not whether such labeling has negative effects, but how these effects compare to the alternative. Is it worse to be assigned to a slow learners class, or to be a slow learner in a heterogeneous classroom? To what extent does placement in lower ability groups become a self–fulfilling prophecy, producing lower ability students with little motivation to improve, and to what extent might students be more motivated to improve when they are better able to compete with their classmates? The relative amounts of stigmatization present in homogeneous and heterogeneous classrooms have not been clearly demonstrated, but neither have the educational benefits of tracking.

All of this is not to say that individualized instruction should be, or has been, eliminated. The trend these days is toward "mainstreaming," in which students work closer to their own pace, but within heterogeneous classrooms. (Being among the slowest students in a mainstreamed class may or may not be less stigmatizing than being an average student in a low–ability track, but these ill effects cannot be blamed on IQ tests.) At the high school level, tracking is still quite common, but generally involves the student's own choice between career– and college–oriented curricula (though counselors, who have access to test scores, obviously influence these decisions). Nor should the stigmatizing effects of tracking be blamed entirely on intelligence tests. Even in 1963, when two–thirds of high school students reported being tracked in elementary school and three–quarters in high school,[25] an experiment in which teachers were asked to assign imaginary students to regular or advanced classes revealed that most teachers were at least as influenced by recommendations from other teachers and counselors as by aptitude and achievement test data.[26] A more recent review indicates that only a small percentage of school systems practicing ability grouping use test scores as the sole criterion for placement, and among the rest tests play only a secondary role in tracking decisions.[27]

Also, many of the tests that are used in counseling and curriculum decision making are tests of achievement or interest inventories, and not IQ or aptitude tests.

An area where intelligence tests continue to be used heavily, and where stigmatizing effects are believed to be great, is in the placement of students into special–education programs for the mentally handicapped. Recommendation for placement in special classes is usually made by a school psychologist or similar professional after a student has been referred for examination by a teacher, counselor, or parent as a result of extreme difficulty in the classroom. The examination almost invariably involves an individually administered IQ test such as the Stanford–Binet or WISC, but also generally includes sensory–motor and other psychological testing, an investigation of social background, and tests of adaptive behavior. The original Binet–Simon test was developed primarily to aid in the identification of mentally retarded students, and such diagnoses remain one of the fundamental legitimate uses for IQ tests. In many states, IQ must fall below a certain score (usually 75 or 80) before an individual can be considered mentally retarded, and thus eligible for special placement, but low IQ is not the sole criterion for such placement even in these jurisdictions. For example, one study of a California school district found that only 52 percent of those students with scores below the cutoff were assigned to classes for the educable mentally retarded (EMR).[28] Among the additional factors influencing placement are often achievement test scores; in general, students placed in EMR and other special education classes tend to have achieved less (before placement) than students of similar IQ not so placed.

The controversy over the use of intelligence tests in the labeling of the retarded usually is concerned with those individuals labeled educable mentally retarded (EMR), whose IQs are at the low end of the distribution, representing mild retardation, but are not so low (e.g., less than 55) as to be considered moderately or profoundly mentally retarded. In the latter group, known as clinical retardates, retardation usually is associated with a specific neurological or physiological deficit. Such retardation generally is diagnosed early in life, and these individuals rarely find themselves in public schools, having difficulty coping with even the most rudimentary tasks. It is clinical retardation, such as among those suffering from Down's syndrome, that most of us think of when we hear "mental retardation."

This is not the group to which the EMR label applies. The educable mentally retarded are classified primarily as sociocultural retardates and appear to represent the low end of the normal IQ distribution. (Clinical retardates represent a hump at the low end of the distribution of IQs, and are equally likely to be found in families of all racial, ethnic, and socioeconomic classifications. Sociocultural retardates, on the other hand, are much more common among lower–scoring groups such as blacks, Hispanics, and members of lower socioeconomic classes.) These individuals have little difficulty coping with the normal demands of early childhood, but demonstrate their retardation once they start school. Such retardation generally is not associated with any specific physiological abnormalities. The label "retardate" for these children is an unfortunate one, both because it tends to be associated with more extreme conditions and because parents and others who see that children are well adapted in other areas of life are then told by school officials that the child is retarded. The anger and frustration produced by such an obvious contradiction leads to action like the *Larry P.* case, in which intelligence tests are singled out as an easy target, though tests clearly are not the cause of the EMR diagnosis.

There has been much criticism of EMR classes and placement methods, including the claim that these classes offer little in the way of positive education and in the end do more harm than good through the stigmatizing effects of the label "mentally retarded."[29] In fact, there is little evidence for either positive or negative long–term effects of EMR placement. The possible stigmatizing effects of EMR placement have been examined from numerous perspectives, including the child's self–perception, the opinions of his peers and teachers, and effects on academic competence. A review of this research by Donald MacMillan, Reginald Jones, and Gregory Aloia reveals that the data are at best equivocal; there is no "support for the notion that labeling has long–lasting and devastating effects on those labeled."[30] Neither, however, was another review able to find substantial positive effects on either academic achievement or social adjustment from placement in EMR classes.[31] At present, EMR placement seems to be on the decline, as the Education for All Handicapped Children Act of 1975 (which requires that all handicapped children, including the mentally handicapped, be given individualized education) has put the emphasis on special education and services within mainstreamed classes. Further regulations established in 1977 require that no single procedure, including tests, be used for placing students in EMR classes.

An important element in Judge Peckham's decision in *Larry P.* was his belief that black children were being deprived of educational opportunity by being placed in "stigmatizing" and "inferior" EMR classes. The data do not support such a conclusion, nor should the evidence presented to Judge Peckham have led him to such a belief. Witnesses for the plaintiffs had few comments about the actual content of EMR instruction, despite the insistence of the plaintiffs' attorneys that these classes were educationally inferior dead ends. Defense witnesses, on the other hand, described EMR classes as carefully monitored, much slower forms of the regular curriculum, including vocational training (for older students) in addition to traditional academic subjects.[32] Whether or not this description is accurate, Judge Peckham should have had little choice, given the evidence he heard, but to conclude that EMR classes are not inferior dead–end tracks. Particularly compelling with regard to stigmatization is that when four of the named plaintiffs, all teenagers and all veterans of EMR placement, took the stand, only one expressed awareness of being labeled mentally retarded.[33] But the facts never mattered much in the *Larry P.* case, as they have not throughout much of the IQ controversy. Samuel Guskin, in concurring with the conclusions of the Macmillan et al. review of stigmatization research, accurately assessed the situation: "The labeling controversy is in actuality a political argument between those who support the current suystem of special education and psychological diagnosis as a constructive and altruistic arrangement and those who wish to break up that system because they see it as oppressive and destructive."[34]

22. Assuming that placement of white children into classes for the educable mentally retarded (EMR) is to continue, are you in favor of the use of individually administered intelligence tests as one of the criteria for such placement?

23. Assuming that placement of black children into EMR classes is to continue, are you in favor of the use of individually administered intelligence tests as one of the criteria for such placement?

In the *Larry P.* case, Judge Peckham found intelligence tests biased and invalid, and placed a moratorium on the use of such tests for the placement of students into EMR classes. We assessed expert opinion of this conclusion. Eighty–three percent of those surveyed responded to each of the questions above. Among those experts responding, 95 percent believe IQ tests should be used for white students, and 92 percent believe they should be used for black students. These results indicate that the racial bias experts perceive in IQ tests is not sufficient in their eyes to justify discarding them.

Admissions Testing in Higher Education

One of the most frequent uses of standardized tests is for admission to colleges, and graduate and professional schools. During 1982–1983 over 1 million people took either the SAT or American College Testing Program (ACT) exam at least once. Approximately 90 percent of all U.S. colleges and universities require that applicants take one or the other test. The proportion of graduate and professional schools requiring tests like the Graduate Record Examination (GRE), Law School Admission Test

(LSAT), and Medical College Admission Test (MCAT) is similar.[35] Few things provoke more anxiety in students than contemplation of SATs and similar exams, yet standardized tests are a necessary evil to nearly all those who seek higher education.

There remains some question as to the status of admissions tests as measures of aptitude or achievement. The publishers of the SAT and GRE, the Educational Testing Service (ETS), over the years have changed their public stance about the status of their tests, largely in response to public criticism. Christopher Jencks and James Crouse, in a 1982 critique of the SAT, point out that a 1959 ETS publication tells ten–year–olds that "Your scholastic ability is like an engine. It is the source of your power and speed in school: It tells you how fast and how far you *can* go."[36] Jencks and Crouse join others in criticizing ETS for misleading test takers into thinking their scores reflect a relatively permanent attribute.[37] More recent ETS statements explicitly recognize these difficulties:

> A common misconception is that these tests somehow measure innate unchanging abilities. In fact, they measure learned skills. They are described as aptitude tests because they are not tied to a particular course of study, curriculum or program, and because they are typically used to assess students' relative abilites to perform well in future academic work.[38]

This definition of aptitude tests is consistent with that put forth in Chapter 2. As long as the ETS admissions tests are dependent on knowledge common to virtually all test takers (e.g., in the case of the SAT, English usage and mathematics to which all second–year high school students have been exposed), these tests will act as measures of aptitude, and we may treat them as such. (The problem of student perception remains, however. Warner Slack and Douglas Porter, echoed by Jencks and Crouse, argue that the belief that there is little one can do to improve SAT scores undermines student motivation to take more challenging courses and to study harder in high school.)[39]

Despite their widespread use, aptitude tests are not the most important determinant of admissions to colleges, a position reserved for high school grade point average (GPA). Rodney Skager has reviewed the relevant evidence for the National Academy of Sciences, and found that most undergraduate institutions surveyed indicate that test scores are a very important factor in admissions decisions, but not as important as high school grades. Absolute test score cutoffs are almost unheard of. Interviews and letters of recommendation, while often used, generally are not as influential as grades or test scores.[40] This rank–ordering of criteria seems to be an accurate reflection of their validity in predicting college GPA, at least during the first year. High school GPA correlates about 0.50 with first–year–college GPA, while the correlation between SAT score and college GPA is approximately 0.40.[41] Using high school GPA and SAT scores together provides better prediction than using either alone. (First–year grades in graduate and professional schools actually seem to be predicted somewhat better by admissions test scores than by college GPA, but even here, the two together provide superior prediction.)[42]

The use of the SAT and other aptitude tests in admissions to higher education has been criticized because of the tests' relatively small predictive accuracy for first–year grades (only 16 percent of the variance accounted for in the case of the SAT), and because test scores predict other criteria of success, like later grades, probability of graduation, and later–life accomplishments, even less well. But the use of a selection device is always a relative question: how does selection with the device compare to selection without it? The fact is, we cannot predict these other criteria for success very well at the time a student is applying for admission, regardless of the selection instruments used. Robert Klitgaard's recent *Choosing Elites* is a careful study of selection procedures at selective colleges and graduate programs. Klitgaard reviews research on the ability of numerous criteria, including GPA, test scores, interviews, and biographical data, to predict academic performance and several later life intellectual, economic, and personality variables. He concludes that the only variable we seem able to predict with any reasonable validity is academic performance, primarily early in school, and that using test scores as one criterion for selection provides significantly better prediction than does selection without test scores.[43] He also demonstrates that the apparently small improvement in prediction offered by admissions tests can make a significant difference (almost one–third of a standard deviation for selective colleges) in the average academic ability of students at a university.[44]

Moreover, the relatively low validity coefficients between admissions test scores and subsequent GPA are misleading for at least two reasons. First, there is the problem of restriction of range. A correlation of 0.40 represents the relationship between SAT score and GPA of only those students admitted to college—students with higher SAT scores. Including all applicants would increase the range of SAT scores and, presumably, the range of GPAs, thus increasing the correlation and the test's apparent predictive power. Robert Linn has demonstrated, through an examination of 726 LSAT validity studies, that the higher the variance in LSAT score in the validation sample, the higher the predictive validity of the test.[45] Second, validity coefficients are depressed by the fact that they are not corrected for the unreliability of the test and sampling fluctuations among validity studies.[46]

That admissions tests provide predictive validity over and above that of GPA alone is probably a result of variation in the quality and grading standards of high schools and colleges. Standardized tests give admissions officers a measure of student ability that cuts across differences in schools and in nonacademic factors affecting grades. Despite recent accusations, most notably by Allan Nairn and his associates in *The Reign of ETS*, that the ETS tests are primarily a means of propagating existing social stratifications, these tests historically have acted as a democratizing force. The advent of the SAT and other admissions tests actually increased minority enrollment in schools of higher education, as students were no longer drawn only from the most prestigious private and public schools, and on the basis of more subjective criteria. As Robert Linn puts it:

> At a time when tests are under attack because they allegedly give some students an unfair advantage relative to other students, especially the poor and minority students, it is desirable to recognize that the lack of comparability of grades from one school to another, from one curriculum to another, or from one college to another is a potentially important source of unfairness. The student who attends a school with less demanding standards for grades is given an advantage [in GPA] relative to his or her counterpart attending a school with more demanding standards.[47]

Admissions officers are aware of these inequities, and are likely to downplay a high GPA from a minority student in an inner–city high school without corroborating evidence from test scores.

Regardless of the essential fairness or validity of admissions tests, the controversy over these tests is moot for the vast majority of applicants. As mentioned in Chapter 1, most colleges are not very selective. A survey conducted by the College Entrance Examination Board reveals that the median proportion of applicants accepted by public 4–year colleges in the United States is 80 percent (70 percent for private colleges), thus undercutting much argument about overreliance on aptitude test scores for important life decisions.[48] The only places where admission seems to be highly selective are in the most prestigious, and in graduate and professional schools, where many more apply than can be accepted.

Stiff competition for places in highly selective colleges and graduate and professional schools means that a large number of applicants will have high GPAs and aptitude test scores. Other admissions criteria therefore become important, and graduate and professional schools typically put more weight on interviews, essays, and letters of recommendation than do most colleges, though still not as much weight as they put on test scores and grades.[49] The narrow range of grades and test scores among those accepted means, however, that accurate measures of predictive validity are very difficult to obtain. There is also the potential for abuse, as admissions decisions may be made on the basis of score differentials that have little meaning given the test's measurement error.

In an effort to reduce such misuse, the LSAT recently has been changed from a 200–800 grading scale to a 10–48 scale, so that differences in test score are more meaningful. Beyond this, admissions officers must be careful not to base any decision too heavily on a single measure known to have limited predictive validity. (In what is otherwise an exceedingly glib discussion of the "myth" of scholastic aptitude, David Owen admits in *None of the Above* that "[e]very admissions officer I've ever talked to has told me that no student with good grades was ever rejected solely because his test scores were low.")[50] *All other things being equal,* one is statistically better off choosing a student with a 700 verbal SAT over one with a 690. But other things are rarely equal, and the wise decision in such a case is to treat these two scores as equivalent, and look to other criteria. (In the typical large–scale admissions situation, this translates into near–exclusive reliance on grades and test scores for those with very high or very low numbers, and increasing use of other criteria near the margin.) The situation is potentially more serious in those situations where test scores are used for admissions to graduate programs for which no validation studies have ever been done. Such programs that use tests with a black–white score differential (which includes just about every admissions test currently in use) are prime targets for legal action.

24. Predictive validity of admissions tests.

Respondents were asked, for each of six commonly used admissions tests, whether they believe the test adds sufficient predictive validity to that available from other nontest criteria to justify its continued use in highly selective admissions decisions. Nonresponse rates are high (> 35%) for all tests but the Scholastic Aptitude Test (SAT) and the Graduate Record Examination (GRE), a result not surprising in a population consisting mostly of members of college and university departments of psychology and education. Nonetheless, the percentage of those answering who advocate continued use is remarkably high and consistent across tests. Results are: SAT, 89.6%; American College Test (ACT), 87.8%; GRE, 82.2%; Law School Admission Test (LSAT), 86.6%; Medical College Admission Test (MCAT), 87.2%; and Graduate Management Admission Test (GMAT), 86.7%.

Related to the question of admissions test validity is the controversy over the effects of coaching, particularly on SAT performance. For years the ETS has vehemently denied that short–term coaching programs have any significant effect on test score, yet coaching programs like Stanley Kaplan continue to be profitable. A large proportion of the population apparently believes that coaching works. Critics see the coachability of the SAT as undermining the claim that it is a test of aptitude, as well as affecting the fairness of the test for those who cannot afford a coaching program.

The empirical research on coaching effects is extremely messy. The major problem is that most studies compare the test scores of those voluntarily in coaching programs with those who have not received coaching. The obvious difficulty here is that those who enter coaching programs may differ in other ways from those who don't, most notably in the motivation to succeed. Studies that have examined before- and after-coaching scores within groups have more often than not failed to include proper controls.[51] Two recent reviews have attempted to summarize this research, eliminating or controlling for studies using inadequate methodology.[52] The conclusions of these reviewers are nearly identical: the effect on SAT score of short-term coaching programs, while demonstrable, is too small to be of practical importance. The results of the review by Samuel Messick and Ann Jungeblut, two ETS researchers, have become the official ETS line: score gain is an increasing function of amount of time spent studying; truly meaningful (in terms of admission to college) score differences do not appear until study time is equivalent to several high school courses, preparation the ETS has always maintained is relevant to SAT performance.

In 1976, the Federal Trade Commission (FTC) began an investigation to determine whether companies offering SAT coaching courses were defrauding their customers. The initial FTC report, completed in 1978, indicates that substantial score gains are possible through commercially available coaching courses.[53] Public release of the report was held up, possibly as a result of pressure from ETS, while the data were reanalyzed. The final report, issued in 1979, contains many of the controls found in the reviews cited above, and concludes that small but significant gains are possible.[54] At the time the report was released, an FTC spokesman stressed that the report was not to be interpreted as an endorsement of coaching. This disavowal, along with the delay for reanalysis (the staff attorney at the Boston FTC office in charge of the investigation resigned while his report remained unreleased) raises numerous unanswered questions about the political climate surrounding this government report.

Much of *None of the Above* is devoted to David Owen's contention that the SAT is a highly coachable test that can be "beat" if one understands the way the test makers are thinking. Owen praises the Princeton Review, a coaching program that uses many of these principles, and that has reported great success in producing very large SAT gains among its students. The Princeton Review is the kind of program that has been downplayed in reviews of coaching effects, due to lack of proper controls. Thus far, however, no scientific studies of Princeton Review effects have been reviewed. That there are large differences between coaching programs in degree of reported improvement seems to indicate that there is something that some programs do better than others. Glossing over these differences in concatenating research results may obscure important variables; not all coaching programs are created equal. As David Owen puts it, "Having heard that the Wright brothers have taken off at Kitty Hawk, ETS samples the general state of aviation and announces that man, on average, can't fly."[55] Of course, many of those who examine the Princeton Review results may not find this demonstration quite as compelling as the Wright brothers'.

If the SAT is coachable, it may be economically unfair. Those who cannot afford a coaching program, or whose high schools do not provide them, will be at a disadvantage when taking the test. The fairness of this situation, however, depends on the relation between coaching effects and the validity of the test. Critics assume that coaching undermines test validity (apparently, so does the ETS), but this has not been empirically demonstrated. The question is, does a student who has raised his SAT verbal score from 500 to 600 as a result of some coaching program do more poorly in college, on average, than a student who received a 600 without coaching? If not, and test scores mean the same thing for both the coached and uncoached, then coaching is a legitimate way to improve the actual college-relevant aptitude the test is measuring. Those who do not receive coaching would be at a *disadvantage* relative to those who do, but the test is not biased or unfair toward them.

The controversy over admissions testing has entered the public policy arena in recent years with the debate and subsequent passage of the 1980 Truth-in-Testing Law in New York State. This law requires test makers, who are not subject to the Buckley Amendment, to release the contents and answers of their tests to the general public shortly after administration of an exam. In addition, test takers have the right to see their exams in order to determine which questions they answered incorrectly. (A similar but slightly less stringent law has recently been passed in California.) The ETS, against whose tests the law was primarily directed, argued against the law, not because they felt that the general public would misuse results (SAT scores are routinely reported to test takers, though this was not the case early in the test's history), but because the development of a completely new test for each administration would significantly increase the cost to the test taker, putting a disproportionate burden on the economically disadvantaged. In addition, by being forced to produce tests at a more rapid pace without reusing test questions, test makers argued that test validity would be reduced, increasing the chance of bias and unfair selection.

The law's proponents, led by members of the Nader organization, felt that test takers' have a right to know as much as possible about their performance on tests that play such a critical role in important life decisions, and they presented evidence that test development represents only a small fraction of the cost of each test to ETS.[56] There was also the hope that complete disclosure would lead to great improvements in the quality and fairness of admissions testing, as test makers were forced to reveal more of their practices and rely on less secretive methods of test validation. (It is apparent from *The Reign of ETS* that the real agenda of Nader and his supporters is far more ambitious than increased accountability; they share with other egalitarian social reformers the desire to undermine testing.) There is little to indicate, however, that the law has had much effect on test practices, other than the elimination of a few ambiguous questions and the correction of clerical errors in scoring.[57] The ETS has gone to a policy of voluntary disclosure nationwide, probably to avoid what they feared would be an even harsher pending federal law. When the New York law had teeth, however, less than 2 percent of SAT takers requested to see their exam.[58] From a public relations standpoint, complete disclosure is probably in the best interests of the testing industry. By presenting an image of secrecy and distrust rather than complete candor, test makers only intensify the present crisis in public confidence about testing.

25. Do you approve or disapprove of complete disclosure laws such as New York's truth–in–testing law, which require admissions test makers to release the contents and answers of their tests to the general public within a specified time afer test administration?

Most expert respondents are not in favor of truth–in–testing legislation. Fifty percent of experts surveyed either somewhat or strongly disapprove, compared to 32 percent who either somewhat or strongly approve. Six percent are indifferent, and 12 percent did not respond.

Employment Testing

The incidence of aptitude and intelligence testing in employment is difficult to measure, particularly in the private sector. Some information can be drawn from a 1975 survey of approximately 1,300 personnel officers of companies ranging widely in size and type of business.[59] Test use is broken down by type of decision (ranging from hiring decisions for unskilled hourly workers to entry–level and promotion decisions for supervisory, managerial, and professional positions) and by type of employer (including manufacturers, retail stores, banks, and transportation and communications companies). Nearly half of all companies surveyed report using some form of test in hiring decisions, while 24 percent use tests in determining promotions. Large companies are more frequent test users, but even among companies with fewer than 100 employees, 30 percent administer tests as part of their hiring procedure, and 18 percent use them in determining promotions. Nonetheless, most employers do not use tests for most employment decisions. (Nor are these tests usually vital to the employment decision, as fewer than one in five companies report disqualifying applicants on the basis of test scores alone.) The notable exception is in the hiring of clerical workers, where more than two–thirds of all firms use at least one employment test, the bulk of such testing involving clerical achievement and work samples.

Across all categories of decisions and employers, the majority of tests used are nonaptitude tests, including tests of achievement (job–specific knowledge), work samples, and personality inventories. Rarely is the proportion of employers reporting the use of general aptitude tests for any of these employment decisions greater than 5 percent. However, because in most of these categories over 70 percent of companies report using no tests at all, general aptitude tests represent a sizable proportion of all tests given.

Employment testing is much more common in the public sector than in private industry. Most federal, state, and municipal employees work under a merit system involving civil service examinations.[60] These exams are primarily job–specific achievement tests, but aptitude testing is not uncommon in government employment. The most widely used employment test in the country is the Armed Services Vocational Aptitude Battery (ASVAB), given annually to all candidates for American military service, as well as to hundreds of thousands of high school seniors.[61] The test is used to find promising candidates for the military, as a screening device, and to guide enlistees into appropriate occupational categories. Prior to 1981, the Professional and Administrative Career Examination (PACE), another aptitude battery, was taken each year by over 150,000 applicants for entry–level positions in the federal government.[62]

The elimination of PACE by a 1981 consent decree is but one example of the state of employment testing since the Supreme Court decision in *Griggs v. Duke Power Co.*[63] The *Griggs* decision, discussed in Chapter 1, established the two–step process necessary for demonstrating discrimination in testing litigation brought under Title VII of the Civil Rights Act of 1964 (prohibiting unfair labor practices): the plaintiff carries the burden of establishing a prima facie case of discrimination through adverse impact. (The Supreme Court has ruled that in Title VII cases involving testing, plaintiffs do not have to show discriminatory intent, only adverse impact.)[64] Once established, the burden is on the defendant to show that the test in question is a "reasonable measure of job performance."

The Court left unanswered the questions of precisely what constitutes adverse impact and a reasonable measure of job performance, but in *Griggs* and subsequent litigation courts have interpreted adverse impact broadly, while requiring strict validity criteria.[65] Consequently, only a small fraction of employment tests have ever withstood legal challenge. Establishment of the prima facie case requires statistical evidence, but whether one compares pass/fail ratios between groups or notes differences in the racial composition of the successful and unsuccessful applicant pools, inferior performance by minority groups on standardized tests is not difficult to document. The burden of proof in Title VII litigation therefore generally falls on the test user to demonstrate that the test is sufficiently related to job performance to justify its use.

While sufficient validity criteria have never been clearly established, the Supreme Court, in a subsequent case (*Albemarle Paper Co. v. Moody*)[66] endorsed the Equal Employment Opportunity Commission's (EEOC) *Guidelines on Employment Testing Procedures*. As noted, the EEOC *Guidelines* rely heavily on the APA's *Standards for Educational and Psychological Tests*, establishing a set of minimum validation procedures that most employers find impossible to satisfy completely. The *Guidelines* require either criterion, content, or construct validation relating to important aspects of job performance, as well as an investigation of "fairness" (differential prediction or validity) to minority groups in appropriate circumstances. The validation studies generally must meet the APA *Standards*, which were intended for test developers with sufficient resources for sophisticated psychometric analyses. In situations where adequate validation is not possible for the job in question, representing the vast majority of cases, the employer must demonstrate sufficient similarity between the job and those for which the test is adequately validated. With such stringent criteria, and the courts' own discretion, tests with adverse impact have been struck down by virtue of almost every failure at justification imaginable.[67] In 1973, the Iowa Supreme Court, in a review of federal decisions, "failed to disclose a single example of a written test passing muster under the [EEOC] guidelines for validation."[68]

While there has been some loosening of these requirements in post–*Albemarle* decisions, the recent history of employment testing litigation is marked by a great deal of inconsistency and judicial misunderstanding of the nature of validation.[69] (Part of the problem stems from the 1976 Supreme Court decision in *Washington v. Davis*,[70] in which the Court accepted validation methods inconsistent with the *Guidelines* in a case involving a constitutional challenge. Lower courts are split as to whether less stringent requirements may also be acceptable in Title VII actions.)[71] Because most employers are not able to provide the kind of criterion validation necessary to justify the use of general aptitude tests for most jobs, employers have more and more had to rely on achievement tests and narrow work samples for which they can show content validity. Moreover, even the existence of extensive criterion validation may be insufficient to defend a test against charges of discrimination; witness the cases of PACE and the New York City police sergeant's exam described in Chapter 1. For many employers, the response to the climate of fear created by testing litigation and government pronouncements about testing has been to eliminate employment testing altogether. The employer survey presented at the beginning of this section was conducted in 1975. Three-quarters of the employers surveyed reported that they had reduced the size of their employment testing programs during the previous five years. No doubt a similar survey conducted today would find the incidence of employment testing further diminished.

Tests of intelligence and general aptitude are probably the easiest targets of Title VII suits, because they bear the least obvious relation to job performance; they lack both face and content validity, and are also less likely to have been validated against specific job-related criteria. The irony of court decisions in this area is that tests of general intellectual ability are probably the best available criterion of job performance. John Hunter and his colleagues have reviewed the available evidence on the validity of various predictors of job performance, including peer ratings, interviews, biographical data, college GPA, and achievement and work-sample tests.[72] For entry-level positions, across all job categories, general ability tests are the best predictor of job performance. For promotion decisions, work samples are slightly better predictors. Moreover, general ability tests have the advantage over specific achievement and work sample tests in that they are valid predictors of successful performance for nearly all jobs in all settings. Thus, an employer using only work sample tests in hiring employees may be able to select those who will perform well at a certain entry level position, but loses much of the ability provided by general aptitude tests to discriminate between those who will be most promotable to other jobs.

The elimination of employment tests that bear little relation to job performance, but which have adverse impact on certain minority groups, is an admirable goal. Such test misuse undoubtedly occurs, as employers, much like teachers, are often too quick to assume that a given test measures abilities important to their purpose. In this sense the EEOC and Title VII have been successful watchdogs. Unfortunately, overzealous interpretation of Title VII by the courts has led to the elimination of many useful testing programs as well. The original motivation behind standardized testing in employment, as in education, was to promote the allocation of resources according to merit, and thus provide more equal opportunity with regard to race, class, and ethnic background. Ironically, selection on the basis of merit thus defined has quite often led to underrepresentation of minority groups in society's most desired positions. Through strict enforcement of Title VII, along with cases like *Larry P.*, the courts have chosen to value equality of outcome over equality of opportunity.

26. Approximately what proportion of all employment tests given do you believe are improperly validated for the purpose for which they are used?

Nonresponse rate to this question is high (34.3 percent), but among those who respond, 76 percent feel that the proportion of employment tests that are not properly invalidated is moderate or worse. Only 4 percent of respondents believe that the incidence of improperly validated employment tests is insignificant, and 19 percent say the proportion is small but significant. The response to this question is the most negative rating of tests in the entire survey. Those who are conducting research or who have written articles on employment testing (N = 121) do not give significantly different responses to this question.

Two aspects of question 26 deserve comment. First, the question asks about employment tests in general, most of which are not tests of general aptitude or intelligence. Second, "improperly validated" is not necessarily "invalid." It may be that many current tests that have not been subjected to appropriate validation studies may turn out to be valid when such studies are done. The work of John Hunter et al. indicates that this is probably the case for tests of general aptitude. This possibility does an employer little good, however, when he is in court trying to defend himself against charges of racial discrimination.

Should Intelligence Testing Be Banned?

Intelligence testing has no shortage of critics who are ready to call for its immediate abolition in all or most of its applications. In 1968, the Association of Black Psychologists (ABP) called for a moratorium on the use of psychological and educational tests in schools. Two years later, 650 members of the National Education Association (NEA) made a similar request. *Larry P. v. Wilson Riles* led to the imposition of just such a ban on intelligence testing in California. Ralph Nader and associates, and others, have severely criticized the use of aptitude tests in admissions to higher education, asking for a reduction in the importance placed on tests in admissions decisions, and the replacement of aptitude tests with tests of achievement. Finally, the elimination of employment testing becomes a reality with almost every piece of Title VII testing litigation. Not included in these examples are the multitude of published critiques of testing that at least implicitly call for its elimination.[73]

A serious appraisal of the question posed in the title of this section requires an examination of the alternatives to intelligence testing in each of its applications. We have seen that intelligence tests are in many instances economical tools that aid in the assignment of resources according to an objective criterion of merit. We have also seen that these tools can be abused, and that they often have adverse impact on the educational and occupational status of members of minority groups. The critical question is whether the social cost of making important educational and occupational decisions without the use of aptitude and intelligence tests is less than we are now paying with them.

As a direct result of the ABP's request for a moratorium on testing in schools, the APA commissioned a panel to investigate the uses and abuses of testing in schools and for admissions to higher education.[74] The panel identified many abuses in test practice, and recommended steps be taken to curb misuse and misinterpretation. They also examined the question of racial bias in tests, the ABP's primary contention, and found no evidence for substantial differential predictive validity for blacks and whites on standard tests of intelligence. Finally, a number of alternatives to commonly used intelligence tests were discussed, including random lotteries, prior experience, demographic categories, subjective evaluations, and grades. The panel's conclusion was that none of the alternatives was capable of performing the function of objective assessment in curriculum placement and college admissions at a reasonable cost:

> the available alternatives to testing require either that we abandon the functions supported by testing or that we abandon the only techniques available for even-handed appraisal under conditions which make educational opportunity widely available at a cost that is within reach of both the prospective applicant and the educational institutions.[75]

One solution to the dilemma posed by the panel is to abandon certain of the functions supported by testing, as in the abolition of tracking and separate EMR classes. The alternative, chosen by the court in *Larry P.*, is to "abandon the only techniques available for even-handed appraisal." The court in this case, as in other instances of affirmative action, placed the social benefits to be derived from equal representation in special classes above the benefits of more objective assessment. Put another way, the costs of adverse impact were seen as greater than the costs of mentally retarded children not being placed in EMR classes.

In the case of admissions to higher education, the alternatives may not be as drastic. Until the number of applicants to colleges and professional schools becomes equal to or less than the number of spaces, admissions decision making cannot be eliminated, but there may be reasonable alternatives to aptitude tests. It has been noted that achievement tests developed by the ETS may actually predict college grades better than the SAT.[76] In addition to increased predictive validity, the use of achievement rather than aptitude tests has the advantage of better public image. Not only are charges of test bias less likely, but, it is argued, students will be more inclined to take test preparation, and hence high school, more seriously.[77] The complete elimination of testing for college admissions is probably not feasible as long as academic performance remains a criterion of selection. The elimination of testing will necessarily lead to a decrease in predictive validity (though this may be irrelevant for those schools that accept the vast majority of applicants). Our expert sample is nearly unanimous in the belief that admissions tests should continue to be used in making selective admissions decisions.

The Committee on Ability Testing of the National Research Council (NRC) has recently published its report on the uses, consequences, and controversies surrounding ability testing.[78] A large part of the report is concerned with testing practices in employment, and much as the APA panel did with test use in schools, the NRC committee considered alternatives to employment testing. Despite obvious abuses in employment testing, the committee was able to find "no evidence of alternatives to testing that are equally informative, equally adequate technically, and also economical and politically viable."[79] John and Ronda Hunter have recently attempted to measure the utility, in dollars of productivity, of using various predictors in employment decisions.[80] They estimate that if the federal government were to use general aptitude tests as the sole criterion for hiring decisions, it would realize a net gain in utility of $15.61 billion per year over random selection of employees. The next best alternative, actual job tryouts, improves utility by $12.49 billion. Thus, by using general aptitude tests rather than the next best alternative, which is often not feasible, the federal government would be $3.12 billion more productive each year.

27. Test use.

For each of seven common intelligence and aptitude test uses, respondents were asked to indicate the importance they felt such tests should have, relative to the role they now have. Ratings were made on a 7–point scale, where 1 represented a "Severely reduced role," 4 was "Remain about the same," and 7 was "Severely increased role." Mean ratings for each test use

TABLE 5.2
Preferred Level of Intelligence and Aptitude Test Use

Use	Mean Rating[a]	% Responding
Diagnosis and special education planning in elementary and secondary schools	3.98 (1.22)[b]	79.6
Tracking decisions in elementary and secondary schools	3.43 (1.43)	77.9
College admissions	3.94 (1.14)	85.3
Graduate and professional school admissions	3.96 (1.27)	84.4
Vocational counseling	4.01 (1.32)	77.3
Hiring Decisions	3.36 (1.5)	74.3
Promotion decisions	2.89 (1.54)	73.2

[a]1 = "Severely reduced role," 4 = "Remain about the same," and 7 = "Severely increased role."
[b]Numbers in parentheses are standard deviations.

are presented in Table 5.2. With the exception of testing in employment, and to a lesser extent in tracking decisions in elementary and secondary schools, experts seem generally satisfied with the status quo in test use. (Of course the status quo, particularly in employment testing, represents less test use than it did twenty years ago.) There appears to be a general belief in the validity of intelligence and aptitude tests for various educational purposes, despite the perception that these tests are often misused in elementary and secondary schools.

Unlike the previous question, those who are conducting research or who have written about employment tests have better things to say about them than the rest of the expert population. Employment testing experts (N = 121) rate the use of aptitude tests for both hiring decisions (4.11 vs. 3.11, p < .0001) and promotion decisions (3.56 vs. 2.67, p < .0001) higher than do the rest of the sample. These results notwithstanding, and examining the responses to this section of the questionnaire as a whole, employment testing appears to be the area in which experts perceive the most problems (even employment testing experts favor decreased use of tests in making promotion decisions).

The Effects of Demographic and Background Variables

Specific Expertise

In addition to substantive questions about testing, the questionnaire contained two sections of demographic questions. The first concerned

"Professional Activities and Involvement with Intelligence Testing." We asked these questions about specific topics of research and authorship and other experiences with testing, and sampled from a wide variety of expert groups, in order to examine the effects of more specific expertise on questionnaire responding. For each of the substantive questions discussed in this and the previous three chapters, comparisons were made between the responses of those experts whose experiences were of particular relevance and the rest of the sample. Thus, for example, those who were conducting research or who had written on bias in intelligence tests served as specific experts for the test bias questions. For some questions, specific experiences and affiliations, such as having administered a group or individual intelligence test, or being a member of the Cognitive Science Society, also served to classify respondents a experts. For the most part, the results of these comparisons are not statistically significant. The important exceptions have been described with the general results from each question. Even when these differences are significant, they are not large.

The relative lack of influence of specific expertise may be partially the result of self–selection on the part of respondents. Subjects were asked to respond "NQ" to all questions that they did not feel qualified to answer. To the degree that subjects were honest in their self–assessments, respondents are even more expert than the sample as a whole. Thus, for example, only 1 of the 168 subjects who answered NQ to question 9 on the sources of heritability evidence is a member of the Behavior Genetics Association, or is conducting research on or has written about the heritability of intelligence. On the other hand, 83 of the 493 who answer this question are experts on heritability by one of these criteria. Such restriction of range due to self–selection makes any attempt to account for within–sample variation more difficult.

Principal–Component Analysis

In order to facilitate further analyses, supervariables were created from substantive question responses via principal–component analysis, a method of partitioning variance very similar to factor analysis. (See Appendix B for the details of the principal–component and subsequent multivariate analyses.) Four interpretable factors emerge from this analysis, accounting for 12.1%, 11.3%, 9.2%, and 6.3% of the variance. They were labeled "Test Usefulness," "Test Bias," "Personal Characteristics," and "Test Misuse." The first factor reveals the following pattern: belief in a consensus about intelligence, in an adequate theory of intelligence and ir the importance of IQ in determining SES, opposition to truth–in–testing laws, and particularly high loadings for all test uses. The substantial loadings for factor two are almost entirely for the various test bias questions. Factor three has high loadings for all of the nonintellectual characteristics in question 8, as well as for the sections of question 16 dealing with bias caused by anxiety and motivation. The fourth factor picks up all four sources of test misuse (question 19) that were included in the analysis. The only questions that do not load on any of the four factors are numbers 5, 6, and 9 on acquired knowledge, stability, and the sources of heritability evidence, the latter no doubt the result of too little variation in responding.

Supervariables were formed corresponding to each of the four factors by combining normalized responses to each of the questions loading on each factor. Table 5.3 presents correlations between the four supervariables and various demographic and background variables. Many of these correlations are highly significant, but few are very large. The effects of demographic and background variables were also examined for each of the substantive questions separately, and correlations are not substantially different. Other background variables not shown, such as ethnic background and religious preference, show only very low correlations (–.10) with supervariables.

Gender. Seventy–two percent of respondents are male. Males hold significantly more traditional pro–testing attitudes: they are more in favor of test use, less likely to rate tests as misused or biased, and less likely to rate nonintellectual personal characteristics as important to test performance.

Age. The mean age of respondents is fifty–two years. Age also bears a significant positive relation to traditional pro–testing views concerning test use and misuse. The negative correlation between age and Test Bias is marginally significant ($p < .015$).

General Expertise. Defined as the number of articles or chapters written on testing and related issues, general expertise, like age and masculinity, is associated with traditional pro–testing views. Authorship has a significant positive correlation with Test Usefulness and a significant negative correla-

TABLE 5.3
Correlations Between Supervariables and Demographic and Background Variables

Variable Misuse	Test Usefulness	Test Bias	Personal Characteristics	Test
Gender[a]	−.15**	.22**	.18**5st	.15**
Age	.30**	−.10	−.06	−.12*
General Expertise	.15**	−.06	−.13**	−.07
Political Perspective[b]	.31**	−.38**	−.06	−.17**
Media Exposure	.08**	−.11*	−.11*	.00
Childhood Family Income	−.10*	.04	.00	.00

[a]1 = Male, 2 = Female. [b]Higher numbers correspond to conservatism.
*$p < .01$. **$p < .001$.

tion with Personal Characteristics. As with specific expertise, the size of the general expertise correlations are small relative to those of other demographic and background variables such as gender, age, and political perspective.

Political Perspective. This variable in Table 5.3 represents the same supervariable described at the end of the last chapter. Political perspective is significantly related to all supervariables except Personal Characteristics, and has the strongest correlation with these supervariables among all demographic and background variables. Political conservatism is associated with traditional views about the validity and usefulness of intelligence tests and low levels of bias and test misuse. Despite being the best single predictor of substantive question response, political perspective accounts for less than 10 percent of the variance.

Media Exposure. Thirty–three percent of respondents had served as a source of information for the news media on intelligence testing or related issues at least once during the two years previous to the survey. Small but significant negative correlations are found between media exposure and Test Bias and Personal Characteristics. There is a marginally significant positive correlation with Test Usefulness ($p < .03$). Media exposure is thus associated with slightly more pro–testing views.

Childhood Family Income. On a 5–point scale with 1 as "Well below average," and 5 as "Well above average," in comparison to other American families at the time, the mean rating of childhood family income is 2.83 (s.d. $= 1.07$, r.r. $= 96.8\%$), or slightly below average. There is a small but significant negative correlation between childhood family income and Test Usefulness. In other words, those who were poorer as children hold slightly more favorable views toward intelligence test use. Making the not unreasonable assumption that both present income and IQ among respondents are above average for the American population, it is possible that those with below average childhood family incomes see their performance on intelligence tests as having helped improve their economic condition.

Multivariate Analysis

Stepwise multiple regression analyses were performed with each of the supervariables as dependent variables and the demographic and background variables as predictors. Given the small size of the correlations in Table 5.3, it was not expected that a combination of demographic and background variables would account for a large proportion of the data variance. In fact, none of the regression analyses accounts for more than 19 percent of the variance in any of the supervariables.

Two explanations for the weak predictive power of demographic and background variables suggest themselves. The supervariables used as dependent variables in the regression analyses were formed from factors accounting for a relatively small amount of the data variance (39 percent total). These factors therefore do not represent strong patterns of responding, and one might expect the supervariables based on them to be resistant to prediction. Similarly, the formation of supervariables necessitated the coding of missing values (nonresponses) as the mean of the remaining cases, thus reducing data variance and making prediction more difficult. These explanations apply only to supervariables. Unfortunately, regression analyses performed at the level of the individual question do not reveal substantially higher proportions of variance accounted for.

While in some sense disappointing, the failure to substantially predict substantive question responding is informative in its own right. The low percentage of variance accounted for by the four factors emerging from principal component analysis reflects, at best, only moderate correlations between questions. These weak intercorrelations, together with the inability to predict responding from demographic and background variables, even at the individual question level, indicate that variance in responding is largely idiosyncratic. This is not to say that there are no explanations for the data variance, only that they are more likely to reside at the level of the individual respondent than in any general demographic or background variables, or in underlying factors. Fortunately, this haze of unexplained variance is not so substantial as to obscure a clear picture of expert opinion.

The survey results described over the last four chapters reveal that those with expertise in areas related to intelligence testing hold generally positive attitudes about the validity and usefulness of intelligence and aptitude tests. These experts believe that such tests adequately measure most important elements of intelligence, and that they do so in a way that is basically fair to minority groups. Intelligence, as measured by intelligence tests, is seen as important to success in our society. Both within- and between-group differences in test scores are believed to reflect significant genetic differences; for within-group differences, a majority of the variation in IQ is felt to be associated with genetic variation. Finally, there is support for the continued use of tests at their present level in elementary and secondary schools, and in admissions to schools of higher education.

The picture that emerges from this survey is not wholly positive, however. Our sample of experts perceive problems with the influence of nonintellectual factors on test performance both within and between groups, and particularly with certain test use practices. There is a widespread belief in frequent misinterpretation and overreliance on test scores in elementary and secondary schools, practices that may have a significant effect on student performance. Yet psychologists and educational specialists a e generally in favor of the continued use of intelligence and aptitude tests in schools. The use of improperly validated employment tests is believed to be common, and our sample, as a whole, favors reducing the use of intelligence and aptitude tests for this purpose. Those with specific expertise about employment testing do not, however, advocate decreased use, despite an equivalent perception of improper validation in employment testing. The attitude of these experts towards employment tests is similar to that of the rest of the sample towards testing in schools: there are significant difficulties with test use, but they are of insufficient magnitude to warrant an overall curtailment of otherwise useful decision–making tools.

One of the more puzzling aspects of our results is the relative lack of effect of within–sample variability in expertise. Our sample would seem to vary rather broadly in expertise, at least as measured by authorship, research, and academic specialty. The sample ranged from emeritus professors in the APA Division of Evaluation and Measurement with hundreds of articles and chapters written on a broad range of testing issues to members of the American Sociological Association with no measured experience in testing, yet substantive question responding was more or less the same among all these groups. Some of the diminished effect of expertise can be attributed to self–selection, as outlined earlier. It is also possible that expertise simply is not a major factor in opinions about testing. The implication of this hypothesis is that the general public's view of testing is not significantly different from that of the experts. We will have more to say about this possibility in Chapter 8.

Our inability to successfully predict differences in e ert opinions about intelligence and testing on the basis of political and social attitudes is an even more interesting finding. We described in the ast chapter how the relationship between political perspective and opinic s about test bias may help explain the discrepancy between these opinic s and the empirical data. Experts are not immune to the influence of pc itical ideology. Overall, however, ideology does not have a large influence on expert opinion, despite the highly political climate surrounding testing. That political perspective accounts for so little of the data variance, and that experts hold generally pro–testing attitudes despite being slightly left of center politically, are important points, and must be contrasted with the heavy political influence apparent in public discussion about intelligence and aptitude testing. The relative immunity of expert opinion about testing to political influence, coupled with their knowledge of the empirical literature and first–hand experience, makes it imperative that the expert voice be heard in the public arena, particularly where important decisions are being made.

Political decisions that affect the lives of almost every member of society, as those about intelligence and aptitude testing do, need not be made entirely, or even primarily, on coldly rational grounds, but they must be informed.

One of the primary mechanisms by which the public and public policy makers become informed on issues of importance is the news media. We have seen that expert opinion often contrasts sharply with criticisms of intelligence and aptitude testing and with many of the decisions about testing being made in the courts and legislatures. That policy makers seem more influenced by the critics of testing than by the opinions of experts is an indication that the expert voice is being lost somewhere between the halls of academia and public policy arenas. An examination of news media coverage of testing related issues reveals that the news media are at least partially to blame for this state of affairs.

Notes

1. Martin G. Holmen and Richard Docter, *Educational and Psychological Testing: A Study of the Industry and Its Practices* (New York: Russell Sage Foundation, 1972), p. 14.
2. Beverly Anderson, "Test Use Today in Elementary and Secondary Schools," in *Ability Testing: Uses, Consequences, and Controversies*, part II, eds. Alexandra K. Wigdor and Wendell R. Garner (Washington, DC: National Academy Press, 1982), pp. 232–285; Carl Dimengo, "Basic Testing Programs Used in Major School Systems Throughout the United States in the School Year 1977–78," Akron Public Schools, March 1978; Janie Hall, "Survey of Large Urban Districts Regarding Use of Mental Ability Tests, 1981," Oklahoma City Public Schools, 1981; National Education Association, *Nationwide Teacher Opinion Poll, 1979* (Washington, DC: Author, September 1979) (ERIC ED 178 533).
3. Dimengo, p. 7.
4. Orville G. Brim, Jr. et al., *American Beliefs and Attitudes About Intelligence Testing* (New York: Russell Sage Foundation, 1969).
5. Anderson, p. 238.
6. National Education Association, p. 21.
7. Anderson, p. 238.
8. David A. Goslin, *Teachers and Testing* (New York: Russell Sage Foundation, 1967), p. 127.
9. James G. Ward, *Teachers and Testing: A Survey of Knowledge and Attitudes* (Washington, DC: American Federation of Teachers, July 1980) (ERIC ED 193 258), p. 4.
10. J. Yeh, "Test Use in Schools," Center for the Study of Evaluation, Graduate School of Education, University of California at Los Angeles, cited in *Ability Testing: Uses, Consequences, and Controversies*, part I, eds. Alexandra K. Wigdor and Wendell R. Garner (Washington, DC: National Academy Press, 1982).
11. T. Anne Cleary et al., "Educational Uses of Tests with Disadvantaged Students," *American Psychologist* 30 (1975):21–22; Eric Gardner, "Some Aspects of the Use and Misuse of Standardized Aptitude and Achievement Tests," in *Ability Testing: Uses, Consequences, and Controversies*, part II, eds. Alexandra

K. Wigdor and Wendell R. Garner (Washington, DC: National Academy Press, 1982), pp. 315–332; Holmen and Docter; Arthur R. Jensen, *Bias in Mental Testing* (New York: Free Press, 1980), pp. 717–718.

12. Anderson, p. 238; Hall, p. 2.
13. Jensen, pp. 717–718.
14. Holmen and Docter, pp. 129–131.
15. Marjorie C. Kirkland, "The Effects of Tests on Students and Schools," *Review of Educational Research* 41 (1971):303–350.
16. Orville G. Brim, Jr., "American Attitudes Towards Intelligence Tests," *American Psychologist* 20 (1965):125–130; Brim et al.
17. Goslin, p. 133.
18. Robert Rosenthal and Lenore Jacobson, *Pygmalion in the Classroom* (New York: Holt, Rinehart, & Winston, 1968).
19. e.g., J. D. Elashoff and R. E. Snow, *"Pygmalion" Reconsidered* (Worthington, OH: Charles A. Jones, 1971); Robert L. Thorndike, "Review of *Pygmalion in the Classroom*," *American Educational Research Journal* 5 (1968):708–711.
20. S. W. Raudenbush, "What Can Research Tell Us About the Effects of Teacher Expectancy on Pupil IQ?" unpublished thesis, Harvard Graduate School of Education, 1982.
21. Robert L. Ebel, "The Social Consequences of Educational Testing," in *Testing Problems in Perspective*, ed. Anne Anastasi (Washington, DC: American Council on Education, 1966).
22. Jensen, p. 718–723.
23. Daniel Resnick, "History of Educational Testing," in *Ability Testing: Uses, Consequences, and Controversies*, part II, eds. Alexandra K. Wigdor and Wendell R. Garner (Washington, DC: National Academy Press, 1982), p. 184.
24. W. G. Findlay and M. M. Bryan, *The Pros and Cons of Ability Grouping* (Bloomington, IN: Phi Delta Kappa, Inc., 1975).
25. Brim et al.
26. Goslin, pp. 98–106.
27. Findlay and Bryan.
28. D. I. Ashurst and C. Edward Meyers, "Social System and Clinical Model in School Identification of the Educable Mentally Retarded," in *Sociobehavioral Studies in Mental Retardation*, eds. R. K. Eyman, C. Edward Meyers, and G. Tarajan (Washington, DC: American Association of Mental Deficiency, 1973).
29. Jane R. Mercer, *Labeling the Mentally Retarded* (Berkeley: University of California Press, 1973).
30. Donald L. MacMillan, Reginald L. Jones, and Gregory F. Aloia, "The Mentally Retarded Label: A Theoretical Analysis and Review of Research," *American Journal of Mental Deficiency* 79 (1974):241.
31. Donald L. MacMillan and C. Edward Meyers, "Educational Labeling of Handicapped Learners," in *Review of Research in Education*, vol. 7, ed. D. C. Berliner (Washington, DC: American Educational Research Association, 1979), pp. 223–279.
32. Rogers Elliott, "The Banning of IQ Tests in California," unpublished manuscript, Dartmouth College, 1983.
33. Ibid.
34. Samuel L. Guskin, "Research on Labeling Retarded Persons: Where Do We Go From Here?" *American Journal of Mental Deficiency* 79 (1974):263.
35. Rodney Skager, "On the Use and Importance of Tests of Ability in Admission

to Postsecondary Education," in *Ability Testing: Uses, Consequences, and Controversies*, part II, eds. Alexandra K. Wigdor and Wendell R. Garner (Washington, DC: National Academy Press, 1982), pp. 286–314.

36. quoted in Christopher Jencks and James Crouse, "Aptitude vs. Achievement: Should We Replace the SAT?" *The Public Interest* 67 (Spring 1982):22.

37. Ibid.; Allan Nairn and Associates, *The Reign of ETS: The Corporation That Makes Up Minds* (Washington, DC: Learning Research Project, 1980); David Owen, *None of the Above: Behind the Myth of Scholastic Aptitude* (Boston: Houghton Mifflin, 1985); Warner V. Slack and Douglas Porter, "The Scholastic Aptitude Test: A Critical Appraisal," *Harvard Educational Review* 50 (May 1980):154–175.

38. Educational Testing Service, *Test Use and Validity* (Princeton, NJ: Author, 1980), p. 7.

39. Slack and Porter, p. 170; Jencks and Crouse, pp. 32–35.

40. Skager, p. 294.

41. S. F. Ford and S. Campos, *Summary of Validity Data from the Admissions Testing Program Validity Study Service* (New York: College Entrance Examination Board, 1977).

42. W. W. Willingham and H. M. Breland, "The Status of Selective Admissions," in *Selective Admissions in Higher Education*, ed. Carnegie Council on Policy Studies in Higher Education (San Francisco: Jossey–Bass, 1977).

43. Robert Klitgaard, *Choosing Elites* (New York: Basic Books, 1985).

44. Ibid., p. 114.

45. Robert L. Linn, "Admissions Testing on Trial," *American Psychologist* 37 (March 1982):282.

46. Ibid.

47. Ibid., p. 284.

48. cited in Skager.

49. Skager; Richard I. Badger, "Prediction and Selection in Law School Admissions," *The University of Chicago Law School Record* 31 (Spring 1985):16–21.

50. Owen, p. 239.

51. Samuel Messick and Ann Jungeblut, "Time and Method in Coaching for the SAT," *Psychological Bulletin* 89 (1981):191–216.

52. Ibid.; Rebecca DerSimonian and Nan M. Laird, "Evaluating the Effect of Coaching on SAT Scores: A Meta–Analysis," *Harvard Educational Review* 53 (February 1983):1–15.

53. Federal Trade Commission, Boston Regional Office, *Staff Memorandum of the Boston Regional Office of the Federal Trade Commission: The Effects of Coaching on Standardized Admission Examinations* (Boston: Author, September 1978).

54. Federal Trade Commission, Bureau of Consumer Protection, *Effects of Coaching on Standardized Admission Examinations: Revised Statistical Analyses of Data Gathered by Boston Regional Office of the Federal Trade Commission* (Washington, DC: Author, March 1979).

55. Owen, p. 109.

56. Nairn.

57. Wigdor and Garner, part I, pp. 194–195.

58. Linn, p. 289.

59. Prentice–Hall, Inc., *P–H Survey: Employee Testing and Selection Procedures— Where Are They Headed?* (Englewood Cliffs, NJ: Author, 1975).

60. Mary L. Tenopyr, "The Realities of Employment Testing," *American Psychologist* 36 (October 1981):1120–1121.
61. Wigdor and Garner, part I, pp. 122–123.
62. Ibid., pp. 123–127.
63. *Griggs v. Duke Power Co.*, 401 U.S. 424 (1971).
64. Donald N. Bersoff, "Testing and the Law," *American Psychologist* 36 (October 1981):1051.
65. Alexandra Wigdor, "Psychological Testing and the Law of Employment Discrimination," in *Ability Testing: Uses, Consequences, and Controversies*, part II, eds. Alexandra K. Wigdor and Wendell R. Garner (Washington, DC: National Academy Press, 1982), pp. 39–69.
66. *Albermarle Paper Co. v. Moody*, 422 U.S. 405 (1975).
67. Wigdor, pp. 63–64.
68. Quoted in Wigdor, p. 59.
69. Bersoff, pp. 1049–1053.
70. *Washington v. Davis*, 426 U.S. 229 (1976)
71. Walter B. Connolly, Jr. and David W. Peterson, *Use of Statistics in Equal Employment Opportunity Litigation* (New York: Law Journal Seminars–Press, 1982), pp. 8.17,8.21; *Clady v. County of Los Angeles*, 770 F.2d 1421 (9th Cir. 1985).
72. John E. Hunter and Ronda Hunter, "Validity and Utility of Alternative Predictors of Job Performance," *Psychological Bulletin* 96 (1984):72–98; Frank L. Schmidt and John E. Hunter, "Employment Testing: Old Theories and New Research Findings," *American Psychologist* 36 (October 1981):1128–1137.
73. e.g., N. J. Block and Gerald Dworkin, "IQ, Heritability, and Inequality," in *The IQ Controversy*, eds. N. J. Block and Gerald Dworkin (New York: Pantheon, 1976), pp. 410–542; D. L. Eckberg, *Intelligence and Race: The Origins and Dimensions of the IQ Controversy* (New York: Praeger, 1979); Stephen Jay Gould, *The Mismeasure of Man* (New York: Norton, 1981); Banesh Hoffman, *The Tyranny of Testing* (New York: Collier, 1962); Paul L. Houts, ed., *The Myth of Measurability* (New York: Hart Publishing, 1977); Joint Committee on Testing, *Testing, Testing, Testing* (Washington, DC: American Association of School Administrators, 1962); Leon J. Kamin, *The Science and Politics of IQ* (Potomac, MD: Lawrence Erlbaum, 1974); Clarence J. Karier, "Testing for Order and Control in the Corporate Liberal State," *Educational Theory* 22 (1972):154–180.
74. Cleary et al.
75. Ibid., p. 35.
76. Slack and Porter, pp. 167–169; Jencks and Crouse, pp. 27–30.
77. Slack and Porter, p. 170; Jencks and Crouse, pp. 32–35.
78. Wigdor and Garner, parts I and II.
79. Ibid., part I, p. 144.
80. Hunter and Hunter, pp. 91–94.

6

It's All There in Black and White: The Extent of News Media Coverage

The Armed Services Vocational Aptitude Battery (ASVAB) is currently administered to all applicants for U.S. military service in order to determine eligibility for enlistment and subsequent classification into various military occupations. The ASVAB is, as its name implies, a battery of ten aptitude subtests in areas ranging from numerical operations and word knowledge to general science and automotive/shop information. Different service areas combine and use these subtests in various ways, depending on their classification requirements. Four of the subtests—word knowledge, paragraph comprehension, arithmetic reasoning, and numerical operations—are combined to yield a single score, and are called the Armed Forces Qualifying Test (AFQT). The AFQT is the primary screening device for all military services; applicants must achieve a certain minimum AFQT score in order to be eligible for enlistment.

In 1979, the Department of Defense contracted with the National Opinion Research Center (NORC) to administer the ASVAB to a representative sample of eighteen to twenty–three year olds drawn from the American population as a whole. The purpose of this exercise was to obtain a normative sample with which to compare armed services applicants. These data would allow the services to set standards for enlistment and would address claims that the all–volunteer military was recruiting a relatively unskilled group.

The NORC administered the test in 1980 to nearly 12,000 Americans, and submitted its report, *A Profile of American Youth*, in early 1982.[1] The report focused on two aspects of the data: (1) a comparison between the *Profile* sample and 1981 military recruits on AFQT score and such demographic variables as sex, race/ethnicity (white, black, and Hispanic), and level of education; and (2) an analysis of demographic influences on ASVAB test performance. The first of these revealed, no doubt much to the

175

relief of the Defense Department, that within racial/ethnic groups, military recruits had slightly higher AFQT scores than their counterparts in the general population. More distressing, but by no means surprising in light of data from other standardized tests, was that both in the *Profile* sample and among military recruits, whites on the average outscored Hispanics, who outscored blacks. In the general population, the white norm was at the 56th percentile, meaning that 56 percent of all test takers scored worse than the average white. Hispanics were at the 31st percentile, blacks at the 24th percentile.

The Pentagon naturally wanted to emphasize the comparison between military recruits and the general population (as well as that the average recruit had become increasingly educated over the past ten years), but was worried about the impact of the racial/ethnic data. As a result, private meetings were held between Reagan administration officials and representatives of various minority groups in anticipation of public release of the *Profile* study.

A *Washington Post* reporter, George Wilson, obtained information about the contents of the report and the minority group briefings before the Defense Department had made any public statement on the matter. Pentagon officials, upon being informed by Wilson on Friday, February 19, 1982, that he intended to print a story two days later, agreed to meet with Wilson on that day and the next to discuss the study results. Meanwhile, the Pentagon quickly called in various specialists to help prepare materials for public release on Monday.

Wilson's story appears on the front page of the *Washington Post* for Sunday, February 21, under the headline "Blacks Score Below Whites on Pentagon Test." The article discusses the comparison between recruits and the general population, as well as demographic data, and provides background for the *Profile* study, but the lead and focus of Wilson's story is the racial differences in test score. It begins, "Young black men and women did less than half as well as whites" on the tests, and three paragraphs later reports the results as blacks scoring an average of 24 "percent," compared to 56 "percent" for whites and 31 "percent" for Hispanics. Wilson had confused "percent," indicating raw score on the test, with "percentile," referring only to an individual's ranking among all test takers, thus inflating the actual score differentials. (The average score, in percentage, was in fact 49 for blacks and 72 for whites.)

Pentagon officials are cited as stressing that the tests "do not measure natural intelligence or learning potential," but only "what has been learned" and "capability to be trained as a soldier." The explanation for these results is clearly placed on the inferior quality of black education.

Wilson also describes the Reagan administration's fears about releasing the test results, and notes the meetings with minority representatives.

Lynne Sussman has provided an extensive analysis of press coverage of the *Profile of American Youth* study, including interviews with the journalists, government officials, and social scientists involved and an examination of almost fifty news stories from newspapers, magazines, and television broadcasts around the country.[2] She notes that Wilson's story, carried on the *Washington Post* and Associated Press wires on the day of publication, became a major source for Sunday night television news broadcasts and many Monday morning newspaper stories.[3] Among these is a *New York Times* story by Charles Mohr entitled "Volunteers in Armed Forces Test 'Above Average'," in which Mohr repeats Wilson's error by reporting "percent" instead of "percentile" and claims that "black youths scored only about half as well as whites."

Nonetheless, the *Times* story, though reporting the racial data, represents a change of focus from the *Post* report. Sussman identifies four different angles chosen by journalists in covering the *Profile* story.[4] They are, in order of frequency: (1) racial/ethnic differences in AFQT score, (2) comparison of civilian and recruit test scores and the representativeness of the all–volunteer force, (3) the possible genetic basis of racial/ethnic score differentials, and (4) the failure of U.S. schooling for minorities.

The civilian–recruit comparison angle, exemplified by the *Times* story, was, of course, the Pentagon's line. It was the point Pentagon spokesmen tried to emphasize in their Monday press conference, though a flood of questions about the black/white score difference precluded as complete a statistical explanation as the report authors would have liked. Inadequate understanding of the statistics involved may explain a rather remarkable omission in press reports of the *Profile* study. Journalists presumably are disinclined to believe much of what they are told by government agencies trying to defend current practices. Yet reporters repeated the Pentagon claim that recruits were equal or superior to the general population on the AFQT. This repetition occurred despite the facts, known to reporters, that the civilian–recruit comparisons were made only within racial/ethnic groups, that blacks scored substantially lower than whites in both populations, and that blacks are greatly overrepresented in the military in comparison to their proportion of the general population. These data, taken together, indicate that the average AFQT score across *all* military recruits was lower than in the general population. This conclusion is not reached in any of the *Profile* news stories.

A more grievous statistical error is George Wilson's confusion over the percent/percentile distinction. Wilson's mistake is unfortunate because it exaggerated an already pernicious problem and made the *Profile* data seem even more inflammatory. The uncritical manner in which this error was propagated throughout the country by other equally uninformed journalists is an example of how technical issues are misrepresented by the popular press, often with potentially damaging consequences. The *Post* 's erratum, published five weeks later, is a case of too little too late.

The racial/ethnic differences in test scores were not, however, the most volatile aspect of the *Profile* report. That distinction belongs to the authors' attempt to explain these score differentials. Emphasis was placed on sociocultural differences, but the possibility of genetic influences was raised. Neither the *Post* story, nor any of the others published or broadcast that Sunday or the following day makes any mention of this issue, but subsequent stories sent out over the *Los Angeles Times* news service, in the *Boston Globe*, and in the Hispanic–oriented *La Raza* highlight the genetic hypothesis. In the *La Raza* story, what had been one possibility raised in the context of many explanations, became the Pentagon's "assumption that the poor results of Hispanics and blacks in the test are caused by hereditary and genetic differences."

(Shortly after the NORC report on demographic influences on ASVAB scores was released to the press, one of the authors of the report expressed his dismay to Lynne Sussman over the way the genetic hypothesis had been handled by the press. In a longer version of the *Profile* report made available to the general public by the Defense Department in February 1984, the possibility of genetic influences is explicitly ruled out.)[5]

Numerous aspects of press coverage of the *Profile of American Youth* study demonstrate the way in which organizational constraints placed on journalists, as well as their own values, can interfere with accurate and balanced coverage of scientific issues:

1. The decision by George Wilson and the editors of the *Washington Post* to emphasize the racial differences in test scores, and to put the story on the front page. It is virtually axiomatic among those who study the news media that decisions about news coverage are influenced by the desire to attract readers and viewers.[6] "Newsworthiness" is therefore enhanced by the shocking and/or controversial nature of any story. As George Wilson explained to Lynne Sussman:

> [the black–white score differential] was the most explosive part of the report—the part that worried the White House and Pentagon the most as evidenced by their efforts to brief black organizations before the report became public. Here was the first in–depth documentation of the differences, according to the Pentagon, which have provoked debate for decades. This made that part of the report more newsworthy and more interesting to readers than what turned out to be the Pentagon's lead in its news release—

basically a self–endorsement of the representativeness of its All–Volunteer Force.[7]

That other news sources did not choose to cover the story as the *Post* did, but rather repeated the Pentagon line about civilian–recruit comparison, or emphasized the hotter topic of genetic influences, is an indication both that Wilson's perspective is not an inevitable result of journalistic constraints and that reporting of any given story is influenced by many factors other than the events themselves.

Among these factors are journalists' own views of what events are important and their ideological visions of the way the world should be. Herbert Gans has identified a series of enduring values and reality judgments that guide the selection of news stories and the focus of coverage.[8] These values, no doubt shared by many other Americans, include a belief in individualism—an emphasis on the uniqueness of each person and on individual initiative—and an official norm of racial integration. Robert Lichter, Stanley Rothman, and Linda Lichter, in their recent *The Media Elite*, note how the rise to prominence of a powerful national media was significantly influenced by coverage of the civil rights movement, in which the news media's role as "patrons of the oppressed" had a substantial effect on the passage of the Civil Rights Act of 1964.[9] The testing enterprise and the data it generates often appear to violate these standards. By rank–ordering people according to score, standardized tests imply that some people are better than others. The possibility that there is a genetic basis to these scores further implies (in the minds of many) that there is little the individual can do to improve the situation. Data on differences in average test score between racial and ethnic groups are detrimental to the achievement of full racial integration as long as these scores are used to make important educational and occupational decisions. Discussion of a possible genetic influence on racial differences in test score is antithetical to both individualism and racial integration, and is therefore most newsworthy and most likely to be reported pejoratively (see the discussion of the *Boston Globe* story, below).

2. By putting the story on the front page of the paper and over the wire with a headline emphasizing black–white differences, the *Post* ensured that the story would receive national attention. In his study of network TV news and national newsmagazines, Herbert Gans reports that the major newspapers are often the source of stories for these institutions, particularly when these papers have "scooped" the rest of the media. On the evening of the *Post* story, the NBC *Nightly News* reported that "young blacks did only half as well as whites in a government–sponsored test of math and verbal skills."[10] These results were similarly reported on the CBS *Evening News* and in *Newsweek* and *U.S. News and World Report*.

3. Wilson's percent/percentile error and its propagation reflect at least three aspects of news media reporting that can have particularly deleterious consequences when technical issues are involved. First, time constraints, as a result of which journalists feel a responsibility both to report news as quickly as possible, and to scoop the competition, are more likely to leads to errors in those aspects of stories that require more time to comprehend fully. Because Wilson gave the Pentagon only two days' notice before the publication of his story, social scientists working for the Defense Department had to rush their press release and were unable to explain the statistical data as carefully as they had planned.[11] These time constraints also give journalists fewer opportunities to verify their information and check the accuracy of important details.

Second, few reporters of social-science data have training in statistics and other mathematical and scientific subjects.[12] Many newspapers, magazines, and TV stations have dedicated science or medical reporters with training in relevant topics, but the same is not true for social science. Because so much of the news involves various of the social sciences to greater or lesser degrees, these stories are covered by general beat reporters without expertise in any particular area. More technical social science topics, like testing, are often short-changed by such an arrangement.

Third, as Carol Weiss and Evelyn Singer have discovered in their recent examination of social science reporting, most journalists covering social science issues are more concerned with readability and impact than thoroughness of coverage. In fact, journalists are often frustrated by the dry style and highly qualified comments made by most social scientists in their writings and encounters with the press. One journalist told Wess and Singer that

> [social scientists] are terrible writers, very boring. They don't use flesh and blood, they use graphs and bar charts. They should ham it up. . . . Make it into drama. They have no talent for telling stories.[13]

Social scientists do not "tell stories" precisely because story telling requires that a dramatic structure be imposed on a series of facts that may not warrant it. "Young black men and women did less than half as well as whites in math and verbal tests given by the U.S. government . . ." is an attention-grabbing introduction, the kind of thing an editor might want to put on the front page of the Sunday paper. Too much clarification detracts from dramatic appeal.

4. Journalists are in the business of gathering information about certain issues and events for the purpose of reporting to an audience. This information is gathered and presented principally in the form of statements

made by individuals (sources). The selection of sources is therefore of primary importance in the quality and content of any given news story. Many observers of the news media have noted that the selection of sources for controversial issues, particularly those involving scientific data, often involves considerations other than the source's representativeness of the group holding that position, or of the individual's specific expertise.[14] Edward Jay Epstein discusses this tendency in television network news:

> [S]pokesmen are selected to represent sides in controversy at least partly because they fit in with the organizational needs of the program. It is assumed that spokesmen must be articulate, easily identifiable and dramatic in order to hold the interest of viewers to whom the subject of the controversy may be of no interest. Since the "average" person in a group cannot be depended on to manifest these qualities—as Reuven Frank [then producer of the NBC *Nightly News*] pointed out, "most people are dull as far as their television image is concerned"—producers are expected to select spokesmen who are capable of retaining the audience's interest, even if they are not what social scientists would consider to be representative.[15]

The frequent use, in both print and broadcast, of the outspoken Leon Kamin as a representative of the environmentalist position, despite his extreme stance in the heritability debate, is an example of this tendency.

In addition to organizational constraints, the choice of sources for news stories is influenced by journalists' values, often at the expense of accurate representation. In 1979 and 1980, Robert Lichter et al. interviewed 238 journalists at major newspapers and national newsmagazines. As part of each interview, respondents were asked to list the major sources to which they would turn for information on four different topics: welfare reform, consumer protection, environmental issues, and nuclear energy. In each case, the most frequently mentioned sources (and the only ones mentioned by a majority of journalists) are those associated with what may be called the liberal side of each of these issues, e.g., the Urban League and PUSH in the case of welfare reform, Ralph Nader on consumer protection, the Sierra Club and Barry Commoner for environmental issues, and the Union of Concerned Scientists and *Progressive* magazine for information on nuclear energy.[16] Subsequent content analyses of elite media coverage of these controversial issues found the major newspapers and newsmagazines giving "greater weight to the anti-nuclear than the pro-nuclear side" of the nuclear energy issue, "greater credence to the advocates of busing than [to] its opponents," and "more sympath[y] to the critics of the oil industry than [to] its supporters. In every instance the coverage followed neither the middle path nor the expert evidence."[17]

In an article in the September 12, 1982, *Boston Globe*, Frank Greve discusses the controversy caused by the genetic hypothesis briefly mentioned in the *Profile* study. There is little doubt where Greve stands on the issue of the possible genetic basis of group differences in test scores. Several paragraphs are devoted to the contention of Darrell Bock and Elsie Moore, the *Profile* authors, that their statement was misconstrued, and the presentation of evidence in support of their conviction that the group differences are entirely environmental in origin. There is also a lengthy discussion of claims by groups representing blacks and Hispanics that the *Profile* study and the tests used were biased.

The story does not contain a word in defense of the tests, nor is any evidence presented in favor of the genetic hypothesis. Instead, the names of Shockley and Herrnstein are invoked. Following a statement that the *Profile* study "has been seized upon by certain behavioral geneticists who argue that there are inherited intellectual differences between racial groups," Shockley's abortive California Senate campaign is mentioned, along with his "assertion of inherent racial differences." A later paragraph tells us that in the 1920s "some scientists inferred the alleged 'inferiority' of Russians, Jews and other immigrant groups from lower scores on aptitude tests." Finally, Herrnstein is described as a Harvard psychology professor who "believes the majority of intellectual variation is inherited," followed by a quote in which he discusses the substantial overlap between black and white test scores. The clear implication is that Herrnstein is one of those "behavioral geneticists who argue that there are inherited intellectual differences between racial groups." But Herrnstein has never made such a claim, speaking only of heritability within groups and across social classes. In Greve's choice of sources, Herrnstein's Harvard affiliation and "name" status in the IQ controversy apparently outweighed his irrelevance to the topic at hand.

The *Profile* case is not unique. In October 1986, Prime Minister Nakasone of Japan made a statement implying that American blacks and Hispanics are of lower average intellige than whites or Japanese. His remarks were picked up and prominently displayed by the national media. The treatment of the issue in the October 6 *Time* magazine is representative. Reviewing the IQ controversy, *Time* identified William Shockley as typical of that very small group of scientists who believe that black–white IQ differences are genetic in origin. The story's authors, after noting that IQ tests have been used in the past to support racial stereotypes, point out that the vast majority of experts in the U.S. and elsewhere believe that differences in intelligence are environmentally determined, and that most standardized tests used to measure intelligence have a pronounced white, middle-class bias. Leon Kamin and Stephen Jay Gould are presented as typical examples of the mainstream expert view on the subject.

Press coverage of the *Profile of American Youth* study and of Nakasone's remarks are two examples of the important role played by the news media in public discussion of social science issues and the ways in which journalistic constraints and values may interfere with objective and accurate reporting. The IQ controversy is full of such cases. While the news media did not create the issues of the nature of intelligence, IQ heritability, and racial differences in test scores, they have, by the nature of their coverage, contributed significantly to the propagation of the public controversy surrounding these issues.

This chapter and the next describe the results of a content analysis of news media coverage of the IQ controversy. The purpose of this content analysis is to describe the way in which the elite print and television media have characterized various testing–related issues. Specifically, we are interested in categorizing which position(s) on the various controversial issues are represented by press accounts and the manner in which these positions are characterized, paying particular attention to the news media's portrayal of expert opinion about testing. Comparison of these data with the results of the expert survey reported in Chapters 2 through 5 will serve as one measure of news media accuracy in coverage of testing issues. More generally, this content analysis should allow us to better understand the mechanisms by which the news media have contributed to the IQ controversy.

Content Analysis Methodology

The following is a basic outline of the content analysis methodology. A detailed description can be found in Appendix C.

Sample

The sample for the content analysis includes the small number of national or near–national news sources believed to have the most influence on public opinion and public policy. These are the three major national newsweeklies (*Time, Newsweek, U.S. News and World Report*), the three commercial television networks (ABC, CBS, NBC), and three major newspapers (the *New York Times*, the *Washington Post*, and the *Wall Street Journal*). The television networks are included because of their overwhelming popularity as sources of national news. The choice of print media sources is based on a 1974 survey by Carol Weiss of American leaders in politics, business, academia, the news media, and various civic, religious, and public interest organizations.[18] The six print media sources analyzed here are the most widely read among these decision makers.

The time frame for the content analysis is the IQ controversy in its recent manifestation. The modern controversy, particularly the public debate, may be defined as beginning with the publication of Arthur Jensen's "How Much Can We Boost IQ and Scholastic Achievement?" in the *Harvard Educational Review* (*HER*), in early 1969. The public debate continues to the present day. The content analysis therefore includes articles published and television news programs broadcast during the 15 years betwen January 1, 1969, (The *Washington Post Index* began publication in 1972; our analysis of the *Post* therefore does not begin until that year.) and December 31, 1983, the last complete year for which news indices were available at the time this analysis was begun.

Within each source, the analysis includes *all* articles and broadcast segments uncovered by a search of the appropriate indices (individual indices for each newspaper, the *Reader's Guide to Periodical Literature* for newsmagazines, and various archival sources for the television broadcasts) using the search terms "Intelligence," "Intelligence testing," "IQ," "Aptitude testing," "Admissions testing," "SAT," and "Employment testing," as well as other categories such as "Schools," "Mental tests," "Educational tests," and "Ability tests," to which the original search items may have led.

The total number of articles and broadcast segments analyzed from each source is listed in Table 6.1. It is fortunate that news media coverage of the IQ controversy, while extensive, has not been so pervasive that there are more articles and broadcasts than can reasonably be coded. By coding *all* relevant news stories from each source, sampling problems were eliminated. While the search for news stories undoubtedly missed some relevant items (this is more true for television than for print media), the overwhelming majority of such stories from the elite news media have been coded. We are confident, therefore, that the inclusion of any relevant but uncoded items from these sources would not significantly alter the results.

Coding

The two fundamental concerns in developing any content analysis (CA) are reliability and validity. Reliability is the sine qua non of content analysis; the purpose of content analysis is to *objectively* describe the contents of the items being coded, independent of the idiosyncrasies and biases of the individual observer. Ideally, a satisfactory coding scheme should result in identical code from all properly trained coders examining the same article or broadcast. Reliable code is of no use, however, if it is not relevant to the purposes of the research (i.e., if it is not valid). Unfortunately, reliability and validity usually work at cross purposes; as CA coding captures more relevant information, it becomes less reliable. To take two extremes, if coders in the present analysis had been asked simply to record the number

TABLE 6.1
Articles and Broadcasts Coded from Various News Sources

Print Media (N = 479)

New York Times: 267
Wall Street Journal: 22
Washington Post (1972-83 only): 123

Newsweek: 32
Time: 22
U.S. News and World Report: 13

Television (N = 65)

ABC:
Daily news broadcasts: 7
News magazine segments: 1
News specials: 0

CBS:
Daily news broadcasts: 38
News magazines segments: 5
News specials: 1

NBC:
Daily news broadcasts: 12
News magazine segments: 1
News specials: 0

of times the words "intelligence" or "intelligence tests" are listed in an article, code would be very reliable, but practically worthless. On the other hand, coders' general impressions about how each of the controversial issues is being characterized represent the central purpose of this research, but would be highly subjective and useless for a scientific analysis. A balance must be struck between these two important but competing goals. How much reliability one must and should give up in order to produce valid code depends both on the nature of the coding problem and on the researcher's opinion of the relative importance of reliability and validity. Content analyses are always open to second–guessing. In the present case, we attempted to maximize both goals through extensive coder training and editing of the CA code sheets and by consultation with content analysis experts.

The coding scheme for the present analysis is hierarchical. In reading through print articles and examining television broadcasts, it was discovered that the relevant information contained in these sources could be classified into thirteen categories, corresponding to general issues of concern within the IQ controversy. The code sheets were therefore set up so that coders first decided which of the categories (Issues) was present, and then moved to individual code sheets containing more specific items within each Issue.

The General Code Sheet, which contains the list of possible Issues considered, is divided into three sections. The first asks for basic information about the article or broadcast such as source, date, length, location, and type. The second section is the list of Issues considered. A given article or broadcast might consider any one or more of these Issues. The thirteen Issues are (see Appendix C for a more detailed description):

    I. The Nature of Intelligence.
   II. What Intelligence Tests Measure.
  III. The Usefulness of IQ.
  IV. Test Misuse.
    V. The Heritability of IQ.
  VI. Group Differences in IQ.
 VII. Other Issues Concerning Herrnstein, Jensen, or Shockley.
VIII. The Meaning of SAT Scores.
  IX. SAT Use and Misuse.
   X. SAT Coaching.
  XI. Group Differences in SAT Score.
 XII. Employment Testing.
XIII. Intelligence and Aptitude Testing Outside the U.S.

This list of Issues is itself an analysis of news media coverage of testing issues, as it is based on an examination of all relevant print and television stories. While there is considerable overlap between the issues considered in our expert survey and in news media coverage, the two are not identical. The questionnaire was developed based upon a review of the social–scientific literature as well as the more public aspects of the IQ controversy. The Issues listed above are derived entirely from elite news media coverage from 1969 to 1983. In general, the media are not as concerned as the social scientists with highly technical issues like the evidence for heritability or the reality of "g," and are much more concerned, particularly in recent years, with SAT issues. The differing emphases of the social science and news media versions of the IQ controversy are relevant to the question of how the news media are characterizing expert opinion. The focus of the news media is generally less technical and more practical than that of testing experts (there is also an obsession with Herrnstein, Jensen, and Shockley), placing limits on the accuracy with which expert concerns can be transmitted through the media.

The third section of the General Code Sheet asks coders to make two simple subjective judgments as to the general tone of the article or broadcast regarding testing and the heritability of intelligence. Testing tone could be "pro–testing," "anti–testing" or "neutral," and heritability tone could be "learned," "innate," or "neutral." As these two judgments are the least objective part of the coding scheme, coders are instructed to assume that all articles and broadcasts are neutral, unless the evidence to the contrary is overwhelming.

Following completion of the General Code Sheet, coders move to Individual Issue Code Sheets corresponding to each of the Issues considered by the article or broadcast being coded. The Individual Issue Code Sheets consist of series of position statements related to the Issue at hand. For example, the "Test Misuse" Code Sheet contains six statements, including:

1. Students are often misclassified, mislabeled, or stigmatized on the basis of intelligence test scores.
4. The use of tests creates a narrow set of educational objectives.
6. Test scores are overrelied upon (are too important in people's lives).

For each statement, the coder must make an initial judgment of whether the position is in any way represented in the article or broadcast being coded. If it is not, the statement is coded as Not Mentioned (NM). If the position is represented, it might be supported, rejected, or both. These possibilities are coded as Positive (Pos), Negative (Neg), or both.

For some of the statements on some of the Individual Issue Code Sheets, there are more options than simply Pos or Neg. Item 1 on the "Heritability of Intelligence" Sheet reads:

1. The heritable component of (genetic influence on) intelligence, as measured by intelligence tests is:
——(NM).
——total (no mention of environmental determination, or environmental determination ruled out).
——significant (including environmental determination).
——insignificant or nonexistent.
——cannot be determined or is undetermined.

An article or broadcast that addresses the question of heritability may receive any one or any combination of the four non–NM codes.

Finally, for each representation of a given position (Pos, Neg, or some other option), coders are required to determine what sources the journalist used. Was the position simply asserted or implied by the journalist, was it attributed to one or more expert or nonexpert others, or was the position characterized as being widely held by the expert population? (See Appendix C for a detailed description of the source codes.)

General Code Sheet Data

Number of Articles or Broadcast Segments

Newspapers. Table 6.1 presents the number of relevant articles or broadcast segments coded from each news source. The three newspapers contribute the lion's share of such stories. The *New York Times* (*NYT*) and *Washington Post* (*WP*) account for 72 percent of all stories coded. No doubt this is primarily a function of the much greater number of stories of all types carried in these daily newspapers, compared to weekly newsmagazines and television news programs. (The small number of *Wall Street Journal* [*WSJ*] articles reflects its specialized news status.) Between the *Times* and *Post*, however, the *Times* has published a much larger number of stories relevant to intelligence testing (even correcting for the three missing years of *Post* articles). Nearly half of all code in the present analysis is of articles from the *New York Times*.

Figure 6.1 presents the number of articles or broadcast segments coded from each news source for each of the fifteen years of the present analysis. *WSJ* data are not shown because there are too few articles for meaningful trends to appear. The *NYT* shows a peak in 1969, reflecting the immediate backlash from the publication of Jensen's *HER* article, followed by a three–

FIGURE 6.1.

Number of relevant articles or broadcasts by year for each news source

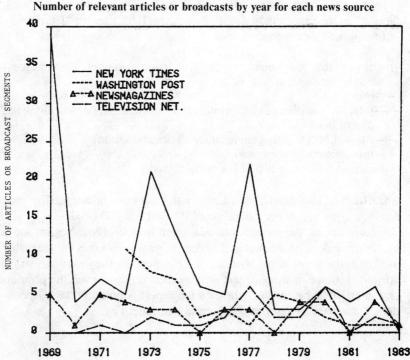

year lull, and somewhat renewed interest in the mid 1970s. This second wave is largely created by coverage of William Shockley and his attempts to debate and to procure funding for research on racial differences in intelligence. It was also during this period that Leon Kamin and other critics became most vocal. Most of the coverage in the late 1970s and early 1980s is concerned with SAT issues. The peak in 1977 is a result of the thirteen relevant articles published in the *NYT* "Spring Survey of Education" on May 1 of that year. With the exception of 1977, the trends in the *WP* graph approximately parallel those of the *NYT* for the years of *WP* coverage analyzed.

Newsmagazines. Because the three newsmagazines contribute a total of only sixty-seven stories to the analysis, we examined the possibility of combining these sources for further analyses. It was discovered that IQ-relevant stories from *Newsweek, Time,* and *U.S. News and World Report* do not differ significantly in average length, location, testing and heritability tone, or in their representation of ten key items (i.e., those concerning critical topics in the controversy such as heritability, the genetic basis of group differences, and the overuse of tests) selected from the Individual Issue Code Sheets. Moreover, the rank-order correlations between the newsmagazines for Issues considered are all greater than 0.60. We therefore concluded that the three newsmagazines do not differ in any important way for the purposes of this analysis, and could be combined in further discussion. Figure 6.1 reveals no substantial time trend in quantity of coverage of IQ-related topics by newsmagazines, with the exception of a slight increase in variability of coverage in later years. This later coverage is primarily SAT related.

Television networks. As with the newsmagazines, the small number of broadcast segments (sixty-five) prompted an analysis of the differences between the three networks. No significant differences were found in average broadcast length and in the representation of three of the ten key items, and rank-order correlations between the networks for Issues considered average above 0.60. (Insufficient sample sizes from ABC and NBC precluded statistical comparisons of broadcast type, tone, and seven of the key items.) The three networks were therefore combined for the purpose of further analyses. Data from this concantenation primarily reflect CBS news coverage, as this network contributes 68 percent of all coded segments. It is unclear precisely how much of this discrepancy between the networks reflects greater coverage of IQ-relevant issues by CBS and how much is a function of the superior indexing available for CBS news broadcasts (see Appendix C). That this disproportionality is reflected in the index of all network evening news broadcasts is an indication that CBS probably has had substantially more coverage of these issues.

FIGURE 6.2.
Number of articles or broadcasts considering each Issue, for each news source

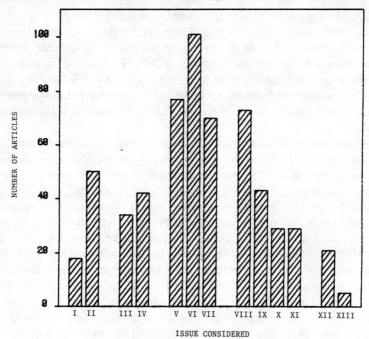

6.2a. *New York Times*

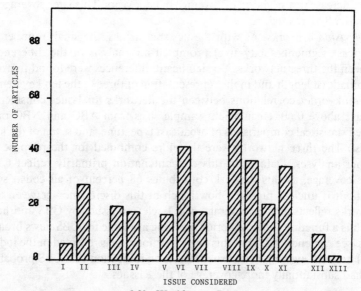

6.2b. *Washington Post*

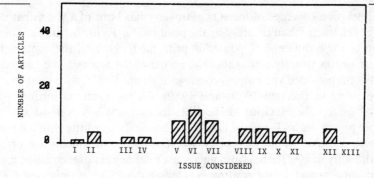

6.2c. *Wall Street Journal*

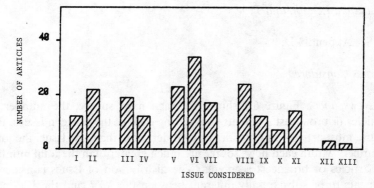

6.2d. Newsmagazines

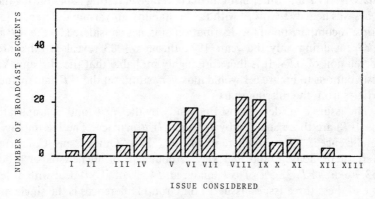

6.2e. Television Networks

Television coverage of the IQ controversy has been of a somewhat different character than coverage by the print media. Figure 6.1 is one indication of these differences. While the print media covered the controversy more or less steadily throughout the period of the analysis, the television networks provided virtually no coverage at all until 1973, with most stories appearing in the late 1970s and 1980s. As the examination of Issue coverage reveals, television has been almost exclusively concerned with the more pragmatic SAT–related Issues, and has dealt very little with the more theoretical and technical problems of the nature of intelligence or the heritability of IQ. There is also an almost total neglect of the earlier, more emotional aspects of the controversy (Jensen, Shockley, Kamin et al.). *The IQ Myth* and a subsequent segment of *60 Minutes* dealing with the Burt scandal constitute the bulk of television coverage of these issues.

Location, Length, and Type

See Appendix D.

Issues Considered

Newspapers. Figure 6.2 shows, for each news source, the number of articles or broadcast segments considering each of the thirteen Issues. Because most articles and broadcasts consider more than one Issue, the total numbers within each news source are much greater than the total number of articles or broadcast segments. The distribution of Issues considered appears to be substantially different between the *NYT* and the *WP*, particularly regarding Issues V, VI, and VII, but this discrepancy can be accounted for by the absence of the years 1969 through 1971 from the *WP* analysis. *NYT* and other print media coverage of testing issues during these years was heavily involved with the heritability and group difference questions. A comparison of the distribution of Issues considered by the *WP* and *NYT* including only the years 1972 through 1983 reveals a rank–order correlation of 0.58. It is therefore highly probable that the *WP* and *NYT* distributions in Figure 6.1 would look very similar if the *WP* data included articles from the missing years.

The Issues considered most frequently by the *NYT* (and by implication the *WP*) are those sparked by Jensen's *HER* article: "The Heritability of Intelligence," "Group Differences in IQ," and "Other Issues Concerning Herrnstein, Jensen, and Shockley." About half of all newspaper articles (53.9% of *NYT*, 32.5% of *WP* analyzed, 54.5% of *WSJ*) deal with at least one of these three Issues. Issue VI on Group Differences is the single most common Issue considered by both the *NYT* and *WSJ*. The second most common Issue considered (first among the analyzed *WP* articles) is VIII on the Meaning of SAT Scores. As a group, the SAT–related Issues ("The Meaning of SAT Scores," "SAT Use and Misuse," "SAT Coaching," and "Group Differences in SAT") are considered by approximately 40% of all newspaper articles (36.3% of *NYT*, 61% of *WP*, 36.4% of *WSJ*). Another frequently considered Issue is "What Intelligence Tests Measure," which, together with "The Nature of Intelligence" corresponds to the topics discussed in Chapter 2. One of these Issues is considered in more than 20% of all newspaper articles (19.9% of *NYT*, 23.6% of *WP*, 18.2% of *WSJ*). Issues III ("The Usefulness of IQ") and IV ("Test Misuse") form the heart of Chapter 5, and are considered by about 20% of newspaper articles (18.7% of *NYT*, 21.1% of *WP*, 13.6% of *WSJ*). "Employment Testing," also discussed in Chapter 5, has not been the subject of much newspaper coverage, though, not surprisingly, it is considered in 23% of all relevant *WSJ* articles. Because Issue XIII, "Intelligence and Aptitude Testing Outside the U.S.," is so infrequently of concern in news media coverage, it will be dropped from further analyses of Issues considered. The contents of the eight relevant articles (six of which concern Japan) will be briefly discussed in Chapter 7.

Figure 6.3 presents the time trends from each news source for each of four Issue groups: I and II on "The Nature of Intelligence," III and IV on "Intelligence Test Use and Misuse," V, VI, and VII on "Heritability and Group Differences in IQ", and VII through XI on the "SAT." These groupings are both conceptually and empirically based; individual time–trend graphs for each Issue within a group do not look substantially different. Once again, the *WSJ* is not included because there are too few articles for meaningful trends to appear.

In the *WP*, "The Nature of Intelligence" and "Test Use and Misuse" have been a fairly constant source of concern throughout the modern IQ controversy. The same is true in the *NYT*, with the exception of a noticeable peak in 1977 as a result of the education supplement.

More interesting trends are apparent in coverage of "Heritability and Group Differences in IQ," and the "SAT," where it becomes clear that the relative absence of trends in Figure 6.1 is the result of the simultaneous waning of one Issue Group and waxing of the other. Like the Figure 6.1 graph, the *NYT* shows a noticeable peak in "Heritability and Group Differences" coverage in 1969 following the publication of Jensen's *HER* article, followed by a three–year lull, and renewed interest as Shockley, Kamin et al. became active. Beginning in the mid 1970s there is a steady decline in articles on these Issues, with the exception of a peak in 1977 (the education supplement again). The *WP* presents a cleaner picture on these Issues, peaking in the early to mid 1970s, and declining thereafter.

FIGURE 6.3.
Number of articles or broadcasts considering each Issue group by year,
for each news source

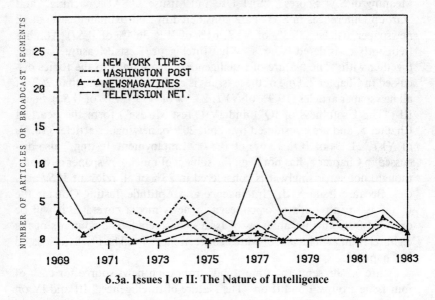

6.3a. Issues I or II: The Nature of Intelligence

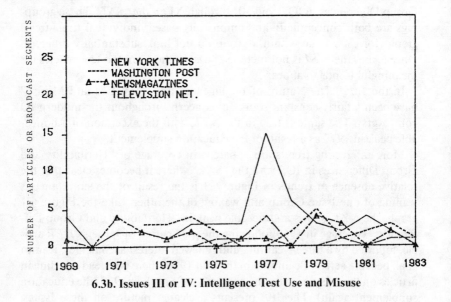

6.3b. Issues III or IV: Intelligence Test Use and Misuse

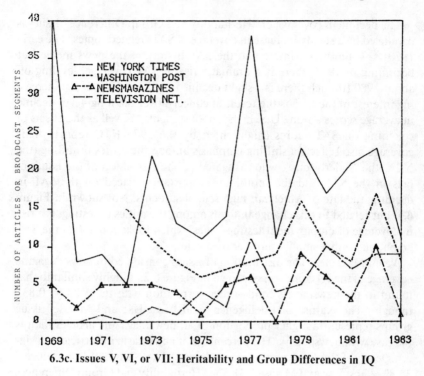

6.3c. Issues V, VI, or VII: Heritability and Group Differences in IQ

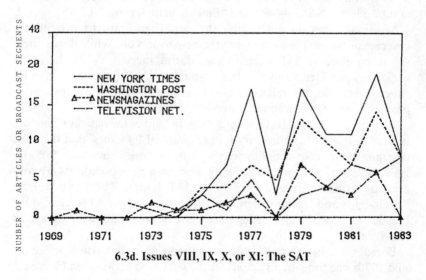

6.3d. Issues VIII, IX, X, or XI: The SAT

The decline in coverage of "Heritability and Group Difference" Issues is paralleled by a steady increase in coverage of SAT–related topics. The early 1970s saw almost no interest in the SAT by any of the news media but beginning in 1975, there is a dramatic rise in SAT coverage, leveling off about 1980 (though there is a slight decline in 1983). Much of the increasing interest in the SAT is the result of concern over the long–term decline in average scores among U.S. high school students, as well as the effects of coaching on SAT scores (highlighted by the 1979 FTC report). This coverage also reflects a shifting emphasis among the critics of testing (the NEA, the Nader group), who instigated public discussion of the issues of bias in the SAT and the inordinate importance placed on the SAT in deciding the fate of American high school students. Not shown in Figure 6.3, but related to this change in focus among the critics of testing, is a rise in coverage of employment testing issues, which looks much like the SAT graph, but with a smaller number of articles.

Newsmagazines. The distribution of Issues considered in newsmagazine coverage of the IQ controversy, shown in Figure 6.2, is highly similar to that found in the newspapers (rank–order correlation with the $NYT = 0.83$), though "The Nature of Intelligence" and "Test Use and Misuse" Issue groups represent a higher proportion of all newsmagazine articles than is the case with newspapers. The percentage of newsmagazine articles considering each of the Issue groups is as follows: "The Nature of Intelligence," 35.8%; "Test Use and Misuse," 31.3%; "Heritability and Group Differences in IQ," 59.7%; "SAT," 44.8%; and "Employment Testing," 4.5%.

Newsmagazines do not exhibit the same significant time trends in coverage of Issues (Figure 6.3) that the newspapers do. While displaying a rise in coverage of SAT–related topics during the late 1970s, the newsmagazines provided a more or less constant level of coverage of other IQ issues. Of course, the relatively small number of newsmagazine articles precludes any highly prominent trends.

Television networks. It is not surprising, in light of the data in Figure 6.1 indicating television's late entry into coverage of IQ issues, that the most common Issues considered in television news stories have been SAT–related. Nearly 57 percent of all relevant television news broadcasts are concerned with one or another of the SAT Issues. The controversial "Heritability and Group Differences" Issues account for 40 percent of the broadcasts. Other IQ and testing Issues have received minimal coverage on television.

Because television was so little concerned with testing issues before the mid 1970s, the time–trend graphs for the television networks in Figure 6.3 are restricted in range. Nonetheless, even the networks show a rise in coverage of SAT-related Issues over the second half of the analyzed time period.

The distribution of Issues in Figure 6.2 reflects both the actual occurrence of news events, and decisions by those in the news media about the relative importance of various issues in the IQ controversy. The differences between news sources in Figures 6.1 through 6.3 are the result of differences in these decisions. The similarities are determined both by the occurrence of events and the similarity of decisions reached about the importance of those events. There is a circularity inherent in these decisions, however, as the news media, by the nature of their coverage, help both to create events and to make them important. Would Jensen's *HER* article have caused such a stir on college campuses and elsewhere had every major print news source not run at least one story on Jensen's thesis? On the other hand, would the media have been so quick to pick up on the story had there not been at least some violent reaction?

The decision to run a story is determined both by what media personnel believe their audience should know and what they believe the audience is interested in. Herbert Gans, on the basis of his analysis of national newsmagazine and television network news coverage, concludes that the newsworthiness of a story is in part determined by certain enduring values shared by those making news decisions. Among these are a belief in individualism (individual worth) and racial integration. Stories about IQ heritability and racial differences in test scores become newsworthy when one holds such values.

Gans also discovered that journalists base what they believe to be of interest to their audience on what is of interest to themselves.[19] The SAT is perhaps the predominant aptitude test in America, of interest to millions of high school students and their parents, particularly if those students are applying to selective colleges. Members of the elite media have disproportionately attended elite (selective) colleges, meaning that the SAT was probably important in their lives. Many are also parents whose children are or soon will be applying to such colleges. In the words of William Schneider and I. A. Lewis, describing the results of a 1985 *Los Angeles Times* poll of over 2,700 newspaper journalists and nearly 3,000 members of the general public:

> Thus, what we end up with is an impression of newspaper journalists as something like "superyuppies." They are emphatically liberal on social issues and foreign affairs, distrustful of establishment institutions (government, business, labor), and protective of their own economic interests.[20]

Besides the personal interest of journalists, the extraordinary amount of coverage of SAT–related issues (relative to the interest in these issues in the professional literature) undoubtedly is dictated by certain organizational constraints of the media. Journalists must be able to tell a readily understandable story on issues of major national and community interest. For better or worse, SAT scores have been accepted by large portions of the news media as a simple metric of the quality of America's high schools. The very large number of stories describing the twenty–year decline in SAT scores almost invariably address the issue of the quality of the schools. Thus SAT stories become more than merely a description of test results.

The desire to tell a readily understandable story may also explain the smaller amount of coverage of Issues concerning "The Nature of Intelligence" and "Test Use and Misuse." These Issues have played a major role in professional discussion of testing, but they tend to be among the most technical of testing–related topics, involving factor analyses, reliability and validity coefficients, and large–scale studies of testing effects. It is often difficult to tell a good story with these data given the production constraints and sometimes inadequate technical training of journalists. Gans notes that the journalists he studied explicitly reject from consideration members of the audience they consider "'would–be intellectuals' who are thought to want more detailed or more analytic—and thus boring—stories than the journalists are willing or able to supply."[21] Reporters for the television networks, whose ability to tell a detailed story is severely limited by the available time, hold this view even more strongly than those at the newsmagazines, which may explain the almost total absence of network coverage of Issues I through IV. Consistent with these considerations, when technical issues like heritability are considered by the various media, they are usually oversimplified, and often grossly inaccurate.

General Tone of Coverage

Table 6.2 lists coder ratings of testing and heritability tone of articles and broadcast segments from each news source. The testing tone data include all coded news stories, the heritability tone data include only those articles and broadcasts considering Issues V, VI, VII, or XI ("The Heritability of IQ," "Group Differences in IQ," "Other Issues Concerning Herrnstein, Jensen, or Shockley," and "Group Differences in SAT Score"), that is, only those stories in which heritability could possibly be considered.

Ratings of general tone (i.e., author's or reporter's attitude) are potentially the most subjective part of the content analysis. Therefore, coders were instructed to be as conservative as possible in making tone ratings, coding tone as anything other than neutral only when absolutely certain

TABLE 6.2
General Tone of Articles and Broadcast Segments

Testing:	New York Times	Washington Post	Wall Street Journal	News Magazines	Television Networks
Pro-Testing	18	15	2	6	0
Anti-Testing	35	18	0	7	3
Neutral	214	90	20	54	62
Heritability of Test Scores:[a]					
Innate	13	0	1	1	1
Learned	39	16	0	4	3
Neutral	119	60	12	45	28

[a]Includes only articles and broadcast segments considering Issues V, VI,VII, or XI.

(see the instructions, Appendix C). As a result, ratings of tone are extremely reliable, but are rarely coded as anything other than neutral.

Newspapers. Nearly 20 percent of all *NYT* articles are rated as having other than a neutral tone regarding testing in general. Of these, almost two–thirds are anti–testing. The difference in the proportion of *NYT* articles rated pro– and anti–testing is statistically significant. *WP* articles are slightly more likely to be rated as other than neutral (26.8 percent), but these articles are no more likely, statistically, to be pro– than anti–testing. The *WSJ* had too few articles for meaningful results.

The heritability tone results present clearer evidence for a slant in the reporting of testing related issues, though once again, the vast majority of articles are rated as neutral. Slightly more than 30 percent of all relevant *NYT* articles are rated as other than neutral with regard to the heritability of test score. Of these, articles emphasizing that skills measured by intelligence and aptitude tests are learned are three times more common than those stressing innate factors. In the *WP*, 21 percent of articles are other than neutral with regard to heritability, and all of these are rated as emphasizing the learned nature of intelligence.

The dichotomous nature of the heritability ratings (innate *vs.* learned) might seem counterfactual in light of the gene–environment synthesis discussed in Chapter 3, but these ratings were designed to reflect the realities of news media coverage, not the facts of human development. The news media have a strong tendency to cast all "controversies" in black–and–white terms in which only the most extreme positions are represented, often at the expense of scientific accuracy. The heritability issue is a prime example of this style, where the idea of the equal importance of genes and environment in development seems often to be lost (see the discussion of question 5 in Chapter 2). Consider, for example, the March 31, 1969 *News-*

week article on Jensen, which begins, "Is intelligence inherited or determined by the environment?" and then attributes to Jensen the belief that "intelligence is fixed at birth;" or the *Time* article of December 19, 1977, in which the author claims that "[f]ew support Harvard Psychologist Richard Herrnstein's position that intelligence is primarily an innate ability, *rather than* an evolving capacity resulting from the interplay of mental quickness and environmental conditioning." (emphasis added) Not only have the news media been guilty of oversimplification, but they are more likely to stress to their readers one side of this false dichotomy.

Strong attitudes are, by definition, more likely to be expressed in editorials, letters to the editor, and book reviews than in feature articles. In fact, there are some striking differences in tone between each of these article types. Table 6.3 shows the number of newspaper articles receiving each of the tone ratings for each article type. Editorials are significantly more likely to be pro–testing than feature articles (when editorials, letters to the editor, and book reviews are excluded, newspaper articles are much more frequently anti– than pro–testing), though no more likely to favor the innate than the learned position on the heritability of test scores. Letters to the editor are also significantly more pro–testing than feature articles, and significantly more likely to take the innate stance on heritability, often in response to the support of the learned position found in feature articles, editorials, and book reviews. Book reviews are, quite clearly, the most opinionated of all newspaper articles. Nearly 40 percent are rated as other than neutral on testing tone, and over 60 percent are not neutral on heritability. In both cases, all non–neutral book reviews are anti–testing and favor the learned position on heritability. Tone ratings for book reviews are based on both the description of the book being reviewed and the comments of the reviewer. These ratings reflect both a predominance of

TABLE 6.3
General Tone of Newspaper Articles by Article Type

Testing	Feature Article	Editorial	Letter to the Editor	Book Review
Pro-Testing	5	17	13	0
Anti-Testing	25	9	10	9
Neutral	228	40	42	14
Heritability of Test Scores:[a]				
Innate	3	1	10	0
Learned	21	12	11	14
Neutral	234	53	44	9

[a]Includes only articles considering Issues V, VI, VII, or XI

anti–testing and anti–genetic books and a group of book reviewers sympathetic to these viewpoints.

Newsmagazines. Slightly less than 20 percent of newsmagazine articles are rated as other than neutral in general testing tone. These ratings are no more likely to be pro– than anti–testing. Only five of fifty relevant newsmagazine articles receive other than neutral heritability–tone ratings. These numbers are too small for any significant differences to appear.

Television networks. Television broadcasts are rated as overwhelmingly neutral with regard to testing in general and the heritability issue, and there are no significant differences among the non–neutral ratings, though the trends are consistent with those from the newspapers (anti–testing and learned).

Despite some indication that the news media may be presenting stories concerning testing in a somewhat slanted manner, the majority of all print and broadcast stories are rated as neutral in the overall impression with which they leave the reader. This is not to say, however, that the media are generally accurate and objective in their coverage of testing issues. As many of those who have studied the news media have noted, media bias is more often reflected in the selection of stories than in a biased accounting within any given story. To this we add that inaccuracies in technical stories result when there is more concern with appealing to the audience than with objectively reporting what the technical experts have to say. The determination of such bias and inaccuracy in media accounts of testing requires a more detailed analysis of the specific content of news stories and, particularly, the media's use of expert opinion. That analysis is the subject of the next chapter.

Notes

1. Office of the Assistant Secretary of Defense, *Profile of American Youth* (Washington, DC: Author, 1982).
2. Lynne Sussman, "Press Coverage of the 1982 *Profile of American Youth* Study: The Intersection of Journalism, Social Science Research, and the Pentagon." Paper presented at the convention of the American Association of Public Opinion Research, Buckhill Falls, PA, May 1983.
3. Ibid., p. 4.
4. Ibid., p. 6.
5. R. Darrell Bock and Elsie G. J. Moore, *Profile of American Youth: Demographic Influences on ASVAB Test Performance* (Washington, DC: GPO, 1984), pp. 268–271.
6. Edward Jay Epstein, *News From Nowhere* (New York: Random House, 1973); Herbert J. Gans, *Deciding What's News* (New York: Pantheon, 1979); June Goodfield, *Reflections on Science and the Media* (Washington, DC: American Association for the Advancement of Science, 1981); Carol Weiss and Elinor

Singer, *The National Media Report Social Science* (New York: Russell Sage Foundation, forthcoming).
7. Sussman, p. 5.
8. Gans, pp. 42–52.
9. S. Robert Lichter, Stanley Rothman, and Linda S. Lichter, *The Media Elite* (Bethesda, MD: Adler & Adler, 1986), p. 14.
10. Sussman, p. 7.
11. Ibid., p. 9.
12. Weiss and Singer, Chapter 6.
13. Ibid., Chapter 10.
14. For example, Goodfield, p. 22; Lichter et al, pp. 52–86.
15. Epstein, pp. 271–272.
16. Lichter et al, p. 54.
17. Ibid., p. 284.
18. Carol Weiss, "What America's Leaders Read," *Public Opinion Quarterly* 38 (1974):1–22.
19. Gans, p. 230.
20. William Schneider and I. A. Lewis, "Views on the News," *Public Opinion* 8 (August/September 1985):8.
21. Gans, p. 240.

7

No News Is Good News: The Nature of
News Media Coverage

The purpose of this content analysis is to describe objectively the way in which the elite print and television media have characterized the various issues constituting the IQ controversy. In the last chapter we examined the extent of media coverage of the controversy, including the distribution of issues considered. This chapter focuses on the specific representation of key topics. What do the news media have to say about each of the issues considered in their coverage of testing? What positions on controversial topics are represented, and how are they characterized? We are particularly interested in the news media's characterization of expert opinion about testing, and in a comparison between news media coverage and the results of our expert survey.

The chapter is organized around a series of six Issue groups, corresponding to the Issues described in the last chapter, as well as to the discussion in Chapters 2 through 5. These Issue groups are the Nature of Intelligence (Issues I and II; Chapter 2), Intelligence Test Use and Misuse (Issues III and IV; Chapter 5), Heritability and Group Differences in IQ (Issues V through VII; Chapters 3 and 4), the SAT (Issues VIII through XI; Chapter 5), Employment Testing (Issue XII; Chapter 5), and Testing Outside the United States (Issue XIII). The emphasis placed on each of these subjects in news media coverage is very different from that to be found in the empirical literature, a fact of some importance, but the issues themselves remain the same. Therefore, the following account of the media's characterization of testing related topics should be directly relevant to the question of news media accuracy in describing expert opinion and in conveying empirical facts about testing.

The Nature of Intelligence

Newspapers

Comments on newspaper coverage are based on the fifty–three articles considering topics related to the nature of intelligence in the *New York Times* (*NYT*) and twenty–nine such articles in the *Washington Post* (*WP*). Coverage in these two newspapers is highly similar; the four relevant *Wall Street Journal* (*WSJ*) articles provide too little code for meaningful analyisis.

In general, the *NYT* and *WP* portray intelligence as a poorly defined, poorly measured concept, and intelligence tests as narrowly focused, poorly developed measures of achievement. For example, eleven articles (eight *NYT*, three *WP*) consider the question of the definition of intelligence; all report that intelligence is not well defined. Eight articles (five *NYT*, three *WP*) report that intelligence is too broad a concept to be measured by a single test; only one of these articles gives the other side of the argument as well. There are eighteen accounts (eleven *NYT*, seven *WP*) describing how intelligence tests measure only a narrow range of mental ability; no newspaper article provides any information to counter this assertion.

Consider the following statement from an August 29, 1971, *NYT* feature article:

> There is little agreement among scientists as to what intelligence really is, and it is readily conceded by most psychologists that the I.Q. tests measure a relatively narrow range of mental attributes.

The author uses as his source the expert population as a whole. Usually, journalists are careful not to attribute statements to most or all experts; more common is the use of a quotation or citation from a single expert, or an unattributed assertion by the author. Among all sources for statements concerning the nature of intelligence in the *NYT* and *WP*, 39 percent are a single expert (including Herrnstein, Jensen, or Shockley), and 32 percent are simply stated or implied by the author. Another 21 percent are nonexpert others, such as the NAACP and other critics of testing. As one might expect, author assertions are more common in editorials, letters to the editor, and book reviews than in feature articles; assertions or implications represent only 20 percent of feature article source codes.

In the last chapter we reported that book reviews received the highest proportion of anti–testing ratings (Chapter 6, Table 6.3). A good example is provided in the December 2, 1972, "Books" section of the *WP*, in which

Wilson C. McWilliams, a professor of political science, reviews five books about intelligence, including one each by Jensen and Herrnstein. Mc-Williams sets up Jensen and Herrnstein as the bad guys against the remaining authors and the rest of behavioral science. Most of the comments concern heritability and group differences, but there is discussion of the nature of intelligence:

> [Jensen and Herrnstein] and their confreres have devoted their lives to IQ testing and, despite a few disclaimers, they equate IQ with intelligence. Ask the Emperor if his new clothes are real, but do not expect Jensen or Herrnstein to consider that the equation may be false. But that is the real point at issue. IQ measures something, but it is not at all clear that the something is intelligence. . . . In fact, IQ is as defective in what it omits from a definition of intelligence as it is in what is included.

In fact, most experts would disagree, as the response to survey questions 3 and 4 indicates. Moreover, both Jensen and Herrnstein came to the question of intelligence late in their careers, and neither has a vested interest in testing.

Other statements about the nature of intelligence in newspaper coverage include ten descriptions (seven *NYT*, three *WP*) of intelligence tests as primarily measures of test–taking skills (only one of these articles also reports the opposite), and five statements (two *NYT*, three *WP*) that test questions are poorly conceived or ambiguous (no arguments to the contrary). Eighteen times the *NYT* (eight articles) and *WP* (ten articles) report that intelligence tests are primarily measures of exposure to relevant environments (i.e., measures of achievement). In only one of the *NYT* articles is any other opinion represented. When a February 10, 1982, *WP* editorial reports that the National Academy of Sciences panel had recently concluded that standardized ability tests are useful predictors of academic and job performance, the editors also claim that "[t]his holds true for both achievement tests and so–called aptitude tests, which largely measure the same thing—what a person knows at the time he or she takes the test, not inherent ability to learn. . . . Nor do the differences in average scores say anything about individual potential." Even when reporting good news about tests, the editors' confusion over the aptitude–achievement distinction (and their belief in human equipotentiality) prevent them from getting the facts straight.

Newspaper coverage of the nature of intelligence is not completely inaccurate, however. Our expert sample generally believes that such factors as attitude and motivation can have a significant effect on test performance (question 8). Newspaper coverage reflects this consensus: nine articles (seven *NYT* and two *WP*) report a significant effect of attitude and motivation, one of the *NYT* articles reports the opposite opinion as well, and one *WP* article reports only that attitude and motivation have little effect. Even when newspaper coverage is consistent with expert opinion, however, the facts often are reported in a way that makes the situation look worse than it probably is. Under the heading "Stories That Test Scores Don't Tell," in the May 1, 1977, *NYT* "Spring Survey of Education," E. J. Dionne Jr. tells the following story:

> For some of [a high school guidance counselor's] students, however, the tests proved to be nightmares. One girl who placed very high in her class panicked on every standardized test. Often, said Mrs. Yeagle, she would lose her place and mark the right answer in the wrong boxes. "Her test scores were disastrous," Mrs. Yeagle said.

Memorable tales like this capture the reader's attention, but they may be misleading in the absence of any information about the prevalence of such horror stories.

Fifty–eight percent of experts surveyed believe that intelligence tests measure learning potential (capacity to acquire knowledge). Two *WP* articles assert this proposition. Four other *WP* articles assert or cite experts who believe the opposite. Our experts see intelligence, as measured by tests, as somewhat less stable an attribute than height (question 6, though it is clear that IQ is, by any absolute standard, highly stable, particularly after age eight). Newspaper coverage split on this question. Five articles (four *NYT*, one *WP*) state that test scores are reliable and stable, and four (three *NYT*, one *WP*) emphasize the possibility of large fluctuations in test score throughout one's lifetime. It is interesting that no article presents both sides of the argument, and that in four of the five articles claiming stability, Jensen is the only source. These articles, like most of those containing positive statements about the nature of intelligence, are reports of Jensen's beliefs about testing, usually accompanied by critical response.

One of few good things newspapers have to say about the content of intelligence tests is contained in eight articles (five *NYT*, three *WP*) reporting that these tests measure abstract reasoning or problem solving (there are no reports to the contrary). The most common source for this position is Jensen, accounting for half the attributions. Finding other expert sources couldn't have been difficult, as 80 percent of our expert survey agree with Jensen. In fact, throughout this Issue group, in those rare cases where positive statements about testing are made, they are almost always attributed to Jensen or, occasionally, Herrnstein. On the other side, one frequently finds such anti–testing psychologists as Leon Kamin, Jane Mercer, Robert Williams, and Jerome Kagan. Such a dichotomy, particularly when coverage of the latter group is predominant, is hardly representative of expert opinion.

Newsmagazines

There are twenty–four relevant newsmagazine articles. Overall, coverage of the nature of intelligence looks very much like that in the *NYT* and *WP*, with one important exception that holds true for all Issues in the content analysis. Newsmagazines are much more likely to draw from expert sources, and less likely to assert or imply something, than are newspapers and television. Seventy–eight percent of all newsmagazine attributions on the nature of intelligence are to one or more experts, while only 9 percent are asserted or implied. Among newspaper feature articles (the more appropriate comparison, since newsmagazine pieces are almost exclusively feature articles) the comparable figures are 51 percent and 20 percent. Television coverage of the nature of intelligence employs only twenty–three total sources, but only 35 percent of these are experts, and 35 percent are assertions or implications.

Newsmagazines, like newspapers, primarily describe tests as narrowly defined measures of a poorly understood conception of intelligence. Five articles cite experts and others claiming that intelligence is not well defined, and one article attributes the opposite opinion to Jensen. Four articles claim that intelligence is too multi–faceted to be measured by a single test, while only one of these cites some experts as believing the contrary. Seven articles tell us that intelligence tests reflect a narrow conception of intelligence, and one also tells us that Jensen believes the opposite. Newsmagazine articles are three–to–two positive on intelligence tests as measures of achievement (the two dissenting articles cite Jensen), four–to–zero on test questions being poorly conceived, and zero–to–four on test scores being stable. Taken together, these data indicate an extremely negative picture of intelligence tests, one very different from the results of our expert survey.

On the positive side, newsmagazine articles are eight–to–zero on intelligence tests measuring abstract reasoning or problem solving, and three–to–zero on learning potential. Newsmagazines also find it easy to reflect the expert consensus on the effects of motivational and personality variables on test performance, being three–to–one positive.

Television Networks

As there are only eight relevant television broadcasts, it is difficult to reach any strong conclusions about network TV coverage of the nature of intelligence. What coverage there is, however, is entirely negative. One broadcast reports that intelligence cannot be measured by a single test, two tell us that tests reflect a narrow conception of intelligence, four equate intelligence with achievement tests, one claims that test questions are poorly conceived, and another that scores are unstable. The sole positive statement about the nature of intelligence in television broadcasts is an interview with Jensen in which he states his belief that intelligence tests measure abstract reasoning and problem solving. That this slanted coverage represents bias on the part of network television reporters and/or executives is indicated in that more than one–third of these negative statements are asserted or implied with no citation.

The television report that intelligence test scores are unstable comes from the CBS News special *The IQ Myth*, originally broadcast on April 22, 1975, and subsequently rebroadcast. Dan Rather explains, "On one important point, however, all but a few of the experts agree: certainly over the span of a lifetime, an individual's IQ can change dramatically." Like many of the statements in this CBS broadcast, Rather's claim is not factually incorrect, but it is highly misleading. While it is true that IQ can change dramatically, such changes are almost always during the first eight years of life, and usually accompany massive environmental changes. Moreover, while IQ *can* change dramatically after age eight, it very rarely happens. By citing expert opinion in this way, Rather gives the impression that experts attach little importance to the IQ, since they know it is liable to change at any moment.

What is most bothersome about news media coverage of topics related to the nature of intelligence is not the amount of print and air space given to criticisms of testing; these criticisms have all been made elsewhere, and the media may feel it is their obligation to report them in light of the important role played by tests. What is bothersome is the exceedingly disproportionate coverage given to these criticisms, including frequent assertions of anti–testing sentiments by journalists, and misrepresentation of expert opinion. It is true, for example, that experts disagree about the nature of intelligence, and that intelligence tests do not measure all important aspects of intelligence. But to stress these points repeatedly while giving virtually no coverage to the rough, but important, equation between IQ and intelligence is to do a great disservice to both expert opinion and the testing enterprise.

That our content analysis coders report frequent negative statements about the nature of intelligence, with almost no statements to the contrary, reflects the absence, in news media coverage, of even so simple a statement as "there is a controversy about . . ." Instead, criticisms are reported and left unanswered. Many of those who study the news media have accused journalists of painting all controversies in black and white, as if there were only two legitimate and polar opposite positions on any issue. For many topics related to the nature of intelligence, the media have not provided even such a simplistic form of balance.

Intelligence Test Use and Misuse

Newspapers

There are fifty *NYT* and twenty–six *WP* articles (only three in the *WSJ*) that deal in some way with intelligence test use or misuse. Many of the trends apparent in coverage of the nature of intelligence are even more prominent in newspaper coverage of these topics. The *NYT* and *WP* uncritically report a wide variety of test misuses, while accepting only the most widely recognized of test uses. Jensen and Herrnstein are once again the primary spokesmen for test validity.

The one fact about intelligence and aptitude tests that virtually everyone accepts is that they are good predictors of performance in school. Twenty–two newspaper articles (nineteen *NYT*, three *WP*) consider intelligence tests as predictors of academic success, and all of them are coded positive, while three articles also consider the opposite opinion. These positive statements about testing are, however, almost always in the context of a discussion of test misuse. For example, in an article entitled "I.Q. Tests Once Again Disturb Educators" in the *NYT* education supplement of May 1, 1977, Paul J. Houts explains that many educators believe that the use of intelligence tests to identify the learning disabled will lead to the mislabeling of large numbers of children, that "an I.Q. can literally determine a child's future," and that tests measure a limited body of middle class knowledge. Finally, he admits:

> To a certain extent the tests do predict how well children will fare later in school, although at its best an I.Q. score is only a very rough guide—the correlation is about the same as that between height and weight.

> But the correlation itself is predictable. After all, it is reasonable to assume that if children perform well on certain kinds of puzzles and questions, the chances are that they will perform well on future puzzles and questions of a similar nature. In this sense, I.Q. tests children's test–taking skills as much as anything.

The only other intelligence test uses newspapers seem willing to accept are as discoverers of hidden talent, and as diagnostic tools for identifying children with specific problems, but these are rarely mentioned. Two *NYT* articles report that intelligence tests can discover hidden talent, and nine newspaper articles (five *NYT*, four *WP*) are positive about test use for diagnoses, though two of these also give the contrasting opinion. The most common source for these test uses are not experts, but others, like school board members and teachers who report on their practical experience with tests.

In question 6 of the expert survey, over 75 percent of respondents indicate they believe IQ to be an important determinant of socioeconomic status (SES). No doubt even a greater percentage would admit that IQ is a good *predictor* of SES, regardless of its causal role. The balance of coverage in the newspapers does not reflect this consensus. Two *NYT* and two *WP* articles contain statements indicating that IQ is a good predictor of SES. Five *NYT* articles and one *WP* article present arguments to the contrary. Two *NYT* and four *WP* articles present the position that IQ is an important determinant of SES, and three *NYT* and two *WP* articles disagree. The most common sources on the positive side of both these arguments are Herrnstein and Jensen, while the negative side tends to be more often stated or implied than anything else. (There is one *WSJ* article dealing with these topics, which presents Herrnstein's arguments about the relation between IQ and SES without rebuttal.) Two *NYT* (Jensen as source for both) and one *WP* article report that intelligence tests are good predictors of job performance. Another *WP* article disagrees.

"Controversy Over Testing Flares Again," the lead article of the *NYT* May 1, 1977, "Spring Survey of Education," is written by *Times* education editor Edward B. Fiske. Its first paragraph reads:

> Controversy over the use and misuse of standardized tests is once again raging through American education. Four years ago, the National Education Association, the country's largest teacher organization, called for a moratorium on the use of standardized intelligence, aptitude and achievement tests on the ground that their results were usually "misleading and unfair." Minority groups have attacked them for cultural bias and consumer groups for excessive secrecy. Legislators have moved to give students greater access to testing data, and at least one court has awarded damages for what amounted to misuse of test scores by school officials.

The remaining sixteen paragraphs of the article document each of the claims made in the introduction, citing numerous examples of test misuse and criticisms from both experts and nonexperts. Not one of these charges of mislabeling, teaching to the tests, overreliance on test scores, poorly worded questions, cultural bias, and excessive secrecy in test administration is answered by Fiske, or by anyone he cites. Such one–sided treatment of the testing "controversy" is typical of the remaining twelve articles in the *NYT* survey, and of news media coverage of test misuse in general.

Our expert sample agrees that test misuse in elementary and secondary schools is prevalent (question 19), but they believe that test use should continue (question 27). It is also the case that almost half of all experts believe test misuse to be an infrequent phenomenon. Yet in all the news media coverage of test misuse, there is virtually no indication that misuse is not highly prevalent or that it does not completely invalidate test use. Instead, we are told, as in William Raspberry's June 12, 1974, editorial in the *WP*, that when IQ tests "are used to predict academic success, to group children according to whether they test out slow, average, or bright, or to determine which children are taught how much of what, then they can do more harm than good."

The most commonly reported abuse of testing involves the misclassification or mislabeling of children on the basis of test scores, with subsequent detrimental effects on self-image and life chances. Twenty–nine *NYT* and nine *WP* articles discuss the frequent occurrence of such abuse, and only two articles in each source also present the possibility that misclassification is not a common phenomenon. The most frequently used sources for the existence of frequent misclassification are nonexpert others (e.g., "critics of testing," "minority groups," and plaintiff attorneys in the *Larry P.* case) and assertions or implications by the author. The most commonly cited experts are Jane Mercer, and the ubiquitous "many educators." The use of assertion or implication by article authors is often in the form of story telling, in which the plight of one or more abused test takers is chronicled. The following is from "Questions Parents Should Be Asking" from the *NYT* 1977 "Spring Survey of Education":

> Youngsters have often been kept out of honors courses or even placed in classes of slow learners because of the results of standardized achievement or aptitude tests.
>
> In one such case, the parents of a teen-age girl whose grades ranked her in the upper quarter of her class were dismayed when their daughter was kept out of the classes for intellectually gifted pupils of her school.
>
> Meeting with the pupil's adviser, the parents got the impression he had never before looked at their daughter's file.
>
> There was a simple explanation for her exclusion, he told the couple. Their daughter's test scores fell below the admission requirements. Yes, he agreed when pressed, the results did seem surprisingly low when compared with the girl's academic grades. Perhaps, he suggested, their daughter was an over-achiever who should not be pushed beyond her abilities.

Table 7.1 shows the number of articles from each news source in which each of five test abuses is coded as being supported (Pos), contradicted

TABLE 7.1
Code for Intelligence Test Misuse

1. Students are often misclassified, mislabeled, or stigmatized on the basis of their intelligence test scores.

	NUMBER OF ARTICLES OR BROADCASTS				
	NYT	WP	WSJ	Newsmags	TV
Positive	21	6	1	7	4
Negative	0	0	0	0	0
Both	2	2	0	0	0

2. A student's knowledge of his or her intelligence test score often results in negative self-concepts and expectations (acts as a self-fulfilling prophecy).

	NYT	WP	WSJ	Newsmags	TV
Positive	3	3	1	1	0
Negative	0	0	0	0	0
Both	0	0	0	0	0

3. A teacher's knowledge of a student's intelligence test score has a significant effect on student performance.

	NYT	WP	WSJ	Newsmags	TV
Positive	6	1	1	1	0
Negative	0	0	0	0	0
Both	0	0	0	0	0

4. Tests are or have been deliberately used to racist or other inegalitarian ends.

	NYT	WP	WSJ	Newsmags	TV
Positive	15	6	1	1	3
Negative	0	0	0	0	0
Both	1	0	0	1	0

5. Test scores are overrelied upon (are too important in people's lives).

	NYT	WP	WSJ	Newsmags	TV
Positive	11	7	0	5	1
Negative	1	0	0	0	0
Both	0	1	0	0	0

(Neg), or both. It is obvious from these data just how uncritical the *Times* and *Post*, and the elite media in general, have been in reporting test misuse. Comparing these data to the relevant survey responses in Chapter 5 is particularly distressing, especially since experts are often used as sources for claims of test abuse.

The use of expert sources for test misuse is not as common, however, as it is for test use. Newspaper authors, particularly in the *NYT*, apparently feel more comfortable asserting or implying various test misuses than test usefulness. Assertions or implications represent 42 percent of *NYT* and 30 percent of *WP* source codes for test misuse, but only 29 percent and 21 percent for test use. The use of experts, on the other hand, increases from 41 percent in the *NYT* and 17 percent in the *WP* for test misuse to 59 percent and 52 percent for test use.

Special mention should be made of test misuse 4 in Table 7.1, concerning the use of tests for racist or inegalitarian ends. Some of this code represents claims of racism on the part of the State of California made by plaintiffs in the *Larry P.* case, but the bulk of the code corresponds to various accounts of the use of World War I Army test results by eugenicists and immigration restrictionists. This history is very often told by the article author, or else Leon Kamin or Stephen Jay Gould are cited as sources. We discussed in Chapter 1 how this history has been repeatedly misrepresented. The news media are no exception.

Newsmagazines

There are twenty–one relevant newsmagazine articles. Newsmagazine coverage is similar to that from the newspapers, with the exception that the magazines tend to be slightly more positive on test use. Newsmagazine coverage is five articles positive, one both for intelligence test scores predicting school performance, five–to–zero for discovering hidden talent, four positive to one both as a diagnostic tool, three positive to one negative as a predictor of SES (all positive sources are Herrnstein) and as a predictor of job performance, and two positive to one negative as a determinant of SES (two of three positive sources are Jensen). The negative code for SES determination is quite remarkable, as Richard Boeth, writing in the December 17, 1973, issue of *Newsweek* states that "it has never been shown that a 15–point difference in conceptual intelligence [*sic*], as measured by IQ, has any significant effect on performance in a complex society." Over 75 percent of expert respondents disagree.

Newsmagazine coverage of test misuse topics is shown in Table 7.1. The only notable difference between newspaper and newsmagazine coverage of these topics is the proportionally less frequent reference to the racist history of tests. Misclassification is the most frequently mentioned form of abuse, as it is for newspapers, and the tendency toward storytelling and drawing generalizations from specific instances remains. A November 25, 1974, *U.S. News and World Report* article, "School Ability Tests Flunking Out?" answers its own question:

> Group IQ—intelligence quotient—tests have been banned from public
> schools in New York City and Washington, D.C., because critics claimed they

mislabeled too many children as "slow" or retarded. In Washington, a study showed that two–thirds of the allegedly deficient students placed in special education classes didn't belong there.

Lawrence Plotkin, a psychologist and educational researcher at New York's City College recalled the case of a well–known colleague who went on to a Ph.D. and a highly successful career after scoring low on tests and being tracked into a vocational school.

The *U.S. News* reporter may be right that critics believe mislabeling is so bad that test use should be suspended, but there is no indication anywhere else in the article that anyone disagrees.

As with topics concerning the nature of intelligence, newsmagazine authors are far less likely to assert or imply conclusions about testing than are their colleagues at the newspapers. Only 11 percent of newsmagazine sources for test use and misuse are assertions or implications, 62 percent are one or more experts, and the remainder are nonexpert others, generally various "critics" of testing.

Television Networks

There are only nine television broadcasts related to intelligence test use and misuse, but these data are consistent with those from other news sources. There is one positive broadcast each for IQ tests as a predictor of school performance, as a predictor of job performance, as a discoverer of hidden talent, and as a predictor of SES. There is one negative broadcast for predictor of job performance, SES, and discoverer of hidden talent. All of this negative code comes from *The IQ Myth*. An interchange between reporter Robert Schakne and psychologist David McClelland informs us of the value of tests:

> *Schakne*: Does an IQ provide in . . . any information of real value about a person's ability?
>
> *McClelland*: Yeah, I think a very limited value, sure. I think it . . . it shows you some very limit . . . limited specific abilities that are . . . that are probably appropriate for certain occupations, yes, I would say that.
>
> *Schakne*: Such as?
>
> *McClelland*: Very limited. Making up tests.

Table 7.1 shows a very small number of positive codes in television coverage of most test misuse, except misclassification, for which there are eight. Half of these represent coverage of the *Larry P.* case. On November 11, 1977, Don Oliver reported on the *NBC Nightly News* that "[a]ttorneys for the children [in the *Larry P*. case] will contend the State fostered racial segregation by placing more blacks in mentally retarded classes, and that the children have been scarred for life because of it." As with the *U.S. News* quote, above, Oliver is probably reporting the attorneys' contention correctly. Apparently, NBC did not feel that the charge that placing black children into EMR classes on the basis of IQ scores would "scar them for life" deserved some form of rebuttal.

Heritability and Group Differences in IQ

Newspapers

This Issue group, comprising "The Heritability of IQ," "Group Differences in IQ," and "Other Issues Concerning Herrnstein, Jensen, or Shockley" is considered in 144 *NYT* articles, 46 *WP* articles, and 12 articles in the *WSJ*. Newspaper coverage of these issues most frequently focuses on the views about IQ heritability and group differences of Jensen, Shockley, and Herrnstein (as well as Cyril Burt), with contradictory views expressed by the article author, other experts, or nonexpert others. These articles often contain accusations of cultural bias in intelligence and aptitude tests, a topic also widely discussed in accounts of other test criticisms (as in the Edward Fiske *NYT* education supplement article discussed above). Charges of cultural bias are rarely contradicted, while the claims of Herrnstein, Jensen, and Shockley are more often than not presented in conjunction with opposing views. There is also widespread misunderstanding about the nature of heritability, as well as misrepresentation of the views of controversial pro–testing scientists.

Table 7.2 lists the code from each news source from four key items in this Issue group. The first item concerns the heritability of IQ. An article or broadcast receives a "total" for statements like that in a December 10, 1973, *WSJ* editorial, "Professors Herrnstein and Jensen both surmised that intelligence was passed on genetically," where there is no indication that Herrnstein or Jensen believes the environment also plays a role. Similarly, when critics are said to believe in environmental determination, with no mention of genetic effects, these views are coded as insignificant or nonexistent heritability. Across the three newspapers, 19 percent of the statements about IQ heritability are coded as "total," 43 percent as "significant," and 25 percent as "insignificant or nonexistent." Among expert survey respondents, 94 percent believe there is evidence for a significant within–group IQ heritability, and among the 214 providing white heritability estimates, one gives an estimate of 1.0 and one gives an estimate of 0.

TABLE 7.2
Code for Key Items on Heritability and Group Differences in IQ

1. The heritable component of (genetic influence on) intelligence, as measured by intelligence tests, is:

	NYT	WP	WSJ	Newsmags	TV
	NUMBER OF ARTICLES OR BROADCASTS				
Total (no mention of environmental determination, or environmental determination ruled out)	19	3	1	5	1
Significant (including environmental determination)	37	10	5	18	4
Insignificant or nonexistent	24	3	3	11	4
Cannot be determined (or undetermined)	15	1	0	2	3

2. The effect of genetic differences on the black-white IQ difference is:

	NYT	WP	WSJ	Newsmags	TV
Total (no mention of environmental determination, or environmental determination ruled out)	16	17	3	10	4
Significant (including environmental determination)	23	6	5	10	4
Insignificant or nonexistent	25	9	3	5	5
Cannot be determined (or undetermined)	17	1	3	5	3

3. The effect of genetic differences on SES differences in IQ is:

	NYT	WP	WSJ	Newsmags	TV
Total (no mention of environmental determination, or environmental determination ruled out)	4	2	0	3	0
Significant (including environmental determination)	2	1	1	3	0
Insignifcant or nonexistent	1	0	0	0	0
Cannot be determined (or undetermined)	0	0	0	0	0

4. Intelligence tests are culturally biased (are largely a measure of exposure to white-middle-class culture).

	NYT	WP	WSJ	Newsmags	TV
Positive	24	12	3	15	9
Negative	1	1	0	1	0
Both	5	7	0	5	3

Sources for total IQ heritability are most frequently Shockley, followed by Jensen, Herrnstein, Cyril Burt, and Hans Eysenck. There are no other sources in the newspapers. Jensen represents more than half of all sources for significant heritability. Shockley and Herrnstein are frequently cited, but other experts are used as well. Nonetheless, because Jensen, Shockley, and Herrnstein are so frequently the sole source(s) for total or significant IQ heritability, the view that genes are important to individual differences in IQ is made to look like a reactionary position held by only the most hard–line testing supporters. Philosopher David Hawkins, reviewing Jensen's book *Bias in Mental Testing* in the July 6, 1980, *New York Times Book Review*, explains how "A decade ago Arthur Jensen stirred up an old controversy, and numerous critics brought it to the boiling point." It seems the "old controversy" involves Jensen's argument "that I.Q. tests yield a reliable measure of mental ability" and his claim that "[t]he fact that test scores are most similar among identical twins and least similar among unrelated persons . . . support[s] the old belief that such abilities are mostly hereditary."

For insignificant or nonexistent heritability, expert sources are most common, along with the nonexpert group labeled "environmentalists." With the possible exception of Leon Kamin, we can be confident that none of the experts cited here actually believes that genes play no role in individual differences in IQ, but their positions are represented as such by newspapers that divide the world into hereditarians and environmentalists, and often fail to clarify for their readers that the argument is over the degree of genetic influence, not its existence or exclusive control. Because newspaper journalists either cannot or do not want to understand this distinction, readers will not either. Writing on the op–ed page of the December 13, 1976, *WP*, Godfrey Hodgson discusses Cyril Burt's "assertion that differences in intelligence were the consequence of hereditary rather than environmental factors."

In response to the disagreement over heritability, many *NYT* authors conclude that the question cannot be answered; the most common source for undetermined IQ heritability in the *NYT* is assertion or implication, usually in feature articles. There are also a considerable number of assertions or implications for significant and insignificant heritability in the *NYT*, but most of these come from the series of letters to the editor following the 1969 *NYT Magazine* "jensenism" article.

One reason Jensen's position on IQ heritability is more accurately reported than Shockley's (they both believe it is significant, but Shockley is more often coded as total) is that Jensen provides a heritability estimate of 0.80 in his 1969 *HER* article. Even if the numbers are not given in descriptions of Jensen's argument, and they rarely are, journalists are usually aware that Jensen does not believe that environment is totally unimportant. Ten of the nineteen sources for heritability estimates in the newspapers (eleven *NYT*, four *WP*, two *WSJ*) are Jensen at 0.80. Most of the rest are Christopher Jencks' estimate of 0.45 in his 1972 book *Inequality*. Herrnstein and Shockley are each cited once as agreeing with Jensen. Environmentalists do not give heritability estimates.

Lee Edson's *New York Times Magazine* "jensenism" article is one of the more accurate media accounts of Jensen's position; Jensen himself praised the piece, but it suffers from at least two errors common to such articles. First, there is the assertion in the title that Jensen believes that "I.Q. is largely determined by the genes." IQ is entirely determined by both the genes and the environment. Jensen believes that *individual differences* in IQ are largely determined by the genes. Second, Edson extrapolates from Jensen's contention that large–scale compensatory education programs have not worked to raise IQs substantially to the conclusion that "[Jensen] adds that [abstract reasoning and problem–solving] ability (which he equates with the ability measured by I.Q. tests) is largely inherited, a matter of genes and brain structure, and therefore no amount of compensatory education or forced exposure to culture is going to improve it substantially." Thirteen *NYT*, three *WP*, and three *WSJ* articles report that a significant IQ heritability would exclude the possibility of successful compensatory education. In all but one *WSJ* and three *NYT* articles, the source for this claim is Jensen. Four of the *NYT* articles deny this claim, and in all four the genials are asserted or implied by the author. These numbers are fascinating both because they so misrepresent Jensen's beliefs (Jensen understands that even a heritability of 1.0 does not rule out the possibility of environmental remediation) and because the newspapers have printed such an obviously hereditarian position with so little contradictory evidence. Jensen and Shockley's belief in the innate inferiority [*sic*] of blacks is also printed, in general, without rebuttal. That all the contradictory statements about Jensen's supposed position on compensatory education are asserted or implied indicates that journalists may find some contentions so absurd as to serve as their own best criticism.

The *NYT* correctly reports in seven articles that Jensen does not believe compensatory education programs have worked (as opposed to the previous statement that they can never work) to raise IQ. In two of these, Jensen is contradicted by other experts. In three other *NYT* articles, the results of successful compensatory education programs (including the Milwaukee Project) are reported with no countervailing evidence from Jensen or anyone else.

Arthur Jensen would not be news, of course, if he had concerned himself only with within–group IQ heritability. News accounts concerning IQ heritability almost always deal with the causes of group differences, primarily the black–white difference, in IQ as well. Most common are discussions of the views of Jensen or Shockley, in which their opinions about within–group heritability and the possible genetic basis for the black–white IQ difference are run together (or within–group heritability is not mentioned at all), often at the cost of considerable confusion about the independence of within– and between–group differences. More often than not, the impression is given that Jensen's or Shockley's (or Herrnstein's or Burt's or Eysenck's) views about genetic involvement in group differences in IQ are a direct result of, or even the same thing as, their belief in substantial within–group heritability. Professor Hawkins, following his statement (quoted above) that Jensen believes IQ to be "mostly hereditary," continues, "Since in the United States blacks, on the average, score less well on the tests than whites, Professor Jensen concluded that these average I.Q. differences were also mainly biological in origin." This syllogism is neither valid nor an accurate description of Jensen's argument. Yet in most media accounts, the views that there is a substantial within–group heritability to IQ and that genetic factors play a role in group differences in IQ are inextricably linked.

Two more examples, both from the *NYT*, demonstrate not only that the within– and between-group issues are linked, but also the kind of language used to describe the views of Jensen, Shockley, and their co–conspirators. Boyce Rensberger's November 18, 1976, article on the Burt scandal explains:

> Because Dr. Burt's writings [on within–group heritability] had been a major buttress of the view that blacks have inherited inferior brains, his discrediting is regarded as a significant blow to the school of thought espoused by such persons as Arthur Jensen of the University of California, Richard Herrnstein of Harvard and William Shockley of Stanford.

In his review of the "important and valuable book" *The Legacy of Malthus* by Allen Chase in the March 13, 1977, *New York Times Book Review*, historian George M. Frederickson[1] concurs with Chase's description of

> those educators and psychologists who use I.Q. tests and rigidly hereditarian conceptions of "mental retardation" to deny poor children a chance to overcome remediable deficiencies, and of course the new breed of pseudo–scientific advocates of white superiority over blacks—namely Professor Arthur R. Jensen, William Shockley (a Nobel laureate in physics) and their fellow travelers.

The second item listed in Table 7.2 concerns the source of the black–

white difference in IQ. The coding scheme is essentially the same as in the first item concerning IQ heritability. Note the general similarity to the distribution of code for heritability, with the exception that the *WP* has nearly twice as many coded articles on group differences in IQ as on heritability, and they are much more likely to report that the effects of genes on the black–white difference are total. In those seventeen *WP* articles, Shockley is ten times the source for total genetic determination, Jensen nine times, and Herrnstein once. In the *NYT*, it is Shockley nine times, Jensen six, and Herrnstein once. In the *WSJ*, Shockley twice and Jensen once. These representations are wrong, particularly for Herrnstein, who has taken an agnostic position on the issue. As with heritability, the newspapers are somewhat more accurate for Jensen than for Shockley; for a significant genetic effect on the black–white difference, Jensen is the source twenty–five times, Shockley five times, and Herrnstein three times across all newspapers. There are only three other expert citations (one of these is Cyril Burt), despite the fact that most expert respondents in the survey agree with Jensen on this point.

In contrast, the claim that genetic effects do not play a role in the black–white IQ difference is attributed most often in newspapers to single experts, and almost as often is asserted or implied by the article author. Nonexpert others ("blacks," "critics of testing") are also common sources. The indeterminate stance is usually attributed to experts, and occasionally is asserted.

Compared to the black–white IQ difference, the subject of genetic effects on SES differences in IQ has received very little media attention. The relevant code is displayed as the third item in Table 7.2. Despite the small numbers, the *NYT* devoted a long piece to the conclusions in Herrnstein's controversial *Atlantic* article. The August 29, 1971, *NYT*, article focuses on Herrnstein's belief that "inborn lack of ability [is] virtually the only factor barring the way to success in careers and in earning power." Richard Herrnstein is coded as a source for total genetic determination once each in the *NYT* and *WP*, and once as significant in the *WSJ*. Arthur Jensen is coded as total once in the *WP*, and as significant twice in the *NYT*. Cyril Burt receives two total codes in the *NYT*. The view that genetic factors play a role in SES differences in IQ is contradicted in only one *NYT* article.

The most common nongenetic explanation for group differences in IQ is cultural bias. The final item in Table 7.2 concerns the existence of cultural bias in intelligence tests. The data here look very much like those for various forms of test misuse shown in Table 7.1. Charges of cultural bias are most often reported without the presentation of opposing viewpoints. Sources for positive bias code are frequently experts and assertions or implications, but the most common source across all media is nonexpert others (NAACP, "critics of testing," *Larry P.* plaintiffs, etc.). Arthur Jensen is a frequent source for negative bias code, as are the *Larry P.* defendants, and the National Academy of Sciences study panel.

The overwhelming support for the existence of cultural bias is not in itself inconsistent with the expert survey data. After all, the vast majority of experts believe there is at least some racial and socioeconomic bias in intelligence and aptitude tests (questions 14 and 15). But these experts also believe that this bias is insufficient to invalidate the tests. In many newspaper accounts, on the other hand, cultural bias is presented as vitiating the use of tests for minority groups. The news media are not to be blamed for reporting that the NEA and NAACP have called for a moratorium on testing, or that certain school systems have discontinued test use because they believe tests are biased. But why are there no reports that most experts disagree with these decisions? Worse yet are the opinions blatantly expressed in book reviews and letters to the editor. Allan Chase, the author of *The Legacy of Malthus*, reviews *The Race Bomb* by Paul R. Ehrlich and S. Shirley Feldman in the July 17, 1977, *NYT Book Review*. *The Race Bomb* is an exposé of the racial bias inherent in intelligence tests. But Chase doesn't like the book because it doesn't go far enough: "While there are a number of good books available to help the lay reader understand the continuing tragedy of using the socially caused low I.Q. test scores of the disadvantaged to freeze their social class, 'The Race Bomb' is not one of them."

The negative character of letters to the editor published by the *NYT* after the "jensenism" article may very well be representative of the extraordinary number of letters it received. It may also help explain why Jensen is treated so badly in subsequent *NYT* book reviews and feature articles. On May 12, 1971, for example, it is reported that "[t]he theory of Dr. Arthur Jensen, a California psychologist, that blacks are inherently less intelligent than whites [no mention of the environment], was attacked yesterday by four professors who said it was causing a 'grave negative effect' on how black children are taught." On November 2, 1973, the *Times* reports a Thanksgiving fast announced by a group of Cambridge, Massachusetts social activists to protest the "'racist' teachings of such sociologists [*sic*] as Richard J. Herrnstein, William H. Shockley and Arthur Jensen." The *NYT* did not invent such stories, but it does report them, over and over again. When opinions about the views of Jensen and others are expressed by *NYT* authors, we get statements like the following from house reviewer Christopher Lehmann–Haupt's December 17, 1975, review of two books critical of testing. After describing two apparently unfair intelligence test questions, one involving avoiding bad company, Lehmann–Haupt tells us more about the tests:

Depending on your answers to such questions as these, you get assigned an Intelligence Quotient. And depending on the level of that I.Q., you get earmarked and dogtagged; you are also folded, spindled, and mutilated. You go to the head of the class, or the foot of it, and you stay there. It is predicted whether you are going to become a gynecologist or a movie usher, and you often live up to that prediction, because, as it's been shown, such prophecies tend to self–fulfill. Last but not least, you are told by such authorities as Arthur R. Jensen of the University of California, William Shockley of Stanford, and Richard J. Herrnstein of Harvard, that the ability to answer these questions is a function of your genotype (just fancy! it's good genes that tell you to avoid the temptation offered by bad company); and, what's worse, that black people are 15 percent [*sic*] poorer at it than white people. That is the problem, and frankly it seems so ridiculous that it's a wonder people still bother to write books about it.

Table 7.2 reveals that reports of cultural bias tends to be somewhat more balanced in the *WP* than in the *NYT*. An example of the exception proving the rule is the March 27, 1977, *NYT Magazine* article by Thomas Sowell, "New Light on Black I.Q.," in which Sowell discusses the inevitable cultural context of all testing and the role of cultural deprivation in lower scores of blacks and other minorities throughout American history. Sowell argues that the cultural deprivation of many blacks does not invalidate the tests, which predict equally as well for students of all backgrounds. In the middle of this article, the *NYT* includes a box by Edward Fiske in which he describes the role of testing in the eugenics movement and immigration restriction, as well as the "educational malpractice" of intelligence test misuse. This is one way to achieve balance.

The popularity of Herrnstein, Jensen, and Shockley in press coverage of heritability and group differences in IQ should be clear from results discussed thus far. Table 7.3 contains further information about these three scientists coded from news media accounts. The first item, referring to attributions to Herrnstein, Jensen, or Shockley of black inferiority without any reference to intelligence, is particularly onerous, as none of these scientists speaks of general inferiority, but only differences in intellectual skill (Herrnstein says nothing about racial differences at all), and a belief in the importance of genetic factors is not the same as innate or inherent (read immutable) differences. Most of the other items in Table 7.3 are descriptions of Herrnstein, Jensen, and Shockley attributed primarily to nonexpert critics, with the exception of the educational and political implications of their views, where assertions or implications by authors are also common. These last two items are best explained by example. A March 24, 1973, *WP* article describes how the Southern Regional Council "is worried that acceptance of the newly popular genetic theory [of Jensen] could lead to an end to compensatory education for blacks and the poor," and how

TABLE 7.3
Attributions to and Descriptions of Herrnstein, Jensen, and Shockley

1. Blacks are inherently or innately inferior to whites.

| | NUMBER OF ARTICLES OR BROADCASTS | | | | |
	NYT	WP	WSJ	Newsmags	TV
Herrnstein	2	1	0	0	0
Jensen	5	4	0	1	0
Shockley	11	7	2	2	5

2. Views have adverse implications for educational policy (compensatory education).

	NYT	WP	WSJ	Newsmags	TV
Herrnstein	1	0	0	1	0
Jensen	4	3	1	2	2
Shockley	2	0	0	0	0

3. Views have adverse political implications.

	NYT	WP	WSJ	Newsmags	TV
Herrnstein	1	0	0	2	0
Jensen	5	3	0	6	2
Shockley	1	4	2	1	2

4. Favors eugenic policies.

	NYT	WP	WSJ	Newsmags	TV
Herrnstein	0	0	0	0	1
Jensen	0	0	0	0	1
Shockley	10	3	1	5	8

5. Is a racist.

	NYT	WP	WSJ	Newsmags	TV
Herrnstein	2	0	2	1	1
Jensen	7	1	1	6	2
Shockley	7	2	0	3	4

Leon "Kamin reinforced these fears today by suggesting that government policymakers may turn to Jensen and his allies for statistical evidence to justify attacks on welfare recipients."

That Shockley is the principal villain in most of the items in Table 7.3, and that his views on IQ heritability and group differences are so inaccurately represented, is no doubt the result of the inflammatory nature of his statements. Shockley has dared to speculate about eugenic solutions to the problem of low IQ, and his insistence on debating the racial issue in various public forums across the country engendered a great deal of protest and ill feeling. Also, because he is not a psychologist, his proclamations take on the air of quackery, if not outright racism. For this reason, every time Shockley's name is associated with those of Herrnstein or Jensen in support of a particular position, as it very often is when genetic factors are mentioned, Herrnstein and Jensen's credibility is reduced.

News media coverage of Shockley's "eugenic policies" consists primarily of two items: his speculations about a voluntary sterilization plan for low–IQ individuals and his support of Robert Graham's high–IQ sperm bank. The national news media have been generally accurate in reporting these events, though they apparently need not be. A July 31, 1980, article in the *Atlanta Constitution* by Roger Witherspoon accused Shockley of "envision[ing] the manipulation of races to eliminate people deemed intellectually inferior," and explained how "[t]he Shockley program was tried out in Germany [by Nazi scientists] during World War II. Shockley sued Witherspoon and the owners of the *Constitution* for libel, producing a recording of the interview between himself and Witherspoon in which Shockley made it clear that he was merely speculating about eugenic programs, and that his proposal dealt only with the voluntary sterilization of low–IQ individuals, not a program forced on members of certain racial or ethnic groups. On September 14, 1984, a federal jury in Atlanta ruled in favor of Shockley, but awarded only $1 in actual damages and no punitive damages. Mr. Witherspoon was quoted as saying that he did not "view it as a loss."[2]

Because of their views, Herrnstein, Jensen, and Shockley were all, at one time or another, prevented from speaking publicly. Shockley's was the most newsworthy case because he pushed the issue, insisting on numerous public debates, and forcing the NAS to consider his proposal to fund research into the causes of group differences in IQ. When a topic or viewpoint is considered too menacing to even discuss, First Amendment issues are raised, and the press are naturally interested. None more so than the *NYT*. Between May 2, 1972, and April 18, 1975, the *NYT* published no fewer than thirty articles, editorials, and letters to the editor concerning William Shockley's attempts to discuss racial differences in IQ at Princeton, Yale, and elsewhere and the uncivil, and often violent reaction with which he was met. An *NYT* editorial of November 23, 1973, is typical of views expressed elsewhere in the *Times*, and in the *WP* and *WSJ*:

> Dr. Shockley's theories about intelligence and race are subject to serious question and have been challenged by many scientists whose backgrounds in these areas of research are far more impressive than his. None of these facts can justify what has become a concerted nationwide campaign to silence the physicist and to deprive those who want to hear him of the opportunity to listen.

When the issue of the propriety of studying or discussing group differences in IQ is reported, as it is in coverage of Shockley's petitions to the NAS, the *NYT* is more likely to report viewpoints in favor of freedom of speech and research. Ten *NYT* articles represent only the pro–research side of this debate, six articles present both sides, and only two present just the negative side. More surprising, Shockley and Jensen are not the most common positive sources; other experts and author assertions are. The November 18, 1973, *NYT* reports that a group of college professors told a conference at New York University that the "racist doctrines" of Jensen, Herrnstein, and Shockley "linking intelligence to race by heredity were unfair for college classrooms because they are as untrue as [the contention that] the world is flat." Ironically, in light of one–sided treatment accorded views about race and IQ by the *NYT*, the author of the article ends sarcastically, "None of the participants took the position that a free exchange of ideas should be encouraged."

Newsmagazines

The forty relevant newsmagazine articles provide coverage of heritability and group differences in IQ comparable to that from the newspapers, as the data in Tables 7.2 and 7.3 reveal. While reporting of these issues is often accurate, there are the same tendencies to simplify the heritability issue, to misrepresent Herrnstein, Jensen, and Shockley, to pit them against the rest of the world, to confuse within– and between–group genetic effects, and to accept the notion of cultural bias in intelligence tests as axiomatic. The newsmagazines are less concerned with Shockley than are the newspapers and, as with other Issue groups, are more likely to use expert sources and less prone to assertion or implication than are newspapers (even when compared to newspaper feature articles).

The first *Newsweek* article concerning the Jensen affair, dated March 31, 1969, begins, "Is intelligence inherited or determined by the environment?" Thus the false dichotomy is established, and Jensen comes down clearly on one side: "Since intelligence is fixed at birth anyway, [Jensen] claims it is senseless to waste vast sums of money and resources on such remedial programs as Head Start which assume that a child's intellect is malleable and can be improved." Not all newsmagazine reports are so inaccurate (articles in the same year in *U.S. News* and *Time* correctly describe Jensen's position on heritability) but there are five newsmagazine articles in which an attribution to total heritability is made. Three sources are Herrnstein, two Jensen, and one Shockley. For the more frequently reported significant heritability, Jensen represents one–third of all sources, and the three scientists together account for one–half. Nearly all the other expert sources for significant IQ heritability come from two 1969 *U.S.*

News articles that reprint excerpts from rebuttals to Jensen in the *Harvard Educational Review*. These scientists criticize Jensen for overstating his point, but agree that genes play a role. More common among news-magazines is the portrayal of Jensen as a loner. After reviewing various pieces of evidence counter to Jensen's claims, an April 11, 1969, *Time* article asserts, "Too little is known of the genes to justify positive state-ments about their contribution to the intelligence of mankind at large, much less to any division of mankind." Overall, the distribution of opin-ions about IQ heritability in newsmagazine reporting, particularly the sub-stantial percentage of "insignificant" attributions, is vastly different from that among experts surveyed.

Jensen's position on compensatory education is as often correctly as incorrectly reported by newsmagazines. Three articles tell us that Jensen's position on heritability rules out the possibility of successful compensatory education, and three correctly report that Jensen believes remediation is still possible, albeit of a different sort than has been tried in the past. Jensen is the only source used in three newsmagazine articles that report that compensatory education has not worked to raise IQs. Jensen is once rebut-ted by other experts, and three independent articles describe the Mil-waukee Project and other successful programs.

All sources for a genetic contribution to the black–white IQ difference are Jensen and Shockley (the newsmagazines correctly leave Herrnstein out of the racial debate), who are just as likely to be ascribed a belief in total genetic determination as one in which the environment also plays a role. All sources for insignificant and undetermined genetic effects are experts, with one *Newsweek* article properly noting Herrnstein's belief that the issue is unresolved.

Confusion over the independence of within– and between–group genetic effects is prevalent. The 1969 *Newsweek* article cited earlier attributes the following to Jensen: "The reason [for the fifteen–point black–white IQ differential,] he argues, is that intelligence is an inherited capacity and that since a prime characteristic of races is that they are 'inbred,' blacks are likely to remain lower in intelligence." The conclusion follows from the premise only if one has already assumed that the cause of the black–white differential is genetic; if it is environmentally caused, the degree of "in-breeding" is irrelevant.

The author of a March 24, 1980, *U.S. News* article attempts to sum-marize the beginnings of the modern IQ controversy:

> It was in 1969 that Arthur R. Jensen, a psychologist at the University of California at Berkeley, declared that heredity is responsible for between 60 and 80 percent of the IQ score. That assertion made "Jensenism" a code

word for racism in the minds of many, because it largely discounted the effects of a child's family background, schooling and economic welfare.

Not only does this statement demonstrate a misunderstanding of the nature of heritability (the 80 percent refers to *differences* in IQ score), but the heritability estimate applies only within groups and does not by itself say anything about the possible effects of environmental manipulation on group differences.

The effects of genetic differences on SES differences in IQ are more accurately handled by newsmagazines, albeit in only three articles, one in each of the magazines. In each case, opposition to Herrnstein's arguments about the possibility of an IQ caste system are attributed to both experts and others who fear Herrnstein's thesis may be used to "rationalize theories of racial superiority"[3] and reduce "compensatory education, affirmative action, and equal–opportunity programs."[4]

Newsmagazine coverage of cultural bias in intelligence tests is even more one–sided than it appears in Table 7.2. The twenty articles coded as positive for cultural bias use thirty–four different sources, half experts and half others. The six articles coded as negative for bias use only six sources, half of which are Jensen (after the publication of *Bias in Mental Testing*). The following paragraph, from a December 19, 1977, *Time* article entitled "Whatever Became of 'Geniuses'? Downplaying the old IQ numbers racket," manages to disregard expert support for testing, overemphasize test score instability and misuse, misrepresent Herrnstein's position on IQ heritability, and, in this context, make cultural bias look like a sufficient explanation for the black–white IQ difference:

> The more tests that are devised, the more educators seem to doubt their validity. For one thing, individual IQ scores are known to vary considerably. The IQs of children, for example, can change 17 points to 20 points up or down before the age of 18, and there is sometimes a marked change from one year to the next. Many experts even question how much IQ scores have to do with intelligence. Few support Harvard Psychologist Richard Herrnstein's position that intelligence is primarily an innate ability, rather than an evolving capacity resulting from the interplay of mental quickness and environmental conditioning. It is also possible that such personal traits as drive and persistence—factors that IQ tests cannot measure—are as important as inherent reasoning ability. Furthermore, most psychologists agree that the tests are biased in favor of middle–class children (blacks as a group score 15 points lower than whites). And there is a persistent danger that an IQ may become a labeling device.

Time and *Newsweek*, in late 1979 and early 1980, each published one-page articles on Jensen's book *Bias in Mental Testing*. These articles both present a fair summary of Jensen's evidence against cultural bias, and neither presents much in the way of refutation. Instead, the book's implications are attacked. From the September 24, 1979, *Time* we get:

> Jensen's findings clearly have horrendous implications. Indeed, they come close to saying that blacks are a natural and permanent underclass—an idea so shocking that it is likely to spark the most explosive debate yet over race and IQ.

Someone at *Newsweek* must have read the *Time* piece. The *Newsweek* article of January 14, 1980, concludes:

> Yet on any count, the implications of Jensen's book are grim. His work suggests that attempts to raise the educational success rate of black youngsters to parity with whites are ultimately doomed to fall short. If black test results derive overwhelmingly from inherited traits, Jensen's message is bleak: blacks should resign themselves to a role of intellectual inferiority. Jensen's ideas are so radical that they are bound to renew the debate over race and genes. An uglier prospect is that they may lend themselves to those who would chop away at the fundamental principles of equal opportunity.

In light of these and other quotations from newsmagazine articles, it should come as no surprise that the data in Table 7.3 reveal that the newsmagazines have had unkind things to say about Herrnstein, Jensen, and Shockley. Newsmagazines are less likely than the newspapers to make the "innate inferiority" error, but more likely (considering the relatively small number of articles) to discuss adverse political implications. It is also clear that the newsmagazines are more concerned with Jensen than with Shockley.

Like the newspapers, the newsmagazines covered much of the protest that met these three scientists. Seven newsmagazine articles describe uncivil reactions to Jensen, four relate Shockley's problems (far less, proportionally, than the *NYT*, but consistent with coverage in the other newspapers), and one mentions Herrnstein's difficulties. The newsmagazines are also inclined to give positive coverage to the notion that racial differences in IQ should be researched and discussed. Nine newsmagazine articles present the positive side of this debate, but only three also present rebuttal.

One of the articles presenting both sides of the debate over research is a May 10, 1971, *Newsweek* piece dealing with one of Shockley's petitions to the NAS. The conclusion reached by the author, after describing Shockley's presentation and reactions from other NAS members, is:

> On balance, it seems likely that Shockley is over his head in certain areas. But

he seems a conscientious and well–intentioned man, whatever the use less–well–disposed persons may make of his hypotheses. Thus a reasonable judgment would seem to be that even if his arguments tend to make qualified sociologists, psychologists and geneticists wince, they demand organized attention that the academy currently seems willing to give them.

On December 17, 1973, *Newsweek* ran another article about Shockley, this time describing his difficulties in making himself heard at Princeton and elsewhere. In the only charge of racism against Herrnstein, Jensen, or Shockley asserted by an article author in a newsmagazine, Richard Boeth is less well inclined towards Shockley than his colleague of two years earlier, but remains, nonetheless, a firm believer in free speech:

> Anyone who advances the notion of inheritable racial differences in IQ, according to the wilder–eyed environmentalists, is by definition a racist and should be shouted down for this reason. . . . As it happens, an easy case can be made that Shockley *is* a racist (though how this disqualifies him from the guarantees of the First Amendment is a question for academics to ponder at their leisure). [Emphasis in the original]

Television Networks

The story of television network coverage of heritability and group differences in IQ is principally the story of CBS. The first television broadcast in our sample is a September 8, 1971, *CBS Evening News* commentary by Eric Sevareid concerning the reaction to William Shockley by some psychologists at the American Psychological Association convention. The other two networks do not provide any coverage of IQ–related issues until 1977, thus missing entirely the early fireworks. Of twenty–six network television broadcasts concerning heritability and group differences, only eight come from ABC and NBC: two evening news pieces by each network on the *Larry P.* case, one ABC and two NBC stories on Robert Graham's high–IQ sperm bank (and Shockley's support thereof), and an interview with Arthur Jensen on NBC's *Prime Time Saturday* following the publication of *Bias in Mental Testing*. CBS, on the other hand, in addition to similar coverage of *Larry P.* and Robert Graham, broadcast three commentaries concerning Jensen and Shockley, two *60 Minutes* pieces related to the reaction to Shockley, one on the Cyril Burt affair, the hour–long special *The IQ Myth*, and a host of other related news segments. The comments that follow, therefore, refer primarily to CBS, except where noted.

Taken together, the television networks have not reported much about IQ heritability (item 1, Table 7.2), but the relevant broadcasts are consistent with those from other news sources. The sole attribution to total heritability comes from Mike Wallace's statement in the June 26, 1977, *60 Minutes* segment on Cyril Burt, describing "Burt's thesis that heredity, not environment, determines a person's I.Q." Significant heritability is attributed four times to Jensen, twice to Herrnstein, and once to a nonexpert other; no other expert support is given. Sources for undetermined IQ heritability are all experts, as are those for insignificant heritability (twice Leon Kamin).

Then there is *The IQ Myth*. After asking Harvard psychologist Jerome Kagan if IQ tests measure "inherited ability," and receiving a negative reply, Dan Rather concludes "IQ, in other words, is mainly a talent for school work, an ability that can be developed, especially if you start at an early enough age. That's what most psychologists seem to be telling us." Later, Rather hopelessly confuses the within- and between-group issues in describing Jensen's argument, and expert response:

> It is a fact, as Jensen says, that black children, on the average, score 15 points lower than whites in IQ. As we've seen, it is not a fact that a lower IQ means less intelligence, and there is even less evidence to show that intelligence is 80% inherited. Yet, that percentage is the very basis of Jensen's argument [about genetic effects on the black-white IQ differential]. The same evidence that Jensen uses has been studied by psychologist Leon Kamin. Like most of his colleagues, he finds the conclusions unsound.

What "conclusions" is Rather talking about? The possible genetic effect on racial differences in IQ, or substantial within-group IQ heritability? Rather apparently sees them as the same thing, for he next turns to Leon Kamin for his explanation of Jensen's "evidence" (paraphrased by Rather and never explained by Jensen)—that high IQ runs in families. Kamin says that this information

> certainly does not in any sense prove his interpretation . . . when one finds that a child resembles his parents, one doesn't know whether that resemblance is due to the fact that he's inherited genes from the parents or due to the fact that he has learned an enormous amount from the parents."

Kamin clearly is talking here about within-group heritability. Yet Rather's following statement is, "It isn't some natural lack of intelligence, but a cultural handicap that holds poor children back." Coupled with the earlier statement that "most psychologists seem to be telling us" that IQ is a developed ability, the viewer is left to conclude that "most psychologists" and "most of [Kamin's] colleagues" do not believe *either* in substantial within–group IQ heritability *or* in genetic effects on group differences. Both attributions are incorrect, as our expert survey reveals.

In response to these and similar statements in *The IQ Myth*, several prominent psychometricians and other psychologists interested in intelligence testing wrote to CBS to protest the network's inaccurate treatment of expert opinion on IQ heritability. Among them was Richard Herrnstein. His July 3, 1975, letter to CBS includes a citation from the *Encyclopaedia Britannica,* placing the "usually accepted figures" for IQ heritability between 0.75 and 0.80, in order to demonstrate how easy it would have been for researchers at CBS News to obtain a more accurate summary of the empirical literature. An August 11 response from David Fuchs, vice–president of public affairs broadcasts for CBS News, argues that *The IQ Myth* is a fair appraisal of expert opinion on IQ heritability, and explains that "we do not believe that the fact the broadcast resisted embracing the genetics–is–all theory constitutes a reason for dismissing it as 'fraudulent'." By his own words, Fuchs has condemned CBS News' understanding of expert opinion.

Like the other news media, the television networks are just as likely to attribute to Jensen and Shockley the genetics–is–all theory of the black–white IQ differential (total) as they are to get it right (significant–item 3, Table 7.2). Similarly, Jensen, Shockley, and Burt are the only sources for these opinions; all other expert sources are in support of insignificant or undetermined genetic effects. (Nongenetic explanations like cultural deprivation and segregated schools are six times attributed to other experts, and twice asserted or implied.) The *60 Minutes* segment on Cyril Burt ends with the following quotation from psychologist Kenneth Clark regarding Jensen's genetic hypothesis: "It's a political judgment, it's an ideological judgment, it's chauvinism, but it's not science."

Much of the television coverage of cultural bias in intelligence tests appears in reports of the *Larry P.* case. The norm in such coverage is to interview or cite plaintiff attorneys and expert witnesses who claim that the intelligence tests used for EMR placement in California are biased against blacks. In none of these reports is anyone from the defense shown or cited denying this charge. In fact, the only negative source for cultural bias in television coverage is Arthur Jensen. Most prominent among these is an NBC News *Prime Time Saturday* segment of January 12, 1980, devoted to *Bias in Mental Testing.* Jensen, who is said to have "caused a sensation by saying he had proof that black people are less intelligent than white people," is interviewed at length and is allowed a reasonable presentation of his evidence on cultural bias. Opposing views are given by Robert Williams (developer of the BITCH test) and by Jerome Doppelt of the Psychological Corporation, a major publisher of tests. After Dr. Doppelt expresses his belief that it is not possible for any test to be "free of any cultural loading," reporter John Palmer explains, "But, even though a test publisher thinks a test will always show some cultural bias, Arthur Jensen does not." Palmer has misrepresented Doppelt's opinion, and further isolated Jensen, by confusing cultural loading with cultural bias.

The same error is made, more egregiously, by Dan Rather in *The IQ Myth*:

> For both forms [individually- and group-administered], the test makers tell us, the questions are based on the average experience of the average American child—in school and outside—"average" meaning "middle class." And it's economic class that marks the main dividing line on IQ scores. Middle class children tend to do well, in general, whatever their ethnic or racial background. They are the group the tests are geared to. Lower class children— blacks, chicanos and whites—all tend to do poorly. The test are slanted against their social and cultural background.

Psychometrician Lloyd Humphreys wrote to Rather on May 2, 1975, protesting this statement, and including documentation that social class accounts for a very small proportion of IQ variation, most of the variation being within class and racial and ethnic group. Rather's reply is dated June 2:

> There's no desire on my part to engage in a running debate with you. The broadcast speaks for itself. It is *not*, however, "demonstrably false" that I.Q. tests measure essentially middle class learning. Many who write the tests say that it is what they measure and that's good enough for me. (emphasis in the original)

First, it *is* "demonstrably false" that IQ tests measure essentially middle class learning, as Humphreys' evidence shows. Second, it is unlikely that any test maker, while probably admitting his tests are culture dependent, would say that something he has labeled a test of intelligence "measures essentially middle class learning." Third, it is ironic that an investigative reporter gathering information for a news report that trashes intelligence tests should be willing to take test makers at their word about anything. Why look further when you've already received the answer you're looking for?

If IQ tests are essentially a measure of economic class, it should not be surprising that Rather describes William Shockley as the "leading popularizer of the idea that intelligence is basically a matter of race, an old theory originally revived by psychologist Arthur Jensen of the University of California." We see in Table 7.3 that Herrnstein, Jensen, and Shockley are treated by the television networks more or less as they are by the other news media. Five times Shockley is said to believe in the inherent inferiority of blacks, yet his right to display his racism is defended. The Eric Sevareid commentary, and two *60 Minutes* segments in particular, while unfavorable to Shockley, are even less sympathetic to those who would not let him be heard. (A total of six television broadcasts cover the uncivil reaction to Herrnstein, Jensen, or Shockley.)

On July 27, 1973, a "Spectrum" commentary on the *CBS Morning News* by M. Stanton Evans decries the harassment and charges of racism to which Herrnstein and Jensen have been subjected. On August 13, Ethel Payne replies in another "Spectrum" segment. She brings up the name of Shockley, who "contends that blacks are genetically inferior to whites," and asks:

> What becomes of the mass of humanity which does not fit into the Herrnstein–Jensen–Shockley specification of the hereditarily competent human beings? Instead of using that dread word "genocide," I'll ask what selecting out process they propose to produce the master race? Does it include mass sterilization, psychosurgery and rigid police controls?

If the references to fascism and Nazism weren't enough, Ms. Payne makes it clear where these scientists fit in her political view of the world: "Let Shockley, Herrnstein and Jensen do a study of the genes of the leaders who are responsible for making war and exploiting the poor for the convenience of the rich."

In the world as described by the news media, Jensen, Shockley, and Herrnstein (and occasionally Burt and Eysenck) stand virtually alone as defenders of meaningful intelligence tests, substantial IQ heritability, and genetic determinants of group differences in IQ. Many members of the general public and the professional community have severely criticized the views of these scientists. The news media have reported these criticisms, as they have the views of Jensen, Shockley, and Herrnstein. At times journalists have allowed themselves to be influenced by the often vitriolic language used by many of the critics of testing, and have misrepresented Jensen et al. At times, they have even forgotten their responsibility to remain objective and joined the critics. These mistakes are more the exception than the rule, however. The most widespread and grievous error committed by the news media in their reporting of heritability and group differences in IQ is in using expert sources other than Herrnstein, Jensen, and Shockley only to contradict their views, thus leaving readers and viewers with the very clear impression that expert opinion is decidedly environmentalist and anti–testing. Our survey of experts demonstrates that this is not the case. The news media have allowed themselves to be influenced by a minority of vocal psychologists and educators whose radical views are consistent with a set of journalistic values emphasizing human equipotentiality and equality of outcome.

The SAT

Content–analysis code for key items related to the SAT is shown in Table 7.4. News media coverage of SAT issues shares certain features with coverage of intelligence testing, notably the tendency to one–sided reporting of criticisms of testing (e.g., items 2 and 6 in Table 7.4) and the use of a very small number of expert sources in defense of tests. But there are two very important differences. First, the SAT has a built–in set of expert defenders, the Educational Testing Service (ETS), who develop and administer the test, and the College Entrance Examination Board (CEEB), for whom this work is done. These sources are easy to identify and locate, they are public organizations with a long history of dealing with the press, and they can be counted on to be almost unequivocally positive about the SAT. It is no wonder these organizations or their spokesmen are the most common sources for positive statements about the SAT among all news sources. This state of affairs has certain consequences, foremost among which is that coverage of the SAT tends to be more balanced, and even positive, than is coverage of intelligence tests (e.g., items 1, 3, 4, and 5 in Table 7.4). However, because the defenders of the SAT are almost exclusively the ETS and CEEB, there is the impression that these organizations are engaged in an unsupported battle against their critics, just as was the case with Herrnstein, Jensen, and Shockley. Further, as a result of the perceived importance of the SAT in determining college admissions, and the monolithic nature of the ETS and CEEB, those who challenge the SAT are often portrayed as David against the ETS/CEEB Goliath.

A second important distinction between SAT and intelligence test coverage is that the SAT is taken seriously by the news media as a barometer of the quality of American education. The most frequently reported topic in articles and broadcasts related to the SAT is the nineteen year decline and subsequent leveling off of average SAT scores. These news stories were not intended to demonstrate that the SAT is getting less accurate; inevitably, such reports discuss the changing nature of our schools and students. This implicit legitimization contributes significantly to the positive coverage accorded the SAT.

Newspapers

There are ninety–seven *NYT* articles on SAT–related issues, seventy–five *WP* articles, and eight articles in the *WSJ*. The *NYT* and *WP* are predomi-

TABLE 7.4
Code for Key SAT Items

1. The SAT is a sufficiently valid predictor of success in college to justify its continued use.

	NUMBER OF ARTICLES OR BROADCASTS				
	NYT	WP	WSJ	Newsmags	TV
Positive	11	10	0	3	1
Negative	4	4	0	0	0
Both	3	5	2	1	2

2. The SAT is given too much weight in admissions decisions (exert inordinate control over test takers' lives).

	NYT	WP	WSJ	Newsmags	TV
Positive	10	12	1	4	2
Negative	0	0	0	0	0
Both	0	2	1	1	0

3. The SAT is not significantly different from an achievement test (measure preparation, not potential).

	NYT	WP	WSJ	Newsmags	TV
Positive	3	4	0	1	0
Negative	12	2	0	2	0
Both	2	2	0	1	1

4. SAT prep courses (and software) significantly increase SAT scores.

	NYT	WP	WSJ	Newsmags	TV
Positive	5	2	0	0	2
Negative	0	0	0	0	0
Both	15	13	3	3	2

5. The effect of truth-in-testing legislation on test quality (validity or reliability) will be:

	NYT	WP	WSJ	Newsmags	TV
Positive	6	3	0	5	0
Negative	5	3	0	3	0
Insignificant	1	0	0	0	0

6. The SAT is culturally biased.

	NYT	WP	WSJ	Newsmags	TV
Positive	9	11	0	7	2
Negative	0	2	0	0	1
Both	3	3	3	2	0

nantly positive about SAT validity (item 1, Table 7.4), in agreement with 90 percent of expert respondents (question 24). Positive sources are overwhelmingly ETS, CEEB, or someone associated with them. The most common negative source is Ralph Nader or *The Reign of ETS,* but many other critics appear, including NEA spokesmen.

There is a time trend in the coverage of SAT issues by the newspapers, as well as the other news sources. Prior to 1980 the newspapers seemed, at least implicitly, to support the SAT as a useful decision–making tool. Criticism of the SAT reached its peak at the beginning of this decade, and the newspapers, in addition to reporting these critiques, appear to have been won over by them. Nearly all positive assertions and implications in the *NYT* and *WP* concerning SAT validity appear before 1980, while most negative assertions and implications appear during or after that year. *NYT* book reviewer Christopher Lehmann–Haupt, whose low opinion of intelligence tests is apparent in a previous quotation, nonetheless begins his February 3, 1981, book review with a positive attitude toward the SAT. In response to charges in *The Testing Trap* by Andrew J. Strenio that admissions and other tests are biased, stigmatizing, and controlled by an insensitive "Psychometric–Academic Complex," Lehmann–Haupt reports: "My first inclination was to say, No, here is an issue I refuse to get worked up over. The schools have to go on something in deciding who is to qualify and who is not to." But, he continues, "Mr. Strenio . . . slowly but steadily grinds such silly objections to powder," leading the reviewer to conclude that "[t]he standardized test measures nothing more than the ability to take tests."

As with intelligence tests, newspaper coverage of criticisms of the SAT is extremely one–sided. "The SAT measures primarily test–taking skills," "SAT scores reflect primarily SES" (a favorite of the Nairn/Nader report), and "SAT questions are often poorly conceived or ambiguous" are each given predominantly positive code in approximately half a dozen articles in both the *NYT* and *WP.* Positive sources for these criticisms are varied, coming sometimes from experts, sometimes from nonexpert others, and often are stated or implied, usually in articles published after 1979. (The November 20, 1983, *WP* "Educational Review" is an issue devoted to "The Limits of Testing," and includes as its only article on the SAT a piece by David Owen, future author of *None of the Above: The Myth of Scholastic Aptitude.*) The few negative sources are primarily ETS, CEEB, or someone associated with them.

Item 2 in Table 7.4 gives another example of the lopsided reporting of testing critiques. Here the criticism that the SAT is too important in test takers' lives is bolstered by the ubiquitousness of the SAT, and the ETS/CEEB near monopoly on admissions testing. The news media will always side with what they perceive as the cause of individual liberty against unthinking corporate control. An article in the August 7, 1977, *WP Magazine* by Lisa Berger is entitled "Playing the Numbers: How to Beat the SAT and Score Big." The title page illustration shows four test takers, with pencils as balancing rods, walking a tightrope. They are dwarfed by a growling King Kong–sized gorilla who is applying his finger to the rope in an effort to topple the students. The attitude expressed by this drawing is precisely that of the oft-reported Nairn/Nader argument in *The Reign of ETS: The Corporation That Makes Up Minds.*

The third item in Table 7.4 concerns the aptitude–achievement distinction, and is an indication that coverage by the *NYT* and *WP* is not always similar; the *NYT* is much more likely to print statements in support of the idea that the SAT is something other than an achievement test. Some of the SAT–as–achievement-test code comes from coverage of SAT coaching effects, where the ETS is usually on hand to deny that coaching works and that coaching effects imply that the SAT is not a measure of aptitude. Some discussion comes from coverage of SAT critics like Nairn et al., and some from treatment of the Jencks and Crouse 1982 *Public Interest* article, where they argue, among other things, that the SAT essentially is an achievement test. (The critics are a more frequent topic of discussion in the *WP*, while the *NYT* concentrates on coaching.) The large amount of negative code from the *NYT* comes often from the ETS and CEEB, particularly in relation to coaching, but many of the sources for negative code are implications or assertions, as in an August 24, 1977, article describing the results of the CEEB panel appointed to study SAT score decline. As background, Edward B. Fiske explains that the SAT "is taken every year by more than a million college–bound High School [*sic*] juniors and seniors as a means of evaluating their academic promise." In articles like this, where no contradictory evidence is given, the *Times* seems, at least implicitly, to support the notion that the SAT is something other than merely an achievement test. Again, however, these statements are made primarily in the 1970s.

The aptitude–achievement distinction, discussed in Chapter 2, is most confusing in relation to the SAT. The ETS and CEEB are criticized for calling the SAT an aptitude test, and thus leading test takers to believe that the test measures some innate ability. The ETS and CEEB reply that their test does not measure innate ability, but neither is it a measure of exposure to some specific course material; it is a measure of those skills and abilities necessary to do college work, which are acquired over the course of a lifetime's education. The makers and sponsors of the SAT do not believe that scores can be significantly improved through short–term coaching programs. These are subtle distinctions, more subtle than the typical genetics–or–environment news media account. As a result, we get statements like the following from Fred Hechinger in the October 5, 1982, *NYT*:

> [High schools] no longer believe [the SAT] primarily measures inborn aptitude; they have been persuaded, after years of debate, that the tests results reflect two basic ingredients: verbal and mathematical skills the student has learned, and reasoning ability, including the ability to make intelligent guesses.

From where does reasoning ability come? Is it learned, or an "inborn aptitude"? According to Hechinger it is either one or the other, but not both.

The only other reference in the news media to anything like heritability of SAT scores appears in several articles and broadcasts in various news sources concerning the consistently higher average scores achieved by boys than by girls on the mathematical section of the SAT. These reports are notable because explanations given for this difference are overwhelmingly environmental, both in terms of number of articles and numbers of sources. The genetic hypothesis put forth by Camilla Benbow and Julian Stanley of Johns Hopkins University, when reported, is always coupled with statements of extreme disagreement from other members of the expert community. (Though an August 2, 1987, *NYT* piece by Daniel Goleman admits that accumulating evidence makes the Benbow–Stanley hypothesis increasingly plausible.)

The average verbal and mathematical SAT scores of U.S. high school students declined steadily from 1963 to 1981. Both the *NYT* and *WP* provided nearly annual coverage of this phenomenon. Reported explanations for the trends, attributed to experts at ETS and CEEB as well as other behavioral scientists, include student factors (declining ability, election of less rigorous courses), school factors (lowering academic standards, curriculum change, teacher apathy), parents and/or culture (fewer traditional values, less parental concern, more television), and demographic changes (expanding applicant pool, including more low scorers). The 1977 report by the CEEB study panel headed by Willard Wirtz, commissioned to study the SAT decline, received extensive news media coverage. The report supported most of the hypotheses mentioned, and specifically ruled out the possibility that test questions were getting more difficult. Coverage of the leveling off of SAT scores during the last two years of this analysis parallels that for the score decline; the good news is attributed to a reversal of the aforementioned trends, primarily among schools and students.

Partial credit for the good news about average SAT scores occasionally is given to the effects of increasingly available SAT coaching courses and software. Overall, SAT coaching has been a popular topic in newspaper coverage of the SAT, and is generally handled in a balanced fashion, as the fourth item in Table 7.4 reveals. The ETS, CEEB, and their spokesmen represent virtually the only negative sources, while the most frequent positive source is the 1979 FTC report concluding that small but significant gains are possible through SAT coaching courses. (Over 80 percent of all news media coverage of SAT coaching is published or broadcast after the release of the FTC report.) Other positive sources include Stanley Kaplan and other coaching instructors, as well as students, parents, and teachers who believe in the value of coaching. In almost half of all newspaper articles dealing with SAT coaching, it is reported that significant coaching effects would undermine the claim that the SAT is a measure of aptitude rather than achievement. About the same number of articles report, usually through assertion or implication, that significant coaching effects lead to economic unfairness in the SAT because many students cannot afford the cost of coaching schools.

In 1980, New York State passed the nation's first truth–in–testing law, requiring admissions test makers to release the contents and answers to their tests to test takers within a prescribed period of time after test administration. The *NYT* and *WP* provide balanced coverage of the debate over this law (item 5, Table 7.4), in the sense that they just as often report that the law will have a positive effect on test quality as that it will be negative. The participants in this debate, as reported by the newspapers, were Ralph Nader and other nonexpert critics of testing on the positive side, and the ETS, CEEB, and other members of the testing industry on the negative. Absent from the list of sources are other testing experts, who are predominantly opposed to such laws (question 25).

Following the passage of the New York law, ETS adopted a policy of complete disclosure nationwide. One of the consequences of this policy afforded the news media one of its greatest opportunities for the glorification of the oppressed. The front page of the March 17, 1981, *NYT* contains an article entitled "Youth Outwits Merit Exam, Raising 240,000 Scores." The article describes how Florida high school student Daniel Lowen, whose picture is also shown on the front page, was able to demonstrate to the ETS that the approved answer to one of the mathematical questions on its Preliminary Scholastic Aptitude Test (PSAT), used to screen National Merit Scholarship applicants, was wrong, and that his answer was right. Lowen was able to spot the error because he had received a copy of the test and his corrected answers as a result of the ETS disclosure policy.

During the next month and a half, the *NYT* ran six articles in which Lowen was either mentioned or figured prominently, his case used as a springboard for discussions of ambiguous and misleading test questions and the extraordinary and unchecked control the testing establishment has over our lives. While not milked to the same degree, the story also was given extensive coverage in the *WP*, *Time*, *Newsweek*, and on CBS and NBC news programs. The apparent newsworthiness of the story of a single corrected test question is testimony to the importance the news media ascribe to the SAT. In a September 2, 1979, *NYT Magazine* article, "The American Way of Testing," Thomas C. Wheeler asserts:

> Though E.T.S. announces that the SAT is not designed to judge the "worth" of anyone, the test sets implicit standards of worth by becoming a passport to education, income and social status. An SAT score—the score of a single test—can set the direction of a lifetime.

The final item in Table 7.4, "The SAT is culturally biased," looks much like the same item in Table 7.2; charges of SAT bias are frequently reported, and rarely contradicted. (A notable exception is a very careful article on ETS on the front page of the February 28, 1978, *WSJ*.) The unbalanced nature of this coverage seems even more extraordinary when one considers that the ETS and CEEB, readily used in defense of the SAT elsewhere, are so infrequently called upon to deny that the SAT is biased. The black–white SAT differential is often attributed to the inferior quality of segregated black schools. Consequently, the notions of cultural bias and cultural deprivation are confused. A long article on "The College Boards" in the May 4, 1975, *NYT Magazine* explains that the SAT is an equally valid predictor of college performance for both blacks and whites, but concludes:

> The evidence indicates that the tests are culturally biased to the extent that reading ability is culturally linked. Colleges rely on them because the ability to do college–level academic work depends on reading skill. Because reading is a skill that is developed in school and nurtured at home, it is related to educational and economic opportunity.

Not everyone writing for the newspapers confuses cultural bias and cultural deprivation, however. An editorial in the February 7, 1980, *WP* by Jessica Tuchman Mathews takes issue with the recent Nairn/Nader report (Nader and Nairn reply in an op–ed piece two months later), which argues that the SAT is racially and economically biased and should be eliminated. In discussing the SAT, Ms. Mathews demonstrates a degree of understanding about the nature of heritability and test bias rare in news media accounts, and almost completely absent from discussions of intelligence tests:

What is the point of these attacks on standardized tests? Abandoning them could only force colleges to place heavier reliance on measures that are more subject to social and racial bias. .... The aptitude that can be measured after 12 or 13 years of schooling is *not* the native intelligence a student inherits in his genes. It is the product of 17 years of continual interaction between those capacities and the student's environment—including everything from pre-natal nutrition, to conditions in the home, to the quality of the school he attends. If the SAT's are sending bad news, it is as much about the system that determines that total environment as it is about the individual student. The news *is* bad—it does not show the progress that was hoped for. But that is all the more reason to keep hearing it. (emphasis in the original)

Newsmagazines

Coverage of SAT–related issues in the forty relevant newsmagazine articles is, like newsmagazine coverage of the other Issue groups, of the same general form as newspaper coverage, albeit in fewer articles. The data in Table 7.4 show balanced or positive treatment for SAT validity, the aptitude–achievement distinction, SAT coaching, and truth–in–testing, while devoting more articles to critics than defenders concerning inordinate control and cultural bias. Sources are also very similar to those used in newspaper coverage: ETS, CEEB, and their spokesmen almost exclusively in defense of tests, and Ralph Nader and several other nonexpert and expert critics on the offensive. Unlike the newspapers (considering feature articles only), the newsmagazines make very little use of assertion or implication in coverage of these issues.

Without providing the annual reports of the *NYT* and *WP*, the news-magazines do discuss trends in average SAT scores in almost one–quarter of all articles considering the SAT, with explanations linked to students, school, culture, and demography. The Wirtz commission findings are featured in all three newsmagazines, as are the FTC coaching findings (which are always coupled with ETS response).

Persistent problems in newsmagazine coverage of the SAT include the tendency to one–sided coverage of testing criticism and confusion over aptitude and achievement. The latter generally occurs in the context of discussions of SAT coaching. The language used to describe the SAT in a June 11, 1979, *Time* article on coaching is about sixty years out of date: "In theory, there is little that students can do to prepare for the dread day, since the SAT supposedly measures innate ability, not learned skills." Through national exposure, statements like this help to perpetuate myths about testing.

On the whole, however, coverage of the SAT by the newsmagazines is much fairer and more sensitive to expert opinion than is their coverage of intelligence testing. A good example of both the strengths and weaknesses of this coverage is provided by the February 18, 1980, *Newsweek* article "Tests: How Good? How Fair?" which primarily is concerned with the SAT. There is a description of Ralph Nader's "vitriolic study of the Educational Testing Service ... calling it a private regulator of the human mind 'that served as a formidable barrier to millions of students.'" This is counterbalanced by:

> To the test–makers, the harsh—often ill–informed—criticism mistakes both their purpose and influence. "We are both shocked and dismayed by the power critics ascribe to us," says ETS vice president Robert Solomon.

After discussions of the widespread use of the SAT and ACT, the power of the ETS (despite Solomon's demurrer), and SAT validity (including Nader's data and a response of "fraud" from an ETS official), the authors confuse cultural bias with cultural deprivation. Here the journalists are given some help by ETS test developer Richard Adams who, in response to the charge that tests are culturally biased, is quoted as replying "'Tests are biased toward the environment that most people will work in.'" Whether Adams explained to the *Newsweek* reporter that this is not the same thing as cultural bias is not known, for the article follows this quotation with a discussion of the *Larry P.* case. Despite this problem, the article ends with a paragraph that could very well serve as a summary of our survey of expert opinion:

> No one thinks tests are perfect. For all their long history and wide use, they remain badly misunderstood. At best, they provide an essentially objective antidote to grades and teachers' opinions. At worst, they discriminate unfairly against people whose culture does not match that of the mainly middle–class test–makers. Yet college admissions officers and others who count on test results insist that the standardized measures give them a significant tool to judge with reasonable fairness people from all backgrounds and all parts of the country. If tests did not exist, someone would probably have to invent them.

Television Networks

There are thirty–seven television broadcasts (all but nine from CBS, and most of these from the *CBS Morning News*) concerning the SAT, almost as many broadcasts as there are relevant newsmagazine articles, yet there are generally fewer broadcasts than newsmagazine articles listed among the key items in Table 7.4. The small number that exist appear consistent with those from other news media (sources on both sides of the debate are similar to those used in the newsmagazines, with little use of assertion or implication). Reports of test criticism (items 2 and 6), are derived from *CBS Morning News* and *NBC Nightly News* reports of Nader's charges and an ABC *20/20* segment concentrating on cultural bias in the SAT.

The bulk of television coverage of the SAT falls into one of three categories. The first topic, considered by one-third of all SAT-related broadcasts, is the trends in average SAT score, including the Wirtz commission report. Explanations for the decline and leveling off of scores parallel those from other news sources. The second category of broadcasts concerns coaching effects, discussed in a *CBS Evening News* story on the FTC report (in which the ETS is cited in opposition), a CBS *30 Minutes* segment that provides information for children on the meaning and use of the SAT (including a discussion of coaching effects in which the ETS is pitted against the FTC, Stanley Kaplan, and a high school SAT coaching program), a *CBS Morning News* story on SAT coaching software, and *CBS Morning News* and *NBC Nightly News* stories on a successful Florida high school coaching program in which groups of students compete against each other in a military game, complete with battle fatigues and war cries, through the use of computer-administered SAT questions.

The final category of television news broadcasts concerning the SAT falls under the heading of underdog stories in which the individual test taker is dwarfed by the "all-important Scholastic Aptitude Test"[5] and the ETS "testing empire."[6] Foremost among these is the case of Daniel Lowen and the corrected PSAT question. The story was originally covered by both the *CBS Morning News* and *NBC Nightly News*. The *CBS Morning News* followed up the story three weeks later, giving more possible answers to the question, and within the next nineteen months ran two other stories on students finding errors in SAT questions. During the summer of 1983, both the NBC and ABC evening news programs broadcast stories about a trial in New Jersey in which four high school students whose SAT scores had been invalidated for suspicion of cheating were challenging the statistical method by which the ETS determines such invalidation. Typical of the way the television networks treat the ETS and SAT is the July 14, 1983, report on ABC *World News Tonight* describing the trial. The lead-in by Max Robinson begins:

> Each year more than a million high school students take the SAT exams— exams which are crucial in deciding where, or even whether, they'll go to college. Now, in the first trial of its kind, four former high school students from Short Hills, New Jersey are claiming the Educational Testing Service arbitrarily cancelled their test scores because of a rumour they cheated.

Not only does this statement overemphasize the importance of the SAT, but by misrepresenting the facts of the case, it portrays the ETS in the worst possible light. When the case was decided in favor of the ETS, ABC chose not to report the news.

Employment Testing

There is a total of only forty–three articles and broadcasts (twenty–one *NYT*, ten *WP*, five *WSJ*, three newsmagazines, four television networks) from all sources concerning employment–testing. The amount of codeable material is even smaller, as code sheets were set up to record general statements about testing, and most coverage of employment tests concerns specific tests. News media accounts of employment testing generally appear in one of three ways: First, and most frequently, as reports of legal challenges to employment tests such as *Griggs v. Duke Power*, the PACE consent decree (covered in a series of articles in the *NYT*, as well as reports in the other two newspapers), the New York City police sergeant's exam, and a 1978 Supreme Court decision on a South Carolina teachers' test (covered by all three television networks). These reports usually involve descriptions of a suit brought by individuals or organizations representing minority test takers, who claim that the test in question is racially discriminatory; opposing viewpoints are rarely presented. (Reports of the 1978 Supreme Court decision say only that the Court upheld the right of the states to give such tests, despite disproportionate impact.) These statements are codeable only if, in the judgment of the coder, they apply to employment testing as a whole, or if the journalist seems to imply that such problems are widespread. A second way employment tests appear in the press is through letters to the editor regarding the PACE decree (two letters opposing the decree in both the *NYT* and *WSJ*) and editorials on PACE and other employment tests. A January 29, 1981, *NYT* column (by William Safire) favorable to PACE is followed by a February 17 *NYT* editorial supporting the consent decree that eliminated the exam. William Raspberry wrote a series of columns in the *WP* and *Newsweek* dealing with testing, and occasionally touched on employment tests. A September 23, 1974, "My Turn" piece in *Newsweek* provides codeable material:

> Most job tests should be reconstructed to make them more clearly related to the tasks to be performed. The Federal service entrance examination, for instance, is used to screen applicants for more than 100 different jobs. But since the questions have little to do with the specific skills required for those jobs, it's a safe bet that they screen out a lot of people who could perform well on the job. It's a safe bet, too, that they screen out a disproportionate percentage of potentially competent blacks. There *is* cultural bias, you know. (emphasis in original)

The final category of employment–testing stories is that in which employment tests are mentioned in an article or broadcast primarily dealing with educational tests. These include articles on the SAT that also deal with ETS extensive involvement in licensing and professional exams, *The IQ Myth* (where the invalidity of employment tests is described), articles on general criticisms of testing, and those where the omnipresence and omnipotence of testing are stressed, as in the January 16, 1983, *Washington Post Magazine* piece "Testing Anxiety" (with the subheading "Tests can determine what jobs we get, how much money we make, where we live and whom we marry—no wonder we worry"). In these reports, many of the same criticisms leveled against educational tests (bias, overuse) are directed at employment tests.

Codeable statements about employment testing follow the same pattern as reports of other criticisms of testing; employment tests are challenged, and rarely defended. "A significant amount of employment testing is invalid" and "The rejection of a disproportionate number of minority candidates from many jobs can be traced to invalid tests" are each coded ten times as positive, without any rebuttal. "Testing in employment is overused" receives four unanswered positive codes. "Employment tests are often culturally biased" is coded as ten positive, two negative, and two both. The negative code for bias comes from newspaper and newsmagazine coverage of the 1982 National Academy of Sciences report on ability tests that concludes educational and employment tests are generally not biased. These news stories are among the few uses of expert sources in coverage of employment tests. Challenges to employment tests come almost exclusively from nonexpert groups and individuals, and this is reflected in news media coverage. One half of all sources for employment testing code are nonexpert others, and another third are assertions or implications; only 15 percent of all source codes represent experts.

Intelligence and Aptitude Testing Outside the U.S.

The first news report, chronologically, in this content analysis is a January 31, 1969, *NYT* article dealing with the request by a Soviet educator that his government adopt a policy of regular use of objective aptitude tests for selection in education and employment. Such tests, he said, would increase productivity and fairness, consistent with Socialist goals. "'A recognition of capabilities opens the way for their fullest development, and a correct evaluation of aptitudes indirectly helps assess the actual labor, the real contribution that person makes to society,' the Moscow educator said."

A May 19, 1981, *NYT* article on changes in the testing industry contains a one paragraph description of an agreement signed by ETS to test Chinese students planning to attend college in the U.S. The remaining six articles (two *NYT*, two *WP,* one *Time*, one *U.S. News*) that in some way deal with testing outside the United States all concern the superior IQ of the average Japanese schoolchild. In half of these, explanations for the Japanese–American IQ differential are proposed, and they are all environmental. An editorial by Nicholas Wade in the September 10, 1982, *NYT* states, "If Japanese kids score higher than Americans, or white children higher than blacks, the likeliest explanation lies in differences of educational or environmental opportunity."

News Media Accuracy Ratings

As part of the survey of testing experts, we asked respondents for their opinion of the accuracy of various news sources in reporting issues related to intelligence and testing. Table 7.5 presents the results of these ratings, which were made on a 7–point scale, with 1 as "very inaccurate" and 7 as "very accurate." Mean ratings fall in the middle of the accuracy range, reflecting both substantial accuracy and inaccuracy, with the *Christian*

TABLE 7.5
Expert Opinion of News Media Accuracy on Testing Related Issues

News Source	Mean Accuracy Rating[a]	% Responding
Christian Science Monitor	5.08 (1.44)[b]	24.1
Commercial television networks	3.09 (1.18)	68.7
National Public Radio	4.4 (1.41)	49.2
New York Times	4.62 (1.31)	58.2
Newsweek	3.85 (1.2)	51.7
PBS television	4.8 (1.18)	59.5
Time	3.83 (1.21)	54
U.S. News and World Report	3.72 (1.29)	37.4
Wall Street Journal	4.4 (1.28)	37.2
Washington Post	3.98 (1.4)	29.8

[a] 1 = "Very inaccurate," 7 = "Very accurate." [b] Numbers in parentheses are standard deviations.

Science Monitor doing noticeably better (5.08), and commercial television networks doing noticeably worse (3.09) in expert opinion. Unfortunately, commercial television is the single most popular news source among the general public (as it appeared to be among experts, judging by response rates). The *NYT*, long considered by journalists to be the hallmark of fair and accurate reporting, receives a 4.62. Media accuracy ratings are not significantly related to any of the demographic and background variables discussed at the end of Chapter 5, with the exception that political liberalism bears a significant positive relationship to ratings of the Public Broadcasting System (PBS) and National Public Radio.

Caution must be observed in interpreting the ratings in Table 7.5 as measures of accuracy in relation to testing, as opposed to more general ratings or opinion about the quality of news coverage as a whole. The substantial response rate for PBS is particularly troublesome, given our inability to find more than one PBS story on testing in a fifteen–year period.

The foregoing content analysis reveals that the news media, particularly on non–SAT issues, presents a very different picture of testing than that obtained from our survey of expert opinion. By stressing the indeterminacy of a definition of intelligence, the limitations of tested ability, the ubiquitousness of test misuse, the inordinate control exerted by test makers, and cultural bias in tests, the news media have presented to the reading and viewing public a distorted image of testing, one more consistent with the opinion of a disappointed test taker than that of those who know most about tests. The views of the expert community are lost when Herrnstein, Jensen, and Shockley, in addition to being frequently misrepresented, are cast as intellectual loners in their defense of substantial heritability and the validity of tests. Moreover, whether as a result of disinclination to clarify issues that would put testing and its supporters in a better light, or because of inadequate technical training, journalists have done a great disservice to their audience by portraying IQ heritability as an all–or–none phenomenon, and by confusing within– and between–group heritability, cultural deprivation and cultural bias, and aptitude and achievement. Such inaccuracies add fuel to the fires of the IQ controversy just as surely as does portraying Leon Kamin as a spokesman for a substantial portion of the psychological community.

All of this is not to say that the news media could be accurately characterized as spokesmen for Leon Kamin and Ralph Nader. There are many excellent news reports about testing in which the views of critics are placed in the context of an accurate assessment of expert opinion, and there is little doubt that most journalists and editors attempt to be fair. But fairness and accuracy are not the norm in news media coverage of intelligence and aptitude testing. Because of the constraints placed on them by their media, and by their own beliefs and values (see Appendix E) those who report the news are more apt to achieve balance by pitting Arthur Jensen against Leon Kamin and Robert Williams, and Ralph Nader against the ETS, than to attempt a more global perspective of the IQ controversy.

There are many ways to tell the truth. The quote from the *WP* that ends our discussion of newspaper coverage of SAT issues is exceptional because it places criticisms of testing in their proper perspective. Intelligence and aptitude tests have problems, as any schoolteacher or testing expert will tell you, but they are also among the best decision–making tools we have. The news media regularly report the former, but rarely the latter. Tests are gatekeepers; they prevent many people from obtaining the educational and employment opportunities they desire. As a result, tests are an easy target for the rejected, and for those, including the news media, who see themselves as champions of the oppressed. (Ironically, this defender's attitude may also work to favor tests. As this book goes to press, the news media are engaged in widespread and largely sympathetic coverage of Mary Amaya's struggle to have an intelligence test administered to her son in defiance of the *Larry P.* decision.) Through all of this it is forgotten that the tests do not create limited opportunities and resources, they are merely tools intended to achieve the most efficient and equitable allocation of a small pie. When these tools fall short of their goal, it is the business of the news media to report it, but they also have the responsibility to explain the alternatives.

Notes

1. "Shockley Wins $1 in Libel Suit," *New York Times*, 15 September 1984, p. 8.
2. "Is Equality Bad For You?" *Time*, 23 August 1971, p. 33.
3. Stanley N. Wellborn, "A 'Genetic Elite' Taking Shape in U.S.?" *U.S. News and World Report*, 24 March 1980, p. 49.
4. *World News Tonight*, ABC, 14 July 1983.
5. "Testing-True or False," *20/20*, ABC, 24 April 1980.
6. Ibid.

8

Conclusion: The New Sociology of Science

The IQ Controversy and the Informed Public

In the 1950s, those liberal and informed Americans who most influenced public policy believed that intelligence and aptitude tests contributed to social progress. A society in which white Anglo–Protestant notions of character and the right connections had been of key importance in social and economic advancement was being transformed into one in which merit played a far more significant role. During the 1940s and 1950s elite universities began to open their doors more widely to previously excluded groups, and those gaining entrance were being admitted, at least in part, because such institutions were turning to "objective" tests of ability.

Many also saw intelligence and aptitude tests as a way of helping young people with educational deficits and of placing adults in jobs for which they were best suited. As a result, IQ and aptitude tests gained more widespread use in public school systems as one mechanism for locating both talented children and children with special problems. In the workplace the tests were used as an aid in deciding who to hire for positions requiring different skills.

As befitted (so many thought) an advanced or "post–industrial" society, the United States was becoming a meritocracy.[1] There were those who objected to this trend. Some conservatives saw it as eroding traditional values based on notions of character, and radicals of a certain type believed that the goal of a meritocracy violated norms of equality and represented an attempt by a capitalist society to conceal its basic flaws. However, opponents of testing represented a small minority.

During the 1950's, scientists and the informed public accepted as a matter of course the assumption that genetic factors were importantly involved in individual differences in measured intelligence, as well as the argument (against the position taken by many as late as the 1920s) that differences in

249

IQ among various ethnic or racial groups were wholly the result of environmental factors.[2]

In the past twenty-five years this conventional wisdom has changed dramatically. Intelligence and aptitude tests have fallen into disfavor among the literate public, as have attempts to define intelligence. However intelligence is defined, the suggestion that individual differences in intelligence, like individual capacities for painting or composing, may have a genetic component has become anathema.

More significantly, the literate and informed public today is persuaded that the majority of experts in the field believe it is impossible to adequately define intelligence, that intelligence tests do not measure anything that is relevant to life performance, and that they are biased against minorities, primarily blacks and Hispanics, as well as against the poor. It appears from book reviews in popular journals and from newspaper and television coverage of IQ issues that such are the views of the vast majority of experts who study questions of intelligence and intelligence testing.

The new conventional wisdom has not eliminated testing from school systems and employment but, as the result of a series of court decisions and legislative enactments as well as voluntary actions by teachers and administrators, the use of both IQ and ability testing has declined considerably from its heyday in the 1950s. Much of this change may be for the good, as tests have been both misused and overused. But there is also the serious danger of absurdities like the *Larry P.* case or the New York City Police sergeant's exam, when policy decisions regarding testing are based on popular misconceptions rather than informed opinion.

Expert views have not undergone the fundamental change characteristic of the attitudes of the informed public, despite the expansion of environmentalism within the expert community. On the whole, scholars with any expertise in the area of intelligence and intelligence testing (defined very broadly) share a common view of the most important components of intelligence, and are convinced that it can be measured with some degree of accuracy. An overwhelming majority also believe that individual genetic inheritance contributes to variations in IQ within the white community, and a smaller majority express the same view about the black–white and SES differences in IQ.

The expert community does have reservations about the definition of intelligence and what intelligence and aptitude tests measure. They do not wish to reify test scores. They recognize that such tests are often misused. Nonetheless, experts continue to believe that, despite problems, testing plays a useful role in our society and that, properly used, IQ and aptitude tests can contribute significantly to social well-being.

What has produced so sharp a disjunction between the views of the literate citizenry and those of the relevant scientific community with regard to testing? How does one explain the distorted image of the views of the scientific community that has become part of the conventional wisdom, including the conventional wisdom of journalists? One key element is the civil rights revolution that began in the 1960s, a revolution that has fundamentally changed the contours of American politics.

Americans traditionally have believed strongly in equality of opportunity. They also have believed that, by and large, success depends upon opportunity, luck, and "character," i.e., the willingness and ability to discipline oneself and work hard. This essentially democratic ethos, with its emphasis upon character, has always been part of the American creed, though historically tempered by beliefs in the innate inferiority of non–Anglo–Saxon peoples, including the Irish, Italians, Poles, Jews and, especially, blacks.[3] Commitments to merit and efficiency were also tempered by a belief that certain kinds of behavior (character) were appropriate while others were not.

During the 1940s and 1950s, a purely meritocratic view was triumphing over traditional notions of character, and an uneasy compromise was reached between these two aspects of American thought. As Bell points out in *The Cultural Contradictions of Capitalism*, the triumph was in part dictated by the requirements of the economic order, which demanded that rewards be based on a combination of ability and effort. Such notions were also implicit in the liberal–capitalist ideology that underlay that order.

At the same time, it was no longer considered reasonable by social scientists (especially in the light of the Nazi experience) to believe that any group differences might involve a genetic component. One could still believe that differences between individuals had something to do with what they inherited, but differences between ethnic or racial groups were entirely the result of the barriers faced by minorities, especially black Americans.

The compromise began to unravel in the 1960s. The shift was in the direction of completely environmental explanations of individual as well as group differences. Arthur Jensen was attacked because he wrote about the possibility of a genetic component of racial differences in IQ, but the attack on the hereditarian position went further. Richard Herrnstein was characterized as a racist because he emphasized the hereditary component of differences among whites, even though he claimed agnosticism as to black–white differences. Hereditarian views about differences among whites were not to be expressed publicly in the manner in which Herrnstein presented them.[4] To many, the admission that intelligence could be defined or that there was any hereditary component to intelligence was tantamount to an assertion that genetic factors also played a role in racial and ethnic differences even if such an assertion was not made.

Thus, the civil rights issue played a key role in undermining the 1950s conventional wisdom about intelligence and intelligence testing. There were, of course, other factors involved. We noted in Chapter 1 that Daniel Bell perceives a "sea change" in the nature of American ideology in the past fifty years.

The United States was created by an elite whose background and perceptions derived from an English Puritan tradition that stressed control of the passions in the pursuit of mundane worldly tasks. Strong commitments to self-discipline and restraint were embedded in this tradition.[5]

As many scholars have pointed out, the tradition gave rise to the hegemony of liberal capitalism in the United States with its emphasis on practical activity, the free market, and political democracy.[6] Anthony Wallace summarizes some of the elements of the dominant American creed of the time in his perceptive discussion of the development of a small American industrial community in the nineteenth century:

> It was in Rockdale, and in dozens of other industrial communities like Rockdale, that an American world view developed which pervades the present—or did so until recently—with a sense of superior Christian virtue, a sense of global mission, a sense of responsibility and capability of bringing enlightenment to a dark and superstitious world, for overthrowing ancient and new tyrannies, and for making backward infidels into Christian men of enterprise.[7]

By the middle of the twentieth century, however, the traditional American ethos had been eroded by affluence and new ideologies that, with the crumbling of a traditional religious orientation, sought meaning in the satisfactions of increasing consumption.[8]

The ethos was also eroded by the emergence of new strategic elites, themselves a product of an advanced industrial society. These elites included government bureaucrats and various social-service professionals who, along with cultural elites, have been growing rapidly in size and influence. Most individuals in these sectors have received college educations, and sometimes doctorates. By the mid 1960s, the U.S. boasted 500,000 college faculty. In 1899/1900, 382 doctorates were granted in the United States. The number granted in 1976/1977 was 33,000, and the total number of such degree recipients was close to 600,000. By 1982 approximately 750,000 Americans held doctoral degrees.[9]

In 1940, approximately 3.4 million Americans over twenty-five years of age had completed four or more years of college, less than five percent of the relevant age group. By 1973, the number was well over 11 million, and by 1985 it had reached 27 million, or almost 20 percent of the population. The number of persons in the work force classified as professionals rose from 4 million to over 12 million between 1950 and 1974, and to just under 16 million in 1980.

The phenomenal growth of this stratum was partly a function of affluence. The American economy grew with unprecedented rapidity in the 1940s and 1950s, providing funds and opportunities for all sorts of service personnel from academics to psychiatrists. The number of those "Metro–Americans," as Eric Goldman has called them, or at least that segment of them which had come to feel somewhat estranged from traditional American institutions and values, had reached a critical mass by the 1960s.[10] It was largely the children of this group who made up the cadres and sympathizers of the 1960s student movement, and they and their parents provide (even when they are not "intellectuals") the readership for the *New York Review of Books*, the *Nation*, and other liberal cosmopolitan journals, as well as the volunteer workers for liberal political candidates. They read the books that criticize the large oil companies or warn about the degradation of the environment. In public opinion polls, they rate as strong supporters of civil rights, civil liberties and new life styles to a far greater degree than traditional middle–class or working–class respondents.

Part of this has to do with their status. Many feel little vested interest in the maintenance of "free enterprise." Indeed, as bureaucrats or lawyers they may well have an interest in increasing the extent of government activity and/or the litigation involved in government regulatory activities.

Just as important, they have been educated at colleges and universities in which they have been taught new ways to look at and evaluate the world.[11] Only a segment of this stratum shares such understandings, but it is just this segment of the population that is responsible for the creation of activist public–interest groups. "Metro–Americans" also play important roles in television and motion picture entertainment and in the national media, where they influence the views of a still larger number of Americans.[12]

Whereas at one point Americans' commitment to production placed an emphasis upon hard work, discipline, and merit, the new generation of professionals and intellectuals has rejected such notions in favor of self–fulfillment and self–realization. These groups were and are alienated from the remnants of American Puritanism and the idea of meritocratic society. To them, meritocracy and instrumental rationality are typical of a system that limits individual freedom to be what one wants to be. The goal of efficiency in corporate enterprise is said to stultify individuals and to make them miserable automatons. Thus, tests of ability and intelligence are simply part of a corporate capitalism that creates robots rather than human beings.[13] Corporate capitalism also produces racism. The use of tests is designed to maintain the necessary racist basis of American capitalist society.

The 1960s and early 1970s were the heyday of such attitudes.[14] They have declined in popularity in recent years, but they have by no means disappeared. Rather, in a moderated form, they have become an important part of the American cultural scene. Most educated professionals, especially those in journalism and the helping professions, are now somewhat alienated from traditional American values. This alienation implies being critical of much of what American culture has stood for in the past.[15]

There is another factor, too. Having been successfully mobilized during the 1960s, blacks and Hispanics have become important political forces in American life. Their votes are to be reckoned with, as is their capacity for organized criticism of those whom they consider racist. To many, if not most, articulate intellectuals in the black and Hispanic communities, IQ tests have been and are still weapons designed to "keep them in their place." Both they and their allies fear (not completely without reason, given the history of racism in the United States) that the public acceptance of the validity of intelligence and aptitude tests can lead to retrograde policies, including the dismantling of affirmative action programs. It is at least partly for this reason that some liberal and black organizations have pressed for a ban on testing and on research dealing with possible genetic differences between ethnic or racial groups with regard to measured intelligence.

Are such fears justified? It is by no means certain that the experts who believe that genetic factors play some role in black–white IQ differences are correct. Assuming for the moment, however, that they are, what might be the consequences? Noam Chomsky makes the quite legitimate point that a finding that some groups have less innate capacity for making it in our society need not serve as justification for discriminating against them or allowing them to remain poor. Indeed, we might come to just the opposite conclusion. We might decide to allocate more resources to such groups simply because of their greater need.[16] In this view the association of discrimination with claims about black inferiority is a historical, not a logical, connection.

Most experts in the field of intelligence and intelligence testing believe that disadvantaged individuals or groups require special assistance, not that they should be deprived of help. Over 60 percent of our expert respondents support strong affirmative action for blacks and a larger percentage of experts than journalists are strongly committed to it. (See Appendix E, where it appears that experts are better able than journalists to reconcile liberal political attitudes with belief in a significant IQ heritability.) Arthur Jensen has always insisted that students (of *all* racial and socioeconomic groups) with lower measured IQs need special assistance, though few have paid attention to such statements, so anxious have they been to attack him.

Finally, the possibility that genetic factors play some role in measured individual or group IQ differences does not imply that individuals should be treated other than as unique persons. For one thing, differences among groups in measured IQ are smaller than within–group differences, making tests a rather inelegant tool for racism. More important, the source of individual and group differences in IQ is relevant only to the question of what we may be able to do to narrow these differentials; that genetic factors may be involved lends no more credence to the idea that all blacks should be treated alike than would be the case if IQ were purely a function of the environment.

Journalists, Academics and the IQ Controversy

Our work demonstrates that, by any reasonable standard, media coverage of the IQ controversy has been quite inaccurate. Journalists have emphasized controversy; they have reported scientific discussions of technical issues erroneously and they have clearly misreported the views of the relevant scientific community as to the interaction between genetic and environmental factors in explaining differences in IQ among individuals and between groups. One would be forced to conclude from reading the newspapers and newsmagazines and watching television that only a few maverick "experts" support the view that genetic variation plays a significant role in individual or group differences, while the vast majority of experts believe that such differences are purely the result of environmental factors. One would also conclude that intelligence and aptitude tests are hopelessly biased against minorities and the poor.

We have suggested several explanations for the media's failure in this regard, including the ignorance of journalists and the nature of the news medium. Journalists generally have very little understanding of social science, especially those segments of social science that involve complex statistics; and they are interested in promoting controversy, as we have seen. However, neither of these factors explains why, with such regularity, Stephen Jay Gould and Leon Kamin are presented as representative of mainstream thought in the profession, while those who stress that genetic elements may play some role in measured IQ are characterized as a small minority within the expert community.

It is difficult to believe that either journalists' ignorance or their penchant for seeking out controversial issues explains the directionality of their coverage of the testing issues. We have suggested that journalists' and editors' perceptions of these issues might play some role. Our hypothesis is based on previous studies of journalists' views on a variety of social and political issues which suggest they are among the new strategic elites that have recently emerged in American society. These elites tend to be critical of traditional American values, along the lines outlined by Daniel Bell.

Journalists perceive equality of group outcomes in income and status as a necessary sign of equality of opportunity; journalists are generally liberal and cosmopolitan, and somewhat alienated (culturally) from mainstream America, while still generally supportive of capitalism. Both their views of equality and their general hostility to traditional patterns of American culture lead national journalists to perceive the IQ issue in a certain manner and to describe it in the manner in which they perceive it.

These attitudes represent a distinct shift from the modis operandi of journalists thirty years ago. As late as the 1950s, the media turned to the scientific establishment for information about issues in which technical expertise played a role. Journalists may not have been well informed about scientific issues, but they had some clear notions of where to look for answers. The 1960s changed all that. As June Goodfield points out, journalists increasingly turned to anti–establishment sources for information on controversial scientific matters.[17]

In their study of nuclear energy, Rothman and Lichter demonstrate that other leadership groups look to the national media as their key source of information about public questions. The media thereby play an important role in the development of elite and popular attitudes, independent of the thinking of the scientific community or, at least, of the scientific establishment. Dissenting scientists, especially activists on the left, receive respectful attention from the media no matter how unrepresentative their views may be.[18] This in turn has had a significant impact on those who formulate policy regarding testing.

The influence of the media has increased dramatically as a result of the communications revolution of the past thirty years. The key factor has been the development of television and the emergence of national television networks. By the early 1960s most Americans owned television sets and were receiving essentially the same kind of news whether they lived in a small town in Iowa or in New York City. Television broke down both regional and class boundaries, and nationalized the transmission of information to an extent never before characteristic of American society.[19]

The weakening of traditional institutions such as neighborhood and church, and the influence of new strategic elites all contributed to changes in American life, and these changes reinforced each other. For example, in the past journalists had mostly come from working– or lower–middle–class backgrounds and had shared the attitudes of these strata. By the 1960s, however, the key national journals and television outlets were staffed increasingly by individuals who had been educated at elite universities and whose liberal and cosmopolitan ideas had been formed at such institutions.[20]

Because they think of themselves as intellectuals, and, despite some skepticism, hold intellectuals in higher esteem than did earlier generations of journalists, this new generation is providing academic and nonacademic intellectuals with opportunities to reach an ever larger public.

At the same time, the interaction between journalists and intellectuals is affecting the universities. Whereas in the past the development of an academic reputation had required peer review and publication in prestigious academic journals, one can now partially bypass such traditional paths. In the social sciences, at least, a favorable review in the *New York Times* or the *New York Review of Books*, or an interview on a popular television program, is, in some cases, a more significant source of recognition and reward than that offered by professional journals. Thus, academic as well as nonacademic intellectuals are themselves caught up in the new cultural milieu. Consequently, while the number of persons at least somewhat familiar with science and social science has grown, the quality of the reporting of science and social science opens the door to new kinds of distortion in the transmission of natural- and social-science information.[21]

The tendency of reporters to dramatize events, to personalize them and to transform them into stories, gives rise to an exaggerated and inaccurate perception of the total picture.[22] Moreover, the media's power to enhance or detract from professional reputations probably encourages scientists and social scientists to tailor their work to a style that is more appealing to the media.

More important, however, journalists quite naturally tend to report those scientific findings that accord with their own judgments and, in so doing, they influence public perceptions of the truth of various scientific propositions. Since most first-rank social and natural scientists prefer to avoid conflictual social situations, they are unlikely to challenge the media's version of the truth.[23]

This is what seems to have happened in the area of intelligence and intelligence testing. The history of racism in the United States demands that any acceptance of a genetic component to measured intelligence be denied; indeed, it demands that the very notion of measuring intelligence be brought into question. The new liberalism seeks the same goals for partly different reasons. In the 1960s and 1970s the two streams of thought merged to form a powerful intellectual current on campuses and in the media, and it continues to play an important role.

Newspaper and television personnel can always find professors or journalists to write articles or book reviews attacking traditional understandings of intelligence and aptitude testing. Given media coverage of the issues, the character of fund–granting foundations, and the mood of students on college campuses, only the unusually combative academic will take an alternative view. Nor can such academics expect much support from their colleagues. The lack of public peer support of Herrnstein and Jensen is probably partly a function of a fear on the part of their colleagues that they will themselves come under direct attack. However, the issue is clearly more complex.

As we have seen, the views of most testing experts are very similar to those expressed by Herrnstein and Jensen. Yet these scientists receive relatively low marks from their professional colleagues (see Chapter 4, Table 4.1). Indeed, Jensen's rating is slightly below the quite low scores of environmentalists Gould and Kamin.[24]

How does one account for this apparent paradox? Several factors are probably involved. First, liberal experts, like liberal journalists, may not be anxious to publicize evidence that genetic factors play some role in group differences because they fear the use that might be made of such data. As supporters of the new liberalism, they may believe that it is better to leave some things publicly unsaid. Their goal may be to do everything possible to eliminate or at least reduce the size of inter–group differences, through, for example, strong affirmative–action programs. In their eyes, public emphasis on genetically based group differences can very well hamper the attainment of such a goal.

Second, some of those working in the field may be angered by those who publicly argue that genetic factors play a role in measured inter–group IQ scores because the publicizing of such views can hamper their own work. If they are protected from public scrutiny, they can continue to pursue their studies without harassment. Moreover, given the current climate of opinion, including the climate on college campuses, some experts may feel it is best to limit to technical, professional journals the publication of findings and conjectures about genetic contributions to individual or group differences. In short, they may be engaging in a subtle form of self–censorship.

Given the history of racial oppression in America and, indeed, in the world as a whole, one suspects that it will be a long time before the question of a possible genetic contribution to measured intelligence—either between individuals or groups—can be discussed in a rational and open manner. For the foreseeable future, the question of defining and attempting to measure intelligence, as well as the exploration of individual and inter–group differences, will probably be discussed only in professional journals and only in the most abstract and technical terms. In the meantime, as the new environmentalist conventional wisdom continues to dominate the views of the informed public and policy makers, one can only hope for the increasing appearance of accurate information in the public sphere.

Notes

1. Daniel Bell, *The Coming of Post Industrial Society* (New York: Basic Books, 1973).
2. Thus Berelson and Steiner could publish a popular inventory of what we know about human behavior and state (without being criticized) that 75 percent of individual differences in IQ is a function of heredity. Bernard Bereleson and George A. Steiner, *Human Behavior: An Inventory of Scientific Findings* (New York: Harcourt, Brace and World, 1964), pp. 208–235. For a discussion of attitudes at the turn of the century and through the 1960s, see Jonathan Harwood, "American Academic Opinion and Social Change: Recent Developments in the Nature–Nurture Controversy," *Oxford Review of Education* 8 (1982):41–67.
3. S. M. Lipset, *The First New Nation* (New York: Basic Books, 1963).
4. See the discussion in Chapter 1.
5. See, among other sources, Edmund Leites, *The Puritan Conscience and Modern Sexuality* (New Haven: Yale University Press, 1986); James A. Henretta, *The Evolution of American Society, 1700–1815* (Lexington, MA: D.C. Heath Co., 1973).
6. On the historical dominance of liberalism in the United States see, among other sources: Louis Hartz, *The Liberal Tradition in America* (New York: Harcourt Brace, 1955); S. M. Lipset, "Why No Socialism in The United States?" in *Sources of Contemporary Radicalism* eds. Seweryn Bialer and Sophia Sluzar (Boulder, CO: Westview Press, 1977), pp. 31–149; S. M. Lipset, "Radicalism or Reformism: The Sources of Working Class Politics," *American Political Science Review* 77 (1983):1–18; Stanley Rothman, "Intellectuals and the American Political System," in *Emerging Coalitions in American Society* ed. S. M. Lipset (San Francisco: Institute for Contemporary Studies, 1978), pp. 325–352; Robert Middlekauf, *The Glorious Cause,* (New York: Oxford University Press, 1981); Lionel Trilling, *The Liberal Imagination: Essays on Literature and Society* (New York: Viking Press, 1950); John Patrick Diggins, *The Lost Soul of American Politics* (New York: Basic Books, 1984).
7. A. F. C. Wallace, *Rockdale* (New York: Alfred A. Knopf, 1978), p. 474.
8. Leo Lowenthal, "Biographies in Popular Magazines," in *Radio Research, 1942–43* eds. Paul Lazarsfeld and F. Stanton (New York: Duell, Sloan and Pearce, 1944), pp. 507–548.
9. The data in this and the next few paragraphs is derived from Bell; The National Center for Educational Statistics, *Digest of Educational Statistics* (Washington, DC: U.S. Government Printing Office, 1982); *The Statistical Abstract of the United States* (Washington, DC: U.S. Government Printing Office, 1942, 1975, 1985 and 1987) U.S. Department of Commerce, Bureau of the Census, *Historical Statistics of the U.S.: Colonial Times to the Present* (Washington: U.S. Government Printing Office, 1975).
10. Eric F. Goldman, *The Tragedy of Lyndon Johnson* (New York: Alfred A. Knopf, 1969). See also Everett C. Ladd, Jr., "The New Lines are Drawn: Class and

Ideology in America," parts I and II, *Public Opinion* 1 (July/August 1978):48–53, and (September/October 1978):14–20; Byron E. Shafer, "The New Cultural Politics," *PS* 18 (Spring 1985):221–231; B. Bruce Briggs, ed., *The New Class* (New Brunswick, NJ: Transaction Press, 1979); Ronald Inglehart, *The Silent Revolution: Changing Values and Political Styles Among Western Publics* (Princeton, NJ: Princeton University Press, 1977); Robert N. Bellah et al., *Habits of the Heart: Individualism and Commitment in American Life* (Berkeley, CA: University of California Press, 1985); Daniel Yankelovich, *Searching for Self Fulfillment in a World Turned Upside Down* (New York: Random House, 1981).

11. James Thomas Barry, *Social Origins and Values of Knowledge-Based Elites in Contemporary Society* (unpublished Ph.D. Dissertation, State University of New York at Buffalo, 1977).

12. Lichter et al., *The Media Elite.*

13. Bell traces the roots of these attitudes to the growth of modernism in nineteenth century Europe with its anti-bourgeois overtones.

14. Rothman and Lichter, *Roots of Radicalism.*

15. Stanley Rothman, "American Intellectuals," *The World and I* (January 1987):555–565; Paul Hollander, *The Many Faces of Socialism* (New Brunswick, NJ: Transaction Press,1983), pp. 253–349. The current public discourse on the need to make American industry more competitive has in no way changed these understandings.

16. Noam Chomsky, "The Fallacy of Richard Herrnstein's IQ," *Social Policy* 3 (May/June 1972):19–25. Chomsky's view could derive support from the arguments advanced by John Rawls in *A Theory of Justice* (Cambridge, MA: Harvard University Press, 1971).

17. June Goodfield, *Reflections on Science and the Media* (Washington, DC: American Association for the Advancement of Science, 1981).

18. See Stanley Rothman and S. Robert Lichter, "Elite Ideology and Risk Perception in Nuclear Energy Policy," *American Political Science Review* 81 (June 1987):383–404. For a contrasting view, see *Science in the Streets*, Report of the Twentieth Century Fund Task Force on the Communication of Scientific Risk (New York: Priority Press, 1984).

19. Lichter et al., *The Media Elite*; Stanley Rothman, "The Mass Media in Post Industrial Society" in *The Third Century: America as a Post Industial Society*, ed. S. M. Lipset (Stanford University, CA: Hoover Institute Press, 1979), pp. 345–368.

20. Rothman, "Mass Media;" Lichter, Rothman, and Lichter, *Media Elite.*

21. See, for example, Russell Seitz, "In From the Cold: Nuclear Winter Melts Down," *The National Interest* 5 (Fall 1986):3–17.

22. D. L. Altheide and R.P. Snow, *Media Logic*(Beverly Hills, CA: Sage Publications, 1979); Michael J. O'Neill *Terrorist Spectaculars: Should TV Coverage be Curbed?* (New York: Priority Press, 1986).

23. Ann Roe, "The Psychology of the Scientist," *Science* 134 (1961):456–459.

24. The very large difference between the proportion of respondents rating Jensen as compared to Gould and Kamin makes the comparison somewhat problematic.

Appendix A

Chronology of Important Publications and Events in the IQ Controversy

1859	Charles Darwin, *Origin of Species*
1869	Francis Galton, *Hereditary Genius*
1884	Galton opens Anthropometric Laboratory at International Health Exhibition in London
1890	Cattell, "Mental Tests and Measurements"
1895	Alfred Binet and Victor Henri, "La Psychologie Individuelle"
1899	Stella Sharp, "Individual Psychology: A Study in Psychological Method"
1901	Clark Wissler, "The Correlation of Mental and Physical Tests"
1904	Charles Spearman, "General Intelligence Objectively Determined and Measured"
1905	Binet and Theodore Simon publish first intelligence scale
1908	Binet and Simon revise intelligence scale
1910	H. H. Goddard translates 1908 Binet-Simon scale into English for use in the United States
1916	Lewis Terman publishes Stanford Revision of Binet-Simon scale
1917	Arthur Otis develops group intelligence test
1918-1919	Army Alpha and Beta tests administered to 1,726,966 recruits during World War I
1921	Report of Army test results indicates lower intelligence for immigrants and blacks, and average mental age of thirteen among all recruits
1922-1923	Lippmann-Terman debate in the *New Republic*
1923	Carl Brigham, *A Study of American Intelligence* Frank Freeman, "A Referendum of Psychologists"

1926	College Entrance Examination Board introduces SAT
1928	Barbara Burks' study of IQ heritability in adopted children
1935	L. L. Thurstone, *The Vectors of Mind*
1937	Terman and Merrill publish revision of Stanford-Binet Newman, Freeman, and Holzinger, *Twins: A Study of Heredity and Environment*
1939	David Wechsler, *The Measurement of Adult Intelligence*
1941- 1945	Army General Classification Test administered to more than nine million recruits in World War II
1956	Frank McGurk, "Psychological Tests—A Scientist's Report on Race Differences" and reply by eighteen social scientists in *U.S. News and World Report*
1958	Audrey Shuey, *The Testing of Negro Intelligence*
1961	J. McV. Hunt, *Intelligence and Experience* Society for the Psychological Study of Social Issues (SPSSI) censures Henry Garrett for criticizing "equalitarian dogma" of no genetic group differences
1962	Banesh Hoffman, *The Tyranny of Testing*
1964	Benjamin Bloom, *Stability and Change in Human Characteristics* Dwight Ingle, "Racial Differences and the Future"
1967	*Hobson v. Hansen*
1968	Association of Black Psychologists (ABP) calls for a moratorium on standardized tests Westinghouse Learning Corporation report on IQ gains in Head Start
1969	Arthur Jensen, "How Much Can We Boost IQ and Scholastic Achievement?" *New York Times Magazine* "jensenism" article SPSSI condemns Jensen Bowdoin College drops SAT requirement
1970	American Anthropological Association (AAA) calls Jensen a racist
1971	Richard Herrnstein, "I.Q." National Academy of Sciences refuses William Shockley's request to fund research on group differences in intelligence AAA calls Herrnstein, Jensen, and Shockley "racist, sexist, and anti-working class" *Griggs v. Duke Power Co. Larry P. v. Wilson Riles* filed
1972	National Education Association (NEA) calls for a moratorium on standardized testing

U.S. Senate Select Committee on Equal Educational Opportunity cancels planned hearings on "Environment, Intelligence, and Scholastic Achievement" because of controversial nature of topic

1973   Leon Kamin points out discrepancies in Cyril Burt's twin data

1974   Kamin, *The Science and Politics of IQ*
Educational Rights and Privacy Act passed

1975   CBS News, *The IQ Myth*
Education for All Handicapped Children Act passed
American Psychological Association panel on testing issues its report

1976   Burt scandal becomes public

1977   Wirtz panel report on decline in SAT scores

1979   L. S. Hearnshaw, *Cyril Burt: Psychologist*
Larry P. decision
New York State passes truth-in-testing law
FTC releases report on coaching for the SAT

1980   Allan Nairn and associates, *The Reign of ETS*
Jensen, *Bias in Mental Testing*
PASE v. Hannon

1981   Stephen Jay Gould, *The Mismeasure of Man*
Consent decree eliminates Professional and Administrative Career Examination (PACE)

1982   National Research Council Committee on Ability Testing issues its report

1984   *Larry P.* decision upheld on appeal

1985   Harvard Business School drops GMAT
Johns Hopkins Medical School drops MCAT
FairTest formed

1986   Peckham directive banning administration of intelligence tests to black children referred for special education in California public schools

1987   Mary Amaya informed that her son, Demond Crawford, cannot be given an intelligence test
U.S. Civil Rights Commission begins to gather facts about the Crawford case

Appendix B

Principal-Component and Multivariate Analyses
of Questionnaire Data

Principal—Component Analysis

In order to facilitate further responding, supervariables were created from substantive question responses via principal–component analysis. Formation of the correlation matrix used as input for this analysis necessitated the elimination or recoding of many questions. There were four criteria for question elimination: (1) if questions contained more than two nominal response categories and were thus not amenable to correlational analysis (e.g., questions 17 and 18 on the sources of group differences in IQ); (2) if there was greater than 25 percent nonresponse rate (e.g., heritability estimates, and validity judgments for all admissions tests but the SAT and GRE); (3) if questions were judged not to be central to general views on testing (ratings of noncontroversial authors); and (4) if inclusion would have unnecessarily complicated the analysis (questions 3 and 4 on elements of intelligence). In addition, the five sources of heritability evidence in question 9 were combined to form one scale corresponding to the number of sources checked. The final pool of items subjected to principal–component analysis contained thirty-nine questions, which included all those from the first four sections of the questionnaire and the author ratings not eliminated by one of the selection criteria. Before the correlation matrix was formed, answers to all questions were normalized, and missing values were set equal to zero. Each cell of the matrix thus contained a correlation coefficient based on 661 cases. The inclusion of missing values coded as the mean of the remaining cases reduces the obtained correlation coefficients. The elimination of all questions with greater than 25 percent nonresponse rate was intended to minimize this problem.

Principal-component analysis with Varimax rotation was performed on the correlation matrix resulting from the recoded and streamlined substantive questions. Four interpretable factors emerged from this analysis, accounting for 12.1%, 11.3%, 9.2%, and 6.3% of the variance. They were labeled "Test Usefulness," "Test Bias," "Personal Characteristics," and "Test Misuse." Questions with substantial loadings (> 0.3 or < -0.3) for each factor are presented in Table B-1. The first factor revealed the following pattern: belief in a consensus about intelligence, in an adequate theory of intelligence, and in the importance of IQ in determining SES; opposition to truth–in–testing laws, and particularly high loadings for all test uses. The substantial loadings for factor two were almost entirely for the various test bias questions. Under factor three, all of the nonintellectual characteristics in question 8 and high loadings, as did the sections of questions 16 dealing with bias caused by anxiety and motivation. The fourth factor picked up all four sources of test misuse (question 19) that were included in the analysis. The only questions that did not load on any of the four factors were numbers 5, 6, and 9 (on acquired knowledge, stability, and sources of heritability evidence).

Supervariables were formed corresponding to each of the four factors. Normalized variables were combined using a weighting system such that only variables loading with an absolute value greater than 0.3 on a given factor were combined to form the corresponding supervariable, positive-loading variables being added and negative-loading variables subtracted. Questions with loadings of absolute value greater than 0.6 were given double weight. Missing values were coded as zero and included in the supervariables.

Multivariate—Analysis

Stepwise multiple regression analyses were performed with each of the supervariables as dependent variables, and the demographic and background variables as predictors. Table B-2 shows the best fitting combination of predictors for each of the four supervariables, in the order in which they loaded, as well as the proportion of variance (R^2) thus accounted for. More detailed regression results (coefficients, partial correlations, etc.) would be relatively meaningless in light of the very low variance accounted for, and are therefore omitted.

TABLE B-1
Factors Underlying Substantive Question Responding

Factor	Loading
I. Test Usefulness	
27. Use in college admissions	.80
27. Use in graduate and professional school admissions	.77
27. Use in tracking decisions	.69
27. Use in vocational counseling	.64
27. Use in diagnosis and special education	.62
24. GRE validity	.61
24. SAT validity	.59
22. Use for white EMR placement	.44
23. Use for black EMR placement	.40
25. Opposition to truth-in-testing	.40
2. Belief in adequate theory of intelligence	.36
6. Importance of IQ as determinant of SES	.35
1. Belief in consensus about definition of intelligence	.34
Respect for Jensen's work on intelligence	.33
II. Test Bias	
14. General racial bias	.76
15. General economic bias	.71
13. Racial content bias	.66
16. Race of the examiner as bias	.60
16. Language of the examiner as bias	.57
16. Attitude of the examiner as bias	.53
12. Improper standardization as bias	.47
20. Effect of teacher's knowledge of test score	.45
Respect for Jensen's work on intelligence	− .45
21. Effect of student's knowledge of test score	.44
16. Anxiety as bias	.41
16. Motivation as bias	.40
10. Sufficient evidence for white heritability estimate	− .33
III. Personal Characteristics	
8. Importance of emotional ability to test performance	.74
8. Importance of physical health to test performance	.71
8. Importance of persistence to test performance	.70
8. Importance of anxiety to test performance	.68
8. Importance of achievement motivation to test performance	.66
8. Importance of attentiveness to test performance	.60
16. Motivation as bias	.49
16. Anxiety as bias	.45
IV. Test Misuse	
19. Improper intelligence-achievement test comparison	.81
19. Improper between-student score comparison	.80
19. Invalid test use	.73
19. Test administration under improper conditions	.48

TABLE B-2
Results of Multiple Regression Analyses Between Supervariables
and Demographic and Background Variables.

Dependent Variable	Independent Variables[a]	R^2
Test Usefulness	Political Perspective + Age + General Expertise + Gender	.18
Test Bias	Political Perspective + Gender + Media Source	.19
Personal Characteristics	Gender + General Expertise + Media Source	.06
Test Misuse	Political Perspective + Gender + Age	.05

[a]Independent variables are listed in the order in which they loaded into the regression equation

Appendix C

Content Analysis Methodology

Sample

The sample for the content analysis includes the three major national newsweeklies (*Time, Newsweek, U.S. News and World Report*), the three commercial television networks (ABC, CBS, NBC),[1] and the *New York Times*, the *Washington Post*, and the *Wall Street Journal*. The analysis includes articles published and television news programs broadcast during the fifteen years between January 1, 1969,[2] and December 31, 1983, the last complete year for which news indices were available at the time this analysis was begun.

Within each source, the analysis includes *all* articles and broadcast segments uncovered by a search of the appropriate indices (individual indices for each newspaper, the *Reader's Guide to Periodical Literature* for newsmagazines, and various archival sources for the television broadcasts)[3] using the search terms "Intelligence testing," "IQ," "Aptitude testing," "Admissions testing," "SAT," and "Employment testing," as well as other categories such as "Schools," "Mental tests," "Educational tests," and "Ability tests," to which the original search items may have led. The following types of articles and broadcasts were excluded:

- Those obviously not relevant to the IQ controversy (e.g., those listed under "Intelligence," dealing with the CIA).
- Those dealing with education or educational policy having little or nothing to do with testing (e.g., discussions of the Coleman report on equal opportunity in education, affirmative action in admissions).
- Those dealing only with achievement testing (e.g., reading scores, minimum competency testing).
- Those dealing only with admissions tests other than the SAT.[4]
- Advertisements.

The total number of articles and broadcast segments analyzed from each source is listed in Table 6.1.

Coding

The coding scheme for the present analysis is hierarchical. In reading through print articles and examining television broadcasts, it was discovered that the relevant information contained in these sources could be classified into thirteen categories, corresponding to general issues of concern within the IQ controversy. The code sheets were therefore set up so that coders first decided which of the categories (Issues) was present, and then moved to individual code sheets containing more specific items within each Issue. Thus, for example, a coder might decide that an article dealt with the Issue of "Group Differences in IQ." Having coded this information on the General Code Sheet, the coder would move to the Individual Issue Code Sheet corresponding to this Issue and code the article's content on more specific items like the presence of bias in tests or the possibility of a genetic component to the black-white difference in IQ.

The General Code Sheet, which contains the list of possible Issues considered, is divided into three sections. The first asks for basic information about the article or broadcast, such as source, date, length, location, and type (e.g., feature article, book review, editorial, or letter to the editor for print media; anchorman story, reporter story, or commentary/editorial for television). The second section is the list of Issues considered. Coders were instructed to read the article or view the videotape at least once before beginning to code, and then to refer back to the source as necessary. After recording basic information about the article or broadcast in the first section of the General Code Sheet, the coder had to decide on the Issue or Issues covered by the item being coded. *All* Issues covered were to be recorded. The thirteen Issues listed fall into four independent categories: IQ and Aptitude Testing (Issues I-VII), SAT (VIII-XI), Employment Testing (XII), and Intelligence and Aptitude Testing Outside the U.S. (XIII). The first three categories refer only to tests given to U.S. populations. The thirteen Issues were described to the coders as follows:

> I. *The Nature of Intelligence*: Discussion of intelligence itself, not merely as it is measured by intelligence tests. Topics to look for: the definition of intelligence, general intelligence (g), multi-factorial intelligence, mental speed, non-test measures of intelligence (e.g., physiological measures and reaction time).

> II. *What Intelligence Tests Measure*: Be sure the article or broadcast deals with intelligence or general aptitude tests, and *not only the SAT or employment tests or testing outside the U.S.*, which should be coded separately. Discussion of achievement or competency testing should be excluded from coding. Topics to look for: test reliability and validity; tests as measures of innate potential, learning, or memory; ambiguous or poorly constructed test

questions; and the importance of nonintellectual factors to test performance. This category does *not* include bias in testing.

III. *The Usefulness of IQ*: Here the issue is not what tests measure, but what they can be used for. Topics to look for: tests as predictors of school performance or social status, as decision making tools (other than in employment), as indicators of the quality of schooling, the importance of IQ as a determinant of eventual social status.

IV. *Test Misuse*: Criticisms of the way tests are used. Criticisms of test content fall under the heading of "What intelligence tests measure." Topics to look for: mislabeling, misclassification, and stigmatization as a result of test scores, overreliance on testing, and teacher expectancies based on test scores.

V. *The Heritability of IQ*: Discussions of heredity versus environment in intelligence. *Do not check this alternative as an issue considered if the article or broadcast deals only with the heritability of the black-white or other group differences in IQ.* Besides inheritance, this issue also includes discussions of the effects of compensatory education (e.g., Head Start, early intervention, or other enriched environments) on IQ.

VI. *Group Differences in IQ*: Discussion of IQ differences between racial or socioeconomic groups, including possible genetic influences. Also, any discussion of cultural bias in intelligence tests, including claims about tests being geared to white, middle-class test takers. Also, this issue should be checked for any mention of gender differences in intelligence test scores.

VII. *Other Issues Concerning Herrnstein, Jensen, or Shockley*: Statements concerning Richard Herrnstein, Arthur Jensen, or William Shockley that are not codeable elsewhere. Most statements attributed to or describing these authors will be codeable under other categories (e.g., statements about heritability attributed to Herrnstein, should be coded under "Heritability of Intelligence."). This category refers to statements such as "Jensen has been the subject of much abuse because of his views," or "Shockley believes that blacks are innately inferior to whites" (note that there is no mention of intelligence here). *Do not* check this category if all statements pertaining to Herrnstein, Jensen, or Shockley are codeable elsewhere.

VIII. *The Meaning of SAT Scores*: Essentially the same as "What Intelligence Tests Measure," except dealing with the SAT. Also includes discussions of changes in average SAT scores over time and truth-in-testing legislation ("sunshine" laws).

IX. *SAT Use and Misuse*: "The Usefulness of IQ" and "Test Misuse" combined into one category and applied to the SAT. Topics to look for: the SAT as a predictor of college performance, and the use of admissions tests in general.

X. *SAT Coaching*: Discussion of the effects of SAT coaching courses and software on SAT scores and on education. *Articles or broadcasts that talk about coaching as a challenge to the claim that the SAT measures aptitude should also be coded under "The Meaning of SAT Scores."*

XI. *Group Differences in SAT Score*: "Group Differences in IQ" applied to the SAT. Includes bias and genetic effects, as well as gender differences in SAT scores.

XII. *Employment Testing*: The use of intelligence and aptitude testing in hiring, placement, and promotion decisions in employment. Includes issues of test validity, and cultural bias in employment tests. *Discussions of IQ as a predictor of job performance, with no mention of the use of such tests in employment decisions, should be coded under "The Usefulness of IQ," not under this category.*

XIII. *Intelligence and Aptitude Testing Outside the U.S.*: Any mention of intelligence or intelligence, aptitude, or employment testing outside the United States. A separate Individual Issue Code Sheet should be completed for each country discussed in the article or broadcast. *This category does not include testing of foreign-born or ethnic Americans* (which should be coded under "Group Differences"), only testing that actually takes place outside the U.S.

The third section of the General Code Sheet asks coders to make two simple subjective judgments as to the general tone of the article regarding testing and the heritability of intelligence. As these two judgments are the least objective part of the coding scheme, coders were provided with the following set of instructions:

The coder is here asked to make a subjective judgment of the overall stance taken in the article or broadcast with regard to *traditional forms* of testing and the issue of the heritability of intelligence.

The decision to label an article or broadcast *pro-testing*, *anti-testing*, or *neutral* should be based on the preponderance of comments made about testing. Only if it is clear that most of the comments are either pro- or anti-testing should a category other than neutral be checked. It is not necessary for every statement in the article or broadcast to be pro- or anti-testing, only a clear preponderance.

Similarly, the decision to label an article or broadcast's stance toward the issue of heritability of intelligence as *learned*, *innate*, or *neutral* should be based on the preponderance of comments made about heritability. If the general tone of the article or broadcast *either* clearly disagrees with the theory that intelligence is largely inherited *or* clearly agrees that intelligence is largely learned, then *learned* should be checked. The article or broadcast does not have to make an explicit statement that intelligence is learned in order for *learned* to be checked. Alternatively, if the general tone of the article or broadcast either clearly disagrees with the theory that intelligence is largely learned or agrees that intelligence is largely inherited, then *innate* should be checked. Again, an article or broadcast does not have to make an explicit statement that intelligence is inherited in order for *innate* to be checked.

The critical questions the coder should be asking here are the following: What is the overall picture of testing the article or broadcast dos not have to make an explicit statement that intelligence is learned in order for *learned* to be checked.

The critical questions the coder should be asking here are the following: What is the overall picture of testing the article or broadcast presents to the reader? Is it clearly positive or negative? What is the overall attitude concerning the heritability of intelligence? Is it clearly that intelligence is learned or innate? Assume all articles and broadcasts are neutral unless it is clear to you that they are otherwise.

Following completion of the General Code Sheet, coders move to Individual Issue Code Sheets corresponding to each of the Issues considered by the article or broadcast being coded. The Individual Issue Code Sheets consist of series of position statements related to the Issue at hand. For example, the "Test Misuse" Code Sheet contains six statements, including:

1. Students are often misclassified, mislabeled, or stigmatized on the basis of intelligence test scores.
4. The use of tests creates a narrow set of educational objectives.
6. Test scores are overrelied upon (are too important in people's lives).

For each statement, the coder must make an initial judgment of whether the position is in any way represented in the article or broadcast being coded. If it is not, the statement is coded as Not Mentioned (NM). If the position is represented, it might be supported, rejected, or both. These possibilities are coded as Positive (Pos), Negative (Neg), or both. An article whose only mention of the stigmatization issue is of the form "Many critics have called IQ tests stigmatizing" would receive a Pos code for item 1, above. If the article continued "Others disagree," it would also receive a Neg code. Similarly, statements of the type "There is a debate (controversy) over the stigmatizing effects of IQ" would also receive both Pos and Neg codes, because "debate" implies that there are at least two sides. For some of the statements on some of the Individual Issue Code Sheets, there are more options than simply Pos or Neg. Item 1 on the "Heritability of Intelligence" Sheet reads:

1. The heritable component of (genetic influence on) intelligence, as measured by intelligence tests is:
   _____ (NM).
   _____ total (no mention of environmental determination, or environmental determination ruled out).
   _____ significant (including environmental determination).
   _____ insignificant or nonexistent.
   _____ cannot be determined or is undetermined.

An article or broadcast that addresses the question of heritability may receive any one or any combination of the four non-NM codes.

It is possible for an Issue such as "The Nature of Intelligence" to be dealt with in an article or broadcast, while none of the specific positions presented on the Individual Issue Code Sheet are mentioned. Indeed, it is possible for an Issue to be only briefly mentioned in an article or broadcast. In cases such as these, the appropriate Issue(s) are checked on the General Code Sheet, and all statements on the Individual Issue Code Sheet(s) are coded as NM.

For each representation of a given position (Pos, Neg, or some other option), the coder is to indicate the source or sources for that representation. There are eight possible source codes, described to the coders as follows:

1. *Assertion or implication.* If a position is simply asserted or implied by the author of the article or by an anchorman, reporter, or commentator in a broadcast with no reference to another individual or group, the number 1 should be written in the appropriate space on the code sheet. One of the more difficult decisions you will have to make involves positions that are implied but not stated by the author or broadcaster. There is no easy solution to this problem; you have to use your own judgment as to whether the implication is clear. Do not code an implication unless you are *certain* that the author or broadcaster is implying something.

2. *Single expert.* If the position is attributed to a single expert other than Herrnstein, Jensen, or Shockley, the number 2 should be written, along with the name of the expert and his or her affiliation (e.g., psychology professor at Columbia). For our purposes, *an expert is any individual with a professional label or affiliation related to testing* (i.e. an educator, psychologist, or geneticist, not just a student, high school teacher, lawyer, judge, or government official). Statements or research attributed to more than one individual should be coded as 2 if the name of each individual is given; otherwise, code as 3.

3. *Some experts or specific expert group or organization.* Includes statements like "many psychologists believe . . . ," or "An APA report concludes . . ." In the latter case be sure to specify "APA" in addition to writing down the number 3. Be certain that the statement or opinion is attributed to the organization as a whole, and not just to a particular member. Also, specifically delineated expert groups such as "test makers" fall under this category.

4. *Most or all experts.* Includes statements like "Most social scientists believe . . . ," or "The general feeling among psychologists is . . ." There should be no need to specify a particular group here, as the reference should clearly pertain to most or all experts.

5, 6, and 7. *Herrnstein, Jensen, and Shockley.* This should be self-explanatory.

8. *Other.* Any attribution that does not fall under 1-7 above, including political organizations, ethnic groups, government agencies, and public opinion. *When coding an 8, be sure to specify the source.*

It is possible for any given representation of a position to be attributed to more than one source. Thus, an article on racial differences in test scores might cite a number of sources claiming that tests are biased.

Coders were instructed to try very hard to fit each source into one of the existing categories before using Others. In such cases, as with Single Experts and Some Experts, coders provide a written description of the particular source in addition to providing the source code. The inclusion of separate source codes for Herrnstein, Jensen, and Shockley, like the inclusion of an Issue specific to them, reflects the prominent role these three scientists play in news media coverage of the IQ controversy.

In some cases when analyzing television broadcasts, the coder adds to the source code a second digit that identifies whether an individual is shown during the broadcast and how he or she is shown. These digits are used only when coding television broadcasts and only when the first digit of the source code is either 2 or 5-8 (i.e., only when the source is an individual and not a group). These codes are as follows:

1. *Interviewed.* The individual source must actually be shown on the screen either in a still photo or film footage and be heard making the codeable statement.
2. *Shown/Cited.* The individul source is shown on the screen either in a still photograph or in film footage, but he or she is either quoted, paraphrased, or cited in voiced-over narration by the anchorman or reporter rather than being heard.
3. *Not Shown/Cited.* The individual source is not shown in any way on the screen, but he or she is either quoted, paraphrased, or cited by the anchorman or reporter.

Thus, for example, a filmed interview with psychologist Leon Kamin would have 21 as a source code (coders would also write down his name, profession, and affiliation), while a reporter mentioning William Shockley without accompanying film footage or photograph would have 73 as a source code.

The coding process may be made clearer by working through an actual example. On January 22, 1974, the *New York Times* ran an article on page 16, written by George Goodman Jr., entitled "I.Q. Scores Linked to Environment." The article location is coded as Other page (i.e., not front page, editorial page, etc.), type as Feature article, and length as thirteen paragraphs. (Information about article source and date is part of the code number assigned to each article and is written on both the article and on all code sheets.) The story reports the results of a study by Dr. Peggy Sanday, an associate professor of anthropology at the University of Pennsylvania, that suggests that the black-white IQ difference can be accounted for entirely by environmental factors, including differences in culture and quality of education. There is also some discussion of possible genetic effects on within-group IQ differences and the views of Jensen and Shockley on black-white differences. There is no other IQ-relevant discussion. Issues considered are therefore The Heritability of IQ (V) and Group Differences in IQ (VI). Because Jensen and Shockley are only mentioned in relation to black-white IQ differences, there is no need to check Other Issues Concerning Herrnstein, Jensen, or Shockley (VII).

On the Heritability of IQ Code Sheet, the only item mentioned is the first (shown above), concerning the heritable component of intelligence (the other items on the sheet concern heritability estimates and compensatory education). In the ninth paragraph of the article, Dr. Sanday says, "I.Q. differences between racial groups is [sic] exclusively a matter of environment while differences within racial groups is [sic] determinant on genetics and environment." Therefore a "significant" heritable component of intelligence is coded (see item 1 on the Heritability Sheet, above), with source code 2, single expert, and Dr. Sanday's name, title, and affiliation.

On the Group Differences in IQ Sheet, item 2 reads:

2. The effect of genetic differences on the black-white IQ difference is:
   _____ (NM).
   _____ total (no mention of environmental determination, or environmental determination ruled out).
   _____ significant (including environmental determination).
   _____ insignificant or nonexistent (is entirely environmental).
   _____ cannot be determined or is undetermined.

This item is coded "insignificant or nonexistent" with source code 2, as above, corresponding to Dr. Sanday's statement. The item is also coded "total," with source codes 6 and 7, Jensen and Shockley, because of the following statement in paragraph six: "Thus the findings oppose the theories of Arthur Jensen, the educational psychologist, and William Shockley, the Nobel Prize-winning physicist, which suggest that genetic factors are determinant." Notice that there is no indication that Jensen and Shockley also believe the environment to be an important determinant of racial differences in IQ. In fact, the first paragraph of the article states that Sanday's data indicate that the black-white IQ difference is the result of "environmental factors rather than genetics," as if the two were mutually exclusive.

Other items on the Group Differences in IQ sheet not mentioned include those on cultural bias in tests, SES differences in IQ, and the propriety of studying group differences. The article does describe Sanday's findings that "[c]hanges in I.Q. score seem to reflect changes in students' educational environment rather than racial aptitude," and "[t]est score differences between blacks and whites are a function, among other factors, of the degree and nature of contact that blacks have as a group with the mainstream—white middle-class America." A Pos code was thus assigned to items attributing the black-white IQ difference to "cultural deprivation" and "inferior education," with a Source code of 2, correspondig to Dr. Sanday, in both cases.

Because the article attempts to present both sides of the black-white genetic issue (and recognized genetic effects on within-group differences), the coder rated the story as "Neutral" with regard to general tone, both toward testing and heritability.

Coders and Reliability

Nine graduate and undergraduate students coded newspaper and magazine articles, and three of these students also coded television broadcasts. Many of the coders were involved in the early stages of code sheet development, coding hundreds of articles with earlier versions of the code sheets. Their problems and suggestions were instrumental in the evolution of the final coding scheme and coder instructions. All articles and broadcasts were coded using the final version of the code sheets, regardless of any code they had previously received.

Before coding in earnest, all coders went through an extensive training period in which they were briefed on the important elements of the IQ controversy and given a set of lengthy instructions on the coding procedure, some of which have been reprinted above. Trainees were then asked to code at least twenty articles or broadcast segments in order to gain experience with the coding scheme, and to ensure that coding instructions were being followed. This training was followed by the first reliability check, in which the same ten articles were examined by all coders. Coders whose reliability was significantly lower than the group average were given further training in problem areas. Reliability checks were also conducted throughout the development period. Code sheets were revised to produce the maximum reliability consistent with a valid portrayal of news media coverage of the IQ controversy.

Reliability in content analysis is a measure of the degree to which different individuals, properly trained, agree in their coding of the same articles or broadcasts; it is a measure of the objectivity of the analysis. The simplest measure of reliability, and the one most frequently used in content analyses, is percent agreement between coders. It indicates the proportion of all categories on the code sheets that are identical between two coders coding the same article or broadcast. The problem with percent agreement as a reliability measure is that it greatly inflates reliability estimates because it does not take into account percent agreement expected by chance. This is a potentially serious problem in the present analysis, as the bulk of the code for any given article is NM (there are thirteen Individual Issue Code Sheets, each with at least five items—most of these will not be mentioned in any given article or broadcast). Therefore, most of the code between two coders will agree for any given article or broadcast, even if the coders are distributing their code randomly throughout the code sheets. Scott's pi[5] is a measure that takes this expected agreement explicitly into account:

$$\frac{\% \text{ observed agreement} - \% \text{ expected agreement}}{1 - \% \text{ expected agreement}}$$

Pi is essentially a correlation coefficient between each pair of coders. When agreement is no better than one would expect by chance, the value of pi is 0. When agreement is perfect, pi is 1.0.

Three sets of reliability checks, including the one at the beginning of coding, were run on newspaper and magazine articles using the final version of the code sheets. None of these checks included all nine coders, as the same individuals were not coding simultaneously throughout the run of the project. Nonetheless, all nine coders participated in at least one print reliability check, and there were no fewer than four coders in each check. The small number of television broadcasts allowed only two reliability checks with the three coders involved. Each reliability check involved a different set of ten articles or television broadcasts.

Pi was computed separately for the three levels of coding: Issues considered (on the General Code Sheet), representation of items on the Individual Issue Code Sheets (NM, Pos, Neg, etc.), and source codes. The average pi values across all coders for the three reliability checks on print media are Issues considered, 0.81; representation, 0.68; and source codes, 0.84. The values for representation and source codes have been corrected to take into account the hierarchical nature of the coding scheme. Representation of items on Individual Issue Code Sheets cannot be expected to agree if two coders do not agree on whether the Issue was even considered. The proper calculation of pi for representation involves only those Issue Code Sheets used by both coders. In a similar fashion, the source code values are based on only those items where coders agree on representation.

The average pi values for the TV reliability checks are Issues considered, 0.88; representation, 0.75; and source codes, 0.73. The values for representation and source code are corrected as described.

Fifty-two (11%) of the newspaper and magazine articles, as well as fifteen (23%) of the TV broadcast segments were deemed to have a large enough content relevant to the IQ controversy (e.g., the *New York Times Magazine* "jensenism" article and the CBS News special *The IQ Myth*) to warrant multiple code. These articles and broadcasts[6] received three sets of code from separate coders, and the final code sheets were concantenated by coding only those items on which at least two coders agreed.

Notes

1. The analysis originally included public television (PBS) as well, but a search of *Nova*, the *MacNeil-Lehrer News Hour*, and other nationally syndicated PBS programs for the time period under study revealed only one report on intellegence—and aptitude-testing issues, as part of a December 6, 1981 *Nova* program on "Twins." PBS was therefore dropped from the analysis.
2. The *Washington Post Index* began publication in 1972. Our analysis of the *Post* therefore does not begin until that year.
3. The *Television News Index and Abstracts*, published by Vanderbilt University, indexes all network weekday evening news broadcasts, and a composite videotape of relevant segments was obtained from Vanderbilt. For weekend and morning network news broadcasts, television newsmagazine segments (e.g., *60 Minutes*, *20/20*, and network specials, only CBS News publishes an index. At ABC and NBC, the research staffs were able to provide assistance in locating appropriate broadcasts. Unfortunately, videotape availability is both limited and generally very expensive at the networks and at various archives around the country. For six of these broadcasts (four segments from the *CBS Morning News*, one from CBS's *30 Minutes*, and one from ABC's *20/20*), therefore, we were able to obtain transcripts only. We were unable to obtain either videotapes or transcripts from relevant segments on NBC's *Today* and *Tomorrow* programs.
4. Well over 95 percent of news media coverage of admissions testing concerns the SAT. Coding the very limited amount of discussion of other admissions tests would have required a substantially longer and more complicated coding scheme, so these data were dropped from the analysis.
5. Ole R. Holsti, *Content Analysis for the Social Sciences and Humanities* (Reading, MA: Addison-Wesley, 1969), p. 140.
6. For important broadcasts, one coder viewed the videotape and the other two coders used the transcripts.

Appendix D

Location, Length, and Type of News Stories

Newspapers

Table D-1 presents location, length, and type data from each news source. Most of the IQ controversy stories from each of the newspapers (53 percent of all newspaper stories) are found inside the newspaper, approximately one–quarter are to be found on the editorial or op-ed pages, and only rarely (10 percent) are such stories placed in positions of prominence on the front–page or the first page of a section within the paper. Prominent stories, which were more common in the latter years of the analysis, are predominantly concerned with the decline and recent leveling off of average SAT scores. Other front page stories of note are *WP* stories on Shockley (3/12/72) and on the Burt scandal (10/29/76), an *NYT* story on the mislabeling of Hispanic test takers (9/16/79), and two *WSJ* articles on troubles

TABLE D-1
Location, Length, and Type of News Stories

Newspapers	New York Times	Washington Post	Wall Street Journal
Location:			
Front page of paper or section within paper	16	18	4
Editorial or Op-Ed page	46	39	11
Sunday magazine (including *New York Times Book Review*)	51	10	0
Other page	154	56	7
Length (mean no. of paragraphs)	12.5	15.2	14.3
Type:			
Feature article	173	74	11
Editorial	21	37	8
Letter to the editor	58	5	2
Book review	15	7	1

Newsmagazines
Length (mean no. of pages): 1.1 (s.d. = .94)
Page number of first page (mean): 64.8 (s.d. = 24.8)
Type:
 Feature article: 65
 Commentary/Editorial: 2
Television Networks (Newscast segments only)
Broadcast time slot:
 Morning: 22
 Evening: 31
 Weekend: 4
Total time (mean no. of minutes): 1.8
Type:
 Anchorman story: 23
 Reporter story: 28
 Commentary/Editorial: 6

at CEEB and ETS stemming from criticisms of testing (9/5/72 and 2/28/78). Comparison of high (front page of paper or section, editorial or op-ed page, or Sunday magazine) versus low visibility (other page) locations across newspapers reveals that the *WP* places a significantly higher proportion of IQ stories in high visibility locations than does the *NYT*.

Newspaper article type parallels the location data, as 63 percent are feature articles and 32 percent are editorials or letters to the editor. The remaining 5 percent of articles are classified as book reviews. The average length of an IQ-relevant newspaper story is 13.4 paragraphs.

Newsmagazines

Newsmagazine stories on intelligence testing and related issues are very rarely found in positions of prominence within the magazine. The average beginning page number of all such stories is 65, corresponding to such "back-of-the-book" sections as education and science. Virtually all relevant newsmagazine stories are feature articles (as opposed to editorials or commentaries), averaging one page in length. There are no significant time trends in location, length, or type of newsmagazine article with the exception of 1969, the year of the Jensen coverage, in which articles average two pages.

Television Networks

The televison data in Table D-1 represent only segments from morning, evening, and weekend newscasts. These data do not include the seven TV newsmagazine segments (average length 13.3 minutes) or the one news special (the hour long CBS special *The IQ Myth*). Relevant newscast segments are somewhat more common on evening than on morning newscasts (though this may reflect better indexing for evening newscasts) and are approximately equally divided between anchorman stories (in which the story is read entirely by the anchorman) and reporter stories (in which the anchorman introduces a filmed story narrated by another reporter). Commentaries and editorials are rare. Relevant newscast segments average nearly two minutes in length.

Appendix E

Ideology, Journalists, and the IQ Controversy

Studying journalists' coverage of such issues as nuclear energy, busing and oil companies, Lichter, Rothman and Lichter discovered that the tilt of such coverage often correlated closely with reporters' personal, social and political outlooks. Indeed, journalists often reported the views of experts in these fields rather inaccurately as falling in line with their own perspectives on the issues involved. These findings are not surprising, given that journalists tend to seek out experts who share their views when researching issues of public policy.[1]

In an attempt to determine whether similar factors play a role in coverage of IQ and testing issues, we polled a sample of national media personnel, to whom we directed a number of questions designed to tap their social and political outlook, as well as specific questions on intelligence and aptitude testing. The sample consisted of randomly selected names of accredited journalists working for national publications listed in the 1985 *Congressional Directory*. To move beyond Washington we also randomly sampled names of news editors from the 1985 edition of *Editor and Publisher*. From a universe of 1,200 names we drew a sample of 207 journalists employed by the *New York Times*, the *Washington Post*, the *Wall Street Journal*, *Time*, *Newsweek*, *U.S. News and World Report*, AP, UPI, ABC, CBS, NBC, and PBS. One hundred and nineteen journalists responded to our questionnaire, a response rate of 57%.

Because popular science journals have proliferated in recent years and influence the views of both journalists and the general public, we also drew a sample of science editors from *Scientific American*, *Nature*, *Bulletin of the Atomic Scientists*, *Science Digest*, *Science 86*, *Omni*, *Technology Review*, and *American Scientist*. We sampled the full universe of editorial staff for each of the journals. Our questionnaire was sent to 86 editors, of whom 50 responded, a response rate of 58%.

As we hypothesized, journalists and science editors are far more attached to an environmentalist view of intelligence and far more skeptical of IQ tests than are experts, though the differences were not as large in some areas as we had anticipated. For example, while 94% of our expert respondents believe that genetic factors play at least some role in measured IQ differences in the white population, only 74% of science editors and 67% of national journalists believe the same.[2]

Differences among journalists, editors, and experts are even more substantial on the sources of the black-white difference in IQ. As we saw in Chapter 4 (question 10), 53% of expert respondents believe that genes and environment are both involved in this differential. This compares to only 27% of journalists and 23% of the science editors. In short, twice as many experts as journalists believe that genetics plays some role in the black-white difference in measured IQ. The flip side is the proportion of those questioned who believe that the differences are purely the result of environmental factors. Only 17% of expert respondents are complete environmentalists, as compared to 34% of the journalists and 47% of science editors.

Experts are less likely to believe that IQ tests are biased against blacks than are either journalists or editors. Only 28% of the experts rate such tests as either moderately or extremely biased against blacks, as compared to 42% of journalists and almost half of the science editors. Surprisingly, however, experts are somewhat more likely than journalists and science editors to believe that IQ tests have been misused in making decisions about individuals. Sixty-five percent of our expert respondents believe that intelligence and aptitude tests used in elementary and secondary schools are often or almost always used for making decisions for which they have limited or unknown validity, as compared to only 40% of journalists and 46% of science editors.

Our expert sample is more supportive of the continued use of SATs as one criterion for college admission than are journalists or science editors, although all groups are relatively supportive of the SAT. Thus 90% of the experts responding believe that the SAT is sufficiently valid to be used as a basis for college admissions, as compared to 72% of journalists and 68% of science editors (see note 2).

In general, then, both science editors and journalists are less supportive of the hereditarian position (especially on the racial issue) than is the expert community, as well as being less supportive of the validity of both IQ and SAT. These positions are associated with a liberal, cosmopolitan social and political outlook. Science editors are both somewhat more inclined to an environmentalist position on the racial issue and somewhat more liberal and cosmopolitan than the journalists we sampled.[3] Thus, while 63% of the journalists agree or strongly agree that American economic exploitation has contributed to third world poverty, that view is supported by 75% of the science editors. Similarly, only 26% of the journalists questioned agree or strongly agree that it would be good for the

TABLE E-1

Individual differences in IQ among white Americans are at least partially caused by genetic differences.*

	Strongly Agree	Agree	Disagree	Strongly Disagree	N
Journalists	13%	54%	22%	11%	108
Editors	16%	58%	18%	8%	50

Which of the following best characterizes your opinion of the source of the black-white difference in IQ?

	Entirely Environment	Entirely Genetic	Both	Data Are Insufficient	N
Journalists	34%	1%	27%	38%	112
Editors	47%	2%	23%	28%	47
IQ Experts	17%	1%	53%	28%	566

On the whole, to what extent do you believe the most commonly used intelligence tests are biased against American Blacks?

	Not At All or Insignif.	Somewhat Biased	Moderately Biased	Extremely Biased	N
Journalists	19%	40%	33%	9%	116
Editors	13%	40%	36%	11%	47
IQ Experts	21%	50%	24%	4%	556

In your opinion, how often are intelligence and aptitude tests used in elementary and secondary schools for making decisions for which they have limited or unknown validity?

	Rarely	Sometimes	Often	Almost Always	N
Journalists	9%	51%	39%	1%	99
Editors	2%	51%	41%	5%	41
IQ Experts	4%	31%	51%	14%	534

The SAT is a sufficiently valid predictor of college performance to justify its continued use in college admissions decisions in which there are many more applicants than places.*

	Strongly Agree	Agree	Disagree	Strongly Disagree	N
Journalists	6%	66%	21%	7%	112
Editors	7%	61%	26%	7%	46

*See footnote Appendix E, Note 2, re IQ experts' responses to these questions.

United States to move toward socialism. On the other hand, 52% of the science editors hold to that position. Both groups are about equally supportive of strong affirmative action measures for blacks, but only 5% of journalists (as compared to 20% of science editors) "strongly agree," rather than just "agree," with affirmative action. Furthermore, 77% of journalists as compared to 48% of editors, agree or strongly agree that the American private enterprise system is generally fair to working people. Lastly, 23% of journalists compared to 33% of editors agree or strongly agree that the structure of our society causes most people to feel alienated.

As one would expect, both groups are much more likely to view themselves as liberal than middle of the road or conservative on a 7-point scale, although, again, the liberalism of science editors far outstrips that of journalists. Approximately 64% of the latter group rate themselves as liberal (a ranking of 1, 2, or 3), 21% as middle of the road, and 16% as conservative (a ranking of 5, 6, or 7). On the other hand, 86% of science editors place themselves on the liberal side of the political scale as compared to a mere 8% who classify themselves as middle of the road, and an even smaller percentage who see themselves as relatively conservative.

The most interesting findings from our point of view, however, are not the differences between science editors and journalists, but the similarities between journalists and experts. As Table E-2 demonstrates, on almost all questions of social and political outlook, the views of these two groups coincide fairly closely, though the expert community is characterized by a somewhat wider range of opinions than are journalists.

Thus, 60% of our expert respondents agrees or strongly agrees that American economic exploitation of the third world contributes to its poverty; 25% hold similar attitudes about the United States moving toward socialism. Sixty-three percent are supportive or strongly supportive of affirmative action programs for blacks. Indeed, the experts are somewhat more strongly committed to affirmative action than are the journalists.

Fifty-four percent of the expert respondents agree or strongly agree that the private enterprise system is generally fair to workers, while 36% agree or strongly agree that the structure of society causes alienation. Finally, 63% rate themselves as liberal, 17% as middle of the road, and 20% as conservative. Their self–ratings are not quite as liberal as those of journalists. However, the proportion of liberal responses they give on individual questions differs little from national media personnel.

We believe that these data help explain the manner in which information about intelligence and intelligence testing is communicated to the broader public, and that they also throw light on some other issues. Our hypotheses in this area must necessarily be regarded as tentative.

First, it is clear that reporters and IQ experts are sympathetic to the new

TABLE E-2
American exploitation has contributed to Third World poverty.

	Strongly Agree	Agree	Disagree	Strongly Disagree	N
Journalists	13	50	30	8	119
Editors	13	62	23	2	47
IQ Experts	16	44	22	17	590

The United States would be better off if it moved toward socialism.

	Strongly Agree	Agree	Disagree	Strongly Disagree	N
Journalists	8	18	55	19	114
Editors	9	43	39	9	46
IQ Experts	5	20	33	42	532

Strong affirmative action measures should be used in hiring to assure black representation.

	Strongly Agree	Agree	Disagree	Strongly Disagree	N
Journalists	5	60	29	6	114
Editors	20	46	33	2	46
IQ Experts	17	46	24	12	621

The American private enterprise system is generally fair to working people.

	Strongly Agree	Agree	Disagree	Strongly Disagree	N
Journalists	4	73	21	2	114
Editors	4	44	44	6	49
IQ Experts	9	45	36	10	621

The structure of our society causes most people to feel alienated.

	Strongly Agree	Agree	Disagree	Strongly Disagree	N
Journalists	4	19	65	12	113
Editors	6	27	55	9	45
IQ Experts	8	28	36	28	593

	Most Liberal 1	2	3	4	5	6	Most Conservative 7	N
Journalists	22	23	19	21	9	5	2	115
Editors	30	46	10	8	6	0	0	50
IQ Experts	7	25	31	17	16	3	1	632

(Political Ideology)

liberalism. The finding is not surprising. Other studies demonstrate that individuals entering the social sciences or the service professions share certain common views about the society.[4] Experts differ from journalists only in their own specialties, where they reject the overall claims of the new ideology with, one suspects, some cognitive dissonance.

Second, it is clear that journalists' reporting on IQ issues more closely reflects their own views than it does that of the expert community. As with nuclear energy issues, journalists seem to draw their image of what scientists believe from those scientists who share their views, whatever the standing of such persons in the relevant expert community.[5]

It is possible that the views of journalists have been at least partially formed by science journals written for the educated public. The editors of such journals are socially and politically further to the left than either journalists or experts, and they are, in general, less sympathetic to hereditarian views on IQ and to the validity claims of various measures of intelligence and ability. In so far as journalists obtain their information from such journals, and the views of editors of these journals dictate a certain type of coverage of the issues involved, journalists' perception of the views of the expert community will be less accurate than might otherwise be the case.

Journalists' views alone, however, cannot explain the generally negative coverage of the hereditarian position by the national media. While journalists are less supportive of hereditarian arguments than are the experts, they are not as hostile to this position as the almost universally negative coverage of such views would suggest. Clearly, not all journalists share Dan Rather's or *Time* magazine's conviction that the evidence so fully supports an environmentalist anti-testing position that alternate views have little to recommend them.

Our sample may simply not distinguish those most responsible for reporting on IQ issues. It may be that journalists who tend to write about such subjects have stronger anti-hereditarian and anti-testing views than does the average reporter. This is not unusual. In academia, for example, those working on peace studies or in the field of ethnic and race relations tend to be to the left of those who specialize in Greek or medieval history. Indeed, those who seek out areas that are involved with contemporary social issues tend to enter them with a reformer's zeal.

There is another possibility. Perspectives often become dominant because those who support them are more militant than are opponents. Thus, the energy with which egalitarians and anti-hereditarians press their position may have silenced many who believe that individual differences in measured IQ do involve a genetic component. In addition, the history of racism in America has been so flagrant an injustice by America's own standards that even journalists who have reservations about the new environmentalism may hesitate to give any creedence to the hereditarian position for fear of possible social consequences.

These last two hypotheses are conjectural. They are compatible with our findings, but the data we have gathered can not prove or disprove them. Whether they are correct or not, our IQ study, as well as other studies of the communication of information about controversial scientific issues to the larger public, leads us to the conclusion that some profound changes have taken place in this process during the past twenty-five years. As discussed in Chapter 8, such changes have also affected the manner in which scientific (and social scientific) reputations may be enhanced or weakened, at least when it comes to dealing with scientific findings that overlap with controversial issues of public policy.[6]

Notes

1. Robert S. Lichter, Stanley Rothman, and Linda S. Lichter, *The Media Elite* (Bethesda, MD: Adler & Adler, 1986).
2. The wording on questions 1 and 5 was not exactly the same for the expert community as for journalists and science editors. Thus the expert community is not listed for those questions in Table E-1. However, the meaning was close enough to allow for at least a rough comparison (See Chapter 4 and 5).
3. Our samples of journalists is slightly more conservative than the one developed by Lichter, Rothman, and Lichter in *The Media Elite*. However, this is probably a function of sample differences. The sample reported here includes the wire services and is more heavily weighted toward editorial staff than was the one developed by Lichter, Rothman, and Lichter. See *The Media Elite*.
4. Steven Brint, "New Class and Cumulative Trend Explanations of Liberal Political Attitudes of Professionals," *American Journal of Scoiology* 90 (1984):30–71. Alan Mazur, "The Development of Political Values in Management, Engineering and Journalism," *Research in Political Sociology*, vol. 2 (Greenwich, CT: JAI Press, 1986), pp. 225–241.
5. During the 1970s and 1980s, the relevant scientific community overwhelmingly supported the development of nuclear energy. Journalists, on the other hand, gave the impression that the community was sharply divided, and sometimes even that a majority of "experts" were skeptical about such development. In so doing, the national media often relied upon groups or "experts" with very little standing in the scientific community. These were "experts" who shared the views of the journalists. See Stanley Rothman and S. Robert Lichter, "Elite Ideology and Risk Perception in Nuclear Energy Policy," *American Political Science Review* 81 (June 1987):383–404.
6. Stanley Rothman "American Intellectuals," *The World and I* (January 1987):555–565.

Appendix F

Survey Questionnaire

<u>NOTE</u>: Throughout the questionnaire, "NQ" stands for Not Qualified, and should also be interpreted as Don't Know and No Opinion. Also, please ignore numbers in brackets and parentheses, as these will be used for coding purposes only.

THE NATURE OF INTELLIGENCE

1. If you do not feel qualified to answer questions about the nature of intelligence and the reliability and validity of intelligence tests, please check here, and go to question 11. ___ NQ

2. It has been argued that there is a consensus among psychologists and educators as to the kinds of behaviors that are labeled "intelligent." Do you agree that there is such a consensus?

    (1) ___ Strongly agree   [8]
    (2) ___ Somewhat agree
    (3) ___ Somewhat disagree
    (4) ___ Strongly disagree
    (9) ___ NQ

3. Do you believe that, on the whole, the development of intelligence tests has proceeded in the context of an adequate theory of intelligence?

    (1) ___ Yes   (2) ___ No   (9) ___ NQ   [9]

4. Please check <u>all</u> behavioral descriptors, listed below, which you believe to be an important element of intelligence.

    ___ Abstract thinking or reasoning   ___ Memory   [10-27]
    ___ Achievement motivation   ___ Mental speed
    ___ Adaptation to one's environment   ___ Problem solving ability
    ___ Capacity to acquire knowledge   ___ Sensory acuity
    ___ Creativity   ___ Others (Please list)
    ___ General knowledge   _____
    ___ Goal-directedness   _____
    ___ Linguistic competence
    ___ Mathematical competence   ___ NQ (Go to question 6)

5. What important elements of intelligence, checked above, if any, do you feel are <u>not</u> adequately measured by the most commonly used intelligence tests.

    ___ Abstract thinking or reasoning   ___ Memory   [28-45]
    ___ Achievement motivation   ___ Mental speed
    ___ Adaptation to one's environment   ___ Problem solving ability
    ___ Capacity to acquire knowledge   ___ Sensory acuity
    ___ Creativity   ___ Others (Please list)
    ___ General knowledge   _____
    ___ Goal-directedness   _____
    ___ Linguistic competence
    ___ Mathematical competence   ___ NQ (Go to question 6)

291

6. For each personal characteristic listed below, please circle the number, 1-4, which best represents your view of the importance of that characteristic to performance on intelligence tests:

	Of little importance	Somewhat important	Moderately important	Very important		
a. Achievement motivation	1	2	3	4	(9) ___ NQ	[46]
b. Anxiety	1	2	3	4	(9) ___ NQ	[47]
c. Attentiveness	1	2	3	4	(9) ___ NQ	[48]
d. Emotional lability	1	2	3	4	(9) ___ NQ	[49]
e. Persistence	1	2	3	4	(9) ___ NQ	[50]
f. Physical health	1	2	3	4	(9) ___ NQ	[51]

7. How stable is the attribute(s) being measured by intelligence tests, compared to a purely physical characteristic such as height, when each is expressed relative to the population mean?

(1) ___ Much less stable   [52]
(2) ___ Somewhat less stable
(3) ___ About equally as stable
(4) ___ Somewhat more stable
(5) ___ Much more stable
(9) ___ NQ

8. Compared to success on achievement tests, does success on intelligence tests among American test takers generally depend less, more, or about the same amount on acquired knowledge?

(1) ___ Much less   [53]
(2) ___ Somewhat less
(3) ___ About the same
(4) ___ Somewhat more
(5) ___ Much more
(9) ___ NQ

9. Is intelligence, as measured by intelligence tests, better described in terms of a primary general intelligence factor and subsidiary group or special ability factors, or entirely in terms of separate faculties?

(1) ___ General intelligence and subsidiary factors   [54]
(2) ___ Separate faculties
(3) ___ Neither description is superior
(9) ___ NQ

10. Please estimate the average improvement to be expected on composite (Verbal + Math) Scholastic Aptitude Test (SAT) scores (standard deviation = 200 points) from each of the following, assuming the test taker has some general familiarity with standardized tests.

___ a. Practice taking SAT exams   (999) ___ NQ   [55-57]

___ b. Small-scale ($\leq$ 50 hours) coaching programs, over and
       above the effects of practice   (999) ___ NQ   [58-60]

___ c. Large-scale ($\geq$ 300 hours) coaching programs, over and
       above the effects of practice   (999) ___ NQ   [61-63]

THE HERITABILITY OF IQ

11. If you do not feel qualified to answer questions about the heritability of IQ, please check here, and go to question 15. ___ NQ

12. Please check <u>all</u> of the sources of evidence, below, which you believe provide reasonable evidence for a significant non-zero heritability of IQ in the American white population.

___ General comparisons between degree of genetic relatedness between [64] various family members, and IQ correlations, that is, kinship correlations.
___ Studies of monozygotic twins reared apart. [65]
___ Studies comparing monozygotic to dizygotic twins. [66]
___ Twin family studies comparing, for example, the children of [67] monozygotic twins.
___ Adoption studies. [68]
___ NQ

13. Do you believe there is sufficient evidence to arrive at a reasonable estimate of the heritability of IQ in the American white population?

(1) ___ Yes [69]
(2) ___ No (Go to question 14)
(9) ___ NQ (Go to question 14)

13A. To one significant decimal place, what is your best estimate of the broad heritability of IQ in the American white population (please give estimate as a number between 0 and 1.0)? ____ (999) ___ NQ [70-72]

14. Do you believe there is sufficient evidence to arrive at a reasonable estimate of the heritability of IQ in the American black population?

(1) ___ Yes [8]
(2) ___ No (Go to question 15)
(9) ___ NQ (Go to question 15)

14A. To one significant decimal place, what is your best estimate of the broad heritability of IQ in the American black population? ____ (999) ___ NQ [9-11]

RACE, CLASS, AND CULTURAL DIFFERENCES IN IQ

15. If you do not feel qualified to answer questions about race and class differences in IQ, or their heritability, please check here, and go to question 24. ___ NQ

16. In your opinion, is the fact that an intelligence test has not been properly standardized for a certain group, by itself, sufficient evidence that the test is biased against that group?

(1) ___ Yes, improper standardization is sufficient evidence of test bias. [12]
(2) ___ No, improper standardization is not sufficient evidence of test bias, but it makes the possibility of bias more likely.
(3) ___ No, there is no relation between test standardization and test bias.
(9) ___ NQ

17. For each factor listed below, please circle the number, 1-4, which best represents your view of the degree to which that factor biases individually administered intelligence test scores, that is, the degree to which it, <u>on average</u>, differentially affects members of certain groups, racial, economic, or otherwise.

	Insignificant biasing effect	Some biasing effect	Moderate biasing effect	Large biasing effect		
a. Race of the examiner	1	2	3	4	(9) ___ NQ	[13]

	Insignificant biasing effect	Some biasing effect	Moderate biasing effect	Large biasing effect		
b. Language and dialect of the examiner	1	2	3	4	(9) ___ NQ	[14]
c. Attitude of the examiner toward the group in question	1	2	3	4	(9) ___ NQ	[15]
d. Test taker anxiety	1	2	3	4	(9) ___ NQ	[16]
e. Test taker motivation	1	2	3	4	(9) ___ NQ	[17]

18. Racial content bias may be defined as either race by item interaction in test scores, or different factor analytic solutions between black and white test takers. According to either of these definitions, how much racial content bias do you believe there is in the most commonly used intelligence tests?

    (1) ___ An insignificant amount of content bias   [18]
    (2) ___ Some content bias
    (3) ___ A moderate amount of content bias
    (4) ___ A large amount of content bias
    (9) ___ NQ

19. On the whole, to what extent do you believe the most commonly used intelligence tests are biased against American blacks? In other words, to what extent does an average black American's test score underrepresent his or her actual level of those abilities the test purports to measure, relative to the average ability level of members of other racial or ethnic groups?

    (1) ___ Not at all or insignificantly biased   [19]
    (2) ___ Somewhat biased
    (3) ___ Moderately biased
    (4) ___ Extremely biased
    (9) ___ NQ

20. On the whole, to what extent do you believe the most commonly used intelligence tests are biased against members of lower socio-economic groups? In other words, to what extent does the test score of an average lower socio-economic group member underrepresent his or her actual level of those abilities the test purports to measure, relative to the average ability level of members of other socio-economic groups?

    (1) ___ Not at all or insignificantly biased   [20]
    (2) ___ Somewhat biased
    (3) ___ Moderately biased
    (4) ___ Extremely biased
    (9) ___ NQ

21. Which of the following best characterizes your opinion of the heritability of the black-white difference in IQ?

    (1) ___ The difference is entirely due to environmental variation.   [21]
    (2) ___ The difference is entirely due to genetic variation.
    (3) ___ The difference is a product of both genetic and environmental variation.
    (4) ___ The data are insufficient to support any reasonable opinion.
    (9) ___ NQ

22. In your opinion, to what degree is the average American's socio-economic status (SES) determined by his or her IQ?

    (1) ___ IQ is not at all important to SES.   [22]
    (2) ___ IQ plays only a small role in determining SES.
    (3) ___ IQ is an important, but not the most important, determinant of SES.
    (4) ___ IQ is the most important determinant of SES.
    (9) ___ NQ

23. Which of the following best characterizes your <u>opinion</u> of the heritability of socio-economic class differences in IQ?

    (1) ___ The difference is entirely due to environmental variation.   [23]
    (2) ___ The difference is entirely due to genetic variation.
    (3) ___ The difference is a product of both genetic and environmental variation.
    (4) ___ The data are insufficient to support any reasonable opinion.
    (9) ___ NQ

THE USE OF INTELLIGENCE TESTING

24. If you do not feel qualified to answer questions about the use of intelligence testing, please check here, and go to question 34. ___ NQ

25. For each item listed below, please circle the number, 1-4, which best represents your view of the degree to which it is to be found in intelligence test administration and interpretation in elementary and secondary schools:

Rarely present	Sometimes present	Often present	Almost always present
1	2	3	4

a. Administration under improper conditions, such as failure to give adequate instructions or follow prescribed time limits, or in an environment with significant distractors.

   1   2   3   4   (9) ___ NQ   [24]

b. Use of English language test results for long-range predictions concerning students for whom English is a second language

   1   2   3   4   (9) ___ NQ   [25]

c. Comparison of test scores between students while ignoring limitations placed on such comparisons by the test's reliability and measurement error

   1   2   3   4   (9) ___ NQ   [26]

d. Comparison of intelligence and achievement test scores as a measure of under or overachievement while ignoring test reliability and measurement error, and differences in the domains of ability covered by each test

   1   2   3   4   (9) ___ NQ   [27]

e. Use of tests in making decisions for which they have limited or unknown validity

   1   2   3   4   (9) ___ NQ   [28]

26. On the average, how much of an effect do you believe a teacher's knowledge of a student's intelligence test score has on the student's academic performance?

    (1) ___ No significant effect   [29]
    (2) ___ Some effect
    (3) ___ A moderate effect
    (4) ___ A large effect
    (9) ___ NQ

27. On the average, how much of an effect do you believe a student's knowledge of his or her intelligence test score has on the student's academic performance?

    (1) ___ No significant effect   [30]
    (2) ___ Some effect
    (3) ___ A moderate effect
    (4) ___ A large effect
    (9) ___ NQ

28. Assuming that placement of white children into classes for the educable mentally retarded (EMR) is to continue, are you in favor of the use of individually administered intelligence tests as one of the criteria for such placement?

    (1) ___ Yes   (2) ___ No   (9) ___ NQ   [31]

29. Assuming that placement of black children into EMR classes is to continue, are you in favor of the use of individually administered intelligence tests as one of the criteria for such placement?

    (1) ___ Yes   (2) ___ No   (9) ___ NQ   [32]

30. For each of the admissions tests listed below, please indicate whether you believe it adds sufficient predictive validity to that available from other nontest criteria to justify its continued use in admissions decisions in which there are many more applicants than places.

a. Scholastic Aptitude Test (SAT)	(1) ___ Yes	(2) ___ No	(9) ___ NQ [33]
b. American College Testing Program (ACT)	(1) ___ Yes	(2) ___ No	(9) ___ NQ [34]
c. Graduate Record Examination (GRE)	(1) ___ Yes	(2) ___ No	(9) ___ NQ [35]
d. Law School Admission Test (LSAT)	(1) ___ Yes	(2) ___ No	(9) ___ NQ [36]
e. Medical College Admission Test (MCAT)	(1) ___ Yes	(2) ___ No	(9) ___ NQ [37]
f. Graduate Management Admission Test (GMAT)	(1) ___ Yes	(2) ___ No	(9) ___ NQ [38]

31. Do you approve or disapprove of complete disclosure laws such as New York's truth-in-testing law, which require admissions test makers to release the contents and answers of their tests to the general public within a specified time after test administration?

    (1) ___ Strongly approve   [39]
    (2) ___ Somewhat approve
    (3) ___ Indifferent
    (4) ___ Somewhat disapprove
    (5) ___ Strongly disapprove
    (9) ___ NQ

32. Approximately what proportion of all employment tests given do you believe are improperly validated for the purpose for which they are used?

    (1) ___ An insignificant proportion   [40]
    (2) ___ A small but significant proportion
    (3) ___ A moderate proportion
    (4) ___ A large proportion
    (9) ___ NQ

33. For each test use listed below, please circle the number, 1-7, which best represents your opinion of the importance intelligence and similar tests (e.g., general aptitude tests like the SAT in the case of college admissions) should play in such decisions, relative to the role they now play.

Severely reduced role			Remain about the same			Severely increased role	
1	2	3	4	5	6	7	

a. Diagnosis and special education planning in elementary and secondary schools

  1   2   3   4   5   6   7   (9) ___ NQ   [41]

b. Tracking decisions in elementary and secondary schools

  1   2   3   4   5   6   7   (9) ___ NQ   [42]

c. College admissions

  1   2   3   4   5   6   7   (9) ___ NQ   [43]

d. Graduate and professional school admissions

  1   2   3   4   5   6   7   (9) ___ NQ   [44]

e. Vocational counseling

  1   2   3   4   5   6   7   (9) ___ NQ   [45]

f. Hiring decisions

  1   2   3   4   5   6   7   (9) ___ NQ   [46]

g. Promotion decisions

  1   2   3   4   5   6   7   (9) ___ NQ   [47]

PROFESSIONAL ACTIVITIES AND INVOLVEMENT WITH INTELLIGENCE TESTING

34. Please check one item below which best describes your principal current position.

  (01) ___ Tenured faculty member at a college or university   [48-49]
  (02) ___ Nontenured faculty member at a college or university
  (03) ___ Other university or college staff
  (04) ___ Graduate student
  (05) ___ Psychologist or educational specialist working for private (nontesting) industry
  (06) ___ Psychologist or educational specialist working for testing industry
  (07) ___ Psychologist or educational specialist working for federal government
  (08) ___ Psychologist or educational specialist working for state or local government
  (09) ___ Psychologist or educational specialist working in primary or secondary education
  ___ Other (Please specify) _____

35. How often in the past two years have you engaged in the following activities?

  35A. Given speeches or lectures, delivered papers, or served on panel discussions before the following groups on intelligence testing or related issues?

	never	1-2 times	3-5 times	6-10 times	11+ times	
a. Social or behavioral scientists in your discipline	1	2	3	4	5	[50]
b. Other scientific groups	1	2	3	4	5	[51]
c. General college audiences (aside from teaching)	1	2	3	4	5	[52]
d. Business or industry groups	1	2	3	4	5	[53]
e. Public meetings or demonstrations	1	2	3	4	5	[54]

	never	1-2 times	3-5 times	6-10 times	11+ times	
f. "Public interest" groups	1	2	3	4	5	[55]
g. Other (Please specify)	1	2	3	4	5	[56-58]

35B. Served as a source of information for the news media on intelligence testing or related issues?

(1) ___ Never   [59]
(2) ___ 1-2 times
(3) ___ 3-5 times
(4) ___ 6-10 times
(5) ___ More than 10 times

35. How often in the past two years have you engaged in the following activities?

35C. Declined to serve as a source of information for the news media on the subject of intelligence testing or related issues?

(1) ___ Never   [60]
(2) ___ 1-2 times
(3) ___ 3-5 times
(4) ___ 6-10 times
(5) ___ More than 10 times

35D. Written letters to or phoned newspapers or magazines on the subject of intelligence testing or related issues?

(1) ___ Never   [61]
(2) ___ 1-2 times
(3) ___ 3-5 times
(4) ___ 6-10 times
(5) ___ More than 10 times

35E. Administered an individual intelligence or aptitude test?

(1) ___ Never   [62]
(2) ___ 1-5 times
(3) ___ 6-20 times
(4) ___ 21-50 times
(5) ___ More than 50 times

35F. Administered a group intelligence or aptitude test?

(1) ___ Never   [63]
(2) ___ 1-2 times
(3) ___ 3-5 times
(4) ___ 6-10 times
(5) ___ More than 10 times

36. Please check all areas below in which you are currently planning or carrying out research.

___ The nature of intelligence or other cognitive abilities   [8]
___ Test development or validation   [9]
___ The heritability of IQ   [10]
___ Bias in intelligence tests   [11]
___ Group differences in IQ   [12]
___ Testing in elementary and secondary schools   [13]
___ Testing in admissions to schools of higher education   [14]
___ Employment testing   [15]
___ Other aspects of intelligence or testing
      (Please specify)

                                                                                     [16-18]

37. Approximately how many articles or chapters have you <u>ever</u> written for either academic/professional or general audiences dealing with the following aspects of intelligence and intelligence testing? (Please answer <u>all</u> that apply)

	Academic/ professional	General audience	
a. The nature of intelligence or other cognitive abilities	___	___	[19-22]
b. Test development or validation	___	___	[23-26]
c. The heritability of IQ	___	___	[27-30]
d. Bias in intelligence tests	___	___	[31-34]
e. Group differences in IQ	___	___	[35-38]
f. Testing in elementary and secondary schools	___	___	[39-42]
g. Testing in admissions to schools of higher education	___	___	[43-46]
h. Employment testing	___	___	[47-50]
i. Other aspects of intelligence or testing (Please specify)	___	___	[51-62]
_____	___	___	
_____	___	___	

38. For each news source listed below please circle the number, 1-7, which best represents how accurately you believe their reporting to be on issues related to intelligence testing.

	Very innaccurate						Very accurate		
a. Christian Science Monitor	1	2	3	4	5	6	7	(9) ___ NQ	[63]
b. Commercial television networks	1	2	3	4	5	6	7	(9) ___ NQ	[64]
c. National Public Radio	1	2	3	4	5	6	7	(9) ___ NQ	[65]
d. New York Times	1	2	3	4	5	6	7	(9) ___ NQ	[66]
e. Newsweek	1	2	3	4	5	6	7	(9) ___ NQ	[67]
f. PBS television	1	2	3	4	5	6	7	(9) ___ NQ	[68]
g. Time	1	2	3	4	5	6	7	(9) ___ NQ	[69]
h. U.S. News and World Report	1	2	3	4	5	6	7	(9) ___ NQ	[70]
i. Wall Street Journal	1	2	3	4	5	6	7	(9) ___ NQ	[71]
j. Washington Post	1	2	3	4	5	6	7	(9) ___ NQ	[72]

39. Have you ever hesitated in expressing your opinion on an issue related to intelligence testing?

(2) ___ No   [8]
(1) ___ Yes. If yes, why did you hesitate? _____ [9-13]
_____
_____

40. For each author listed below, please circle the number, 1-7, which best represents how highly you regard his or her work on intelligence and intelligence testing.

	Very low regard						Very high regard		
a. Anne Anastasi	1	2	3	4	5	6	7	(9) ___ NQ	[14]

	Very low regard						Very high regard			
b. Cyril Burt	1	2	3	4	5	6	7	(9) ___ NQ	[15]
c. Raymond Cattell	1	2	3	4	5	6	7	(9) ___ NQ	[16]
d. Lee Cronbach	1	2	3	4	5	6	7	(9) ___ NQ	[17]
e. Hans Eysenck	1	2	3	4	5	6	7	(9) ___ NQ	[18]
f. Stephen J. Gould	1	2	3	4	5	6	7	(9) ___ NQ	[19]
g. J. P. Guilford	1	2	3	4	5	6	7	(9) ___ NQ	[20]
h. Richard Herrnstein	1	2	3	4	5	6	7	(9) ___ NQ	[21]
i. Lloyd Humphreys	1	2	3	4	5	6	7	(9) ___ NQ	[22]
j. Arthur Jensen	1	2	3	4	5	6	7	(9) ___ NQ	[23]
k. Leon Kamin	1	2	3	4	5	6	7	(9) ___ NQ	[24]
m. Robert L. Thorndike	1	2	3	4	5	6	7	(9) ___ NQ	[25]
n. Philip Vernon	1	2	3	4	5	6	7	(9) ___ NQ	[26]
o. David Wechsler	1	2	3	4	5	6	7	(9) ___ NQ	[27]

PERSONAL AND SOCIAL BACKGROUND

41. Sex: (1) ___ Male   (2) ___ Female   [28]

42. Age: ____   [29-30]

43. Current marital status:

    (1) ___ Single   [31]
    (2) ___ Married
    (3) ___ Divorced
    (4) ___ Widowed

44. For each statement listed below, please circle the number, 1-4, which best represents the degree to which you agree or disagree.

Strongly agree	Somewhat agree	Somewhat disagree	Strongly disagree
1	2	3	4

a. American economic exploitation has contributed to third world poverty.

   1   2   3   4   (9) ___ No Opinion   [32]

b. The American private enterprise system is generally fair to working people.

   1   2   3   4   (9) ___ No Opinion   [33]

c. Strong affirmative action measures should be used in job hiring to assure black representation.

   1   2   3   4   (9) ___ No Opinion   [34]

d. The United States would be better off if it moved toward socialism.

   1   2   3   4   (9) ___ No Opinion   [35]

e. The structure of our society causes most people to feel alienated.

   1   2   3   4   (9) ___ No Opinion   [36]

Strongly agree	Somewhat agree	Somewhat disagree	Strongly disagree

f. It is wrong for a married person to have sexual relations with anyone other than his or her spouse.

   1   2   3   4   (9) ___ No Opinion   [37]

45. Please circle the number, below, which best represents your political perspective.

Very <br> liberal   Very <br> conservative

   1   2   3   4   5   6   7   [38]

46. From which ethnic or nationality group or groups are you mainly descended? (Check no more than two)

(01) ___ Afro-American   (10) ___ Polish   [39-42]
(02) ___ English, Scottish, Welsh (11) ___ Russian
(03) ___ French   (12) ___ Scandinavian
(04) ___ German   (13) ___ Central or South American
(05) ___ Irish   (14) ___ Mexican-American (Chicano)
(06) ___ Italian   (15) ___ Peurto Rican
(07) ___ Jewish, Eastern European (16) ___ Other Hispanic
(08) ___ Jewish, German or Austrian   ___ Other (Please specify)
(09) ___ Native American   _____

47. Compared to other American families at the time, how would you characterize your childhood family income?

(1) ___ Well above average   [43]
(2) ___ Above average
(3) ___ Average
(4) ___ Below average
(5) ___ Well below average
(9) ___ Don't know/No response

48. Please indicate your current religious affiliation, and that in which you were raised.

	Current	Childhood	
CATHOLIC	01	01	[44-47]
PROTESTANT			
Baptist	02	02	
Congregational	03	03	
Episcopalian/Anglican	04	04	
Lutheran	05	05	
Methodist	06	06	
Mormon	07	07	
Presbyterian	08	08	
Quaker	09	09	
Unitarian	10	10	
Other Protestant (Please specify)	11	11	
Protestant, no demonination	12	12	
JEWISH			
Orthodox	13	13	
Conservative	14	14	
Reform	15	15	
Jewish, no branch	16	16	
BUDDHIST	17	17	
HINDU	18	18	
MUSLIM	19	19	
NONE	20	20	
OTHER (Please specify)	21	21	

49. Do you wish to receive a summary of our findings?   ___ Yes   ___ No

Thank you for taking the time to complete this questionnaire. If you have any additional comments, please use this page.

Index

ABC *World News Tonight*, 243
Ability grouping. *See* Tracking
Ability testing, 117
Abstract reasoning, 44, 53, 56, 59, 74
Achievement motivation, 56, 59, 73
Achievement test, 60
Acquired knowledge, 44
Adams, Richard, 242
Adaptive behavior, 73
Adoption studies, 21, 87, 90-93, 128
Affirmative action programs, 227, 254
Akron, Ohio, Public Schools survey (1964), 3, 140; (1977), 4, 140
Albermarle Paper Co. v. Moody, 160
Alpha test (U.S. Army), 17, 19, 21
Alternative form testing, 62
Amaya, Mary, 6, 248
American Anthropological Association (AAA), 2, 28
American College Testing (ACT), 10, 22, 151, 155
American Educational Research Association (AERA), 46-47, 142
American Federation of Teachers (AFT), 141
American Psychological Association, (APA), 2, 143, 160, 163, 170, 229; Committee on Educational Uses of Tests with Disadvantaged Students, 45; Committee on Mental and Physical Tests, 13; 46-47
American Scientist, 283
American Sociological Association (ASA), 46-47
"American Way of Testing, The," 240
Analysis-of-variance model, 83
Anastasi, Anne, 61, 64, 110, 132
Anxiety, 73, 121
Aptitude-achievement distinction, 59-62, 237, 241
Aptitude test, 59-61
Armed Forces Qualifying Test (AFQT), 175-77

Armed Services Vocational Aptitude Battery (ASVAB), 117, 159, 175
Army General Classification Test (AGCT), 21
Associated Press, 177
Association of Black Psychologists (ABP), 3, 5, 29, 162-63
Assortive mating, 84, 86, 125
Atlanta Constitution, 224
Atlantic, 28, 125, 220
"Attention" tests, 14
Attentiveness, 72-73

Banfield, Edward, 125
Behavior Genetics Association, 46-47, 95, 166
Behavior genetic studies, 94-95
Bell, Daniel, 26, 31, 251-52, 256
Benbow, Camilla, 238
Berg, Cynthia, 53
Berger, Lisa, 237
Beta test (U.S. Army), 17, 21
Bias in Mental Testing, 117, 217, 227, 229, 231
Binet, Alfred, 13, 16, 51, 81-82
Binet-Henri approach, 13-14, 51
Binet-Simon scale, 14-16, 67, 141
Biodata, 8
Biometrical analysis, 86, 93-94
Black-white IQ difference, 105-34, 182, 254
Black-white test score differences, 4-7, 105-34, 175-80, 182
Block design test, 72
Block, N.J., 53, 55, 57, 66, 72-73, 119
Bloom, Benjamin, 25
Bock, R. Darrell, 126, 182
Boeth, Richard, 213, 229
Boston Globe, 178, 181
Bouchard, Thomas, 87, 90, 94
Bowdoin College, 10
Brigham, Carl, 18-20

Brim, Orville, 140, 147
Brown v. the Board of Education, 23
Buckley Amendment. *See* Educational Rights and Privacy Act of 1974
Bulletin of the Atomic Scientists, 283
Burt, Sir Cyril, 30-31, 51, 75, 89-90, 94, 132, 134, 192, 215, 217, 219-20, 230-31, 233, 281

California Test of Mental Maturity, 142
Capacity, innate, 44
Capacity to learn, 43, 56, 58-59, 74
Carroll, John, 70
Carter-Saltzman, Louise,, 97
Cattell, James McKeen, 12-13
Cattell, Raymond, 70, 132
Cattell-type testing, 12-13
CBS *Evening News,* 179, 229
CBS *Morning News,* 233, 242-43
CBS *30 Minutes,* 243
Century Magazine, 44
Civil Rights Act of 1964, Title VI, 4, 7
Civil rights movement, 26, 179
Chase, Allen, 219, 221
Chinese civil service examinations, 11
Chomsky, Noam, 254
Choosing Elites, 153
Christian Science Monitor, 246-47
Civil rights, 251-52
Civil Rights Act of 1964, Title VII, 159-62, 179
Clark, Kenneth, 231
Class differences, 121, 124-25,
Cleary, T. Anne, 52-53
Coaching, SAT, 241; software, 243
Coding, study, 184-92, 270-79
Coding, test, 72
Cognitive Science Society, 46-47, 57, 166
College Entrance Examination Board (CEEB), 9, 22, 154, 234, 241
Colvin, S.S., 43-44
Committee Against Racism (CAR), 125
Compensatory education, 26-27, 100, 218, 222, 226-27
Comprehension, 13
Congressional Directory, 283
Content analysis, 183-201, 203-48
Content bias, 113-15
Continuum of Cultural Specificity, 110
Continuum of Experimental Specificity, 110

"Controversy Over Testing Flares Again," 210
Crawford, Demond, 6
Creativity, 56, 58-59, 108
Crimson, 1
Cronbach, Lee, 132
Crouse, James, 152, 237
Cultural bias, 3, 27, 72, 105, 107-9, 111, 113-14, 122, 220-21, 227, 240, 242-43
Cultural Contradictions of Capitalism The, 26, 251
Cultural deprivation, 240
Cultural differences, 127
Cultural disadvantage, 107-9, 111
Cultural familiarity, 113
Culture-fair test, 23, 61, 110
Culture-free test, 23
Culture loading, 110-11, 114, 232
Culture specificity, 107, 110

Darwin, Charles, 11
Davis, Allison, 23
Department of Defense, U.S., 175-76, 178, 180
Detterman, Douglas, 45, 52, 54-55
Differential Aptitude Test, 142
Differential Prediction bias, 115-19
Differential validity bias, 115-19
Digit span tests, 72
Dionne, E.J., Jr., 206
"Disjunction of realms," 26, 31
Docter, Richard, 139
Dominance, 84, 86
Doppelt, Jerome, 231-32
Dworkin, Gerald, 53, 55, 57, 66, 72-73, 119
"Dysgenic trends," 29

Eaves, L.J., 94
Ebbinghaus, 13
Ebel, Robert, 146
Eckland, Bruce, 125
Economic bias, 121
Editor and Publisher, 283
Edson, Lee, 218
Educable mentally retarded (EMT), 5, 149-51, 163
Education for All Handicapped Children Act of 1975, 6, 29, 150
Educational Rights and Privacy Act of 1974 (Buckley Amendment), 147, 157

Educational Testing Service (ETS), 3, 10, 60, 114, 152, 164, 234, 241-43, 248; disclosure policy, 239
Efficiency, 31, 33
Egalitarianism, 32-33
Ehrlich, Paul R., 221
Employment testing, 7-8, 11, 22, 46, 117, 244-45
Encyclopedia Britannica, 231
Environment, 20-21, 25
Environmental adaptation, 56, 58-59
Environmental variance, 84-85, 96-100, 121, 127-28
Equal Education Opportunity Commission (EEOC), 7, 160-61
Equality, 31
Epistasis, 84
Epstein, Jay, 181
Erlenmeyer-Kimling, L., 94
Essay-type achievement test, 22
Ethnic group differences, 106, 124, 179-83
Expert opinion, politics of, 130-34; survey, 45-49, 55-75
Eugenics, 11-12, 18, 24, 29, 213
Evans, M. Stanton, 233
Eysenck, Hans, 94, 125, 131-32, 134, 217, 219, 233

Factor analysis, 68-69
Factor X, 127
"FairTest," 3, 10
Federal Service Entrance Examination (FSEE), 8
Federal Trade Commission (FTC), 144, 155, 196, 243
Feldman, M.W., 96-97
Feldman, S. Shirley, 221
Figure analogies, 70
Fine, Benjamin, 22-23, 25
Fiske, Edward B., 210, 215, 222, 237
Flynn, James, 80
Frank, Reuven, 181
Fredrickson, George M., 219
Free enterprise, 253
Freeman, Frank, 44
Friedrichs, Robert, 129
Fulker, D.W., 93-94
Fulks, David, 231

Galton, Francis, 11-12, 51

Gans, Herbert, 179, 197
Gardner, Howard, 37, 52
Garrett, Henry, 24
Gene-environment covariance, 85-86
Gene-environment interaction, 79, 86, 122, 128
General knowledge, 56, 59
General psychology, 12-13
Genetic determinants, 1, 105
Genetic influences, 121-30
Genotype, 79, 85
Goal-directedness, 56, 59
Goddard, H. H., 15-17, 19, 82
Golden Rule Insurance Company, 114
"Golden Rule" procedure, 114-15
Goldman, Eric, 253
Goleman, Daniel, 238
Goodfield, June, 256
Gordon, Robert, 61
Goslin, David, 141, 145-47
Gould, Stephen Jay, 18-19, 122, 131-32, 134, 182, 213, 255, 258
Gourlay, Neil, 94
Grade point average (GPA), 152-54
Graduate Management Admission Test (GMAT), 10, 155
Graduate Record Examination (GRE), 151, 155
Grady, Judge, 34-35
Graham, Robert, 29, 224, 229
Greve, Frank, 181-82
Griggs v. Duke Power Co., 7, 159, 244
Guidelines on Employment Testing Procedures (EEOC), 7, 160
Guilford, J.P., 69-70, 132
Guskin, Samuel, 151

Half-sibling studies, 89, 91
Hammond, Ray, 120, 130
Harvard Business School, 10
Harvard College, 10
Harvard Educational Review (*HER*), 1-2, 29, 93, 184, 188, 192-93, 197, 226
Hawkins, David, 217, 219
Hawthorne Works project, 22
Head Start program, 25, 27, 97, 127-28, 225
Hearnshaw, L.S., 31
Hebb, Donald, 79
Heber, Richard, 97, 99-100, 145
Hechinger, Fred, 238

Henri, Victor, 13
Hereditary Genius, 11
Heredity, 20-21
Heritability of intelligence, 1-3, 27, 30, 36-37, 44, 79-100, 123-24, 193, 196, 199, 215-34; estimates of, 93-96
Hernstein, Richard, 28-31, 33-34, 65, 100, 106, 125, 131-32, 134, 182, 200, 204-6, 213, 215, 217-34, 247, 251, 258, 276
Hilliard, Dr. Asa, 114
Hispanic test takers, 175-76, 178, 182, 281
Hobson v. Hansen, 4-5
Hodgson, Godfrey, 217
Holmen, Martin, 139
Holziger, Karl, 83
"How Much Can We Boost IQ and Scholastic Achievement?", 1, 26, 29, 184
Howard, Jeff, 120, 130
Houts, Paul J., 209
Humphreys, Lloyd, 132, 232
Hunt, J. McV., 24
Hunter, John, 65, 117
Hunter, Ronda, 65

Idiot savants, 71
Illinois Insurance Agent Licensing Test, 14
Imagination, 13
Imaginativeness, 14
Immigrant data, 18-19
Immigration Act of 1924, 18-19
"Innate inferiority" error, 228
Individualism, 197
Individual psychology, 13
Inequality, 74, 218
Ingle, Dwight, 24
Intelligence and Experience, 24
"Intelligence and Its Measurement" symposium, 43
Intelligence, definition of, 51-57, 75
Intelligence, general (g), 67-72, 75
Intelligence, nature of, 35-37, 43-75, 193, 196, 198
Intelligence quotient (IQ), 15
Intelligence test, 59-60
International Health Exhibition (London, 1884), 12
Interpersonal sensitivity, 108
Intervention programs, 97-100, 128. *See also* Head Start
Interviewing, 8

Iowa Child Welfare Research Station, 97-98
"IQ," 28
IQ Controversy, The, 53
IQ Heritability, and Inequality, 53
IQ Myth, The, 192, 208, 214, 229, 231-32, 245, 279, 282
"I.Q. Tests Once Again Disturb Educators," 209

Jarvik, Lissy, 94
Jencks, Christopher, 65-66, 74, 85, 87, 94, 152, 218
Jensen, Arthur, 1-3, 11, 26-29, 31, 33, 63, 70-71, 93, 97-98, 100, 105-6, 110-11, 117, 119, 122-23, 125, 127, 129, 131-32, 134, 147, 184, 188, 192-93, 197, 200, 204-8, 213, 215, 217-34, 237, 247-48, 251, 254, 258, 276, 282
"jensenism, n. The Theory that IQ Is Determined Largely by the Genes," 2, 79
Jinks, J.L., 93-94
Johns Hopkins Medical School, 10
Journal of Educational Psychology, 43, 45
Jungeblut, Ann, 156

Kagan, Jerome, 206, 230
Kamin, Leon, 18-19, 30, 89-90, 92-93, 98, 131-32, 134, 181-82, 189, 192-93, 206, 213, 217, 223, 230, 247-48, 255, 258
Kaplan, Stanley, 239, 243
Klitgaard, Robert, 153
Koch, Edward, 9
Konner, Melvin, 122

L'Annee Psychologique, 13
"La Psychologie Individuelle," 13
La Raza, 178
Larry P. v. Wilson Riles, 4-6, 11, 30, 34, 82, 114, 141, 144, 150-51, 162-63, 211, 213-15, 221, 229, 231, 242, 248, 250
Lawrence, E.M., 124
Law School Admissions Test (LSAT), 9, 151-53, 155
Layzer, David, 85
Leahy, Alice, 124
Legacy of Malthus The, 219, 221
Lehmann-Haupt, Christopher, 221, 236
Lewis, I.A., 197
Lewontin, Richard, 86, 96-97, 123
Licensing exams, 245

Lichter, Linda, 179, 283
Lichter, Robert, 179, 181, 256, 283
Lindzey, Gardner, 85
Linguistic competence, 56, 59
Linn, Robert, 117, 153
Lippmann, Walter, 20, 44, 52
Loehlin, John C., 85, 87, 94, 126
Lorge-Thorndike Intelligence test, 142
Los Angeles Times, 178, 197
Lowen, Daniel, 239, 243

Machine scoring, 21
MacKenzie, Brian, 126
MacMillan, x, 151
Mainstreaming, 29
Master Plan for Special Education. *See* Education for All Handicapped Children Act of 1975
Mathematical competence, 56, 59, 70, 74
Mathews, Jessica Tuchman, 240
Mazes, 72
McClelland, 214
McGue, Matthew, 87, 94
McGurk, Frank, 24
McNemar, Quinn, 98
McWilliams, Wilson C., 205
Measurement error, 63, 85
Measurement, error-free, 63
Media Elite, The, 179
Medical College Admission Test (MCAT), 9-10, 152, 155
Memory, 56, 59; rote, 69-70
"Mental quotient," 15
Mental speed, 56, 59
"Mental tests," 12
Mercer, Jane, 114, 206, 211
Meritocracy, 31-33, 125, 249, 251
Messick, Samuel, 156
"Metrical Scale of Intelligence." *See* Binet-Simon scale
"Metro-Americans," 253
Milwaukee Project, 97, 99-100, 128, 145, 218, 226
Mismeasure of Man, The, 3, 18, 122
Misuse, test, 36-37
Mohr, Charles, 177
Moore, Elsie G.J., 126, 182
"More and More, the IQ Idea is Questioned," 23
Morton, G. Newton, 94

Motivational bias, 119-21
Motivational variables, 22-23
Moynihan, Daniel Patrick, 125
Multiple choice test, 22
"Multiple intelligences," 37
Multi-factor theory, 69-71
Multivariate analysis, 265-66
Musical aptitude, 108
Myth of Measurability, The, 3

Nader, Ralph, 3, 9, 114, 157-58, 196, 236-37, 239-42, 247-48
Nairn, Allan, 9, 154, 236-37, 240
Nakasone, Prime Minister, 182-83
Nation, 253
National Academy of Sciences (NAS), 29, 117, 152, 205, 221, 228, 245
National Association for the Advancement of Colored People (NAACP), 3, 114, 221; Legal Defense Fund, 5
National Council on Measurement in Education (NCME), 46-47
National Education Association (NEA), 3, 141, 162, 196, 210, 221
National Opinion Research Center (NORC), 175
National Public Radio, 246-47
National Research Council (NRC), 164
Nature, 283
NBC *Nightly News*, 179, 214, 243
NBC *Prime Time Saturday*, 229, 231
"Night Light on Black I.Q.," 222
New Republic, 20
News media accuracy, 246-48
"New Snobbery," 20
Newsweek, 179, 183, 185, 189, 199-200, 213, 225-29, 242, 244, 246, 283
New York City Police Department sergeant's exam, 8-9, 244, 250
New York Review of Books, 253, 257
New York Times, 2, 28-30, 34, 177, 183, 185, 188-89, 192, 193, 196, 199, 204-7, 209-13, 215-17, 234-239, 241, 244-47, 257, 281-83
New York Times Book Review, 219, 221
New York Times Magazine, 2-3, 22-23, 79, 217, 222, 240, 279
None of the Above, 155-56, 236
Numerical ability, 69. *See also* Mathematical competence

Numerical operations, 175

Object assembly tests, 72
Oehrn, 13
Oliver, Don, 214-15
Omni, 283
On the Origin of Species, 11
Otis, Arthur, 16
Owen, David, 155-57, 236

Paragraph comprehensions, 175
PASE v. Hannon, 34
Payne, Ethel, 233
Peabody Picture Vocabulary Test (PPVT), 110-11
Peckham, Judge Robert, 5-6, 34-35, 82, 150-51
Perceptual speed, 69
Persistence, 73
Phenotype, 79, 84
Physical health, 73
Piaget, Jean, 24
Picture completion, 72
Picture description, 14
Plomin, Robert, 85
Porter, Douglas, 152
Poverty, 25
Practical intelligence, 45
Primary mental abilities, 69
Princeton Review, 156-57
Principal-component analysis, 265-66
Problem comprehension, 72
Problem solving, 44-45, 56, 74
Professional and Administrative Career Examination (PACE), 8, 159, 244
Profile of American Youth, A, 175-78, 182-83
Psychological Bulletin, 98
"Psychological Tests—A Scientist's Report on Race Differences," 24
Psychological Testing, 64
Psychologists for Social Action, 2
Psychometics, 25, 52, 57, 68, 75
Public Broadcasting System, 246-47
Public Interest, 237
Pygmalion in the Classroom, 145-46

"Questions Parents Should Be Asking," 211

Race Bomb, The, 221
Racial bias, 4, 8. *See also* Cultural bias

Racial differences, 124, 127-128
Racial discrimination, 4-5, 7-8, 124. *See also* Racial bias
Racial integration, 197
Racism, 2, 254-55
Raspberry, William, 244
Rather, Dan, 208, 230, 232, 288
Raudenbush, S.W., 145
Ravens Progressive Matrices, 61, 110-11
Reagan administration, 176-77
Reaction-time measurement, 12-13, 71, 110
Reader's Guide to Periodical Literature, 184, 269
Reasoning, deductive, 69
Reasoning, inductive, 69
Reasoning, arithmetic, 175
Reasoning, quantitative, 106
Regression analyses, 168-69
Reign of ETS, The, 9, 154, 158, 236-37
Reliability, 62-63
Rensberger, Boyce, 219
Restandardization, 112
Robinson, Max, 243
Rose, Richard, 91
Rothman, Stanley, 179, 256, 283

Safire, William, 244
Sanday, Peggy, 276-77
Scarr, Sandra, 97, 127-28, 130
Schakne, Robert, 214
Schneider, William, 197
Scholastic Aptitude Test (SAT), 3, 9, 22, 60, 107, 151, 153, 155, 164, 193, 196-198, 234-44
"School Ability Tests Flunking Out?", 213
Science, 24, 30
Science and Politics of IQ, The, 3, 18, 30
Science Digest, 283
Science 86, 283
Science for the People, 122
Scientific American, 283
Scott, Walter Dill, 22
Selection model bias, 118
Selective breeding. *See* Eugenics
Sensory acuity, 56
Sensory measurement, 12-13
Series completion, 70, 110
Sevareid, Eric, 229
Sharp, Stella, 13
Shockley, William, 28-29,, 33, 125, 182, 189,

192, 204, 215, 217, 219-226, 228-29, 231-34, 247, 276, 281
Shuey, Audrey, 24
Sibling studies, 84, 89-90, 92
Simon, Theodore, 14, 16, 51
Singer, Evelyn, 180
60 Minutes, 30, 192, 229-31, 233
Skeels, Harold, 97-98
Skodak, Marie, 97-98
Slack, Warner, 152
Social competence, 45
Social mobility hypothesis, 124-25 (also Herrnstein, Chapter 2)
Social variables, 22
Society for the Psychological Study of Social Issues (SPSSI), 2
Socioeconomic status (SES), 66, 72, 106 (and intelligence), 124
Solomon, Robert, 242
Sommer, Barbara, 99
Sommer, Robert, 99
Southern Regional Council, 222
Sowell, Thomas, 222
Spatial ability, 56, 69
Spatial-visual ability, 106
Spearman, Charles, 67-69
Special needs students, 5-7, 14-15, 17, 34
Spencer, Herbert, 51
Sperm bank, high IQ, 224
"Spring Survey of Education," 210-11
Spuhler, J.N., 85
Stability, 62-63
Stability and Change in Human Charac- teristics, 25
Stanford Revision of the Binet-Simon scale (Stanford-Binet test), 16, 20-21, 59, 67, 70-71, 80, 112, 114, 149
Standards for Educational and Psychologi- cal tests (APA), 7, 160
Standardization, test, 111-13
Stanley, Julian, 238
Stern, William, 15, 58
Sternberg, Robert, 37, 45, 52-53
Strenio, Andrew J. 236
Students for a Democratic Society (SDS), 1
Study of American Intelligence, A, 18
Suggestibility, 14
Survey of expert opinion, 46-51
Sussmann, Lynne, 177-78

Tangled Wing, The, 122

Technology Review, 283
Terman, Lewis, 16-17,, 20-21, 43-44, 53, 57, 67, 82, 98
Test administration: group, 16-17; individ- ual, 16-17, 21
Test bias, 3, 34, 36, 105, 107-21, 182, 245
"Testing Anxiety," 245
Testing international, 245-46
Testing of Negro Intelligence, The, 24
Testing Trap, The, 236
Test misuse, 209-15
Test overuse, 245
Test-retest, 62
"Tests: How Good? How Fair?," 242
Test use, 209-15
Thurstone, L.L., 69-70
Time, 34, 182-83, 185, 189, 200, 225, 227-28, 241, 269, 283, 288
Times (London), 30
Titchener, E. B., 13
Thorndike, Robert L., 132
Tracking, 4-5, 17, 29, 163
Triarchic Theory, 37, 45
Truth-in-testing, 241; law, 9, 157-58, 239
Twins, dizygotic (DZ) (fraternal), 83-84, 87, 91-93
Twins, monozygotic (MZ) (identical), 83-84, 89-93
Twin studies, 21, 30, 83-93
Two-factor theory of intelligence, 68

United States Army: Methods of Psycholog- ical Examining of Recruits committee, 17; tests, 16-21, 33
United States Civil Rights Commission, 6
United States Civil Service Commission, 8
United States Employment Service, 22
U.S. News and World Report, 24, 179, 183, 185, 189, 213, 215, 225-26, 246, 269
United States Supreme Court, 244

Validation, 7, 53, 160
Validity, test, 18, 21, 27, 34, 37, 62, 64-68, 74
Vectors of Mind, The, 69
Verbal ability, 45, 69, 106
Verbal analogies, 70
Verbal intelligence, 45
Verbal memory, 14
Verbal similarities/differences tests, 70, 72
Vernon, Philip, 70, 86, 90, 99, 126, 132

Vocabulary tests, 72

Wade, Nicholas, 246

Wallace, Anthony, 252

Wallace, Mike, 230

Waller, Jerome, 66

Wall Street Journal, 183, 185, 188, 192-93, 199, 204, 209, 212, 215-16, 234, 244, 246, 269, 281, 283

Ward, James, 141

Washington, D.C. public schools, 4

Washington Post, 28, 176-79, 183-85, 188, 192-93, 199, 204-7, 209-13, 215-17, 234-41, 244, 269, 281-83

Washington Post Magazine, 245

Washington v. Davis, 160

Wechsler Adult Intelligence Scale (WAIS), 21, 73

Wechsler Block Design test, 91

Wechsler, David, 21, 73, 132

Wechsler Intelligence Scale for Children (WICS-R), 71-73, 112-14, 142, 149

Wechsler tests, 73, 80, 114

Westinghouse Learning Corporation, 27

Weinberg, Richard, 128, 130

Weiss, Carol, 180, 183

Weiss, John, 3

"Whatever Became of 'Geniuses'?", 227

Williams, Robert, 206, 231, 248

Wilson, George, 176-80

Wirtz, Willard, 238, 241, 243

Wissler, Clark, 13, 67

Witherspoon, Roger, 224

What is Intelligence?, 45

Wheeler, Thomas C., 240

Word fluency, 69

Word knowledge, 175

Wright, Judge Skelly, 4

Wrong criterion bias, 119

Wundt, Wilhelm, 12-13

Yerkes, Robert, 16-17